MW00667601

Causes and effects of twentieth-century wars

Second edition

Andy Dailey and Sarah Webb

HODDER
EDUCATION
AN HACHETTE UK COMPANY

Dedication
AD: To my parents, Ken and Angie Burress Dailey, and friends: Ridley and Irene Wills, Kay Mongardi, Sue Eby
SW: To my parents, Marcus and Madeleine, with thanks

The material in this title has been developed independently of the International Baccalaureate®, which in no way endorses it.

The Publishers would like to thank the following for permission to reproduce copyright material:

Photo credits: p.28 © DEA/A. DAGLI ORTI/Getty Images; **p.39** © FPG/Hulton Archive/Getty Images; **p.43** © TopFoto; **p.54** © Library of Congress Prints and Photographs Division/LC-USZC4-10986; **p.64** © FPG/Hulton Archive/Getty Images; **p.89** © Hulton Archive/Getty Images; **p.94** © Daily Herald Archive/SSPL/Getty Images; **p.103** © Library of Congress Prints and Photographs Division/LC-USZC4-7447; **p.140** © The Mariners' Museum/Corbis; **p.145** © Bettmann/Corbis; **p.151** © Bettmann/Corbis; **p.156** © Yevgeny Khaldei/Corbis; **p.191** © Keystone/Getty Images; **p.204** © US Marine Corps/Frederic Lewis/Hulton Archive/Getty Images; **p.209** © US Navy/US Navy/The LIFE Picture Collection/Getty Images; **p.215** © Fenno Jacobs/PhotoQuest/Getty Images; **p.237** © Alinari via Getty Images; **p.266** © Bettmann/Corbis; **p.286** © Bettmann/Corbis; **p.301** © John Van Hasselt/Corbis.

The publishers would like to acknowledge use of the following extracts: **pp192, 214, 228** *A Modern History of Japan: From Tokugawa Times to the Present* by Andrew Gordon, published by Oxford University Press, 2003. By permission of Oxford University Press.

The publishers would like to thank the following for permission to reproduce material in this book: **p20** illustration from 'Public finance and national security: the domestic origins of the First World War revisited' by Niall Ferguson in *Past and Present* No. 142, February 1994, page 150, published by Oxford University Press.

Acknowledgements: p25 *Minds at War* by David Roberts, Saxon, London, 1999; **p31** *The Origins of the First World War* by A. Mombauer, Pearson, London, 2002; **p33** *The Origins of the World War* by Sidney Bradshaw Fay, Macmillan, New York, 1929; **p34** *War Aims and Strategic Policy in the Great War* by Fritz Fischer, Rowman & Littlefield, Totowa, 1977; **p34** *The Experience of World War One*, by J.M. Winter, Greenwich Editions, London, 2000; **p45** *The Battlefields of the First World War* by Peter Barton, Constable & Robinson, London, 2005; **p71** *The Peacemakers* by Margaret MacMillan, Random House, New York, 2003; **p85** *The Coming of the Spanish Civil War* by Paul Preston, Taylor & Francis, London, 2004; **p92** *I Helped to Build an Army* by José Martin Blázquez, Secker & Warburg, London, 1939; **p97** *The Spanish Civil War* by G. Ranzato, Interlink Books, New York, 1999; **p99** *Homage to Catalonia* by George Orwell, Penguin, London, 1938; **pp103, 106** *The Spanish Civil War: A Modern Tragedy* by George R. Esenwein, Routledge, London, 2005; **p123** *The Origins of the Second World War Reconsidered: A.J.P. Taylor and the Historians* edited by Gordon Martel, Routledge, London, 1999; **pp149, 168** Fordham University's Modern Internet History Sourcebook www.fordham.edu/Halsall/index.asp; **p160** *The Origins of the Second World War* by A.J.P. Taylor, Penguin, London, 1991; **p161** *Hitler's Stalingrad Decisions* by Geoffrey Jukes, University of California Press, Berkeley, 1985; **p162** *Russia's War* by Richard Overy, Penguin, London, 2010; **p199** *A World in Flames: A Short History of the Second World War in Europe and Asia, 1939–1945* by Martin Kitchen, Longman, London, 1990; **p218** 'Need, greed and protest in Japan's black market, 1938–1949' by Owen Griffiths in *Journal of Social History*, Vol. 35, George Mason University Press, Virginia, 2002; **pp228, 232** *Modern China: The Fall and Rise of a Great Power, 1850 to the Present* by Jonathan Fenby, HarperCollins, New York, 2008; **p229** *Empires on the Pacific: World War II and the Struggle for the Mastery of Asia* by Robert Smith Thompson, Basic Books, New York, 2001; **p232** *War in the Pacific: Pearl Harbor to Tokyo Bay* edited by Bernard C. Nalty, Salamander Books, London, 1991; **p233** *The Pacific War: Japan Versus the Allies* by Alan J. Levine, Praeger, Connecticut, 1995; **p248** *Throwing the Emperor from His Horse: Portrait of a Village Leader in China, 1923–1995* by Peter J. Seybolt, Westview Press, Boulder, Colorado, 1996; **pp258, 270** *Mao* by M. Lynch, Routledge, London, 2004; **p267** *Wild Swans: Three Daughters of China* by Jung Chang, HarperCollins, London, 1991; **p269** *I Stayed in China* by William Sewell, Allen & Unwin, London, 1966; **p282** *The Military and the State in Latin America* by Alain Rouquié, University of California Press, Berkeley, 1987; **p286** *Capitalists and Revolution in Nicaragua: Opposition and Accommodation, 1979–1993* by Rose J. Spalding, University of North Carolina Press, Chapel Hill, 1994; **p292** *Nicaragua Divided: La Prensa and the Chamorro Legacy* by Patricia Taylor Edmisten, University of West Florida Press, Pensacola, 1990; **p299** *Nicaragua: Dictatorship and Revolution*, Latin American Press Bureau, London, 1979; **p302** *Death of Somoza* by Claribel Alegría and Darwin Flakoll, Curbstone Press, Connecticut, 1996; **p304** *Caribbean Revolutions and Revolutionary Theory: An Assessment of Cuba, Nicaragua and Grenada* by Brian Meeks, University of the West Indies Press, Barbados, 2001; **p311** *Jimmy Carter: Foreign Policy and Post-presidential Years* edited by Herbert D. Rosenbaum and Alexej Ugrinsky, Greenwood Press, Westport, Connecticut, 1994.

Every effort has been made to trace all copyright holders, but if any have been inadvertently overlooked the Publishers will be pleased to make the necessary arrangements at the first opportunity.

Although every effort has been made to ensure that website addresses are correct at time of going to press, Hodder Education cannot be held responsible for the content of any website mentioned in this book. It is sometimes possible to find a relocated web page by typing in the address of the home page for a website in the URL window of your browser.

Hachette UK's policy is to use papers that are natural, renewable and recyclable products and made from wood grown in sustainable forests. The logging and manufacturing processes are expected to conform to the environmental regulations of the country of origin.

Orders: please contact Bookpoint Ltd, 130 Milton Park, Abingdon, Oxon OX14 4SB. Telephone: +44 (0)1235 827720. Fax: +44 (0)1235 400454. Lines are open 9.00a.m.–5.00p.m., Monday to Saturday, with a 24-hour message answering service. Visit our website at www.hoddereducation.co.uk

© Andy Dailey and Sarah Webb 2015

First published in 2012 by
Hodder Education,
An Hachette UK Company
Carmelite House, 50 Victoria Embankment
London EC4Y 0DZ

Impression number   10 9 8 7 6 5
Year   2019 2018 2017

Cover photo World War II Bomber Planes © Aloysius Patrimonio/ImageZoo/Corbis
Typeset in 10/13pt Palatino and produced by Gray Publishing, Tunbridge Wells
Printed in Dubai

A catalogue record for this title is available from the British Library

ISBN: 978 1471 841347

Contents

Dedication

Keith Randell (1943–2002)

The original *Access to History* series was conceived and developed by Keith, who created a series to 'cater for students as they are, not as we might wish them to be'. He leaves a living legacy of a series that for over 20 years has provided a trusted, stimulating and well-loved accompaniment to post-16 study. Our aim with these new editions for the IB is to continue to offer students the best possible support for their studies.

Introduction

This book has been written to support your study of Topic 11: Causes and effects of twentieth-century wars of the IB History Diploma.

This introduction gives you an overview of:

★ the content you could study about several twentieth-century wars

★ how you will be assessed for Paper 2

★ the different features of this book and how these will aid your learning.

① What you will study

assemble

The twentieth century was a century of wars. The First and Second World Wars were the modern world's first total wars in which some nations <u>marshalled</u> their vast economic, political and military forces in an attempt to achieve victory. These wars significantly altered international relations and borders and affected millions of people. Other conflicts, such as the Spanish and Chinese Civil Wars, were also total wars but limited to the confines of a single state, with victors establishing new political or economic systems. The Nicaraguan Revolution was a short, significant conflict without the death and destruction of either the world wars or the Spanish or Chinese Civil Wars, yet also achieved a new political system for the people of that country. This book covers these five wars in detail and gives you the opportunity to study wars across all regions of IB History: the Americas, Europe, Africa and the Middle East and, finally, Asia and Oceania.

Twentieth-century wars are an interesting topic of study. Modern warfare has been caused by a desire to undo results of earlier wars, corruption, nationalism, to expand a state and other reasons. These conflicts have been fought using a variety of strategies and have seen tremendous development in weapons and other technology that continue to have an impact on our world today. Wars have altered the lives of women and national minorities throughout the twentieth century, as well as led to the establishment of two international organizations that worked to prevent conflicts. Many states were created and others destroyed through these conflicts.

Different types of war

In your IB History Guide, you will notice that there are several types of warfare that should be studied:

- civil
- wars between states
- guerrilla.

The Guide provides no definition for these terms, which can be more complicated than they first appear. It is important that you define these terms when writing essays. Through your studies, you will discover limited and total forms of warfare. Although these are not specifically mentioned in the Guide, it is important to understand the concepts of limited and total warfare. These are explained below.

Civil war

Civil wars are generally defined as conflicts that occur within a state. These conflicts may however develop into other forms of warfare, such as limited, if they spread beyond a country's borders. While these conflicts are usually between two groups, many groups may actually be involved. In this book civil wars in Spain, China and Nicaragua are covered. These conflicts were primarily between two groups within each of these countries. In addition, this book covers civil wars which occurred during or as a result of the First and Second World Wars.

Wars between states

Wars between states are simply wars between two or more countries. The First and Second World Wars are clear examples of this. Wars between states may also include other types of war, such as civil when there is fighting within a state. Armies from any state may also utilize guerrilla war against an opposing state.

Guerrilla war

Guerrilla warfare is a way of conducting war, usually by a smaller group on a larger organization. Guerrilla tactics usually involve, but are not limited to:

- assassinations of opponents and their supporters
- attacks on a specific place or group for a limited period of time before retreating to safety
- sabotage of infrastructure, equipment or production
- destruction of enemy supplies and housing.

Guerrilla warfare has been used very effectively throughout the twentieth century, including in both world wars, as you will see throughout the wars covered in this book. This type of hit-and-run warfare is used when a smaller group with limited supplies wishes to attack a larger, better supplied, enemy. Without strategic retreat, part of guerrilla tactics, the smaller force would be surrounded and destroyed. Guerrilla warfare is a cheaper form of warfare as it requires only a few people with smaller types of weapons such as pistols, grenades and rifles, which are easier to smuggle, transport and train fighters to use. Operating in small groups makes it possible to approach targets more stealthily as well as helping in retreat and hiding. Effective use of guerrilla warfare against a larger enemy can mean tying down larger numbers of conventional troops, which can be expensive and provide further targets for guerrillas. Guerrilla warfare has allowed smaller groups to affect international and national politics.

Guerrilla warfare may develop into conventional warfare (see page 5) if guerrillas gain enough support in terms of people and equipment to form regular, organized armies.

Other types of warfare

There are other types of warfare you will see discussed in this book. Limited and total warfare can refer to the extent to which a state mobilized human and economic resources to prosecute a war. The study of trench and conventional forms of land war, as well as warfare in the air and by sea, will help you understand how fighting wars has changed, or not, throughout the twentieth century.

Limited war

Limited warfare can refer to many things, hence the need to specifically define your use and understanding of the term. Limited warfare may mean war:

- limited to a specific area, state or region
- limited in terms of resources consumed by battling groups or states
- limited in terms of results or impact.

One could argue that the Spanish Civil War was limited because it was fought in Spain and had a limited impact on international politics. The Second World War was limited for some participating nations, one could argue, because they:

- participated in few battles
- did not fully employ their national resources in the conflict
- were affected little by the events or results of the conflict
- were conquered by another nation early in the war and then had little active participation in the conflict.

It is important that you clearly define what you mean by limited warfare in your essays.

Total war

Like limited warfare, the term total warfare needs to be defined clearly. This type of warfare generally means that a nation at war uses a substantial amount of its resources. The most commonly cited examples of this are the First and Second World Wars where several nations organized their national economies for war production, drafted millions of men into the military, and fought battles across the world on land, air and sea. Total warfare is often understood to involve huge death tolls, destroyed cities and the targeting of civilians.

While it is important to understand why many historians refer to the First and Second World Wars as total wars, it is also important to understand that the term total warfare is very general. Germany, for example, was involved in the Second World War as it sent millions of troops against its enemies, destroyed the armies and independence of several nations, destroyed cities and millions of civilians and so forth. Yet Germany did not organize its

4

national economy for full war production until early 1943, although the conflict began in late 1939. Women were discouraged from working in factories where they were desperately needed, and the resources of captured areas were not utilized efficiently. Was Germany engaged in total warfare during the Second World War in Europe? Yes.

The USA, by contrast, organized its national economy for war production on a tremendous scale, employing millions of women, supplying its allies with weapons and food, developing new weapons and sending millions of men to fight in the Pacific, north Africa and Europe. The USA, however, suffered only a few hundred thousand deaths and was involved in the war in Europe and north Africa in a limited way compared to its allies. Was the USA engaged in total warfare during the Second World War in Europe? Yes.

Germany and the USA, as well as many other nations, were involved in total warfare in both the First and Second World Wars, although their experiences and participation were different. Make sure you define what you mean by total warfare.

Trench warfare
Trench warfare is generally associated with the Western Front of the First World War, although variations of this type of warfare have occurred in other conflicts. Trenches were essentially ditches <u>excavated</u> by troops to protect themselves from machine-gun and artillery fire, as well as to hold on to territory. Trench warfare led to the development of the tank and other forms of technology and military strategies in an effort to defeat it.

Conventional warfare
Conventional warfare essentially refers to the battling of armies on open ground. This was the type of warfare of the Eastern Front in the First and Second World Wars, for example. Conventional warfare often meant that there was rapid movement of armies and constantly changing lines of battle. Mobile warfare, normally used to describe the use of tanks, trucks and other machine-driven vehicles, is a form of conventional warfare.

Air warfare
Air warfare developed in the twentieth century and the term refers to the use of airborne machines in conflicts. Air warfare initially involved Zeppelins, but soon involved large numbers of aircraft. By mid-century, aircraft were involved in naval and conventional warfare, as well as the bombing of civilians.

Naval warfare
Naval warfare is the use of various types of warships in a conflict. Naval warfare changed greatly during the twentieth century, from battleships fighting battles during the First World War, to carrier groups fighting each other with only aircraft during the Second World War. Submarines, a type of warship designed to travel and attack enemy ships from underwater, were important in the world wars as well, developing throughout the century. Naval warfare is discussed throughout the book.

How you will be assessed

The IB History Diploma can be studied to either Standard or Higher Level. It has three papers in total: Papers 1 and 2 for Standard Level and a further Paper 3 for Higher Level. It also has an internal assessment which all students must do.

- For Paper 1 you need to answer four source-based questions on a prescribed subject. This counts for 20 per cent of your overall marks at Higher Level, or 30 per cent of your overall marks at Standard Level.
- For Paper 2 you need to answer two essay questions on two different topics. This counts for 25 per cent of your overall marks at Higher Level, or 45 per cent of your overall marks at Standard Level.
- For Paper 3 you need to answer three questions out of 36 questions. This counts for 35 per cent of your overall marks at Higher Level.

For the Internal Assessment you need to carry out a historical investigation. This counts for 20 per cent of your overall marks at Higher Level, or 25 per cent of your overall marks at Standard Level.

Topic 11: Causes and effects of twentieth-century wars is assessed through Paper 2. There are twelve topics on Paper 2 and you will answer two questions in total, one each from a different topic. Questions for Topic 11 may ask you to discuss the effect of warfare on women, to compare and contrast wars from different regions, to assess the impact of technology on particular wars or wars generally, to explain the causes or results of wars, and so forth.

Examination questions

You should answer only one question out of the two questions you will find on Topic 11: Causes and effects of twentieth-century wars. Your answer will take the form of an essay. This means that they will not name a specific conflict, but will be broad enough that you will be able to answer them using your knowledge from the wars you have studied. This book prepares you to answer questions using information about the First and Second World Wars, Spanish and Chinese Civil Wars, and the Nicaraguan Revolution. These cover the regions of Africa and the Middle East, Asia and Oceania, Europe, and the Americas.

Questions for Paper 2 are open-ended. These may require you to use material from the study of:

- one war
- two or more wars
- two wars from two different regions
- some aspect of wars of the twentieth century generally

Questions about a single conflict

Your examination may contain questions regarding a single conflict. This conflict may be named, or the question may allow you to choose one to address.

Example 1

To what extent was ideology the cause of a twentieth-century conflict?

Example 2

How did technology affect the outcome of one twentieth-century war?

Example 3

For what reasons, and with what results, were women affected by a war in the twentieth century?

Example 4

Discuss the role of guerrilla warfare in one war you have studied.

Questions about two or more wars

Your examination may contain questions regarding more than one conflict. You can choose the wars you would like to use to address the question.

Example 1

Compare the results of two twentieth-century conflicts.

Example 2

Compare and contrast the causes of two civil wars you have studied.

Example 3

With reference to two wars you have studied, discuss the effectiveness of guerrilla warfare in determining victory.

Example 4

Assess the importance of air warfare on the outcome of two wars in the twentieth century.

Questions that require cross-regional wars

Some questions will require you to address wars from two different IB History regions. A map of these four regions may be found in the History Guide, but also on the cover of your examination paper (see below).

Example 1

Discuss the importance of naval warfare in the conduct of two twentieth-century wars, each chosen from a different region.

Example 2

Analyse the social and demographic effects of two wars that you have studied, each from a different region.

Example 3

With reference to two wars, each from a different region, assess the importance of economics in causing the conflicts.

Example 4

Compare and contrast territorial changes that occurred as the result of two twentieth-century wars, each from a different region.

Questions about twentieth-century warfare generally

Examination papers often have questions that allow you to discuss a particular issue regarding warfare generally, allowing you to use your knowledge from all the wars you have studied.

Example 1

What major political issues occurred after twentieth-century wars?

Example 2

To what extent has naval warfare changed during the twentieth century?

Example 3

Discuss the impact of technology on the conduct of warfare in the twentieth century.

Example 4

How have modern wars affected minority groups?

The appearance of the examination paper

Cover

The cover of the examination paper states the date of the examination and the length of time you have to complete it: 1 hour and 30 minutes. Instructions are limited and simply state that you:

- should not open it until told to do so
- should answer only two questions, each from a different topic
- should make sure that you understand what the paper means by regions.

A map indicates the regions for you.

Topics

Once you are allowed to open your examination paper, you will note that there are twelve topics, each numbered and titled. Each topic has two questions.

Questions

You are required to answer only one of the two questions for Topic 11. Make sure you have read through both questions before starting, selecting the question you know the most about and feel the most comfortable with. It is important to understand that you need to answer the question fully in an essay format. There is more guidance about answering questions in Chapter 8 (page 324).

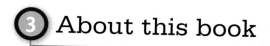

3 About this book

Coverage of course content

This book addresses the prescribed content listed in the IB History Guide for Topic 11 using various twentieth-century conflicts. Each conflict is addressed in a chapter. These chapters cover the following:

- First World War 1914–18
- Spanish Civil War 1936–9
- Second World War in Europe and north Africa 1939–45
- Second World War in Asia and the Pacific 1941–5
- Chinese Civil War 1927–37 and 1945–9
- Nicaraguan Revolution 1976–9.

These chapters start with an introduction outlining the key questions that they address. They are divided into a series of sections and topics covering the course content. Throughout the chapters you will find the following features to aid your study of the course content.

Key and leading questions

Each section heading in the chapter has a related key question that gives a focus to your reading and understanding of the section. These are also listed in the chapter's introduction. You should be able to answer the questions after completing the relevant section.

Topics within the sections have leading questions that are designed to help you focus on the key points within a topic and give you more practice in answering questions.

Key terms

Key terms are the important terms you need to know to gain an understanding of the period. These are emboldened in the text and are defined in the margin the first time they appear in a chapter. They also appear in the glossary at the end of the book.

Sources

Throughout the book are several written and visual sources. Historical sources are important in understanding more fully why specific decisions were taken or what contemporary writers and politicians based their actions on. The sources are accompanied by questions to help you understand them better.

Key debates

Historians often disagree on historical events and this historical debate is referred to as historiography. Knowledge of historiography is helpful in reaching the upper-mark bands when you take your IB History examinations. There are a number of debates throughout the book to develop your understanding of historiography, some of which quote important historians that you may wish to refer to in your examination.

Theory of Knowledge (TOK) questions

Understanding that different historians see history differently is an important element in understanding the connection between the IB History Diploma and Theory of Knowledge. Alongside most historiographical debates is a Theory of Knowledge-style question that makes that link.

Summary diagrams

At the end of each section is a summary diagram that gives a visual summary of the content of the section. It is intended as an aid for revision.

Chapter summary

At the end of each chapter is a short summary of the content of that chapter. This is intended to help you revise and consolidate your knowledge and understanding of the content.

Skills development

Chapter 7 gives guidance on how to make links between wars in order to compare and contrast them, which examination questions often ask you to do. Chapter 8 gives guidance on how to answer examination questions.

Chapter 7: an overview of twentieth-century warfare

This chapter:

- compares and contrasts the causes of the First and Second World Wars
- compares and contrasts the practices of different wars, looking at technology and types of warfare
- compares and contrasts the effects of different wars.

Chapter 8: examination guidance

This chapter includes:

- examination guidance on how to answer different question types, accompanied by a sample answer and commentary designed to help you focus on specific details
- examination practice in the form of Paper 2-style questions.

Glossary

All key terms in the book are defined in the glossary at the end of the book.

Further reading

This contains a list of books, DVDs and websites that may help you with further independent research and presentations. It may also be helpful when further information is required for internal assessments and extended essays in history. You may wish to share the contents of this area with your school or local librarian.

Internal assessment

All IB History diploma students are required to write a historical investigation that is internally assessed. The investigation is an opportunity for you to dig more deeply into a subject that interests you. This gives you a list of possible areas for research.

First World War 1914–18

The First World War was a truly global conflict. It eventually involved 32 nations, with fighting taking place in Europe, the Middle East, Africa and Asia. It was also the first modern total war encompassing entire populations and resources in a way hitherto unknown. New military technologies pitted man against machine on an unprecedented scale. The experience of this war profoundly altered the political, social and economic situation in Europe.

• until now

The following key questions will be addressed in this chapter:

★ To what extent did the long-term causes of the war make conflict likely by 1914?

★ How significant were the short-term causes to the outbreak of war in 1914?

★ To what extent should Germany be blamed for causing the First World War?

★ How far did the nature of fighting in the First World War represent a new type of conflict?

★ How significant was the management of the war in determining its outcome?

★ Did the impact of the First World War make future European conflict more or less likely?

1 The long-term causes of the First World War

▶ *Key question: To what extent did the long-term causes of the war make conflict likely by 1914?*

In August 1914, war broke out between the major European powers. Austria-Hungary and Germany were on one side, against Britain, France and Russia on the other.

The onset of war was triggered by the assassination of the Austro-Hungarian Archduke, Franz Ferdinand, in Sarajevo on 28 June 1914. The assassin was a Serb nationalist. Austria-Hungary blamed Serbia. This led to the following sequence of events which embroiled all the major European powers in war by the middle of August.

→ Guerilla warfare

- 6 July: German offered full support to its ally Austria-Hungary in any action it may choose to take against Serbia.
- 23 July: Austria-Hungary issued an ultimatum to Serbia.
- 24 July: Serbia replied to the ultimatum, rejecting one of the key terms.
- 25 July: Austria-Hungary issued the partial mobilization of its army.

} Immediate causes

- 29 July: Russia issued the partial mobilization of its army. Germany ordered Russia to cease partial mobilization, regarding this as threatening German security.
- 30 July: Russia ordered the full mobilization of its army.
- 31 July: Germany ordered the full mobilization of its army.
- 1 August: France ordered the full mobilization of its army. Germany declared war on Russia.
- 3 August: Germany declared war on France. Germany invaded Belgium.
- 4 August: Britain declared war on Germany.
- 6 August: Serbia declared war on Germany. Austria-Hungary declared war on Russia.
- 12 August: Britain declared war on Austria-Hungary. France declared war on Austria-Hungary.

The enlargement of the conflict continued with the **Ottoman Empire**'s entry into the war in October 1914 on the side of Austria-Hungary and Germany, while Italy joined with Russia, Britain and France in May 1915. Many of the European powers had substantial empires that became involved in the conflict, rapidly giving the war a truly global dimension.

Although the assassination was the trigger, the First World War had its roots in long-term social, economic and political developments in Europe in the decades before 1914. This section will look at these long-term causes of the First World War.

> **How far did economic developments increase the likelihood of war?**

Economic changes in Europe, c.1870–1914

One long-term cause of the First World War lay in the impact of economic developments that had taken place in Europe in the decades before 1914. The **industrial revolution** of the nineteenth century transformed the basis of economic power, giving enormous strength to countries that could increase their production of coal, iron and steel. In this, the former great powers of Austria-Hungary and Russia lagged behind, while Britain, at least initially, took the lead in industrial development. By 1900, however, British dominance was increasingly challenged as competition developed for economic superiority.

Economic growth and competition

Almost all the major powers increased their production of steel and iron in the decades before the First World War. However, economic growth occurred at differing rates, leading to a significant shift in the relative economic strength of the major powers (see Source A), which fuelled economic competition and rivalry between them. Britain, for example, became increasingly concerned by the USA and Germany, the latter by 1910 leading the European powers in industrial output. Russia was also a cause for concern due to its growth rates in the production of pig iron and steel. Although by 1900, Russia's absolute output remained significantly behind the world leaders, it still contributed six per cent of the total world output of iron and steel, ranking it fourth in the world, and given its vast size and largely untapped raw materials its potential for growth was considerable.

SOURCE A

Relative shares of world manufacturing output, 1880–1913 (percentages).

Country	1880	1900	1913
Britain	22.9	18.5	13.6
United States	14.6	23.6	32.0
Germany	8.5	13.2	14.8
France	7.8	6.8	6.1
Russia	7.6	8.8	8.2
Austria-Hungary	4.4	4.7	4.4
Italy	2.5	2.5	2.4

What does Source A indicate about economic growth between 1880 and 1913?

Only the U.S. & Germany were truly growing while other nations were staying stagnant or declining.

Most European countries invested considerably in extensive railway networks. Russia made the most rapid progress between 1870 and 1910, both in growth rate and in absolute terms, so that by 1910 Russia possessed the largest overall railway network. However, the vast size of Russia meant that its rail network was far less efficient in terms of coverage than those of Britain and Germany. The growth rate of Germany's rail network was also notably impressive, increasing by 224 per cent between 1870 and 1910.

Military strength

In the decades before 1914, economic rivalries contributed to profound insecurities as countries feared being overtaken by their competitors. Many countries entered the war believing that if war had to come, it was better to fight sooner rather than later before their adversaries grew stronger.

Economic growth generated such concerns because of its implications for military strength. The increase in output of iron and steel, as well as the development of an effective manufacturing industry, was vital for the production of modern military technology. Similarly, the construction of extensive, efficient rail networks was imperative for the rapid transportation of troops and supplies. For example, the substantial growth of the Russian railway network had significant military consequences since it meant that the Russian army could be mobilized more rapidly, something which it was estimated would take over eight weeks in 1906, but only 30 days by 1912.

Nonetheless, economic growth and its potential implications for military strength were only a source of anxiety in a climate in which military spending was prioritized by European governments (see page 20); tensions and rivalries between nations were already in existence due to other factors such as imperialistic rivalries.

How far did imperialism contribute to war in 1914?

→ Imperialism

Imperialist policies were pursued vigorously by the major European powers at the beginning of the twentieth century. The possession of an empire conferred economic and potential military power as well as prestige. France, Britain and Germany focused on gaining overseas colonies, primarily, but not exclusively, in Asia and Africa, while Russia and Austria-Hungary had substantial interests in extending their empires into the **Balkans** (see Source B). Imperialism stimulated, and clashed with, the growth of **nationalism**, which arose in opposition to the existence of vast multi-ethnic empires.

Imperial rivalries in the Balkans

The Balkan region was the focus of the imperial ambitions of Austria-Hungary, Russia, Serbia and the Ottoman Empire. The Balkan region had been dominated by the Ottoman Empire since the sixteenth century, but the demise of Ottoman strength led to the fragmentation of the region and the formation of smaller Balkan states like Serbia in 1817 and Bulgaria in 1878. The decline of Ottoman strength provided the opportunity for rival European powers to expand their control in the region, thereby intensifying rivalries.

SOURCE B

The Balkans in 1913.

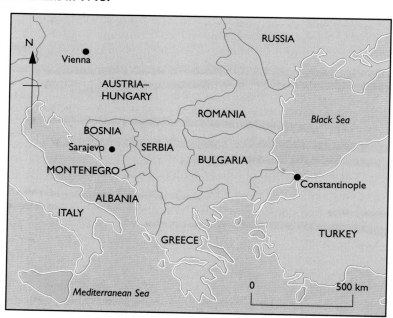

? How useful is Source B in understanding the importance of the Balkans in 1913?

Austro-Hungarian interests in the Balkans

The vast Austro-Hungarian Empire encompassed much of central and eastern Europe and began to extend its control into the Balkans in the early twentieth century; Bosnia-Herzegovina for example had been **annexed** in 1908. Austro-Hungarian ambitions to maintain and extend this control brought it into conflict with Russia and Serbia for influence over the region. Both Serbia and Russia promoted the growth of **pan-Slavism**. Austria-Hungary feared this would encourage revolt and threaten not only Austrian interests in the Balkans, but the very existence of the multi-ethnic Austro-Hungarian Empire which contained substantial numbers of **Slavic** peoples.

Serbian interests in the Balkans

Serbia promoted the nationalistic vision of a greater Serbia in which all Balkan Slavs would be united under Serbian rule. Serbian nationalism had increased in militancy following the rise of the pro-Russian and fiercely nationalistic ruling Karadjordjević dynasty through a military **coup** in 1903. In addition, the Kingdom of Serbia had recently enlarged its territory by 80 per cent as a result of victory in the **Balkan Wars** of 1912–13. Austria-Hungary understandably saw Serbia as a threat to the existence of its multi-ethnic empire and insisted on the creation of Albania, a state for ethnic Albanians, which would prevent Serbia from having access to the sea. Access to ports was essential for economic development as most trade occurred with merchant vessels, so the creation of Albania not only limited Serbia's gains, but hindered its economic development. Key individuals within the Austrio-Hungarian government also promoted the view that the Serbian menace ought to be dealt with sooner rather than later, before Serbia grew more influential, accounting in part for Austria-Hungary's deliberately provocative ultimatum in response to the assassination in June 1914 (see page 28) which did much to escalate the crisis to war.

Russian interests in the Balkans

Russian interests in the Balkans were partly motivated by ideological commitment. Russia, as the most powerful of the Slavic nations, had long promoted the image of itself as the defender of all Slavic peoples. This agenda was popular within Russia since it emphasized, and potentially increased, Russian power and prestige. However, ideological commitment to pan-Slavism was not the primary reason for Russian interests in the Balkans. There were more important strategic and political reasons. An extension of Russian influence in the Balkans would:

- provide important access for Russian merchant and warships through the Black Sea and into the Mediterranean
- limit the territorial expansion of Russia's main rival, the Austro-Hungarian Empire.

KEY TERM

Annex To incorporate a territory into another country.

Pan-Slavism A movement advocating the political and cultural union of Slavic nations and peoples.

Slavic An ethnic and linguistic grouping of eastern European peoples whose languages include Russian, Serbo-Croatian, Polish and Czech.

Coup An illegal takeover of power, often through the use of force.

Balkan Wars Two wars fought between 1912 and 1913 for possession of the European territories of the Ottoman Empire involving Bulgaria, Montenegro, Serbia, Greece and the Ottoman Empire.

Austro-Hungarian and Russian rivalries in the Balkans

Austro-Hungarian and Russian rivalries in the Balkans had almost triggered war on a number of occasions before 1914. In 1878, for example, Austria-Hungary mobilized its army in protest against a substantial extension of Russian influence in the region that had come about in the aftermath of a **Russo-Turkish War**. On this occasion, war was averted through diplomacy, although the final settlement left Russia dissatisfied and increased its animosity towards Austria-Hungary and Germany.

Tensions between Russia and Austria-Hungary over the Balkans flared again when Austria-Hungary formally annexed the region of Bosnia-Herzegovina in 1908. Russia was militarily too weak to contemplate anything more than a diplomatic protest. However, the event increased Russian concerns about the extension of Austro-Hungarian influence in the Balkans and made it more determined to resist any further such occurrences in the future. This contributed to making any issue involving the Balkans, Austria-Hungary and Russia potentially particularly explosive.

Imperial rivalries between Britain, France and Germany

The focus of the imperial ambitions of Britain, France and Germany was the acquisition of colonies outside Europe. The British Empire's imperial possessions constituted 20 per cent of the world's territory by 1900. France had substantial interests in Africa. Germany, a relatively new country having only come into existence in 1871, was keen to exert an influence on the world stage by acquiring its own empire.

German imperial ambitions

German imperial ambitions became increasingly evident during the rule of **Kaiser** Wilhelm II from 1888. The Kaiser was adamant that Germany should be recognized as a world power commensurate with its economic strength and he saw imperial policy as a way to achieve this. In 1896 he declared that 'nothing must henceforth be settled in the world without the intervention of Germany and the German Emperor'. This sentiment informed the new policy of **weltpolitik** in which Germany sought to extend its influence in the world largely through the acquisition of a large navy and colonies. This inevitably threatened French and British imperial interests, especially since the vast majority of key colonial ports were already in their possession. Although the German Foreign Minister, Bernhard von Bülow, issued the assurance to the other Great Powers in 1897 that 'we don't want to put anyone else in the shade, but we too demand our place in the sun', German interventions in global politics in the decades before 1914 all too often caused significant fractures in European power relations.

The Moroccan Crises, 1905 and 1911

The imperial rivalries of the major European powers led to diplomatic clashes over Morocco in 1905 and 1911. North Africa was considered primarily a French sphere of interest, which Britain supported as part of the

Anglo-French *entente* in 1904. When France moved to establish more control over Morocco in 1905, Germany objected, claiming that it had to be consulted. When France ignored German demands, the German military threatened to attack France if its foreign minister was not replaced and if France refused to attend an international conference to resolve the matter. France complied and during the Algericas Conference held in Spain in 1906, Britain firmly supported its *entente* partner, forcing Germany to agree to allow France to extend further control over Morocco under certain minor conditions.

In 1911, France sent troops into Morocco, causing Germany to proclaim the right to do the same in southern Morocco. Again Britain and France resisted German moves and demands, forcing Germany to accept 275,000 km² of French Congo instead. The German government felt that it had been defeated and humiliated.

How far did imperialism contribute to war in 1914?

Imperialism contributed to the growing likelihood of war by generating rivalries between the European powers and by stimulating the growth of nationalism. However, it would take more than rival imperial interests to provoke war. After all, the Moroccan Crises had been resolved diplomatically, as had the Russian and Austro-Hungarian clashes over the Balkans. It was the growing military strength of the major powers (see page 20) which made crises generated by imperial rivalries more likely to trigger the outbreak of real hostilities.

Alliance systems

One of the striking features of the **July Days** (see pages 11–12) was the rapidity with which a conflict between Austria-Hungary and Serbia enlarged to a European war. The existence of rival alliance systems which tied the main countries of Europe together is often cited as an explanation for this escalation. France, Britain and Russia were allied in the **Triple Entente**, while Germany, Austria-Hungary and Italy were joined together in the **Triple Alliance.**

Why were the alliances formed?

Alliances had been formed in a bid to increase security. The **Dual Alliance**, between Germany and Austria-Hungary, agreed in 1878, was largely a response to German insecurity following a fracturing of Russo-German relations (see page 16). The Dual Alliance was enlarged to the Triple Alliance when Italy joined in 1882. It was a defensive military alliance which committed the signatories to providing military support should one of their number be attacked by one of the major European powers. In the case of Germany and Italy, however, they were only committed to helping each other should either be attacked by France.

This is so funny!

> **KEY TERM**
>
> **July Days** The period during July 1914 in which diplomatic efforts failed to avert the outbreak of war.
>
> **Triple Entente** The alliance between France, Britain and Russia established in 1907.
>
> **Triple Alliance** The alliance between Germany, Austria-Hungary and Italy established in 1882.
>
> **Dual Alliance** The alliance between Germany and Austria-Hungary established in 1878.

← **Did the alliance systems make war more likely?**

- Possibly. It is easy to feel threatened when people team up against you, let alone people who are enemies.

Europe in 1914 showing the major alliances.

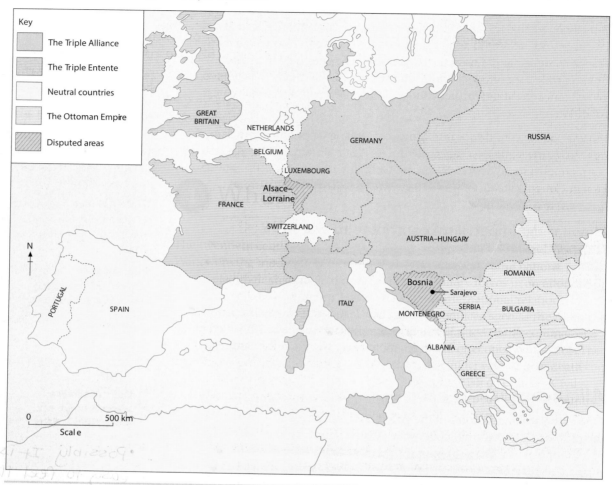

Key

- The Triple Alliance
- The Triple Entente
- Neutral countries
- The Ottoman Empire
- Disputed areas

GREAT BRITAIN
NETHERLANDS
BELGIUM
LUXEMBOURG
GERMANY
RUSSIA
Alsace-Lorraine
FRANCE
SWITZERLAND
AUSTRIA–HUNGARY
PORTUGAL
SPAIN
ITALY
Bosnia
Sarajevo
MONTENEGRO
SERBIA
ROMANIA
BULGARIA
ALBANIA
GREECE

N

0   500 km
Scale

? Look at Sounrce C. Why might Germany have felt particularly threatened by the existence of the Triple Entente?

🔑 **KEY TERM**

Entente Cordiale The agreement signed between Britain and France in 1904 settling their imperial rivalries.

In turn, Russia sought an ally against its main rival Austria-Hungary, who had been strengthened by the alliance with Germany. Russia was also concerned by the growing potential German threat, an anxiety shared by France. In consequence a Franco-Russian military alliance was signed in 1894. This too was a defence alliance, committing each country to support the other in the event that either one of them was attacked by a member of the Triple Alliance. In 1904, Britain and France drew closer by signing the ***Entente Cordiale***. This was not a military alliance but a series of agreements finally settling imperial rivalries and recognizing and agreeing to respect each other's spheres of colonial influence. In 1907, Britain reached a similar accord with Russia, in the Anglo-Russian Convention, which ended animosities generated by their competition for colonies in central Asia. This paved the way for Britain to join with France and Russia in the so-called Triple Entente in 1907. Unlike the Triple Alliance, this was not a military alliance.

How far did the alliance systems contribute to war in 1914?

The impression that the alliance systems led to war by a chain reaction during the summer of 1914 is only superficially compelling. Although by mid-August 1914 all the signatories of the two rival alliances, with the exception of Italy, were at war, the manner in which they entered the war was not in adherence to the terms of the alliance agreements, nor primarily motivated by them. France did not immediately declare war on Germany, despite the German declaration of war against France's ally Russia. Neither did Austria-Hungary declare war on Britain or France, despite their declarations of war on Germany. Italy also failed to enter the war in support of its Triple Alliance partners, despite the British and French declaration of war on Austria-Hungary. The fact that all the major signatories of the alliances, with the exception initially of Italy, ended up at war was more a reflection of their own individual agendas rather than their blindly being pulled into conflict by the existence of the alliance systems. The terms of the Triple Entente in particular did not commit its signatories to military action in any event.

The existence of the Triple Entente did contribute to war, however, by fostering insecurity within Germany since it accentuated fears about the vulnerability of Germany's position as it was now encircled by hostile powers. This added to the appeal within the German military high command of the merits of provoking a preventive war in which Germany would have the advantage through launching a first strike before its rivals were fully prepared. This increasingly came to be seen as the most effective way to improve German security prospects, in part accounting for German decisions during the summer of 1914 which seemed to positively encourage the outbreak of war (see page 30). However, the existence of the Triple Entente alone was not enough to stimulate this agenda, not least because the terms of the Entente were *defensive* and vague, meaning it posed little immediate or direct threat to Germany. German insecurity, if real and not a cloak for a more aggressive agenda, was at least as much prompted by concerns about France and Britain's growing military strength due to increased defence expenditure (see pages 19–22).

Militarism

The growth of **militarism** on the eve of the First World War manifested itself in the glorification of military strength and an **arms race** in which escalating amounts of money were spent on defence, leading to increases in the size of armies and weaponry. In part this was stimulated by economic and technological developments that not only enabled the more effective mass production of weaponry, but also led to the invention of new types of weapons. New weaponry, such as explosive shells and the machine gun,

[Handwritten margin note:] • Although the rival alliances were at war, it wasn't the alliance systems that caused the war because each nation declared war at different times.

[Handwritten margin note:] Pro of Alliance:
- resources
- increase of security
- Support from other countries
- Strenght in numbers
Con:
- creates more conflict

🔑 KEY TERM

Militarism The principle or policy of maintaining a strong military and the glorification of military strength.

Arms race A competition between nations for military superiority.

← **How did militarism contribute to war in 1914?**

massively increased the rate, range and accuracy of firepower so that any nation not prepared to invest in these new technologies, and the railways to transport them, would be at a grievous disadvantage in any future military engagement.

The arms race

There had been a steady increase in defence expenditure in all the major European countries from the mid-1890s that increased more rapidly from 1905 (see Source D). In a large part this increase was prompted by economic and technological developments which made possible a new range and scale of armaments.

? What can be learned from Source D about the defence spending of the major European powers between 1890 and 1913?

• Russia and Britain, both members of the triple entente spent the highest amount on their armies.

SOURCE D

The defence spending (in millions of marks) of the major European powers, 1890–1913.

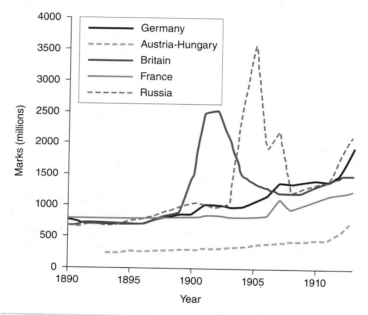

The growth in armed forces

There was substantial investment in increasing the troop numbers in the **standing armies** of most of the major European countries in the decades leading up to the First World War (see Source E). By 1914, all the major European powers possessed mass armies. The Triple Entente, however, had a substantial advantage in terms of the overall manpower of its standing armies, outnumbering the combined troops of Germany and Austria-Hungary by 1.5 million. The rate of increase of the size of the standing armies in the Entente nations was also greater than that of Austria-Hungary and Germany, the latter actually increasing at the slowest rate.

KEY TERM

Standing army A permanent, professional army maintained in times of peace and war.

SOURCE E

Approximate standing army and population sizes of the major European powers in 1900 and 1914.

	Britain	France	Russia	Germany	Austria-Hungary
Number of troops in standing army in 1900	281,000	590,000	860,000	601,000	397,000
Number of troops in standing army in 1914	710,000	1,138,000	1,300,000	801,000	810,000
Population in 1914	46,407,000	39,602,000	167,000,000	65,000,000	49,882,000

How much can Source E tell us about the relative military strength of the major powers on the eve of the First World War?

- Why, even though having the smallest population out of the 6 nations, does France have such a large army

However, the size of the standing armies only gives a partial impression of military strength, for all countries had plans to call up reservists, and then conscripts, in the event of war.

The naval arms race

Naval power was the focus of a particular arms race that developed between Britain and Germany in the decade before 1914. The Kaiser, admiring and envious of the British Royal Navy, sought to build a German navy which would challenge British naval supremacy. An ambitious plan to increase the size of the German navy was drawn up by Admiral Alfred von Tirpitz and implemented in the Navy Bill of 1900. The British interpreted this as a challenge to their dominance of the seas, and an implied threat to the security of their empire for which a strong navy was a prerequisite.

The British, seeking to retain their lead in naval supremacy, increased their own shipbuilding programme, culminating in the launch of a new class of **battleship**, the HMS *Dreadnought*, in 1906. The *Dreadnought* was the first example of a heavily armoured battleship equipped exclusively with large guns capable of destroying enemy ships from great distances, setting a new standard for modern battleships. The Germans, anxious not to be left behind, responded in kind with the launch of their own dreadnought battleship in 1908. An intensification of the naval arms race ensued (see Source F, page 22).

 **KEY TERM**

Battleship Heavily armed and armoured large warship.

?

How valuable is Source F as evidence of the relative naval strength of Britain and Germany in the years before the First World War?

SOURCE F

A comparison of British and German dreadnoughts, 1906–14.

Dreadnoughts	Britain	Germany
1906	1	0
1907	4	0
1908	6	4
1909	8	7
1910	11	8
1911	16	11
1912	19	13
1913	26	16
1914	29	17

How did the arms race contribute to war in 1914?

The German actions which were key in escalating the crisis of July 1914 into war (see page 30) can in part be seen as motivated by anxieties generated by the arms race. In the years leading up to 1914 there was a growing perception within the German government and military that Germany was actually losing the arms race in terms of its long-term ability to keep pace with its rivals. There was some evidence for this fear. Germany was particularly anxious about Russia, whose increase in defence expenditure was rising at a more rapid rate and whose potential resources were far greater than those of Germany.

In consequence, there developed a view within the German military high command that if European war was inevitable in the near future, then Germany's best chance for success lay in a pre-emptive strike while it was still militarily stronger than its rivals. This attitude of 'war the sooner the better' was voiced by General von Moltke at the Kaiser's so-called 'War Council', a meeting held between the Kaiser and his military and naval advisers in December 1912, and can be seen to influence the German decisions in July 1914 which directly contributed to the escalation of military conflict.

→ ## Military plans

New military technologies necessitated a rethinking of military strategy and tactics. New military plans were drawn up by all the major powers in the decades leading up to the First World War. The premise behind all these plans was the importance of the rapid offensive. Military planners were convinced that any war would be short in duration. This belief, mistaken as it turned out, reinforced the view that the decisive battles would be those of the initial offensives. It was therefore crucial that mobilization was achieved quickly, since any delay could give the enemy a potentially insurmountable advantage.

German military plans

German military planners faced a particularly concerning problem, the danger of a two-front war. This became a realistic prospect following the alliance between France and Russia in 1894 (see page 18). In response to this threat, and in accordance with the primacy placed on the offensive, German security came to rest on the plan devised in 1897 by the head of the German army, Count Alfred von Schlieffen. The so-called **Schlieffen Plan** set out that German troops attack France by way of a several-pronged hook advancing through northern France, Belgium and The Netherlands, avoiding the heavily fortified French border with Germany, to surround Paris and defeat France within six weeks (see Source G). This would then enable German troops to turn around and face the Russians to the east before the vast Russian army was mobilized. It was estimated that it would take at least eight weeks for the Russian army to be fully operational. The key to the success of the plan would lie in the swift movement of the hook formations into France; any delay either before or during the offensive would hand the initiative to Germany's enemies. In this context, rapid German mobilization was crucial to its security plans.

[handwritten note:] 1897 is 17 years before the war breaks out.

🔑 **KEY TERM**

Schlieffen Plan The German military plan by which they hoped to win the First World War by avoiding a substantial war on two fronts.

[handwritten note:] assumption

What can be learned about the nature of the Schlieffen Plan from Source G? ?

SOURCE G

The Schlieffen Plan.

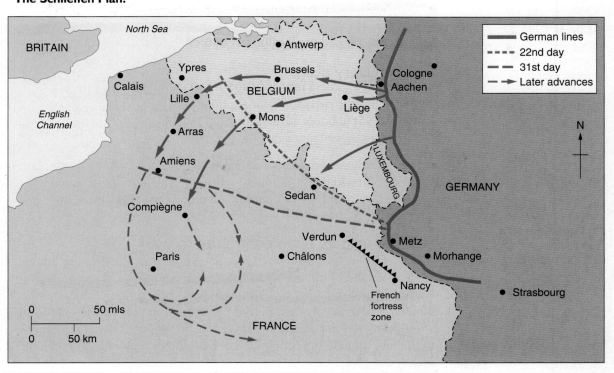

Russian military plans

Russian military plans also emphasized early mobilization in order to compensate for the logistical and organizational difficulties that meant the Russian army would be comparatively slow to reach military readiness. This explains the early Russian order for mobilization on 30 July 1914 that dramatically escalated the crisis. However, unlike the German military plans, mobilization did not have to presage war.

French military plans

French military plans were based on Plan XVII drawn up by the chief of the general staff, Joseph Joffre, in 1913. Again the offensive was emphasized. Central to the plan was a concentrated attack through Lorraine on German forces across the German border. The mismatch of this plan with the nature of the German advance in 1914, which avoided the Franco-German border near Lorraine, revealed the limitations of French military intelligence as well as the exaggerated optimism of the French high command in the comparative strength of its forces.

Austro-Hungarian military plans

KEY TERM

Galicia A region of eastern Europe, now in south-east Poland.

Blockade To prevent enemy ships from reaching or leaving their ports usually to prevent the movement of supplies of food, raw materials or war goods.

Austro-Hungarian military planners, like those in Germany, had to deal with the prospect of a multiple-front war. Austria-Hungary would be likely to have to face Serbian troops to the south, and Russian forces to the east in **Galicia**. If Romania entered the war (which it did from August 1916), Austria-Hungary would have to deal with a three-front war. The Austro-Hungarian army was comparatively weak technologically and would be outnumbered by its enemies. Austria-Hungary therefore certainly hoped for substantial assistance from its German ally.

British military plans

The British had a relatively small standing army on the eve of 1914 (see page 21), but it was planned that this would be rapidly mobilized and transported to France to help counter any German attack. The British Royal Navy would be used to:

- destroy the German navy
- impose a **blockade** on Germany
- protect the Triple Entente's supply shipping from attacks by enemy vessels.

How did military plans contribute to war?

The nature of most of the pre-1914 military plans contributed significantly to the likelihood of war. All were based on the optimistic premise that war was winnable in certainly no more than a few months. This assumption turned out to be deeply flawed. Had this been suspected to any significant extent before war was underway, it is likely that the majority of nations would have tried harder to stay out of war in the summer of 1914 than they actually did.

The German Schlieffen Plan bears particular responsibility for the outbreak of war as its emphasis on swift action immediately following the order to mobilize meant that Germany was more likely to perceive mobilization in other countries as an inevitable prelude to war. It also made war unavoidable once Germany issued the order to mobilize.

Nationalism

The decades before the First World War witnessed the growth of an increasingly strident and aggressive nationalism in the major countries of Europe. This was frequently connected to pride in a nation's military strength as well as its cultural values and traditions.

Reasons for the growth of nationalism

Nationalistic sentiment in the decades before 1914 was not new, but had been encouraged by a number of recent developments. It had been boosted by national pride generated by the growth of militarism and economic strength in these years and the international competition these stimulated.

There were also more subtle ideological reasons behind the inclination to trumpet national superiority. These developed from the gradual assimilation of the naturalist **Charles Darwin**'s ideas about evolution. Darwin's presentation of a process of natural selection, in which the weaker elements of a species die out and in which the 'fittest' survive, gave rise to the idea that some nation's were innately 'fitter' or stronger than others and that it was their destiny to triumph over weaker nations.

Nationalistic sentiment grew too because it was promoted by the press and governments. In part, the press was responding to an already existing nationalism which it knew would appeal to its readership, but its promotion of patriotism served to reinforce and encourage it further. Governments promoted nationalism to justify growing military expenditure.

SOURCE H

Private George Morgan of the 16th Battalion, West Yorkshire Regiment explaining why so many volunteered to enlist. Quoted in *Minds at War* by David Roberts, published by Saxon, London, 1999, page 21.

We had been brought up to believe that Britain was the best country in the world and we wanted to defend her. The history taught to us at school showed that we were better than other people (didn't we always win the last war?).

How did nationalism contribute to war?

The feelings of rivalry and superiority generated by nationalism created an environment in which war was not as assiduously avoided as it might have been, but was rather seen as an opportunity to assert dominance. Indeed, in so far as nationalistic pride encouraged optimism in victory, it may have made the risk of going to war seem more worth taking. Nationalistic

---

← To what extent did the rise in nationalism contribute to war?

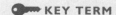 **KEY TERM**

Charles Darwin A British natural scientist (1809–82) who formulated the theory of evolution.

How useful is Source H as evidence of why so many men volunteered to enlist in the army in 1914? ?

• This man explains why and how the governments Promotion of nationalism helped in persuading people to enlist.

sentiment influenced entire populations, diplomats and governments, making the latter increasingly likely to risk war in the belief that their populations would bear the financial burden and mobilize when called to arms. In the case of Slavic nationalism, it contributed to the war in a more direct way by leading to the assassination of Franz Ferdinand, which triggered the escalation to conflict in 1914.

<table>
<tr><td>To what extent had the long-term causes of the war made conflict likely by 1914?</td></tr>
</table>

→ # Conclusion

European conflict was a likely prospect by 1914 but not inevitable. Relations between European countries had become increasingly fragile due to economic and imperial competition, the alliance systems and escalating militarism. These factors simultaneously contributed to increased insecurities and nationalistic pride within the governments of Europe. This, in turn, would make the governments more likely to resort to war in 1914 as the best way to safeguard their power and position before their adversaries became too strong. However, it would take a particular crisis to convert the potential for war into actual conflict.

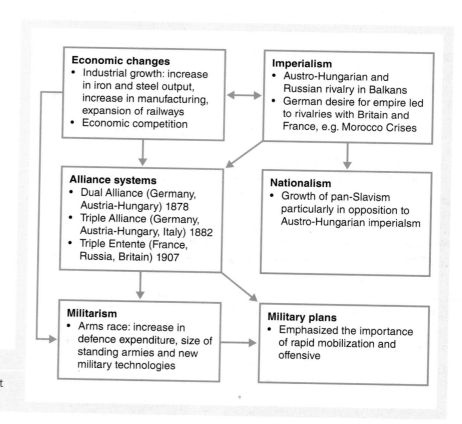

SUMMARY DIAGRAM

Long-term causes of the First World War

The short-term causes of the First World War

▶ *Key question: How significant were the short-term causes to the outbreak of war in 1914?*

Although war had become a likely prospect by 1914, it was the short-term causes that determined the precise timing of the outbreak of war. The main short-term causes were the assassination of the Austro-Hungarian Archduke Franz Ferdinand in June 1914, which provided the trigger for war, and the failure of diplomacy in the following weeks to provide an alternative to military conflict.

The assassination of Archduke Franz Ferdinand, 28 June 1914

> **Why did the assassination of the Archduke trigger war?**

The First World War had its roots in long-term social, economic and political developments in Europe in the decades before 1914. The event which brought together these pressures in such a way as to trigger war was the assassination of the heir to the Austro-Hungarian throne, Franz Ferdinand, in Sarajevo, capital of the province of Bosnia-Herzegovina which Austria-Hungary annexed in 1908. The assassin was a Bosnian Serb nationalist who was a member of the Black Hand, an anti-Austrian terrorist organization that was sponsored and trained by members of the government of Serbia.

The significance of the assassination

The assassination was the spark that ignited the long-term tensions into war. The particular significance of the assassination was that it raised the Balkan issue, which was a source of serious rivalry between Austria-Hungary, Russia and Serbia. This rivalry was long standing, but had not yet triggered war, although it had come close to doing so on a number of occasions (see page 15). In 1914, however, Austria-Hungary did take military action. This was mostly because the changed military and political circumstances made Austria-Hungary more confident in taking provocative action, but in part also due to the nature the assassination itself. Not only was the murder of the heir to the Austro-Hungarian throne of sufficiently serious magnitude to prompt an extreme reaction from Austria-Hungary, but it also provided Austria-Hungary with good reason to hope for international sympathy, encouraging it to risk more decisive action against Serbia without it necessarily enlarging to a wider conflict. In particular, there were grounds to believe that Russia would not intervene on the side of Serbia given the Tsar's abhorrence of terrorist action; Russia's tsars were not infrequently the targets of terrorist violence themselves. This highlights the importance of the assassination in particular as a trigger.

? What can be learned about
the assassination of the
Archduke from Source I?

The assassination of Archduke Franz Ferdinand and his wife in Sarajevo as illustrated in *La Domenica del Corriere*, an Italian newspaper, in 1914.

Diplomatic crisis

The assassination of the Archduke triggered a diplomatic crisis that rapidly escalated into world war. The enlargement of the crisis beyond an internal affair of the Austro-Hungarian Empire began when Austria-Hungary blamed the Kingdom of Serbia for the assassination. Austria-Hungary had long been desirous of war with Serbia, its main rival in the Balkans, and seized on the opportunity presented by the assassination to provoke military action. Austria-Hungary's accusation that Serbia was complicit in the assassination was not without justification, although without formal proof, given the activities of the Serbian-based Black Hand terrorists (see page 27).

Austria-Hungary's ultimatum

Austria-Hungary took the first step in escalating the crisis when it issued a deliberately harsh ultimatum to the Serbian government on 23 July 1914. It demanded, among other things, that the Serbian government open a judicial inquiry into the perpetrators of the assassination and that this investigation be open to scrutiny by Austrio-Hungarian investigators. Since such Austro-

Hungarian intervention would represent a violation of Serbian independence, it was unlikely to be acceptable to the Serbian government. Austria-Hungary gave Serbia just 48 hours to respond, fully expectant of a rejection.

The 'blank cheque' guarantee

Austria-Hungary was emboldened to take such a provocative stance by the encouragement it had received from its ally, Germany, to take decisive action against Serbia, even if this precipitated a war with Serbia. On 6 July, the German government essentially offered unconditional assistance to Austria-Hungary in whatever action it may take against Serbia in the crisis. This unconditional offer became known as the German 'blank cheque' guarantee to Austria-Hungary. Germany's motives in doing so are not entirely clear. Some believe it wished a limited war between Austria-Hungary and Serbia, in which the victory of the former would strengthen Germany's ally Austria-Hungary, and by extension Germany itself. Others believe that Germany wanted a wider European war and saw the crisis triggered by the assassination as an opportunity to provoke one.

Serbia's response

Serbia, on 24 July, accepted all the demands except that relating to Austro-Hungarian intervention in a judicial inquiry into the assassination. Although Serbia was aware that it was likely that military action would result from this refusal, they were perhaps emboldened by hopes that Russia might act to protect Serbia against Austria-Hungary. Russia styled itself as the protector of Slavic interests in the Balkans and public pressure in Russia to honour this role was considerable. In addition, Russia was anxious to prevent any potential extension of the territory of its rival Austria-Hungary in the Balkans. There existed, however, no formal alliance between Serbia and Russia, and so no guarantee of Russian assistance.

The crisis rapidly intensified during the July Days, the name given to the period in which diplomatic efforts were made to try to avert the outbreak of war, and within weeks, despite various initiatives to diffuse the crisis, all the major countries of Europe had become embroiled in conflict (see page 11).

Attempts at diplomacy

> **Why did diplomacy fail to prevent the outbreak of war?**

There were significant efforts to reach a diplomatic solution to the crisis. These negotiations ultimately failed to prevent the outbreak of war.

Communications between the ambassadors and governments of the major powers were continuous in the weeks following the assassination of the Archduke, and various proposals were made to attempt to settle the developing crisis:

- 26 July: a conference to settle the crisis was proposed by Britain. France, Italy and Russia signalled their willingness to attend. Germany rejected the proposal. The conference never met.

Chancellor German equivalent to prime minister.

?
What can be learned from Source J about the intentions of Russia in the days leading up to the outbreak of war?

- 29 July: Britain proposed international mediation, the day after the Austro-Hungarian declaration of war on Serbia.
- 29 July: the German **chancellor**, Bethmann-Hollweg, urged Austria-Hungary to limit its invasion of Serbia to an occupation of the Serbian capital, Belgrade, only, and urged Austria-Hungary to open talks with Russia. These proposals were ignored by Austria-Hungary.

SOURCE J

Tsar Nicholas II to his cousin Kaiser Wilhelm II in a telegram on 28 July 1914.

To try to avoid such a calamity as a European war, I beg you in the name of our old friendship to do what you can to prevent your allies from going too far.

The failure of diplomacy

Germany's opposition, until the last moment, to diplomatic initiatives to resolve the crisis contributed to the failure of a negotiated settlement. Until 29 July, Germany was urging Austria-Hungary to take prompt and decisive action against Serbia, not least by offering its unconditional support through the blank cheque guarantee (see page 29).

Germany's 'calculated risk'?

The motives that informed the German escalation of the crisis have been much debated. Some historians, such as Erdmann and Zechlin, argued that despite appearances, Germany did not want a European war, but a more localized Balkan conflict between Austria-Hungary and Serbia. This could have been advantageous to Germany in that victory by Austria-Hungary would have significantly strengthened Germany's main ally. In this interpretation, Germany was pursuing a policy of 'calculated risk', the 'risk' being that Russia might intervene on behalf of Serbia, necessitating German military involvement, and might even bring in Russia's ally, France.

In the 'calculated risk' interpretation, Germany's misreading of the situation in the early weeks of July emphasizes the significance of short-term diplomatic miscalculations in causing the war. These miscalculations were the German government's flawed assumptions that Russia, France and Britain would not intervene. There is certainly evidence to suggest that the German Chancellor, Bethmann-Hollweg, did not expect the major powers to get involved, and that when Britain and Russia made their intentions more transparent from 29 July he backtracked and urged restraint on Austria-Hungary. By that point, however, Austria-Hungary was already at war with Serbia and could not very well call its troops off without significant humiliation.

Germany may have misinterpreted the Russian mobilization order on 30 July as a direct threat and a prelude to war, since in the German Schlieffen Plan mobilization and war were virtually synonymous (see page 23). This was not the case in Russian military plans, and a German misunderstanding of this may have contributed to the decision to mobilize and the subsequent escalation of the crisis.

Did Germany deliberately seek war?

Other historians reject the view that German diplomatic miscalculations satisfactorily explain German actions in escalating the crisis. They highlight that there was strong evidence to suggest that the war could not be contained throughout July. Indeed, warnings to this effect were issued by the British and Russian governments. They dismiss the German government's last-minute attempt to halt escalation as a mere face-saving measure. Instead, they see German actions as symptomatic of a policy that deliberately sought European war, motivated either by **expansionist** desires (see page 16) or by the desire for a preventive war in which German victory would safeguard its position in Europe before its rivals grew sufficiently in strength to overwhelm it (see page 20).

KEY TERM

Expansionist A policy aimed at the enlargement of territorial/economic control.

SOURCE K

The German Chancellor, Theobald von Bethmann-Hollweg, in August 1914. Quoted in *The Origins of the First World War* by A. Mombauer, published by Pearson, London, 2002, page 21.

Should all our attempts [for peace] be in vain, should the sword be forced into our hand, we shall go into the field of battle with a clear conscience and the knowledge that we did not desire this war.

How useful is Source K in showing German motivations on the eve of the outbreak of the war?

How did the failure of diplomacy contribute to war?

The immediate consequence of the failure of diplomacy was the outbreak of war. Certainly diplomatic miscalculations were important in accelerating the descent into war, but the tensions, insecurities and hostilities generated by the longer-term causes of the war arguably made effective diplomacy unlikely in any event by July 1914. Indeed, the long-term causes contributed to many of the miscalculations made by governments in the July Days.

Conclusion

How significant were the short-term causes in the outbreak of war in 1914?

The short-term causes dictated the precise timing of the outbreak of war, although the fundamental reasons for the conflict lay primarily with the long-term causes. It was, for example, the insecurities, rivalries and hostilities generated by the long-term causes that largely undermined the effective operation of diplomacy in the weeks leading up to the war. Similarly, while the assassination was necessary to trigger war, without the long-term causes, it was probable that the animosity between Serbia and Austria-Hungary could have been contained to a Balkan affair.

It sounds like the long term causes were more influential

Short-term causes of the First
World War

Assassination of Archduke Franz Ferdinand, 28 June 1914
- Triggered conflict between Austria-Hungary and Serbia, which …
- Triggered rivalry and possible war between Austria-Hungary and Russia over the Balkans, which …
- Triggered many of the long-term anxieties and causes of the war, such as the alliance systems and military plans

Failed diplomatic attempts at resolving the crisis
Various conferences proposed and negotiations ongoing but all failed due to:
- long-term mistrust and anxieties (due to long-term causes)
- desire for war (although this is more controversial)
- mistakes and wrongful assumptions in diplomacy

Long-term causes of war
- Economic changes
- Imperialism
- Alliances
- Nationalism
- Militarism
- Military plans

③ Key debate

▶ **Key question:** *To what extent should Germany be blamed for causing the First World War?*

The Treaty of Versailles and German war guilt

The historiography of the origins of the First World War has frequently focused on assessing the actions and motivations of the leading powers. From the outset, German culpability was emphasized. In the Treaty of Versailles (see page 65), German delegates were forced to accept responsibility for the war. However, this verdict was soon challenged as unfair.

Collective mistakes

In the 1920s and 1930s, verdicts about the origins of the war shifted towards an emphasis on collective mistakes.

US historians, such as Sidney Bradshaw Fay (see Source L), took the lead in formulating this interpretation. This is not surprising given the widespread opposition in the USA to the German War Guilt clause; it had been opposed by the US President Woodrow Wilson even in 1919. In Europe, an acceptance of collective responsibility was increasingly embraced in the context of greater efforts at political reconciliation with Germany in the 1920s. These efforts were manifested in the German entry into the **League of Nations** in 1926, something prohibited by the Treaty of Versailles, and a series of financial loans to Germany by the USA which aimed to rescue Germany from financial crisis, which was in large part brought on by the heavy financial penalties imposed by the Treaty of Versailles.

SOURCE L

Excerpt from *The Origins of the World War* by Sidney Bradshaw Fay, published by Macmillan, New York, 1929, pages 547–8.

No one country and no one man was solely, or probably even mainly, to blame … None of the Powers wanted a European War … one must abandon the dictum of the Versailles Treaty that Germany and its allies were solely responsible … Austria was more responsible for the immediate origins of the war than any other Power … [indeed, Germany] made genuine, though too belated efforts, to avert one … the verdict of the Treaty of Versailles that Germany and its allies were responsible for the war, in the view of the evidence now available, is historically unsound. It should therefore be revised.

As the political mood in Europe became more tense in the 1930s with the rise of the **Nazi Party** and the increasing possibility of another European war, the extent of German guilt for the First World War acquired a heightened significance. For those who wished to justify the policy of **appeasement** adopted by the Western **Allies** towards Germany's increasingly assertive and expansionist foreign policy, the interpretation that the Treaty of Versailles' verdict had been too harsh made sense. If Germany had been unfairly blamed and too harsh penalties imposed on it, then it was only fair to agree to some revision of these terms as Germany was demanding and as appeasement allowed.

German responsibility again: the Fischer thesis

The publication of German historian Fritz Fischer's book *Grasping for World Power* in 1961 reignited controversy over the origins of the war. In Fischer's interpretation, European war was the deliberate and desired result of an aggressive and expansionist German foreign policy. Fischer placed particular weight on the 'War Council' held between the Kaiser and his military advisors in December 1912 (see page 34) in order to show that a desire for war was already apparent in 1912. Central to Fischer's arguments that German foreign policy was expansionist was his discovery in the archives of the Reich Chancellery of a memorandum written by the German Chancellor Bethmann-Hollweg's private secretary Kurt Riezler on 9 September 1914. This document, often referred to as the 'September Programme', set out details of Bethmann-Hollweg's views about what Germany could hope to gain from German victory. These gains included the annexation of territory belonging to Germany's European neighbours, a customs union ensuring German economic dominance of Europe and German colonial expansion in Africa.

What view does Source L express about who was to blame for causing the First World War?

KEY TERM

League of Nations International organization established after the First World War to resolve conflicts between nations in order to prevent war.

Nazi Party The German National Socialist Party led by Adolf Hitler, which held power in Germany from January 1933 until April 1945.

Appeasement A policy of giving concessions in order to avoid a more immediate confrontation.

Allies In the First World War, an alliance between Britain, France, the USA, Japan, China and others, including Russia until 1917.

?

What can be learned from Source M about German responsibility for causing the First World War?

SOURCE M

Excerpt from *War Aims and Strategic Policy in the Great War* by Fritz Fischer, published by Rowman & Littlefield, Totowa, 1977, page 109.

War simultaneously seemed [in the eyes of the German élites] to secure the stability of the social order and to guarantee the dissolution of the Entente and freedom to pursue an imperialistic policy on a global scale … Hot on the heels of the mid-November 1912 decision to enlarge the army came the so-called 'War Council' of 8 December 1912 [at which] the Kaiser demanded the immediate opening of hostilities against Britain, France and Russia. Moltke concurred, adding his dictum, 'the sooner the better', since the strength of Germany's land opponents could only continue to grow. But Tirpitz requested a postponement of one and a half years [to ready the German navy] … The 'not before' of the navy and the 'no later than' deadline of the army led to the appointment of a date, of an optimal moment, for the war now held to be inevitable.

T O K

'Historical facts are like fish swimming about in a vast and inaccessible ocean; and what the historian catches will depend partly on chance, but mainly on what part of the ocean he chooses to fish in and what tackle he chooses to use – these two factors being, of course, determined by the kind of fish he wants to catch.' E.H. Carr, historian, 1961.

To what extent does this quotation have relevance in understanding the different interpretations about the origins of the First World War? Can the historian be truly objective? What factors might influence his judgement of historical events? Does this mean we can never really know what happened in the past with any certainty? (History, Language and Reason.)

Fischer's thesis immediately attracted critics, especially in Germany, where one of his strongest challengers was historian Gerhard Ritter. Ritter attacked Fischer's reliance on the September Programme, arguing that given it was written at a time when the war was *already* underway, and when a German victory seemed a real possibility, it cannot be taken as evidence of German pre-war aims. The vehemence of opposition to Fischer's views within Germany was not just motivated by differing interpretations of evidence from the archives. It was also coloured by contemporary politics and an understandable aversion to any interpretation of Germany's role in the First World War, which seemed, in the light of the more recent and substantial German responsibility for the Second World War, to suggest some kind of innate, or at least cultural, aggression on the part of Germany.

Towards a consensus of predominant German responsibility

The prevailing consensus that has emerged tends towards arguments of collective responsibility with a particular emphasis on the relative importance of German actions (see Source N).

SOURCE N

Excerpt from *The Experience of World War One* by J.M. Winter, published by Greenwich Editions, London, 2000, page 38.

On the one hand, somebody had to pull the trigger. That was Germany. But on the other hand, its actions exposed the weaknesses and confusions of both its allies and its adversaries … If Germany may be said to have brought about World War I, it did so as part of a political community which collectively let the peace of Europe slip through its fingers.

?

What view does Source N give about why the First World War began?

I agree with this interpretation mostly. Emphasis should be placed on Germany but it is not only on them. You can't engage in war without having someone to battle.

The course of the First World War

▶ *Key question:* How far did the nature of fighting in the First World War represent a new type of conflict?

In many ways the First World War represented a new type of conflict. It was arguably the first example of modern total war (see page 4). As such, countries mobilized resources on an unprecedented scale towards the war effort, frequently blurring the distinction between civilians and combatants to a new degree. On the battlefield, new weapons played a decisive role in shaping the nature of the conflict, although tactical thinking did not always evolve rapidly enough to maximize their potential.

The land war in Europe 1914

The First World War, contrary to the pre-war expectations of a short war that would 'be over by Christmas', became a prolonged war of exhaustion in which victory ultimately went to the side more able to sustain such conflict. On the Western Front, primarily in Belgium and northern France, the mobile warfare of the opening month rapidly turned into stalemate and trench warfare (see page 37). On the Eastern Front, Russian forces were mobilized for action far more rapidly than had been predicted.

◀ **Why had neither side been able to make decisive gains by the end of 1914?**

The war on the Western Front

Belgium and Luxembourg

The initial phase of the war on the Western Front was characterized by rapid movement in accordance with the Schlieffen Plan (see page 22). Within the first three days German troops had occupied Luxembourg, and the Belgian capital, Brussels, was captured in 20 days.

The German violation of Belgium neutrality, which Britain had promised to protect in the Treaty of London of 1839, was used by the British government as the ostensible reason for its declaration of war on Germany on 4 August. In reality, Britain had more fundamental reasons for entering the war, not least to ensure the defeat of its main rival, Germany. Britain feared that a French defeat would mean German domination of Europe and the capture and use of the French navy against Britain.

The race to the sea

The German advance began to slow through a combination of resistance from Belgian, French and British troops, as well as exhaustion and failing supply lines. Belgian troops held up the Germans at the forts of Liège, which were finally shelled into submission by German artillery. The 150,000 strong British Expeditionary Force (BEF) confronted German troops at the Battles of

? What can be learned from Source O about the fighting on the Western Front?

Mons on 23 August, delaying, but not halting, the German advance. By the end of August, German troops were exhausted trying to keep pace with the ambitious timescales set by the Schlieffen Plan, and supplies were lacking due to the inability of a damaged and incomplete railway system to transport vital food and equipment. By the end of August, the nearest available **railheads** were some 135 km from the leading troops. In particular, the troops of General Alexander von Kluck, occupying the right outside edge of the German advance, were struggling to cope with the 30–40 km per day march stipulated by the plan. This jeopardized the plan's success since it was important that all the 'hooks' advanced in conjunction with each other to avoid creating gaps in the line that could be exploited by the enemy.

The German advance was finally halted by the combined French and British counterattack along the Marne River on 6–9 September. The German armies were forced into retreat and entrenched their positions; initially digging trenches to provide some temporary shelter. Subsequent French and British attempts to break through the German line failed, as did efforts by both sides to advance by **outflanking** each other. A succession of failed outflanking manoeuvres led to the extension of the trench lines from Ostend in the north of Belgium to the Swiss border in the south, in what has become known as the 'race to the sea'. Neither side was able to advance, so more trenches were dug for protection. These trench lines would dominate the war

SOURCE O

The Western Front 1914–17.

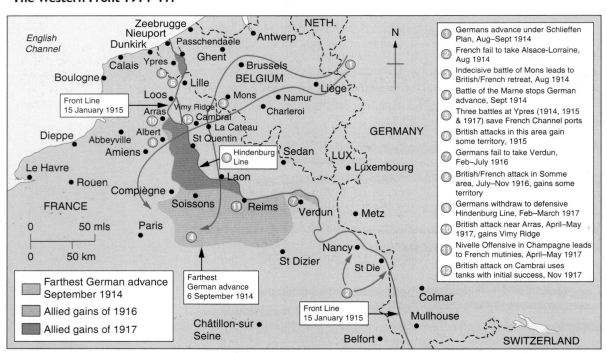

36

on the Western Front for the next four years. The war of manoeuvre was over, at least on the Western Front.

Trench warfare

The construction of trench systems along the Western Front necessitated the development of entirely new strategic and tactical approaches to try to break the stalemate in order to achieve victory. Trench warfare posed particular difficulties for the attacking side since the military technology available conferred huge advantages on the defenders in this type of warfare. The advancing infantry would have to cross the exposed ground of **no-man's land**, in the face of artillery bombardment and machine-gun fire. Even if the infantry succeeded in crossing no-man's land, the enemy trenches were protected by rolls of thick barbed wire which was almost impossible to traverse, making the infantry easy targets for machine-gun or sniper fire. It was little wonder that few offensives resulted in a decisive breakthrough or significant territorial gain.

KEY TERM

No-man's land The unclaimed land between the two opposing trench systems.

Technology of the war: machine guns

Machine guns were mainly used for defensive purposes, given the lack of manoeuvrability of early tripod-mounted machine guns. They were formidable weapons against infantry. Machine guns fired on average over 500 rounds per minute. Later in the war, technological developments led to the creation of machine guns that could be carried by one person, allowing them to be used for offensive purposes.

SOURCE P

Approximate machine-gun production in Britain and Germany 1914–18.

	1914	1915	1916	1917	1918
Britain	300	6,000	33,500	79,700	120,900
Germany	500	1,000	2,000	10,000	13,000

What can be learned from Source P about armament production in Britain and Germany during the First World War?

Offensive strategies in trench warfare

The main basis of attack strategy throughout the war on the Western Front remained the infantry advance in which waves of troops would cross no-man's land in an attempt to capture enemy trenches. New tactics were developed to weaken the enemy defensive positions *before* exposing infantry to an advance and to *support* the infantry once the advance was underway (see the table on page 38).

Britain had significantly more machine guns. Between 1915 and 16 germany only doubled production while Britain produce almost x4 as much.

Soldiers marching or fighting on foot

The key offensive tactics used in the First World War

Offensive tactic	Description of the tactic	Aims of the tactic	Weaknesses with the tactic
Preliminary artillery bombardment	Artillery shells bombarded enemy trenches and defensive positions before the start of an infantry attack. The bombardment halted once the advance had begun	To weaken enemy trench systems To kill enemy troops To destroy enemy machine guns and artillery To cut rolls of barbed wire	The inaccuracy of artillery fire The relatively high proportion of dud shells Many enemy trenches were strongly reinforced with concrete and were not destroyed by bombardment Barbed wire was frequently not cut by artillery shells A preliminary bombardment gave advance warning to the enemy that a probable offensive was imminent, giving them time to bring in reinforcements and supplies
Creeping barrage	Artillery was used simultaneously with an infantry advance. Artillery shells were set to explode just ahead of the advancing troops	To provide continuous cover for advancing troops To kill enemy troops To destroy enemy machine guns, artillery and trench systems To cut rolls of barbed wire	The effective synchronization of artillery and infantry was difficult to achieve due to inaccuracies of artillery fire and the rudimentary field communications that limited the contact which infantry could make with the artillery once the advance was underway. In consequence, creeping barrages sometimes advanced too rapidly to provide any real cover for troops, or too slowly, leading to casualties from friendly fire
Mines	The detonation of mines in advance of an infantry attack which had been laid under the enemy's trenches via underground tunnels	To destroy enemy trenches and troops and create a breech in the enemy front line	The digging of tunnels was hazardous; miners could be killed by collapsing tunnels, lack of oxygen or the build-up of poisonous gases The detonation of mines was not always accurate. Sometimes mines did not detonate at all, sometimes they detonated after a delay once the infantry advance had begun, killing members of their own troops
Poison gas	The release of poison gas, initially from canisters and, later in the war, fired in shells towards enemy trenches	To kill and cause panic among enemy troops	If the wind changed direction suddenly the gas could be blown back towards the trenches of those who fired it Gas masks were quickly developed which offered protection against gas
Tanks	Tanks, first used by the British in September 1916, were used to support an infantry advance	To provide additional firepower To provide cover for infantry advancing across no-man's land	The tank was only available from 1916 and then only in very limited numbers Tanks frequently broke down or became stuck in the uneven ground of no-man's land

*new tech of this war

First used in April of 1915

Given the difficulties of launching a successful offensive in trench warfare, it was unsurprising that infantry casualty numbers were frequently devastatingly high and that a decisive breakthrough was rarely achieved, with stalemate characterizing the war on the Western Front for most of 1915–18. In consequence, First World War commanders have not infrequently been accused of incompetence and callousness. However, what often limited their options and the effectiveness of their tactics was the technological limitations of the military equipment available. This, combined with political and strategic pressure on commanders to continue to launch offensives, makes it difficult to identify alternative tactics that would have worked better.

SOURCE Q

German troops in a trench in 1915.

> How useful is Source Q as evidence of trench warfare? ?

The war on the Eastern Front

On the Eastern Front, Germany and its allies Austria-Hungary and Bulgaria (who entered the war in October 1915) fought against Russia and Serbia. Major confrontation with Russia began sooner than Germany had expected as the result of the quicker than estimated mobilization of the Russian army. The Russians made good progress against the armies of Austria-Hungary, driving deep into Galicia, but were less successful against German troops.

Russian forces invaded East Prussia and pushed the Germans back until the Battle of Tannenberg on 22–29 August 1914 when the Russian army of General Alexander Samsanov was encircled and defeated by the Germans. Never again in the war did Russian troops seriously threaten the German border, although they did tie down huge numbers of German troops on the Eastern Front. Further defeats were inflicted on Russian forces at the Masurian Lakes on 5–15 September 1914.

↗ how did this happen when Germany had a substantially weaker standing army in terms of numbers. (pg. 21 source B

How did the nature of fighting on the Western Front differ from fighting elsewhere during 1915?

KEY TERM

War of attrition A strategy in which the main goal is to achieve victory by wearing down the enemy's strength and will to fight, through the infliction of mass casualties and the limitation of their essential resources.

Theatre In warfare, a major area of fighting.

The land war in Europe 1915

The second phase of the war on the Western Front was characterized by efforts to break the stalemate of trench warfare. The failure to do so led to the development of a **war of attrition**. The lack of progress made on the Western Front encouraged the British to enlarge their commitment to other **theatres** of the war, contributing to the launch of the Gallipoli Campaign (see page 41) against the Ottoman Empire.

The war on the Western Front: stalemate

The Germans attempted to break the stalemate by launching an attack against the Allied line in Belgium at the Second Battle of Ypres between 22 April and 25 May 1915. Germany used poison gas for the first time (see below) against Allied troops. Estimates of the casualties of this first gas attack vary considerably, but an approximate number is 1500, of whom 200 were killed. This first use of gas created panic and the flight of troops from their trenches, leading to a 7-km wide gap emerging in the Allied front line into which the Germans advanced. The Germans, however, were halted before they reached the key city of Ypres. By the close of the Second Battle of Ypres, in a pattern which would become familiar, casualties were high, with the Allies sustaining 69,000, the Germans 38,000, while the territory gained was minimal.

Technology of the war: poison gas

Poison gas became a standard weapon by the end of the war; by 1918 roughly one shell in four fired on the Western Front was a gas shell. Gas released was heavier than air and therefore infiltrated trenches. The impact of gas was rarely decisive in battles and its military effectiveness was limited due to the introduction of gas masks and its reliance on favourable weather conditions (see the table below). Casualties caused by gas from all sides amounted to 88,498 fatalities, less than one per cent of the total killed in the war.

Gas was a potentially lethal weapon, but its psychological impact was often greater than its military effectiveness. It has often received attention beyond its real impact on the fighting as a consequence of psychological aversion to its use due to its potentially horrendous physical effects.

The three types of poison gas used on the Western Front

Type of gas	Effects of gas
Chlorine (the only gas available between April and December 1915)	Suffocation, as inhalation of the gas in significant quantity destroyed the lungs
Phosgene (introduced from December 1915)	Suffocation, as inhalation of the gas even in relatively small quantity destroyed the lungs
Dichlorethyl sulphide or mustard gas: an odourless gas, slightly yellow in colour (introduced from July 1917)	Highly toxic, if inhaled, even in small quantities. If skin was exposed to the gas it caused internal blistering and (usually temporary) blindness

The war on the Ottoman Front: Gallipoli

The Allies launched an assault against Ottoman forces on the Gallipoli peninsula between 19 February 1915 and 9 January 1916. With stalemate dominating the Western Front, it was hoped that the attack on Gallipoli would:

- provide a much-needed success to boost Allied morale
- knock the Ottoman Empire out of the war
- open up Allied supply routes to Russia through the Dardanelles
- weaken Germany and Austria-Hungary by opening up another front to their south.

SOURCE R

The Gallipoli Campaign.

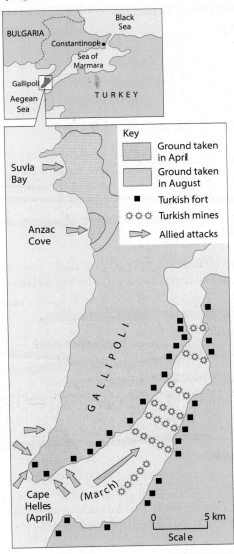

> How useful is Source R in learning about the Gallipoli Campaign?

The campaign

The British army, using troops mostly from New Zealand and Australia, known as ANZACs, was the primary Allied force at Gallipoli. These forces stormed the peninsula in an **amphibious assault** in late April 1915 after a preliminary bombardment of Ottoman forts by Allied warships. Allied troops, eventually numbering almost half a million, made little headway against entrenched Ottoman soldiers, conceding defeat only in January 1916. There were 45,000 Allied deaths at Gallipoli, with Ottoman deaths numbering at least 60,000. With the evacuation of Allied forces from Gallipoli, the possibility of supplying a failing Russia was greatly diminished.

The Italian Front

Italy joined the war on the side of the Allies in 1915 as a result of the secret Treaty of London in which Italy was promised territorial gain at Austria-Hungary's expense at the war's conclusion. Almost immediately, poorly trained and equipped Italian soldiers became bogged down in a form of trench warfare in the mountains between Italy and Austria-Hungary, capturing only a few kilometres. British and French hopes that Austria-Hungary would be successfully invaded from the south evaporated.

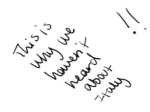
The land war in Europe 1916

The war on the Western Front in 1916 was characterized by huge battles of attrition in which enormous casualties were sustained in return for very little territorial gain. The stalemate remained unbroken. On the Eastern Front, despite some impressive gains by the Russians, it was clear by the end of the year that Russian forces were not winning, nor would be able to win, the war against the Germans.

The war on the Western Front: Verdun

German troops launched a massive assault on the series of French fortresses at Verdun between 21 February and 18 December 1916. Verdun was considered crucial by France for its defence and morale. The German Chief of the General Staff, Erich von Falkenhayn, aware of the importance of Verdun to the French, predicted that a massive German offensive on the fortresses would encourage the French to pour in reinforcements, thereby weakening other points along the Western Front where a decisive offensive could be more easily launched.

The German assault began in February 1916 and soon developed into an epic battle of attrition. Total French casualties are estimated to have amounted to 542,000. Despite these enormous losses, and the temporary capture of several of the major forts, the French held Verdun. By the close of the battle after 10 months, Germany held only 8 km more territory than when it had begun. The Germans also suffered heavy casualties in the offensive, estimated at 434,000 dead, wounded or missing.

The war on the Western Front: the Somme

The British attempted to break the stalemate on the Western Front and to draw some of the German forces away from Verdun, with a large offensive near the Somme River between 1 July and 18 November 1916.

The offensive employed the classic tactics of trench warfare, beginning with a lengthy preliminary artillery bombardment of the German trenches, before an infantry advance across no-man's land towards German trenches. Tanks were used for the first time by Britain, but not effectively and had no real impact on the battle. The preliminary artillery bombardments failed to significantly weaken the German trench defences so that the advancing British infantry suffered horrific casualties from German machine-gun and artillery fire. On the first day alone the British sustained 57,470 casualties (21,392 of them killed or missing). The territory gained was minimal.

How useful is Source S as evidence of the use of the tank in the First World War?

SOURCE S

A British mark I tank on 15 September 1916, the day tanks went into battle for the first time.

Technology of the war: tanks

The tank is an armoured military vehicle with caterpillar tracks, designed to be able to cross difficult terrain. The tank was armed with significant guns; in the First World War, these were cannon and machine guns. It was first used in combat in September 1916 by Britain. It was hoped that the use of the tank would break the stalemate of trench warfare. Tanks were only produced in very limited numbers in the First World War.

Numbers of tanks produced by country in the First World War

Year	Britain	France	Germany	Italy	USA
1916	150	0	0	0	0
1917	1277	800	0	0	0
1918	1391	4000	20	6	84

The early tanks were slow, difficult to steer and liable to break down and get stuck in mud or shell craters. There were also few tanks available for use, with only 49 at the Somme, for example. Tanks also had only a limited range, making it impossible for them to penetrate deeply into enemy lines. Tanks underwent considerable development during the war and were primarily fitted with machine guns, designed to deal with trench warfare. Tanks would eventually be used successfully in large groups to attack enemy positions as at Cambrai in November 1917 when 476 British tanks took control of 9.5 km in just a few hours. In September 1918, this tactic regularly broke through German defensive lines. Some of the main models in production by 1918 are included in the table below.

Country	Tank model (*date first in service*)	Armaments	Speed	Range
Britain	Mark V (from 1918)	Two 57-mm guns and four machine guns	8 km/h	72 km
France	Renault FT (from 1917)	One 37-mm gun and two machine guns	7 km/h	65 km
USA	Mark VIII (from 1918)	Two 57-mm guns and seven machine guns	8 km/h	89 km
Germany	A7V tank (from 1918)	One 57-mm gun and six machine guns	12 km/h (but very unstable over rough terrain)	80 km
Italy	Fiat 2000 (from 1918 but never used in combat)	One 65-mm gun and six machine guns	7 km/h	75 km

SOURCE T

Major-General J.F.C. Fuller, second-in-command and Chief Staff Officer of the Tank Corps Head Quarters, writing after the war. Quoted in *The Battlefields of the First World War* by Peter Barton, published by Constable & Robinson, London, 2005, page 342.

The first period of the war [was] the reign of the bullet, and the second the reign of the shell, and the third was the reign of the anti-bullet. We introduced the tank, and though, until the Battle of Cambrai was fought … our General Head Quarters in France showed a tactical ineptitude in the use of this weapon that was amazing, ultimately it beat their ignorance and stupidity and won through.

What are the values and limitations of Source T as evidence of the importance of the tank in the First World War?

The Somme Offensive continued until 18 November 1916, despite the continuation of high casualties which were in total even greater than at Verdun: 420,000 British, 200,000 French and 500,000 German. The Allies had advanced only 13 km in some places; the Somme had become a battle of attrition despite this not being the intention of Britain's military commanders.

The war on the Eastern Front: the Brusilov Offensive

A major Russian offensive, known as the Brusilov Offensive after General Alexei Brusilov who directed the campaign, was launched predominantly against Austro-Hungarian troops in the region of what is now Ukraine on 2 June 1916. The timing of the assault was in part to relieve the Italians, who were hard-pressed fighting the Austro-Hungarians in northern Italy along the Isonzo River, and to help the French at Verdun. The offensive was initially highly successful for the Russians, who made rapid progress, capturing 96 km by the end of June 1916.

However, the momentum of the Russian advance faltered by July due to insufficient supplies and reinforcements, which meant it was impossible to maintain the gains. In addition, the transfer of substantial numbers of German troops from Verdun to the Eastern Front shifted the balance of forces in the region against the Russians. In consequence, the Russian offensive ended by September 1916. Although Russia's territorial advance had been considerable, in the vast territories of the Eastern Front where mobile, rather than trench, warfare was the norm, even relatively good gains did not often translate to substantial strategic advantage. The cost in casualties and war supplies had also been high; almost a million men were lost. This had a detrimental impact on morale on the Russian home front where discontent against the war and the government's management of it was increasing due to the substantial privations borne by the population (see page 60). The offensive did, however, fatally cripple Austria-Hungary's military, which could no longer operate without substantial help from Germany.

The land war in Europe 1917

Although the stalemate remained unbroken on the Western Front in 1917, there were signs that an Allied victory was increasingly imminent. The Allies were boosted by the USA's entry into the war and by victories achieved through the more effective deployment of their new weapon, the tank. However, on the Eastern Front their ally Russia looked on the point of collapse, beset by military and political problems.

The war on the Western Front: the stalemate continues

Throughout 1917 there were several Allied attempts at a breakthrough but none was decisive. The most significant attempts came with the French Nivelle Offensive between 16 April and 9 May 1917 and the British third offensive at Ypres in Belgium, known as Passchendaele, between 31 July and 10 November 1917. Both failed to achieve significant gains, while casualties were substantial. In the three-month-long Battle of Passchendaele, the Allies gained approximately 8 km while sustaining 325,000 casualties, the Germans 260,000.

The USA joins the war

The USA entered the war on the side of the Allies in April 1917 as a result of Germany's submarine warfare, which increasingly targeted US vessels, and the discovery of evidence that Germany was encouraging Mexico to invade the USA. The impact of US troops and supplies was an enormous boost to the exhausted Allies. Although it would take several months for significant numbers of US soldiers to arrive on the Western Front, by March 1918, 250,000 men were arriving in Europe every month. The knowledge of this had a hugely detrimental impact on German morale, as Germany's own reserves of men were rapidly running out by 1918 (see page 57).

The war on the Eastern Front: the retreat of Russian forces

Russia underwent a revolution in February 1917 in which the tsar, or emperor, was replaced by an army-appointed **Provisional Government**. The Provisional Government attempted to continue the war, launching a failed offensive in July 1917. Conditions in Russia were so poor as a result of hunger and political dissatisfaction that a second revolution occurred in October 1917 by the **Bolshevik Party**. The Bolsheviks ended the war with the **Central Powers**, signing the Treaty of Brest-Litovsk (see page 47), which allowed Germany to move troops from the Eastern to Western Fronts for a major offensive in 1918.

 **KEY TERM**

Provisional Government The government of Russia between March and October 1917.

Bolshevik Party The Russian Communist Party. It seized power in a revolution in October 1917.

Central Powers First World War alliance of Germany, Austria-Hungary, Bulgaria and the Ottoman Empire.

The Italian Front

In October 1917, Austro-Hungarian and German troops launched a major offensive against Italian forces in northern Italy. At the Battle of Caporetto, Italy suffered a crushing defeat with at least 300,000 dead, wounded or captured. The Central Powers took control of a large portion of northern Italy and the Italian government contemplated leaving the war. Britain and France were forced to rush reinforcements to prevent a complete collapse of Allied lines there.

The land war in Europe 1918

The defeat of Germany and its allies in 1918 brought about the end of the war, although fighting at the start of the year seemed to be in their favour. On the Eastern Front, Russia surrendered, while on the Western Front, the stalemate was finally broken by a massive German offensive.

← **Why were Germany and its allies defeated in 1918?**

The war on the Eastern Front: Treaty of Brest-Litovsk

The collapse of the Eastern Front came early in 1918 when the new Bolshevik government of Russia, which had seized power in a revolution in October 1917, sued for peace. This decision was motivated not only by repeated Russian losses on the Eastern Front and the collapse of morale on the home front, but also by the ideological opposition of the Bolsheviks to the war. They condemned a war in which ordinary working men were sent by their rulers to fight other workers. In Bolshevik eyes, the workers of the world should instead be united in struggle against their ruling oppressors. Germany and its allies agreed to an **armistice** but not without imposing punitive peace terms in the Treaty of Brest-Litovsk of 3 March 1918. Thereafter, Russia withdrew from the war.

 **KEY TERM**

Armistice An agreement to stop fighting.

Treaty of Brest-Litovsk, March 1918

Russia lost:

- 2.6 million km² of territory including Poland, Lithuania, Estonia, Latvia, Finland and Ukraine
- 75 per cent of its iron ore and 90 per cent of its coal
- almost half its industry
- 55 million people
- almost half of its best agricultural land.

Most of this territory was placed under Germany's control.

The different fronts 1914–18.

? What can be learned from Source U about the fighting on the Ottoman, Italian and Eastern Fronts?

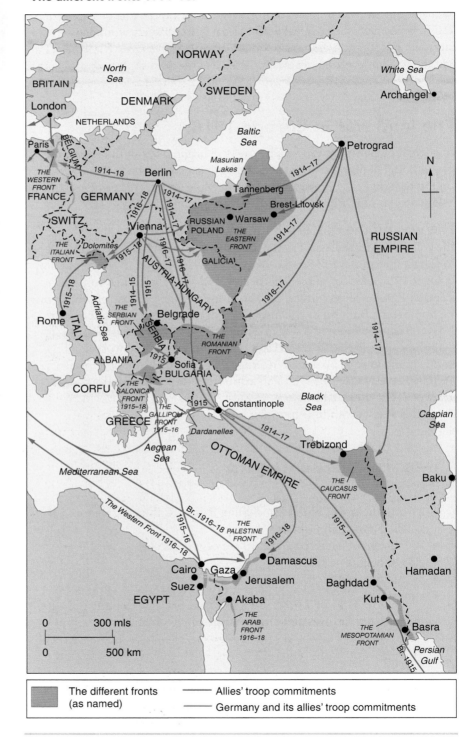

▨ The different fronts (as named)	—— Allies' troop commitments
	—— Germany and its allies' troop commitments

The war on the Western Front: the Ludendorff Offensive

The final phase of the war on the Western Front saw an end to the stalemate due to a massive German offensive designed to bring about a decisive victory. The German campaign, known as the Ludendorff Offensive after the German commander General Erich Ludendorff, took place between 21 March and 3 June 1918. Ludendorff realized that this was Germany's last opportunity to win the war since Germany's manpower and *matériel* resources were not sufficient to sustain the war, especially in the face of US war production.

The Ludendorff Offensive made use of new infantry and artillery tactics to break the stalemate. No lengthy preliminary bombardment was used, but instead a short intensive bombardment, known as a **hurricane barrage**, was employed to saturate Allied lines with explosive and gas shells 30 minutes before the infantry assault began. This was followed not by a massed infantry advance towards the Allied lines, but by the rapid movement of small detachments of **stormtrooper** infantry. These were armed with lightweight sub-machine guns and grenades with the objective of penetrating and infiltrating Allied lines by focusing on taking previously identified weak points, while avoiding strong points which could then be isolated for subsequent attacks by troops with heavier weapons. The stormtroopers, frequently covered by a creeping barrage, had greater flexibility of movement than a massed infantry advance, and the element of surprise and speed was crucial to their success. A second wave of infantry then was sent to consolidate the capture of the Allied line. These tactics became known as **infiltration tactics**.

The German advance initially made significant progress, advancing 65 km in the first week. The breakthrough, however, was not decisive and the advance lost momentum. This was largely due to a lack of **reserve forces** and sufficient supplies to exploit the initial successes. German troops were forced to draw back in the face of Allied counterattacks such as that launched at the Second Battle of the Marne between 15 July and 3 August 1918, and at Amiens on 8 August 1918, which made good use of the new technologies of the tank and aircraft (see pages 44 and 51). For Germany, the retreat was irreversible as their armies were repeatedly forced to draw back until fighting ceased with an armistice on 11 November 1918.

 **KEY TERM**

Hurricane barrage A short, intensive artillery bombardment.

Stormtroopers German specialist infantry used in the First World War.

Infiltration tactics The use of small, mobile detachments of infantry to infiltrate enemy lines by targeting previously identified weak points and thereby isolating strong points on the line for easier attack by more heavily armed troops.

Reserve forces Former, trained soldiers who can be quickly recalled from civilian life to expand a military.

• formal agreement is made between warring parties to stop fighting

Disease

Soldiers lived in crowded conditions with poor sanitation. This meant an increase in disease, with outbreaks of malaria, typhoid and other diseases more common throughout Europe during the First World War. The worst outbreak of disease was Spanish influenza, which lasted from January 1918 to December 1920. This virus killed up to 120 million people around the world or six per cent of the world's population. In 1918, hundreds of thousands of soldiers, including up to half a million German troops, were too ill to fight, weakening armies and the morale of civilian populations.

The collapse of Germany and its allies

The German armistice came shortly after the collapse of its allies, who had all already made armistice agreements:

- Bulgaria on 29 September 1918
- Ottoman Empire on 30 October 1918
- Austria-Hungary on 3 November 1918.

The collapse of the Central Powers was in large part brought about by their inability to sustain conflict any longer. Their combined reserves of manpower and supplies were by 1918 far inferior to those of the Allies, making continued military conflict, let alone the likelihood of victory, impossible. Their collapse was hastened by the difficulties that had beset their home fronts. Extreme privations (see page 59) led to a collapse in support for the war and revolt among the civilian populations and mutiny within the German navy (see page 60).

The war in the Middle East

What was the nature of fighting in the Middle East?

The entry of the Ottoman Empire into the war in October 1914 led to fighting in the Middle East, which formed part of the empire. The conflict in this region primarily involved Russian troops to the north in the Caucasus region, and British and Arab tribes in **Mesopotamia** and **the Levant**. On all fronts, the Ottoman forces were eventually forced into retreat. The nature of the fighting was very different from that on the Western Front, but similar to that of the Eastern Front in that warfare was more mobile.

The Mesopotamian Campaign

The Mesopotamian Campaign was fought between troops from the British and Ottoman Empires and was a highly mobile conflict. Indeed, British troops made significant advances, occupying Basra in November 1914, thereby safeguarding access to vital oil supplies, and capturing the town of Kut in 1915. The subsequent British advance on Baghdad was, however, repelled by Ottoman troops, which led to the Ottoman siege of Kut between December 1915 and April 1916. In April 1916, 13,000 British troops surrendered, becoming prisoners. A later British offensive on Baghdad succeeded in March 1917 (see the map on page 48).

The Arab Revolt

The British were also involved in fighting Ottoman forces in the area around Palestine and Arabia. The conflict was triggered by an Ottoman attack on the **Suez Canal**, a vital supply route for Britain. British forces subsequently pushed the Ottomans back into Palestine.

Arab tribesmen were encouraged by Britain to revolt against the Ottoman government with promises of support for Arab independence after the war. The Arab Revolt began in June 1916 and Arab efforts, in conjunction with British troops, captured Medina in June 1916. Arab fighters, using guerrilla

KEY TERM

Mesopotamia A region of south-west Asia, part of what is now Iraq.

The Levant An area of the eastern Mediterranean, including what is now Lebanon, Syria and Israel.

Suez Canal Canal located in Egypt connecting the Mediterranean and Red Seas, and therefore the Atlantic and Indian Oceans.

tactics (see page 3), attacked Ottoman railways and supply lines, driving Ottoman troops out of Arabia and Palestine and eventually into today's Syria, where Damascus was captured in 1918. In October, the Ottoman Empire surrendered to the Allies.

War in the colonies

The world outside Europe and the Middle East was largely affected by the war through the supply of men, *matériel* and food to the armies of the European powers. The peoples of the British **dominions** and colonies alone suffered 200,000 dead and 600,000 wounded in the fighting. Limited fighting also occurred, primarily in the German colonies.

Conflict in Asia and Africa

In Asia in 1914, fighting focused on German colonial possessions:

- New Zealand forces occupied and quickly took German Samoa.
- New Guinea fell to Australian forces.
- Micronesia, the Marianas and the Marshall Islands were also captured by Allied forces virtually unopposed.
- The German naval base at Tsingtao, in China, was taken by Japanese forces.

There was more sustained fighting in German colonial Africa. German South-West Africa was taken by British Imperial forces in 1915, while German forces in German East Africa did not surrender until 25 November 1918. German forces were able to hold off larger British-led forces by using guerrilla warfare tactics.

The war in the air

The First World War brought about a transformation in air power. There was a significant increase in the range of military usage to which aircraft were put, reflecting innovations and improvements in aircraft technology during the war. Overall, air power did not play a decisive role in the war, but the huge technological and tactical developments made suggested the military potential of aircraft.

> **Technology of the war: reconnaissance aircraft**
> Initially aircraft were used solely for **reconnaissance**, flying behind enemy lines to gather information about troop movements. This remained a significant function throughout the war. The importance of aerial reconnaissance was shown at the Battle of Tannenberg in August 1914 (see page 39) when, as a result of information provided by German/Austro-Hungarian Rumpler Taube aircraft, outnumbered German troops were able correctly predict Russian troop movements in order to encircle and defeat the advancing Russian army.

How was the wider world involved in the war?

 **KEY TERM**

Matériel Equipment used in warfare.

Dominion A country which has its own autonomy (independent government) but which recognizes the sovereignty of a monarch from overseas.

Reconnaissance The gathering of military information.

What impact did air power have on the war?

Technology of the war: fighter aircraft

To try to prevent aerial reconnaissance, both sides developed fighter aircraft to attack enemy aircraft in the skies. Fighter aircraft made use of the newest technological developments which saw planes able to increase their speeds and to carry machine guns. Considerable technological developments were made over the course of the war. In the initial months of the war, aircraft were flimsy, slow and unarmed. By the end of the war, aircraft were faster and more manoeuvrable and had more powerful guns. Some of the main fighter aircraft in operation in 1917 are shown in the table.

Country	Aircraft model (date first in service)	Armaments	Speed	Rate of climb	Number built
Britain	Sopwith Camel (from 1917)	Two machine guns	77 km/h	5 m/s	5490
France	Spad S. XIII (from 1917)	Two machine guns	218 km/h	2 m/s	8472
Russia	Anatra (from 1916)	Two machine guns	144 km/h	3 m/s	184
Germany	Albatros DV (from 1917)	Two machine guns	186 km/h	4 m/s	2500
Austria-Hungary	Aviatik (Berg) DI (from 1917)	Two machine guns	185 km/h	4 m/s	700

By 1918, even though Germany possessed the most technically capable fighters, such as the Albatros DV and the first steel-framed fighter, the Fokker DVII, aerial superiority went to the Allies mainly because their aircraft substantially outnumbered those of Germany. The numbers of aircraft produced increased during the war, reflecting the growing importance of air power and the role of war production in total war.

The total number of aircraft produced by country in the First World War, taken from *World War One* by S. Tucker, *An Encyclopedia of World War One: A Political, Social and Military History*, published by ABC-CLIO, 2005, page 57.

Year	Austria-Hungary	France	Germany	Britain	Italy	Russia
1914	64	541	694	193	NA	NA*
1915	281	4,489	4,532	1,680	382	NA
1916	732	7,549	8,182	5,716	1,255	NA
1917	1,272	14,915	13,977	14,832	3,861	NA
1918	1,989	24,652	17,000	32,536	6,488	NA
Total	4,338	52,146	44,385	54,957	11,986	5,300

*Russian statistics relating to yearly production are not available.
NA, not available.

Technology of the war: Zeppelins and bomber aircraft

At the start of the war aircraft lacked the capability to carry significant bomb loads, so the practice of bombing was limited and was carried out by **Zeppelins**. In total, 51 German Zeppelin raids took place over Britain during the war causing damage and the deaths of 557 people. Zeppelins were often inaccurate, slow moving and easy targets for anti-aircraft fire. As such they sustained high losses, with 60 of the 84 built during the war destroyed.

Over the course of the war, technological developments saw the emergence of specifically designed bomber aircraft. Their capabilities, however, remained limited in terms of range, speed and bomb load.

Examples of bomber aircraft from the First World War

Country	Aircraft model (*date first in service*)	Bomb load	Speed	Range	Number built
Britain	Handley Page O/400 (*from 1916*)	907 kg	157 km/h	1120 km	600
Russia	Iilya Muromets (*from 1913*)	500 kg	110 km/h	550 km	83
Germany	Gotha GV (*from 1917*)	500 kg	140 km/h	840 km	205

Technological developments nevertheless made the tactic of aerial **strategic bombing** possible, and this was practised for the first time in the First World War. The British launched raids on industrial targets in the Saar Basin in Germany from 1916, while German Gotha IV bombers carried out 27 raids on Britain in 1917, for example. Strategic bombing, however, played little military significance in the war overall.

Aircraft also began to be used to provide support for troops on the ground by destroying artillery and supply depots. German squadrons, consisting of aircraft specifically designed for ground-attack, dropped bombs and fired machine guns on ground troops at the Battle of Cambrai in November 1917 and in the Ludendorff Offensive of 1918, for example.

KEY TERM

Zeppelin A large cylindrical airship that uses gas to stay aloft.

Strategic bombing The bombing of targets such as factories, transportation networks and even civilians, in an attempt to gain strategic advantage.

Merchant shipping Non-military shipping, carrying supplies.

The war at sea

Although there was only a very limited number of major naval battles in the First World War, naval power had a decisive impact on the war. This was primarily due to the use of naval power by both Britain and Germany to restrict vital supplies by imposing blockades and targeting **merchant shipping**.

What impact did the war at sea have on the war?

British naval action against Germany

In the naval war, the initial priority of the British was to prevent the German navy from leaving its ports and to end Germany's overseas trade. To this end the British imposed a blockade on German ships by laying mines and having patrols guard the North Sea and English Channel. These manoeuvres resulted in a number of clashes between British and German ships in the early months of the war, such as off Heligoland Bight on 28 August 1914 in which Britain sank four German warships. The naval blockade had a devastating effect on supplies of vital food, fuel and raw materials into Germany, which contributed significantly to the German defeat in 1918 (see page 59).

There was only one major battle between the fleets, the Battle of Jutland on 31 May 1916. In this confrontation, where Germany hoped to break Britain's blockade, Britain lost 14 ships and Germany 11. British losses were not enough to give the German navy any hope of breaking the blockade and the German navy was largely confined to its own ports for the remainder of the war.

German submarine warfare

SOURCE V

A propaganda recruitment poster produced by the British government in 1917 following the torpedoing of the *Lusitania*.

?

What does Source V show about how German submarine attacks were used in British government propaganda?

From 1915, German naval strategy shifted to a much greater emphasis on submarine warfare in order to more efficiently target merchant shipping supplying Britain. On 4 February 1915 Germany declared the seas around Britain a war zone and that shipping there would be targeted by German **U-boats** and sunk without warning. In 1915, U-boats sank 748,000 tons of shipping, mainly merchant ships. This campaign of unrestricted submarine warfare was temporarily halted in the wake of increased criticisms, not least from the neutral USA, which lost many ships (such as the *Lusitania*, see Source V), and citizens as a result of submarine attacks. However, the campaign was relaunched between February and June 1917, by which time U-boat numbers had risen to 152 (in August 1914 Germany had only 28 U-boats). In consequence, in April 1917 alone over 500,000 tons of British merchant shipping was lost. This had a critical impact on food supplies in Britain (see page 59). The introduction of a **convoy system** and new anti-submarine devices helped to reduce the losses caused by U-boats. Ultimately German attempts to force a British surrender by submarine blockade failed.

 **KEY TERM**

U-boats German submarines.

Convoy system The practice of ships sailing in large groups protected by naval destroyers rather than sailing individually.

Depth charge An explosive device fired from a battleship which is designed to detonate at a certain depth.

Technology of the war: submarines

Submarines were a relatively recent innovation and first made a significant impact in the First World War. Submarines were used to target naval warships and increasingly merchant shipping as they became an integral part of the implementation of the strategy of naval blockade used by both Britain and Germany. The strategic importance of submarines was reflected in an expansion in their numbers in both German and British navies.

Submarine numbers from Germany and Britain in 1914 and 1918

Country	Submarine numbers in 1914	Submarines built between 1914 and 1918	Submarines lost during the war
Britain	76	146	54
Germany	28	327	204

Britain introduced a number of measures to minimize the impact of the U-boat menace. One such measure was the Q-ships, well-armed ships disguised as merchant ships, which would lure U-boats into surfacing to make an attack and then attack the submarines themselves. The most significant measure introduced by the British to counter the impact of the U-boats was the convoy system. In addition, naval escorts became increasingly well equipped with more efficient mines and **depth charges** for use against submarines. The German strategy to use U-boats to force Britain into surrender ultimately failed, but the U-boat had demonstrated its considerable potential.

Year	Western Front	Eastern Front	Other theatres
1914	German invasion of Belgium, France and Luxembourg Battle of Marne leading to stalemate and trench warfare	Russian invasion of east Prussia Battles of Tannenberg and Masurian Lakes	British forces occupied Basra in the Mesopotamian Campaign German colonies in Asia taken by Allied forces
1915	Second Battle of Ypres (first use of gas)		Gallipoli Campaign British forces took Kut in the Mesopotamian Campaign German South-West Africa surrendered to the Allies
1916	German attack on Verdun The Somme Offensive	Brusilov Offensive	The Ottoman siege of Kut British and Arab forces took Medina British forces took Baghdad
1917	The French Nivelle Offensive Third Battle of Ypres (Passchendaele) Battle of Cambrai (first use of massed tanks)	Kerensky Offensive	Aqaba captured by the Allies
1918	Ludendorff Offensive	Treaty of Brest-Litovsk	German East Africa surrendered to the Allies Damascus captured by the Allies

The course of the First World War

⑤ Managing the war

▶ *Key question: How significant was the management of the war in determining its outcome?*

It was incredibly significant. The Allies won because they had the resources needed to sustain a prolonged war.

A conflict on the scale and of the duration of the First World War required the management of resources on an unprecedented scale. Governments had to ensure the supply of manpower and *matériel* to the armed forces, and to mobilize the support, and safeguard the needs, of the civilian population. This was particularly true in the context of total war, which affected civilian populations as never before. The ability of some governments to manage these demands better than others had a significant impact on the outcome of the war.

Military manpower

How effectively was each side able to mobilize manpower for their militaries?

The priority for all major powers at the start of the war was the mobilization of manpower into their militaries. All the major powers, with the exception of Britain, had large standing armies in 1914 (see page 21), and had measures in place to enlarge their ranks substantially with reservists and conscripts. The rapid mobilization of these forces would be as crucial as the overall numbers in gaining advantage in the early months of the war. The speed and efficiency of German mobilization, which enabled the 1.5 million men needed for the Schlieffen Plan's 'hook' westwards to be ready for action within days of the mobilization order, compensated in large part for the overall numerical advantage of the Entente powers (see page 21).

However, as the war dragged on, the size of the populations that the major powers could draw on to provide recruits for their armies became increasingly important. As a consequence the advantage swung very definitely in favour of the Allies, who could draw on:

- Russia's huge population
- the British Empire's population, which provided over 2.5 million troops
- US soldiers from 1917.

This increasing imbalance contributed to the German decision to launch the Ludendorff Offensive in 1918, which failed in large part due to the lack of reserve troops (see page 49).

All the powers resorted to **conscription** to fill the ranks of their armies. Britain alone avoided doing so in the early years of the war, but did introduce conscription from January 1916 as the initial flood of volunteers dried up.

KEY TERM

Conscription Compulsory enrolment of civilians into an army.

War production

How successfully were difficulties overcome to ensure the production of sufficient war *matériel*?

The mobilization of men for the military was essential, but without sufficient guns and ammunition this would count for little. The ability to cope with these demands had a significant impact on the outcome of the war.

Munitions

Most countries were not expecting a protracted conflict and were faced with severe shortages of munitions early in the war. In May 1915 the 'shell scandal' broke in the British press, in which shortages of shells were blamed for the failure of the British to achieve a breakthrough on the Western Front. It was estimated that the shortfall in weapons-production targets by June 1915 was in the region of 12 per cent in rifles and a massive 92 per cent in high-explosive shells. However, production was rapidly increased thereafter. France too increased its output of shells from a mediocre 4000 shells per day in October 1914 to 151,000 per day in June 1916. In Britain and Germany, machine-gun production increased, although more rapidly in Britain. This was primarily due to shortages of vital raw materials in Germany, while the Allies also benefited from increased resources and war supplies following the USA's entry into the war in 1917.

SOURCE W

What can be learned from Source W about British and German armaments production during the First World War?

British and German explosives production 1914–18

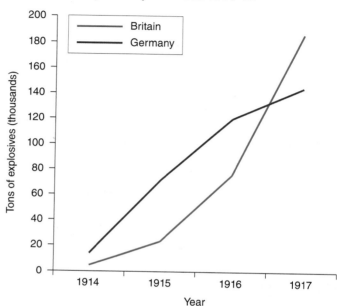

· After 1916 British had a higher amout of explosives made than Germany did but before that Germany's production of explosives was larger. the limited resarces provided to Germany may have been to blame for this.

The less industrialized Russian economy, in particular, struggled to produce weaponry to equip its vast army. In 1915, the production of 70,000 rifles per month was woefully short of the estimated 200,000 requirement. However, even in Russia, sufficient armaments were soon being produced to supply at least the major needs of its troops. By September 1916, 4.5 million shells were made per month, a figure which bears comparison with the German output of seven million shells and far exceeded the Austro-Hungarian production of just one million per month.

Government control

The increase in munitions was the result of continually greater government control over industry. Most governments established departments that oversaw all production which gave priority to war industries in terms of raw materials, labour and investment. They also ensured efficient management and production methods and eventually took control over coalmines and other critical industries.

In Russia, government management was poor. The Russian War Ministry failed to co-ordinate distribution of supplies, resulting in serious munitions shortages by the spring of 1915. The situation improved with the establishment of a new War Industries Committee, contributing to increases in munitions production. Rifle production increased from 70,000 per month in 1915 to 110,000 per month by 1916. Central government's failure to supply Russian soldiers with basic food, clothing and medical supplies led to the creation of civilian-led organizations to make up for the shortfall. Russian troops also suffered from a disorganized and limited rail system which prevented effective distribution of supplies.

The workforce

The increase in production of war supplies was only possible due to an enlargement of the industrial workforce. In most countries this was partly achieved by the employment of women on an unprecedented scale. In Britain, women constituted 23 per cent of the industrial workforce in 1914, rising to 34 per cent in 1918. In France, the percentage of female employees in the industrial and transport sectors rose from 34.8 per cent in 1911 to 40 per cent in 1918. In Austria-Hungary, the percentage of women in industry increased from 17.5 per cent in 1913 to 42.5 per cent by 1916. In Russia, the percentage of women in industry went up from 26 per cent in the pre-war period to 46 per cent by the end of the war. Women in Germany formed 55 per cent of the industrial workforce by 1918. In order to retain sufficient expertise within essential war industries, exemptions were also put in place from conscription for those men employed in certain sectors such as mining, steel and munitions production, as well as shipbuilding.

Food shortages

Most warring European nations suffered from reduced food supplies during the war. This was partly the result of millions of farmers being conscripted into armies, but also resulted from factors such as poor transportation, less fertile soil, weather and blockades.

> To what extent did warring nations ration their supplies?

Britain

Britain imported approximately 60 per cent of its food, in addition to many other products such as rubber and oil. This made it especially vulnerable to Germany's submarine warfare. Britain was reluctant to initiate major rationing and instead focused on growing more food; it farmed an additional 2.1 million acres of land by 1918. Britain also increased its imports of food from the USA, but was forced to establish a rationing system by April 1918 for animal products such as beef and for sugar. The government also tightly controlled food prices and encouraged people to go without certain foods on certain days.

Germany

Germany imported about 30 per cent of its food before the war, in addition to many other products. Britain's naval blockade meant that Germany had to increase food production or face slow starvation of food and raw materials. By December 1915, Germany imported half of what it imported in 1913. Germany attempted to address its food deficiencies by creating substitute foods where flour, grain and mushrooms were made into a meat substitute. To save grain, the government ordered the slaughter of millions of pigs, which actually decreased the amount of protein available to the country, and removed a valuable source of manure that could be used to fertilize fields, which meant even less food was available in the long term. The lack of food in German cities led to strikes and riots, contributed to thousands of deaths by Spanish influenza and other diseases, and was one of the causes of the revolt in Germany at the end of 1918 that established a new government.

Russia

In Russia, food shortages in the major cities were such that huge price inflation developed during the war. The average price of food in the major Russian cities rose by 89 per cent between 1914 and 1916, while the price of meat rose by 232 per cent and salt by a massive 483 per cent. The lack of food in urban areas was the result of a disorganized transportation system as well as the fact that peasants increasingly produced less food throughout the war. Peasants had little incentive to sell their products since all they received in return was increasingly worthless paper money for which there were few consumer goods to spend it on. Hunger was one of the main forces behind mass demonstrations against the government which led to the February 1917 revolution in Russia.

Other nations

Austria-Hungary's transportation system was disorganized and inadequate to ensure proper food distribution throughout the country, leading to severe rationing in cities, as well as riots by 1918. By the end of the war, starving refugees from war zones crowded into Istanbul and other cities of the Ottoman Empire. France suffered far less, producing large quantities of its own food and supplementing these supplies with US imports. The USA was able to feed its own civilians and military, while providing enormous quantities of food to Britain, France and Italy.

Why did the Allies win the First World War?

Outcomes and conclusions

In terms of determining the outcome of the First World War, military strategy and tactics, technology and the management of the home front were all crucial. However, with rough technological parity between the sides, technology did not prove the decisive factor in determining the Allied victory, although it had an enormous impact in shaping the nature of the war itself. Ultimately, the outcome of the war was determined by its management. The Allies won because they had the resources to sustain a prolonged war in a way that Germany and its allies did not. With hindsight, once the Schlieffen Plan failed and a long, two-front war set in, Germany was doomed to fail unless it could strike a decisive strategic victory against the Allies, something that it failed to achieve.

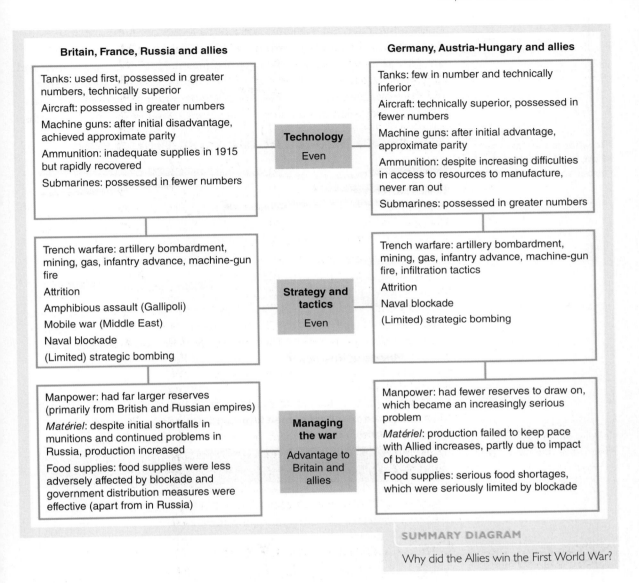

Britain, France, Russia and allies		Germany, Austria-Hungary and allies
Tanks: used first, possessed in greater numbers, technically superior Aircraft: possessed in greater numbers Machine guns: after initial disadvantage, achieved approximate parity Ammunition: inadequate supplies in 1915 but rapidly recovered Submarines: possessed in fewer numbers	**Technology** Even	Tanks: few in number and technically inferior Aircraft: technically superior, possessed in fewer numbers Machine guns: after initial advantage, approximate parity Ammunition: despite increasing difficulties in access to resources to manufacture, never ran out Submarines: possessed in greater numbers
Trench warfare: artillery bombardment, mining, gas, infantry advance, machine-gun fire Attrition Amphibious assault (Gallipoli) Mobile war (Middle East) Naval blockade (Limited) strategic bombing	**Strategy and tactics** Even	Trench warfare: artillery bombardment, mining, gas, infantry advance, machine-gun fire, infiltration tactics Attrition Naval blockade (Limited) strategic bombing
Manpower: had far larger reserves (primarily from British and Russian empires) *Matériel*: despite initial shortfalls in munitions and continued problems in Russia, production increased Food supplies: food supplies were less adversely affected by blockade and government distribution measures were effective (apart from in Russia)	**Managing the war** Advantage to Britain and allies	Manpower: had fewer reserves to draw on, which became an increasingly serious problem *Matériel*: production failed to keep pace with Allied increases, partly due to impact of blockade Food supplies: serious food shortages, which were seriously limited by blockade

SUMMARY DIAGRAM

Why did the Allies win the First World War?

⑥ The effects of the First World War

▶ **Key question:** *Did the impact of the First World War make future European conflict more or less likely?*

The First World War had a profound effect on post-war politics, not least in territorial changes made to the map of Europe in the aftermath of the conflict. The post-war political settlement was an attempt to construct a meaningful peace, but in many ways it left a legacy of resentment and instability which contributed to future unrest. The socioeconomic consequences of the war were no less significant. Huge numbers of men had been killed and the lives of civilians altered through the experience of the war. Post-war European societies, politics and economies bore the influence of the war long after it had ended.

To what extent did the First World War bring about social change?

The social impact of the First World War

The First World War had a profound impact on society across Europe. The casualties were enormous. On the home fronts, women experienced new freedoms and employment opportunities, and the state had intervened to an unprecedented degree in the economy and daily life of its citizens. Not all these changes, however, were long lasting.

War casualties

All countries suffered huge casualties and incurred substantial debts as a result of the war, although some suffered more than others.

Soldiers

The loss of life was far greater than any previous European conflict, with as many as 10 million men killed. Many men had been severely wounded and returned to their homes unable to work.

SOURCE X

? According to Source X, did the Allies or the Central Powers suffer the most dead and wounded?

The estimated numbers of men killed and wounded who served during the First World War.

Country	Number of dead	Percentage killed of men who served	Number of wounded
Russia	1,800,000	15%	4,950,000
France	1,390,000	16%	4,330,000
Britain	900,000	10%	2,090,000
Italy	460,000	7%	960,000
USA	50,000	1%	230,000
Germany	2,040,000	15%	5,690,000
Austria-Hungary	1,020,000	13%	1,940,000
Ottoman Empire	240,000	24%	1,270,000

Civilians

Many civilians were killed in the conflict, although estimates of the numbers vary wildly depending on whether the victims of famine and disease are included. In addition to those killed directly by the war, the Spanish influenza epidemic killed millions around the world.

SOURCE Y

The estimated number of European civilian deaths caused directly by military action, excluding famine and disease.

Country	Civilian dead directly caused by the war
Russia	500,000
France	40,000
Britain	2,000
Belgium	7,000
Italy	4,000
USA	750
Germany	1,000
Austria-Hungary	120,000

> What can be learned from Source Y about the impact of the war on civilians?

Women

Women contributed to the First World War more significantly than in any modern war up to that point.

Employment

The war provided unprecedented employment opportunities for women, as they were needed to perform vital war work and to fill the jobs of men who had joined armies. In consequence, across Europe a larger proportion of the female population was employed than ever before. In France, the numbers of women in employment had risen to 47 per cent in 1918, compared to 35.5 per cent in 1911. In Britain, the rise in overall female employment went from 24 per cent in 1914 to 37 per cent in 1918. In Russia, women constituted almost 45 per cent of the industrial workforce, while Austria-Hungary had over one million women join war production.

Although women were successful as industrial workers, at the war's end many stopped working. By 1920, two-thirds of British women left jobs they had taken during the war. In France, by 1921, the proportion of women working had returned to 1911 levels. The nature of women's employment after the war did, however, see a more permanent shift away from **domestic service** to **white-collar employment**, although this was in part due to the expansion of this sector. Women also continued to receive lower wages than men. There was, however, a new spirit of freedom among many women in the 1920s as they began to challenge conventional expectations about behaviour by living alone, smoking, working and wearing new fashions, among other things.

> **KEY TERM**
>
> **Domestic service** Domestic servants provide household services for others, usually serving as cooks or maids.
>
> **White-collar employment** Non-manual employment, typically office work.

SOURCE Z

SOURCE Z

Women workers inspect high-explosive shells in a British munitions factory in 1915.

Enfranchisement

Women were given the vote for the first time after the war in tacit acknowledgement of their contributions during the war in:

- Russia
- Austria, Czechoslovakia, Poland, Canada and Britain in 1918
- Germany in 1919
- USA in 1920.

France did not **enfranchise** women until 1944, with other nations following in later years.

KEY TERM

Enfranchise To give the right to vote in political elections.

The political impact of the First World War

Post-war peace settlements

Once the fighting ceased, the enormous task of constructing lasting peace out of the ruins of war began. The peace treaties imposed on the losing countries by the Allies were an attempt to create a lasting peace (see page 65). However, these treaties have been criticized as actually contributing towards future instability in Europe by creating huge resentments among the defeated nations. These post-war settlements significantly redrew territorial boundaries in Europe, with all the losing countries losing land, as well as imposing restrictive military terms and punitive economic penalties.

The key terms of the peace treaties signed after the First World War

Country	Treaty (date)	Land	Reparations	Military
Germany	Treaty of Versailles (1919)	Ten per cent of its land was removed and redistributed including: • Alsace-Lorraine to France • West Prussia, Posen and Silesia to Poland • Eupen, Malmedy and Moresnet to Belgium • Northern Schleswig to Denmark • Hultschin to Czechoslovakia • Danzig and the Saarland became mandates of the League of Nations All colonies were lost	Reparations set at 132 billion gold marks (but never paid in full)	Army reduced to 100,000 men No air force, no tanks, no artillery Navy limited to six battleships, 12 destroyers, 12 torpedo boats and no submarines Rhineland became a demilitarized zone
Austria	Treaty of St Germain (1919)	Lost land including: • Bohemia and Moravia to Czechoslovakia • Bosnia-Herzegovina and Croatia to Yugoslavia • Galicia to Poland • The Tyrol to Italy	Before a reparations figure was set Austria went bankrupt	Army reduced to 30,000 men No air force No navy
Hungary	Treaty of Trianon (1920)	Lost over two-thirds of its territory and 64 per cent of its pre-war population including: • Transylvania to Romania • Slovakia, Ruthenia to Czechoslovakia • Slovenia and Croatia to Yugoslavia	Reparations set at 200 million gold crowns (payment suspended due to Hungary's financial difficulties)	Army reduced to 35,000 men No air force, no tanks, no submarines
Bulgaria	Treaty of Neuilly (1919)	Various lands lost to Greece, Romania and Yugoslavia (thereby losing access to the Mediterranean Sea)	Reparations set at £100 million	Army reduced to 20,000 men No air force Navy reduced to four torpedo boats, six motor boats and no submarines
Turkey	Treaty of Sèvres (1920)	Lost land including: • South-western Anatolia to Italy • Western Anatolia to create Kurdish and Armenian states • Smyrna and Eastern Thrace to Greece Middle Eastern possessions became mandates under the control of Britain and France	None	Army reduced to 50,000 men No air force, tanks or submarines

? What can be learned from Source AA about the ways in which Europe was altered after the First World War?

Central Europe after the peace settlements 1919–23

Land lost by Germany

Lost by Austria and Hungary

Lost by Russia

Lost by Bulgaria

To Greece 1920
Recovered by Turkey 1923

The most significant changes to the map of Europe came with the disintegration of the Austro-Hungarian and Ottoman empires. The new countries of Czechoslovakia and Yugoslavia were formed partly out of the former territories of the Austro-Hungarian Empire in the closing weeks of the war and were given formal recognition by peace treaties. As the peacemakers redrew the territorial boundaries of Europe, they often tried to take into account the principle of **self-determination** in efforts to minimize the instability caused by the desire for ethnic groups to rule themselves which had helped to trigger the war in 1914. For example, the new state of Yugoslavia was primarily composed of Slavic peoples. Self-determination was not fully achieved, however, with some three million Hungarians and 12.5 per cent of Germany's pre-war population ending up in other states. It has been argued that this contributed to future instability as nationalist groups fought for independence, particularly in eastern Europe.

The economic and political impact of the treaties

The high **reparations** figures set by the post-war treaties have attracted much criticism for contributing to economic crisis and political instability. One of the first and most vehement critics of the Treaty of Versailles on economic grounds was the British economist John Maynard Keynes who, in his book *The Economic Consequences of the Peace* (1920), condemned the treaty for imposing too harsh a settlement on Germany. He argued that it would harm German prospects of recovery and also longer-term Allied economic interests by limiting prospects for trade, as well as giving Germany grounds for vengeance in the future.

Criticisms of the post-war treaties have largely centred on the accusation that they contributed to political instability in Europe, ultimately leading to the Second World War. This is discussed in Chapter 2 (see pages 111–13).

Change of government and political unrest

Russia

In February 1917, revolution in Russia forced the army to replace the autocratic system ruled by the tsar with the Provisional Government, which worked to continue the war against the Central Powers while attempting to alleviate food shortages caused by the war. This government's failures resulted in another revolution in October 1917 by the Bolsheviks, who signed the Treaty of Brest-Litovsk that ended Russia's war with the Central Powers (see page 47). By this time Russia was collapsing as an organized state and civil war erupted, ending only in 1921 after the death of up to eight million people. The Bolsheviks were victorious and the Soviet Union, as Russia became known, was established as the world's first communist state. As early as 1918, the Bolsheviks helped to sponsor political unrest throughout Europe, hoping that more regions would come under communist control.

Germany

Germany became a republic at the end of 1918. This government was formed by the parties of the *Reichstag* with army approval. The republic survived a series of communist-inspired revolts:

- Berlin in January and March 1919
- Munich until May 1919
- Ruhr valley in March 1920.

It also dealt with two attempts by **ultra-nationalists** to overthrow the government:

🔑 **KEY TERM**

Reparations Payments made by a defeated nation to a victorious one to compensate for war expenses and damage.

Ultra-nationalist Extreme form of nationalism that advocates national or racial superiority of a particular group.

- Kapp Putsch in Berlin in 1920 by a **paramilitary** group
- Munich Putsch in Munich in 1923 by the Nazi Party.

The German Republic stabilized and prospered with multi-party elections after the economy began to recover in 1924, only to suffer a series of political crises as a result of the **Great Depression** (see page 114).

Italy

Italy entered the First World War specifically to gain territory laid out in the secret Treaty of London signed by the Allies in 1915. After the war, Italy was denied some of the land it was promised and other territory it also wanted. Soldiers had been promised jobs and land during the war that was not forthcoming afterwards, instead returning to poverty and poor living conditions. The country was politically divided between industrialists, workers, landowners and impoverished peasants, leading to violence and the formation of armed groups. Benito Mussolini emerged as the leader of the Blackshirts, a paramilitary group sponsored by industrialists and who battled opposing groups. By 1922 many **conservatives**, including Italy's king, believed that Mussolini's group, now formed into a political party, was the only group that could save them from a Bolshevik-style communist revolution. Mussolini was named prime minister and soon established a dictatorship that lasted until 1943.

Central and eastern Europe

Austria-Hungary was dismantled into a series of new republics, while other territories were granted to **constitutional monarchies**. Essentially:

- Austria formed an unstable republic in which socialists and conservatives often battled, leading to a single-party, conservative state in 1933.
- Hungary formed a version of constitutional monarchy with a former naval officer acting as regent, but serving basically as a conservative dictator, for the deposed Habsburg Emperor.
- Czechoslovakia had a stable, multi-party republic dominated by Czech nationals.
- Romania, Bulgaria and Yugoslavia were constitutional monarchies in which kings enhanced their power continually until the outbreak of the Second World War, at the expense of multi-party government.
- Poland established a conservative military dictatorship by the mid-1920s to counter socialists.

Economic effects of the First World War

Germany

Germany lost land and people as a result of the Treaty of Versailles (see page 65), including industrialized areas such as Upper Silesia. These losses compounded Germany's economic difficulties since the nation had also lost most of its merchant ships during the war and its international trade. The country was essentially bankrupt and was after 1921 saddled with

How were countries in Europe affected economically by the First World War?

KEY TERM

Paramilitary A group of civilians organized and operating like an army.

Great Depression Economic depression which began in 1929 and adversely affected the world economy throughout much of the 1930s.

Conservative A political position generally favouring the maintenance of a structured social hierarchy and minimal government intervention in social and economic life.

Constitutional monarchy Governmental system in which a hereditary monarch is head of state, but whose powers are limited by a constitution.

reparations of 132 billion gold marks which Allied states demanded as compensation for their own losses during the war. Germany declared in 1922 that it would be unable to make its annual payment, leading to an occupation of part of the country by French and Belgian troops, known as the Ruhr Crisis. **Hyperinflation** hit the German economy, meaning that Germany's currency lost its value while prices rose. Savings were wiped out, people went hungry and international intervention was required. A US-negotiated resolution of the crisis led to a reorganization of Germany's reparations, the withdrawal of French and Belgian troops, and the extension of loans to Germany which stimulated the economy, leading to major growth in the mid-1920s.

◆━━ KEY TERM

Hyperinflation When the value of a currency falls rapidly and leads to extremely high monetary inflation.

France

Much of northern France was destroyed during the war, including thousands of factories, villages, railways, farmland and much more. These losses were joined by the loss of overseas markets for French products during the conflict and the loss of all funds lent to Russia; the new Bolshevik government of Russia, named the Soviet Union after 1922, refused to honour any of the old government's debt obligations. France had also borrowed huge sums from Britain and the USA. It was the intention of the French government that German reparations would rebuild their northern regions and pay their international war debt. Limited German payments meant that France recovered slowly economically from the First World War with high rates of taxation to pay for the national debt.

Britain

Before the First World War, Britain was a nation that lent far more money than it borrowed. During the war, however, Britain borrowed enormous sums from the USA and left the conflict in huge debt. The USA also took control of many of Britain's overseas markets in the early years of the war when Britain shifted to war production. Parts of Britain's overseas territories, such as India, became much more economically self-sufficient for their own consumer goods during the conflict, leading to a further decrease in demand for British goods at the war's conclusion. In order to pay its debt, Britain needed France to pays its debt and Germany to economically recover so that Britain could export its products there. Britain only began to return to economic prosperity in the late 1920s, just as the Great Depression (see page 114) began.

USA

The USA entered the war in 1917 after years of lending money to Britain, France and Italy, as well as selling these states war supplies and food. The USA also took control of markets around the world which these nations could no longer supply. The US economy, already by far the world's largest, expanded further when the USA joined the conflict. With millions joining the workforce there was demand for construction of factories, homes and infrastructure throughout the country. At the war's conclusion, the USA was more prosperous than at any earlier time in its history, with expanding businesses, markets and investments. By the late 1920s, however, excessive borrowing and collapsing agricultural product prices led to the Great Depression (see page 114).

Central and eastern Europe

Many new states were established in central and eastern Europe. Most of these suffered severe economic problems after the war since they were formerly parts of much larger, economically integrated empires. Poland, for example, had been part of three separate countries and each of these three parts was linked to its former empire by railways, but not to each other. Hungary had been the grain-producing section of the Austro-Hungarian Empire and now found itself with little industry and producing 500 per cent more farm products than it could consume in the first years after the war. Austria had been the administrative district of the same empire and now found itself with factories, little food and a massive government that once managed tens of millions of people that it could not support. This pattern was repeated throughout central and eastern Europe, where hyperinflation destroyed savings, prevented economic recovery and led to political instability. League of Nations loans helped both Austria and Hungary to re-establish some economic stability, while Czechoslovakia, home to 80 per cent of Austria-Hungary's industry, enjoyed prosperity.

Russia/Soviet Union

Russia left the war officially in March 1918 after signing the Treaty of Brest-Litovsk and then descended into civil war in which the Bolsheviks fought various anti-communist groups known collectively as the Whites. War Communism was established in Bolshevik-controlled areas. This was primarily an economic policy in which:

- the use of currency was abolished
- the government owned all property, industries and banking
- peasants were forced to give food to Bolshevik forces
- all production was geared for war.

While the Bolsheviks won the Russian Civil War by 1921, War Communism was a failure. Millions starved as a result of either having food seized by government forces or peasants refusing to grow grain that might be seized. Some Bolshevik soldiers rebelled as a result of privations, and people stopped working in many industries from lack of pay, food and things to purchase. This led to the New Economic Policy in 1921, in which:

- peasants paid taxes in grain and were able to sell for profit anything remaining
- smaller industries could be privately operated
- government industries would produce consumer goods to encourage peasants to grow more grain to buy these goods
- government would export excess grain to purchase modern machinery to build industries to strengthen the nation.

This programme continued through most of the 1920s and restored Russian economic strength, which became known as the **Soviet Union** in 1922, to 1914 levels by 1928.

Conclusion

Verdicts on the post-war treaties are now moving towards the consensus that although they were certainly flawed, they were not too harsh. They certainly could have been harsher. Germany, for example, remained unified in contrast to its division in the aftermath of the Second World War. The fundamental weakness with the treaties is instead increasingly seen to be that they were simultaneously too harsh and too lenient; that they gave reasons for vengeance while not removing fully the means to enact that vengeance in the future. Despite this, the causal links also frequently made to the origins of the Second World War are now also increasingly challenged as being too simplistic (see Source BB).

SOURCE BB

Excerpt from *The Peacemakers* by Margaret MacMillan, published by Random House, New York, 2003, page 500.

[The Allies] made mistakes, of course. If they could have done better, they certainly could have done much worse. They tried … to build a better order. They could not foresee the future and they certainly could not control it. That was up to their successors. When war came in 1939, it was as a result of twenty years of decisions taken or not taken, and not of arrangements made in 1919.

> **Did the impact of the First World War make future European conflict more or less likely?**

> **⚷ KEY TERM**
>
> **Soviet Union** Communist Russia and states under its control, also known as the USSR

> What is the verdict of Source BB about the extent to which the post-war peace treaties should be blamed for future unrest?

Social impact
- Huge casualties
- New opportunities for women during war, but impact not all long lasting
- New role for state intervention during war, but impact not all long lasting

Economic impact
- Government debts
- Manpower and material losses had an adverse impact on manufacture
- Post-war recession: unemployment, inflation
- Defeated countries adversely affected by reparations
- Damage to agricultural land

The effects of the First World War

Political impact
- Post-war peace settlements fundamentally altered the territorial and political map of Europe
- New governments in the defeated nations
- (Contributed to) Communist revolution in Russia in 1917
- Political unrest/revolt in Germany

SUMMARY DIAGRAM

The effects of the First World War

Chapter summary

First World War 1914–18

The First World War was fought between Germany and Austria-Hungary and their allies, against France, Russia, Britain and their allies. In many ways it marked a new era in warfare. It was the first truly global war, involving 32 nations, with fighting taking place in Europe, the Middle East, Africa and Asia. New modern military technologies were employed on a substantial scale for the first time with the first significant military usage of the tank, submarines, aircraft (in fighter and bomber capacities), poison gas and the machine gun. These technologies changed the nature of modern warfare, although in the First World War their tactical deployment and technical capabilities remained highly limited. Military technologies, however, did not determine the outcome of the war. This was decided more by the ability of each state to sustain the enormous material and manpower demands of a four-year-long modern conflict. These demands made it the first example of modern total war which inevitably involved civilians as participants and potential targets to an unprecedented degree.

The origins of the First World War were long in the making. The atmosphere of anxiety, tension and hostility between the major European powers which made war likely by 1914 had been generated by decades of economic, imperial and military competition and rivalry. When, in June 1914, the assassination of the Austro-Hungarian archduke Franz Ferdinand ignited various long-term tensions making the prospect of war in the Balkans a real possibility, many of the major powers became embroiled. This escalated a potentially localized conflict to a world war, the length and horror of which none of the major powers had expected.

The legacy of the First World War was profound. In Russia and Germany, where the war had prompted revolutionary political change, the impact was most strongly and lastingly apparent. The Allied peace settlements that were imposed on the defeated nations brought about fundamental territorial, political and economic changes to Europe. Whether these changes, by fuelling resentments and regrets in defeated and victorious nations respectively, contributed directly to the outbreak of the Second World War is however, more debatable. Regrettably, the First World War's epitaph 'the war to end all wars' was not to be one of its lasting impacts.

Activities

1 In groups represent one of the following countries:

- Germany
- Austria-Hungary
- Russia
- Britain
- France.

Prepare notes to defend your country from the accusation that they were responsible for the outbreak of the First World War.

Each country should take it in turns to be questioned by the class to see how well they defend themselves against claims that they were responsible for the outbreak of war.

At the end of the debate take a vote as to which country was most responsible.

2 Create a list of the ways in which the First World War could be considered to be an example of total war. Include specific examples from a range of countries.

3 Use one of the key questions from this chapter as an essay prompt and, in seven minutes, create an introduction for your essay. Share this with a partner or in a group and discuss what evidence would support your argument.

4 As a class, create a timeline of First World War events. Use a different colour to note events on the various war fronts. Add other details to your graph such as dates that certain technologies were introduced, such as tanks, poison gas and so forth. Create essay questions based on your timeline and use these while revising.

5 Hold a class debate regarding the following question: Which Allied state was most affected by the outcome of the First World War?

6 Hold another class debate regarding the following question: Which Central Power was most negatively affected by the outcome of the First World War? Rank the defeated Central Powers in order of most severely to least severely affected. Justify your answers. Remember that territorial loss is only one possible negative consequence of many for the defeated states.

CHAPTER 2

Spanish Civil War 1936–9

The Spanish Civil War 1936–9 was a struggle between the forces of the political left and the political right in Spain. The forces of the left were a disparate group led by the socialist Republican government against whom a group of right-wing military rebels and their supporters launched a military uprising in July 1936. This developed into civil war which, like many civil conflicts, quickly acquired an international dimension that was to play a decisive role in the ultimate victory of the right. The victory of the right-wing forces led to the establishment of a military dictatorship in Spain under the leadership of General Franco, which would last until his death in 1975.

The following key questions will be addressed in this chapter:

★ To what extent was the Spanish Civil War caused by long-term social divisions within Spanish society?

★ To what extent should the Republican governments between 1931 and 1936 be blamed for the failure to prevent civil war?

★ Why did civil war break out?

★ Why did the Republican government lose the Spanish Civil War?

★ To what extent was Spain fundamentally changed by the civil war?

 ## The long-term causes of the Spanish Civil War

> ▶ Key question: To what extent was the Spanish Civil War caused by long-term social divisions within Spanish society?

 KEY TERM

Spanish Morocco Refers to the significant proportion of Morocco that was controlled by Spain as a colony from 1906.

The Spanish Civil War began on 17 July 1936 when significant numbers of military garrisons throughout Spain and **Spanish Morocco**, led by senior army officers, revolted against the left-wing Republican government. The conspirators were joined by various groups hostile to the Republican government including monarchists, conservatives and fascist paramilitaries. The rebels also received assistance from the right-wing governments of Germany and Italy.

Most of north-west Spain quickly came under army, or Nationalist, control, but the rising was not universally successful. The military rebels failed to take the key cities of Madrid and Barcelona and most of rural southern and eastern Spain. The outcome was that Spain was divided and civil war began (see the map on page 89).

The Spanish Civil War was fundamentally rooted in, but not exclusively caused by, profound social divisions between the wealthy, privileged few and the masses of poor rural and industrial workers. The desire to improve the conditions of the workers, through political action and demonstrations, led to conflict with those who were opposed to such change. But the civil war was a war of multiple conflicts, with long-term **separatist** and anti-clerical agendas also provoking considerable tension and fuelling political conflict. This first section examines these long-term causes of the war.

Economic and social problems 1900–31

← What was the nature of the economic and social problems in Spain?

Rural poverty

There existed extreme polarization of wealth in many rural areas of Spain between the landlords and the landless labourers. This was particularly so in southern Spain where the agricultural system consisted of huge estates, called *latifundia*, which were owned by a few wealthy landlords and worked by labourers hired by the day. This system kept the labourers poor because:

- the hiring of labour by the day gave no financial security and unemployment was common
- the operation of one-crop farming meant that the availability of work was highly seasonal, often representing only 200 days' work per year
- wages were low.

Most rural unrest took place in southern Spain where rural hardships were most severe. Left-wing unions, which organized strikes and demonstrations against exploitative landlords, appealed to the labourers. Particularly popular was the socialist union, the **Union General de Trabajadores** (UGT), and the **anarcho-syndicalist** *Confederacion Nacional del Trabajo* (CNT), the latter of which, by 1918, had over 700,000 members. Attempts to improve conditions through strike action, however, were rarely successful, not least because landlords frequently brought in alternative labourers from outside the region to do the farm work instead.

Agricultural issues had a significant impact on national politics. Agricultural employment constituted 45.5 per cent of the workforce by 1930 and the growth in rural unrest presented a problem for central government. The different possible solutions to the agrarian problems frequently caused serious divisions between left- and right-wing politicians.

Urban poverty

The percentage of the workforce employed in industry increased in the early twentieth century, from 21.9 per cent in 1923, to 25.6 per cent in 1930. Urban centres grew as a consequence, with over a million people migrating to the cities in this period. By 1930, 42 per cent of Spain's population lived in towns of over 10,000 inhabitants. Spain's main industrial regions were:

- the Basque country, for iron and steel

KEY TERM

Separatist Favouring a degree of political independence or autonomy for a particular region.

Union General de Trabajadores General Union of Labourers, the main union of the Socialist Party.

Anarcho-syndicalist An anarchic belief in which proponents desire the central authority of the state to be replaced by the operation of control by trade unions.

Confederacion Nacional del Trabajo National Labour Confederation, an anarcho-syndicalist trade union.

[Handwritten notes in margin:]

- long term cause:
- Poverty
  - Rural:
    - Labourers who were kept poor through the agricultural system wanted a way out of this
  - Urban:
    - Industry workers were payed very little yet had to pay for the basic ...

In trying to find solutions for this, there became more political polarisation,

- the Asturias, for coal mining
- Catalonia, for textile industries.

Industrial workers were frequently housed in inner-city slums where rents were high and living conditions overcrowded and insanitary. There was no social legislation, so there was no minimum wage, no maximum working hours or protection from dangerous working conditions.

The concentration of dissatisfied workers in Spain's cities led to the growth of **trade unions** and strikes. For the more privileged, the increase in unrest was frequently seen as evidence of the growing threat of social revolution following the successful **Bolshevik Revolution** in Russia. Urban issues, as with agrarian problems, therefore contributed to political polarization in Spain.

Political instability

Separatism in Spain 1900–31

Spain was a unified country, but there was a strong tradition of separatism in Catalonia and the Basque country. Both regions prized their distinctive culture, language and history, and sought a significant degree of political autonomy. This separatism was centuries old, but its popularity increased with the growth in the economic importance of Catalonia and the Basque country in the twentieth century. Separatists argued that the significant economic contributions made by their regions were not sufficiently valued by the central government; separatists in Catalonia pointed out that only one-twentieth of Catalan contributions to state revenue were returned in public spending in the region. Separatist parties like the Catalan **Lliga Regionalista** and the Basque **Partido Nacionalista Vasco** (PNV) grew in popularity. The separatist agenda proved to be another divisive issue in Spanish politics with leftist groups prepared to concede some degree of autonomy and rightists determined to preserve the unity of Spain.

The collapse of the monarchy

Instability characterized Spanish politics in the early twentieth century. Until 1923, Spain was governed by a constitutional monarchy, although matters of government were largely carried out by the elected **cortes** or parliament. Despite the operation of **universal male suffrage** the system was not really democratic since elections were strongly influenced by local **caciques**. This political system was unpopular with ordinary people, not least because it failed to introduce reforms to improve their lives. As protests increased, those on the political right, alarmed by the prospect of left-wing government, turned to Miguel Primo de Rivera, a military official who promised to end the unrest in Spain.

What were Spain's political problems?

KEY TERM

Trade union An organization of workers which pursues improvements in pay and working conditions for its members.

Bolshevik Revolution The successful communist revolution in Russia in October 1917 led by the Bolshevik Party.

KEY TERM

Lliga Regionalista Regionalist League, a separatist Catalan political party.

Partido Nacionalista Vasco Basque Nationalist Party, a Basque separatist political party.

Cortes Elected parliament.

Universal male suffrage When all adult males are entitled to vote in elections.

Caciques Influential local 'bosses', usually wealthy landlords or industrialists.

[Handwritten note in left margin:] As separatism grew in popularity due to the growing economic importance of certain countries/regions, there was more of a political divide.

[Handwritten note at bottom:] Spain's voting system was never really democratic. The rich often had more of a say and people w/o money did not like this.

SOURCE A

A map showing the main regions and political groups within Spain.

What does this map show about the political groupings within Spain before the civil war?

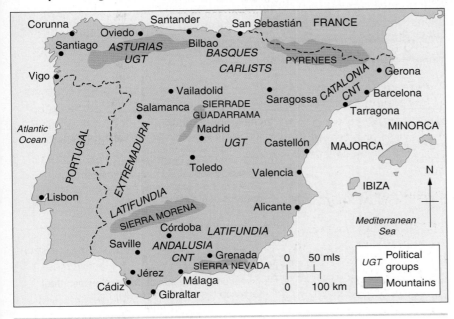

The dictatorship of Primo de Rivera, September 1923 to January 1930

Miguel Primo de Rivera came to power as the result of a military coup. He established himself as a dictator, although a virtually powerless monarch, King Alfonso XIII, remained the head of state.

Primo de Rivera was unable to heal the deep divisions in Spanish society despite introducing a number of reforms. In fact, the reforms themselves proved divisive; they were simultaneously too much for the right and too little for the left. These reforms included:

- Arbitration committees to manage disputes between industrial workers and their employers.
- Government investment in a programme of public works to increase job opportunities. These included the construction of the first trans-Pyrenees rail link between Spain and France.
- Proposals to reform the army and a reduction of the army budget.

The reforms fell far short of what was necessary to resolve Spain's serious socioeconomic problems, but were also costly, alienating both reformers and the conservative élites who resented the increased financial burden. Primo de Rivera became increasingly unpopular, prompting King Alfonso XIII to request his retirement. Primo de Rivera stepped down on 28 January 1930.

Under the dictatorship of Primo de Rivera, reforms were made that did more harm than good

The end of the monarchy, April 1931

After the end of Primo de Rivera's dictatorship, King Alfonso XIII hoped to gain popular support for a continuation of monarchical rule. He arranged for an election to be held on this issue. Contrary to his expectations, the results were an endorsement for a democratic republic. Although he refused to abdicate, he did leave Spain.

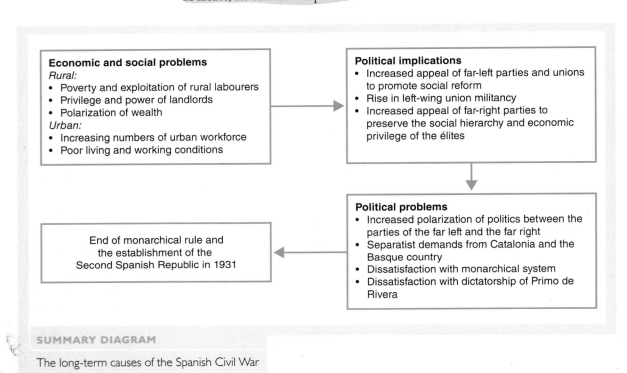

Economic and social problems
Rural:
- Poverty and exploitation of rural labourers
- Privilege and power of landlords
- Polarization of wealth

Urban:
- Increasing numbers of urban workforce
- Poor living and working conditions

Political implications
- Increased appeal of far-left parties and unions to promote social reform
- Rise in left-wing union militancy
- Increased appeal of far-right parties to preserve the social hierarchy and economic privilege of the élites

Political problems
- Increased polarization of politics between the parties of the far left and the far right
- Separatist demands from Catalonia and the Basque country
- Dissatisfaction with monarchical system
- Dissatisfaction with dictatorship of Primo de Rivera

End of monarchical rule and the establishment of the Second Spanish Republic in 1931

SUMMARY DIAGRAM

The long-term causes of the Spanish Civil War

---

2. The short-term causes of the Spanish Civil War

> ▶ *Key question: To what extent should the Republican governments between 1931 and 1936 be blamed for the failure to prevent civil war?*

In 1931, Spain became a republic. The new republican government faced a number of serious social, economic and political problems. The failure of successive governments to provide a satisfactory solution to these problems led to the outbreak of civil war in 1936. This failure was not solely due to the weaknesses of the governments themselves; the problems they faced and the context in which they were operating made the provision of stable government extremely difficult.

The governments of the Second Spanish Republic 1931–6

← **Why was the Second Republic unable to provide long-term political stability?**

The short-lived Spanish Republic underwent significant changes in governments between 1931 and 1936. The three major elections held in this period resulted in dramatic swings between left- and right-wing governments, all of which were **coalitions**:

- left-wing coalition government (June 1931 to November 1933)
- right-wing coalition government (November 1933 to February 1936)
- left-wing coalition government, known as the Popular Front (February 1936 to July 1936).

Substantial problems confronted the government of the Spanish Republic in 1931. These problems included:

- the lack of a tradition of working democracy
- opposition from monarchists hostile to the Republic
- opposition from extreme right-wing groups, like the **Falange**, who did not believe democracy could solve Spain's problems
- serious socioeconomic divisions which meant that any reforming action would leave at least one section of society dissatisfied
- the rise of political extremism in Europe, evident in the establishment of right-wing dictatorships in Italy and Germany
- the fear of communist revolution, encouraged by the USSR; many conservatives in Spain interpreted any social reforms as a step towards communism.

In addition, the Great Depression had just begun. This profoundly disrupted the world economy and worsened the socioeconomic crisis in Spain. During the Great Depression in Spain:

- imports and exports dropped significantly, the former halving by 1935 from 1929 levels; exports were reduced by only slightly less
- industrial productivity decreased, with **gross domestic product** decreasing by 20 per cent in the 1930s
- unemployment rates rose to 12.9 per cent in 1934
- government investment decreased.

The left-wing government's reforms 1931–3

← **How popular were the reforms of the left-wing government?**

The June 1931 elections were a resounding triumph for the left-wing parties. Of the 470 seats in the parliament, the Spanish Socialist Party, the *Partido Socialista Obrero Español* (PSOE), won 116, making them the largest party represented. This, however, was insufficient to ensure the passage of legislation, necessitating they form a coalition government. They joined other left-wing parties including the second largest party, the **Radical Party** led by Alejandro Lerroux, to form a government. The moderate Niceto Alcalá-Zamora was chosen as President. The right-wing parties held only 41 seats.

 **KEY TERM**

Coalition Government formed of a combination of political parties.

Falange Fascist political party established in February 1933 by José Antonio Primo de Rivera, the son of Miguel Primo de Rivera.

Gross domestic product The market value of all goods and services produced in a country in a given time period.

Radical Party Spanish political party founded by Alejandro Lerroux. Its political ideology represented the centre ground, favouring moderate social reform.

The new parliament passed a series of reforms which aimed to address the problems of rural inequality, unemployment and the exploitation of labour. These are shown in the table below.

The left-wing government's reforms 1931–3

Agrarian reforms	Anti-clerical reforms
• Law of Municipal Boundaries of 28 April 1931 which prohibited employers from bringing in workers from outside a given region until all those within the locality had jobs, preventing landlords from breaking strikes • Law of Obligatory Cultivation of 7 May 1931 which aimed to increase employment by forcing landlords to farm their lands to employ more workers • Extension of arbitration committees (see page 77) to the countryside • Introduction of an eight-hour working day on 1 July 1931 • Agrarian Reform Law passed on 9 September 1932 which aimed at dismantling *latifundia* estates through the redistribution of land by expropriating land from landlords whose estates exceeded 300 hectares of arable land or whose yield amounted to over 10,000 pesetas a year • Institute of Agrarian Reform was established to implement the process of redistribution, which included the payment of compensation to landlords	• Teaching by religious orders banned in an attempt to end the Church's traditional monopoly in education • Prohibition of the display of religious images in public buildings, including classrooms • Definition of Spain as a secular state • An end to state financial support to the Church after a period of two years' transition • Legalization of divorce and civil marriage • An obligation to acquire the state's approval for official religious displays These reforms encouraged a spate of violent attacks against Church property throughout Spain in May 1931 in which over 100 buildings were vandalized or looted.
	Military reforms
	• Army officer numbers were reduced • An investigation of promotions of officers during the dictatorship of Primo de Rivera was established • The conservative military academy at Zaragoza was closed • Top military positions awarded to those with strong pro-Republican credentials • All officers were required to swear an oath of loyalty to the Republic or face discharge • Some right-wing officers were moved to minor posts
Urban worker reforms	**Separatist reforms**
• An entitlement to seven days' paid leave per annum • An eight-hour working day, unless overtime was paid • Some social security benefits, although these were restricted to maternity, retirement and insurance against accidents in the workplace • Freedom to strike without the fear of dismissal	• Catalan Statute of September 1932 gave limited autonomy to Catalonia • Established a Catalan Parliament, the *Generalitat*, with legislative power over agriculture, transport, public health and poor relief in Catalonia; other issues remained the preserve of the central government in Madrid • One-third of Catalan taxation was under the control of the Catalan Parliament

Limitations of the reforms 1931–3

Although the reforms achieved much, they fell short of solving many of the problems they set out to address. The Agrarian Reform Law in its first year only succeeded in resettling 10 per cent of the 60,000 families it had aimed to help. In large part this was because the Institute of Agrarian Reform was allocated an inadequate 50 million pesetas (one per cent of the annual budget) with which to carry out the reform, including the compensation payouts. The Law of Obligatory Cultivation was frequently ignored by landlords, in part because they only incurred minimal fines (frequently not exceeding 500 pesetas) for so doing. Rural labourers continued to suffer considerable hardship, and by the early 1930s, 72 per cent of those registered unemployed were from agricultural regions. Unemployment also remained a substantial problem in urban areas. Social security benefits provided only limited assistance to industrial workers, and did not cover those who were out of work. The concessions to separatist demands were also highly limited. Catalonia was granted only a very restricted degree of independence, and no provision was made for the Basque country.

Political reactions to the reforms 1931–3

The reforms generated criticism from both the extreme left and the conservative right. The government became isolated and weakened as Spain's politics polarized and it was abandoned by the extreme left and attacked by a strengthened conservative right. In the general election of November 1933, the left-wing coalition government was voted out of power.

Opposition from the extreme left

The government's defeat in the November 1933 elections was in significant part due to the loss of support from elements of the more extreme left that had formerly backed the government. These included anarchists and the left-wing faction of the PSOE, which was led by Largo Caballero. To these groups, the government's reforms did not go far enough to address Spain's socioeconomic problems. In consequence, their opposition grew. Anarchists abstained from voting rather than give the left-wing parties of the coalition their vote. The PSOE was weakened by divisions caused by criticisms from Largo Caballero's left-wing faction, many of whom refused to co-operate with other left-wing parties in the November 1933 elections, dividing the left-wing vote.

One of the main reasons why the November general elections were called at all was because of a breakdown in co-operation between, and within, the coalition parties which made effective, stable government almost impossible. This persuaded President Alcalá-Zamora to use his power to dissolve the parliament and call new elections. The breakdown of the coalition was prompted by the reform programme, in particular the agrarian reforms. The Radical Party favoured more gradual reform and the defence of property rights, law and order. They employed blocking tactics in the parliament to slow the passage of the reforms. This angered members of the PSOE, especially Largo Caballero's more extreme left-wing faction who demanded an even more radical programme of reforms. Anti-clerical reform also caused difficulties within the leftist coalition government. Some key government ministers were opposed to what was perceived as a radical programme including, crucially, the strongly Catholic President, Alcalá-Zamora.

Many ordinary labourers and workers were dissatisfied with the effects of the reform programme, expressing this not only in their electoral support for the more extreme left-wing parties, but also through participation in street demonstrations. Many of these protests and strikes were organized by the unions of the far-left parties such as the anarchist *Federacíon Anarquista Ibérica* (FAI) and the anarcho-syndicalist union, the CNT, which grew in popularity. One of the most serious uprisings, organized by FAI, occurred in January 1933. Although it was crushed by government forces, in the village of Casas Viejas in Cadiz, 19 peasants were killed when the government's **Assault Guards** opened fire. This was part of the government's increasingly firm stance against militant demonstrations which included the passing of the Law for the Defence of the Republic in October 1931. This banned spontaneous strikes and allowed for the arrest and deportation of suspected instigators. Such repression and violence increased disillusionment towards the government from those on the far left, while doing little to halt the demonstrations.

Opposition from the conservative right

The reforms also provoked hostility from the conservative right on the opposite end of the political spectrum. From their perspective, many of the reforms represented an assault on the traditional social and religious order in Spain, which they fiercely defended, and an undesirable increase in the intervention of the state in economic and social affairs. They feared that both marked first steps towards more radical, socialist reform. These anxieties were given credence by the increase in far-left militant protest that seemed to accompany the reforms. It appeared to the conservative right that the left-wing coalition government had unleashed forces of social revolution that it could not control which would lead to communism. There was also widespread hostility to the perceived fragmentation of the unity of the state through the granting of concessions to Catalonia.

The growth of conservative right opposition was manifested in the formation, and popularity, of the *Confederacion Espanola de Derechas Autonomas* (CEDA), a right-wing party established in February 1933 by José Maria Gil-Robles. It was essentially a union of right-wing opposition groups whose proclaimed agenda was the defence of law, order, property and the Catholic Christian religion. Increased support for CEDA was strikingly apparent in the November 1933 elections when they took 115 seats, making them the single largest party in the parliament.

The conservative right opposition included a significant number of military officers. Their affiliation with right-wing groups was in large part due to the socioeconomic background of many of Spain's high-ranking military, who came predominantly from landowning classes. The military also opposed many of the recent reforms. They feared these were a prelude to a more substantial purge of the traditional military hierarchy. However, there was only one, abortive, military coup in the period 1931–3, led by General José Sanjurjo in August 1932.

Right-wing Republican government, November 1933 to February 1936

← How did the policies of the right-wing Republican government contribute to unrest in Spain?

In the November 1933 elections, CEDA became the largest party in the parliament with 115 deputies. They worked closely with the second largest party, the Radicals, who had shifted considerably to the right since 1931.

Reforms of the right-wing Republic 1933–6

The period of right-wing government saw the reversal of much of the legislation passed by the earlier left-wing government. Their actions included:

- the repeal of the Law of Municipal Boundaries (see page 80) in May 1934
- a refusal to enforce most of the agrarian and industrial reforms, including undermining arbitration committees (see page 77), which led to the eviction of peasant farmers who had recently received land from the reforms
- police searches of trade union premises
- the authorization of force to break up strikes
- a refusal to enforce laws that separated the Catholic Church from the state, allowing it to take control of education.

[handwritten margin note: Basically a reversal of everything the Right-wing gov did.]

The Asturias Uprising, October 1934

The left-wing parties and their supporters were alarmed by the reforms of the right-wing government. Left-wing protests against the government increased. The most serious uprising took place in the Asturias in October 1934. The revolt was intended to be part of a larger national socialist uprising to remove the government, but poor planning meant that the one in Asturias was the only one of significance.

The Asturias was predominantly a mining region that had suffered severely from the effects of the Great Depression. Hundreds of mines had been closed in the 1920s, resulting in high unemployment. The agenda of the far left therefore held significant appeal. During the revolt of October 1934, many of the workers succeeded in establishing an independent workers' republic exercising control over one-third of the province and 80 per cent of its population. There was violence, with revolutionaries burning 58 churches as well as taking hostages, 31 of whom they killed.

[handwritten margin note: Lots of unemployment in the Austrias due to the closing of mines during the GD. Because of high unemployment there was a large population of left wing protesters]

The reaction of the right-wing government was brutal and within two weeks the revolt was ended with 1335 killed and almost 3000 wounded; most of these were from the Asturias. Government suppression continued, and broadened, even after the surrender of the Asturian rebels on 19 October 1934. Catalan autonomy was suspended and thousands of left-wing activists were arrested throughout the region.

The end of the right-wing government, January 1936

The right-wing government came to an end when President Alcalá-Zamora dissolved the parliament and called a general election for February 1936. His decision was precipitated by the virtual collapse of co-operation between the Radical and the CEDA partnership, a situation that made government almost unworkable. The breakdown in this partnership was in large part over policy since the Radical Party became increasingly unsupportive of the CEDA's more extreme right-wing position.

Popular Front government, February–July 1936

The general election of February 1936 resulted in another left-wing government. The victorious coalition, known as the Popular Front, was a broad union of left-wing parties including republicans, socialists and communists. The Popular Front held a substantial majority in the parliament with 286 seats, in comparison to the 132 seats held by the right. However, this distribution of seats, which was in accordance with the rules of the electoral system, obscured the closer split of opinion in Spain. This split was revealed in the division of actual votes cast, which was 4,654,116 for the left, 4,503,524 for the right.

Reforms of the Popular Front government

The Popular Front government resumed the left-wing reformist agenda:

- the restoration of Catalan autonomy
- discussion of granting autonomy to the Basque country
- the resumption of agrarian and military reforms.

Opposition from the conservative right

These reforms were opposed by the conservative right and there was an almost immediate escalation in right-wing inspired violent protest. Many of the more extreme elements of the conservative right expressed frustration with the democratic system and began to advocate a more militant approach to gaining power. Indeed, there was an abortive right-wing plot involving Gil-Robles, the leader of the CEDA Party, to prevent the Popular Front government from even taking power at all. Further evidence of the rightist drift to extremism was the significant increase in membership to the explicitly anti-democratic and fascist Falange Party from 1936.

The conservative right were encouraged into greater opposition by the increasingly radical rhetoric of the extreme left. Conservative politicians claimed a right-wing government was the only way to restore and preserve order in Spain. On the streets, right-wing militants provoked left-wing groups to violence to justify claims that they were needed to prevent lawlessness. The assassination of the right-wing monarchist leader José Calvo Sotelo on 13 July 1936 by government troops confirmed for many that left-wing violence needed to be stopped, by force if necessary.

The inability of right-wing parties to work together led to re-election and the end of a right-wing gov

Though the left held more seats, the overall population of Spain was split

○ The right greatly opposed left-wing reforms

○ They viewed the left as violent and lawless

[handwritten: → Leader of right wing group, CEDA]

SOURCE B

Excerpt of a speech by Gil-Robles in parliament on 15 April 1936 in
***The Coming of the Spanish Civil War* by Paul Preston, published by**
Taylor & Francis, London, 2004, page 254.

Civil War is being brought by those who seek the revolutionary conquest of
power and it is being sustained and weaned by the apathy of a government
which does not turn on its supporters … when civil war breaks out in Spain, let
it be known that the weapons have been loaded by the negligence of a
government which has not been able to fulfil its duty towards groups which have
stayed within the strictest legality.

> According to Source B,
> what was the cause of civil
> war in Spain? **?**

Opposition from the extreme left

The Popular Front government faced opposition from increasingly extreme
left-wing militancy. This was motivated in part by what these groups saw as
an opportunity to exact vengeance on landlords and employers who had
used the previous two years of right-wing government to exploit workers
and peasants. Extreme left-wing unions encouraged labourers who had been
the victims of eviction to take undertake illegal occupations to reclaim land,
resulting in mass land seizures which were later made legal by the
government. The increased militancy of the left was also a consequence of
worsening conditions due to poor harvests and unemployment. The rhetoric
of the leader of the left-wing faction of the PSOE, Largo Caballero, became
increasingly extreme, speaking of a social revolution.

[handwritten: Some left-wing groups wanted greater and quicker change]

The government's ability to provide stable rule was weakened by political
divisions within its ranks. The rift within the PSOE became so serious that
the left-wing faction led by Caballero refused to participate in the
government on the grounds that any coalition would dilute the social reform
agenda they wished to pursue. In addition, animosity between the leaders of
the competing PSOE factions, Caballero and Indalecio Prieto, resulted in
Caballero's supporters vetoing Prieto's appointment as prime minister in
May 1936. The new Prime Minister Santiago Casares Quiroga
underestimated the seriousness of the political situation and failed to save
the fragmenting Popular Front.

[handwritten: Due to this and the gov's inability to make that happen, there was political division between groups in the Popular Front]

The military uprising, July 1936

Throughout 1936, both the extreme left and extreme right had spoken
increasingly of revolution as the only solution to Spain's crisis. But it was the
conservative right who decisively abandoned the path of legality when
members of the military launched an uprising against the Popular Front
government in July 1936. The revolt had its roots primarily in the army and
was chiefly planned by General Emilio Mola. Most colonels and middle-
ranking officers supported the revolt, bringing their garrisons with them. The
Spanish Military Union (*Unión Militar Española*, UME) was a secretive
organization of over 3500 officers that played a key role in the establishment
of cells of conspirators throughout the country. General Mola also

recognized the importance of civilian support and established links with monarchists and CEDA to ensure their participation.

The revolt began with troops in Morocco on 17 July 1936 and soon spread to military units throughout Spain. This action met with armed resistance from left-wing unions, particularly in the rural south and in the key cities of Barcelona and Madrid. These unions quickly mobilized civilians into **militia** units and joined with troops loyal to the Republic. The result was that rebellious garrisons were only able to take control of parts of Spain. Civil war had begun.

 **KEY TERM**

Militia A military force using civilians as opposed to professional soldiers.

Left			Centre		Right
	Socialist Party (PSOE)		Radical Party (– by 1933 →)	CEDA	Falange
FAI	FNTT	UGT			
CNT					
Anarchists: in favour of radical social reform	Socialists: in favour of social reforms to achieve a greater fairness and distribution of wealth in society		Radicals: in favour of moderate reforms, moved increasingly to the right from 1931	CEDA: in favour of the defence of the social hierarchy, religion. Their commitment to democracy was questionable	FALANGE: fascist, anti-democratic

Year	Government	Key policies	Reactions
1931–3	Left-wing coalition (Primarily PSOE and Radicals)	Agrarian reform Urban reform Anti-clerical reforms Military reform Separatist concessions	Rise of right-wing opposition, e.g. formation of CEDA Left-wing opposition, e.g. FAI and CNT uprisings and PSOE split
1933–6	Right-wing coalition (Primarily CEDA and Radicals)	Reversal of left-wing reforms	Increase in left-wing protest: Asturias Uprising
1936	Left-wing Popular Front coalition	Revival of left-wing reforms	Left-wing militancy: land seizures, strikes Increase of right-wing opposition Military uprising (July 1937)

SUMMARY DIAGRAM

The short-term causes of the Spanish Civil War

3 Key debate

▶ **Key question:** *Why did civil war break out?*

The extent to which the left or the right was more responsible for the abandonment of democracy chiefly characterized early accounts about the causes of the Spanish Civil War.

Nationalist interpretations

Naturally, pro-nationalist interpretations, such as those written in the 1960s by Ricardo de la Cierva, a former priest and official in the Ministry of Information, blamed the left. They emphasized left-wing lawlessness, such as the Asturias Uprising and growth of militant unionism, which *forced* the right to take decisive action to safeguard order, property, law and religion against the spectre of social revolution.

Nationalist accounts, such as Joaquin Arraras' *Historia de la Cruzada Espanola* (1943), particularly emphasized the importance of the anti-Church reforms of the left-wing Republic in leading to civil war. These accounts accorded with Nationalist wartime propaganda that presented the civil war as a crusade in which the conservative right fought to preserve traditional Christian values against a godless left-wing Republic. While it was certainly the case that religion had the power to mobilize and inflame opinion, its importance may have been exaggerated by the conservative right, who wanted to present the civil war as a religious crusade instead of a battle to preserve wealth and privilege. Overall, it is difficult to determine to what extent religious conviction contributed to the outbreak of civil war.

Republican interpretations

Pro-Republican interpretations stressed that it was the extreme right who decisively went against the democratic system in launching the military uprising in 1936. They also questioned the extent to which the conservative right had ever really supported the democratic Republic. They presented examples of the Falange and the autocratic CEDA, whose commitment to democracy had always been doubted by their opponents.

Other interpretations

Accounts written by less politically involved historians have tended to emphasize the socioeconomic roots of the conflict. In particular, they highlight the difficulties caused by the long-term agrarian problems. This was evident in Gerald Brenan's *The Spanish Labyrinth* published in 1943, and more recently in the work of historian Paul Preston. They see agrarian issues as at the root of much of the conflict. Agrarian problems increased the growth of left-wing strikes and militancy and influenced the social reform

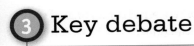

TOK

Photography, both still and motion pictures, was used by the Nationalists and the Republicans in the Spanish Civil War to affect public opinion outside Spain. How would visual imagery of the conflict affect people's understanding of the war? (Perception and Emotion.)

→ Nationalist blamed the left stating that their lawlessness and anti-church reforms led them to wanting to preserve traditional values

→ Republicans say that the right abandoned the democratic system.

→ Many Historians view the long term cause of agrarian issues to be the root of the conflict

programme of the left-wing governments, both of which antagonized the conservative right and played a key role in causing fractures in the left-wing coalitions.

Ultimately, if the war was most profoundly rooted in social and political divisions caused by agrarian problems, it was also a war of multiple conflicts, with separatism, religion and political factors all playing a role.

4 The course of the Spanish Civil War 1936–9

> ▶ **Key question:** Why did the Republican government lose the Spanish Civil War?

The right-wing military uprising against the Republican government quickly developed into civil war. The forces of the conservative right were known as the Nationalists, while those who fought to defend the left-wing Republican government were the Republicans. The civil war quickly acquired an important international dimension with both sides reliant on foreign supplies of weapons. Ultimately, the Nationalists triumphed, leading to the establishment of a right-wing military dictatorship. The role of strategy, tactics, technology and the effective management of the material requirements of war were all important in determining the outcome.

July 1936: Republican and Nationalist Spain

> **Were the Nationalists stronger than the Republicans at the outset of the civil war?**

• troops stationed in a town

 **KEY TERM**

Army of Africa Spanish and Spanish Moroccan troops stationed in Spanish Morocco.

The revolt of military garrisons throughout Spain led rapidly to the division of Spain into Nationalist and Republican areas. The Nationalists controlled the agricultural north-west, except the most northerly regions of the Basque country and the Asturias with its mining and industrial resources. Their area of western control bordered Portugal, whose dictator, António de Oliveira Salazar, was sympathetic to them. The Nationalists also held a small segment of territory in southern Spain around Seville, where 1500 troops from the Spanish **Army of Africa** were airlifted by Germany from Spanish Morocco to bolster Nationalist forces from 29 July 1936. More troops followed, ferried in convoys in co-operation with Italian and German militaries. This army was to prove decisive in the fortunes of the military rebels and was led by General Francisco Franco, who emerged by September 1936 as the leader of the Nationalists.

SOURCE C

A map showing the geographical division of Spain between the Nationalists and the Republicans by the end of July 1936.

What does Source C suggest about how far the Nationalists or the Republicans held the advantage in the civil war in July 1936?

SOURCE D

General Francisco Franco (centre) in 1936.

What does the photo in Source D suggest about Francisco Franco?

Republican-controlled territory in July 1936 centred on southern and eastern Spain, and included Spain's two major cities: Madrid and Barcelona, each with a population of over a million. This, along with the Republican control of the Basque country and the Asturias, meant that the Republic possessed the majority of Spain's industries and raw materials, as well as the areas of greatest population density. These included the territories producing Spain's primary agricultural exports, olive oil and citrus fruit, as well as control over Spain's gold reserves. The Republic also retained the loyalty of Spain's small navy and air force as well as a considerable proportion of the army and Civil Guard.

Why did the Nationalists fail to take Madrid in 1936?

The Nationalist advance to Madrid 1936

The initial strategic priority for the Nationalists in 1936 was to gain the capital city, Madrid, which was held by the Republic. The battle for Madrid led to fierce fighting throughout much of 1936.

Nationalist advance on Madrid, August–October 1936

The Nationalist Army of Africa advanced rapidly through Extremadura in August 1936, heading for Madrid. The troops were transported in trucks, with air cover provided by Italian and German aircraft, ensuring that they had reached the key Republican-held city of Merida, some 320 km from Seville, within a week. The cities of Merida and Badajoz were captured by 15 August 1936 after fierce battles. In what became known as the Massacre of Badajoz, some 2000 people were shot by order of the Army of Africa leader General Yagüe. Nationalist forces were barely delayed by Republican resistance, which was primarily composed of inexperienced and ill-equipped Republican militiamen. The town of Talavera de la Reina, for example, fell to the Army of Africa in a single day despite being defended by several thousand militiamen.

Fortress of Alcázar, September 1936

To the south of Madrid, near Toledo, stood Alcázar, a medieval fortress where 2000 Nationalist troops were besieged by Republicans. General Franco, determined to gain a symbolic victory, was anxious to relieve the fortress and ordered the Army of Africa to divert to Toledo instead of proceeding directly to Madrid. The siege was broken on 27 September, but this diversion meant Republicans had more time to improve Madrid's defences and receive a shipment of military equipment from the USSR.

Republic had help from USSR

Battle for Madrid, October–December 1936

In October 1936, Nationalists began a heavy artillery bombardment of Madrid, supplemented by German aircraft. The Republican government moved to Valencia although the Nationalist advance into Madrid from the west was halted at the **Casa de Campo**.

🔑 **KEY TERM**

Casa de Campo A large urban park to the west of Madrid.

Republican fighters in Madrid were helped by the arrival of weapons from the USSR and Mexico on 4 October. These included Soviet tanks and aircraft (see page 101), which proved superior to the German and Italian aircraft available at that stage to the Nationalists. Republicans also had the advantage in manpower with regular troops, militiamen and the non-Spanish **International Brigades** who arrived on 8 November, providing an additional 3500 men for the defence of Madrid. By the end of November, stalemate had set in to the west of Madrid.

 **KEY TERM**

International Brigades
Military units composed of volunteers from a range of countries.

Technology of the war: aircraft

Aircraft played a crucial role in the Spanish Civil War and were used in a wide variety of capacities including reconnaissance, ground attack and strategic bombing. Foreign-supplied aircraft played the most significant role, with Germany and Italy providing the Nationalists a combined 1253 and the USSR supplying 648 to the Republic. Soviet-supplied Polikarpov I-15 and I-16 fighters were superior to aircraft used by the Nationalists in the first year of the war, helping the Republicans to achieve aerial supremacy in the war's early months. The arrival of more advanced German Messerschmitt Bf 109 fighters in early 1937 gave the Nationalists the advantage. Although the Soviet Tupolev SB-2 bomber was, on paper, the most powerful bomber aircraft in Spain, there were few deployed and they performed poorly; the German Heinkel 111 bomber was superior. Bombers were used for strategic bombing on an unprecedented scale.

A comparison of the main aircraft in the Spanish Civil War

	Republican		**Nationalist**			
Overall number of aircraft *of all types* supplied by the USSR, Italy and Germany to Spain	648*		1253			
Type of aircraft	Polikarpov I-15 (*from 1936*)	Polikarpov I-16 (*from 1936*)	Fiat CR.32 (*from 1936*)	Heinkel He 51 (*from 1936*)	Messerschmitt Bf 109 (*from spring 1937*)	Heinkel He 111 (*from spring 1937*)
Country of origin	USSR	USSR	Italy	Germany	Germany	Germany
Maximum speed	350 km/h	489 km/h	360 km/h	330 km/h	640 km/h	310 km/h
Range	300 km	700 km	781 km	570 km	850 km	2400 km
Armaments	Four fixed forward firing machine guns	Two fixed forward firing machine guns, two 20 mm cannon in wings	Two machine guns	Two machine guns in nose	Two machine guns in wings, two 20 mm cannon in the wings, a 20 mm cannon in the nose	2000 kg as main bomb load, cannon and machine guns
Number of each type supplied to Spain	161*	276*	477	93	139	95

*Inconsistencies in the Soviet statistics mean that there can be variations in citations of the numbers of aircraft supplied.

→ Madrid and northern Spain 1937

The Nationalists made significant territorial gains in 1937, which would prove a decisive year in the conflict. By the end of the year, Nationalists controlled two-thirds of the country, and the ability of the Republic to win the war was in serious doubt.

The Málaga Campaign, February 1937

Nationalists attempted to extend their control over southern Spain in early 1937 with a campaign focused on gaining the southern coastal city of Málaga, which was surrounded by Nationalist troops. Nationalists were joined by 10,000 Italian troops in a co-ordinated attack on the city. The Italians employed *guerra celere* (rapid war) tactics which relied on speed through the use of armoured vehicles and tanks supported by aircraft. Weakened Republicans, cut off in Málaga with only 12,000 militiamen and 16 artillery units, were defeated by 8 February 1937.

SOURCE E

What reasons does Source E give for the defeat of the Republicans at Málaga?

Excerpt from *I Helped to Build an Army* by José Martin Blázquez, published by Secker & Warburg, London, 1939, page 307.

On February 8 [1937] a rebel army, consisting of motorised Italian units, entered Malaga … No ammunition was sent [by the Republicans] to Malaga for the simple reason that there was no ammunition to send. Our forces at Malaga were still less organised than those on other fronts, and they asked not for thousands of shells, but simply for rifle ammunition. We had had three weeks warning of the attack at Malaga. We knew the Italian troops had landed at Cadiz for the purpose, and we knew of the concentration of sixty German bombers. But we could do nothing to avoid the disaster. We hoped that a shipload of munitions might arrive to save us at the last moment. Our forces in Malaga were behind schedule in the transformation from a militia into a regular army, and were worse off than other fronts both in the quantity and quality of war material. Nevertheless I am convinced that if they had had ammunition, the 'glory' of taking Malaga of which Italy boasts would have been less glorious. Indeed, it is doubtful if they ever would have taken it at all.

Battle for Madrid, January–March 1937

A new series of Nationalist attempts to encircle and subdue Madrid were launched from January 1937. These included an attack at Guadalajara, north-east of the city in March.

The Guadalajara campaign, March 1937

The Guadalajara campaign aimed to take Madrid from the city's north-east. Like previous attempts to capture Madrid, infantry was supported by limited numbers of tanks, artillery and aircraft. Guadalajara, like previous Nationalist campaigns around Madrid, resulted in a defensive victory for the Republicans. Republicans benefited from greater manpower and superior quality, although not quantity, of weaponry at this stage of the war, such as Soviet tanks. The Nationalist advance was halted and stalemate once again prevailed around Madrid.

Technology of the war: tanks

The full potential of motorized combat vehicles in military combat was not realized in the Spanish Civil War. At the beginning of the civil war neither the Republicans nor the Nationalists possessed more than a handful of small tanks, although foreign-supplied machines increased these numbers rapidly. The Soviet T-26 tank proved superior to the German Panzer I and Italian CV.33 and CV.35 tanks (see the table below).

A comparison of the main tanks used in the Spanish Civil War

	Republican	Nationalist		
Overall number of tanks and armoured vehicles of *all types* supplied by the USSR, Italy and Germany to Spain	407	400		
Type of tank	T-26	Panzer I	CV.33	CV.35
Country of origin	USSR	Germany	Italy	Italy
Weight	9.4 tonnes	5.4 tonnes	3.15 tonnes	2.3 tonnes
Gun	45 mm cannon, one machine gun	Two machine guns	One 8 mm machine gun	Two 8 mm machine guns
Armour	7–16 mm	7–13 mm	5–15 mm	5–14 mm
Speed	28 km/h	40 km/h (depending on terrain)	42 km/h	42 km/h
Range	175 km	175 km	110 km	125 km/h
Number of type supplied to Spain	281	122	155	

Tanks were primarily used in the war to support infantry, with tanks spread in small numbers across multiple infantry divisions. This usage certainly helped to bolster an infantry advance, as was evident in the Republican defence around Madrid in the early months of the war. This tactic, however, failed to use tanks to their full potential; tanks were better used in mass formations to quickly overrun enemy infantry. New tank tactics were developed later in the conflict by German officers who used tanks concentrated together and supported their rapid attacks with aircraft.

The Vizcaya Campaign, March–June 1937

The repeated failure of Nationalists to take Madrid precipitated a change in strategic focus. Franco shifted his attention to northern Spain, notably the far northern regions of the Basque country and the Asturias, which remained outside of Nationalist control. Franco calculated that these would be easier to take than Madrid and their valuable resources and industries would add to Nationalist strength.

Nationalist use of airpower was crucial in this campaign. Nationalists achieved air supremacy through the support of the German **Condor Legion**. From 1937, this included increased numbers of newly developed aircraft which proved superior to those of the Republicans. The Vizcaya campaign began with aerial bombing raids on the cities of Ochandiano and Durango which were devastated in March 1937, with hundreds of civilians killed. Shortly afterwards Nationalist troops occupied the towns, encountering little resistance.

Guernica, April 1937

Guernica was a provincial Basque town with a population of 7000. It was of limited military significance, containing an armaments factory and occupying one of the main routes to the north. On 26 April 1937 it was targeted by Italian and German bomber and fighter aircraft. Bombers released 27,000 kg of **incendiary bombs**, while German fighters strafed roads full of fleeing

⚷ **KEY TERM**

Condor Legion Units of Germany's air force that fought with the Nationalists.

Incendiary bombs Bombs designed to start fires.

? How much can be learned from Source F about the Nationalist assault on Guernica?

SOURCE F

The destruction of Guernica, April 1937.

civilians. Guernica was left devastated. Over 1500 people were killed, with many more wounded. The bombing of Guernica was one of the first significant examples of the deliberate targeting of a primarily civilian area and the devastation that could be wrought by aerial bombs. This destruction was widely exploited in Republican propaganda within Spain and abroad (see page 102). Three days after the bombings, Nationalist ground troops, facing very little resistance, captured Guernica.

Nationalist conquest of the north, May–October 1937

Rapid progress made by Nationalists through the Basque region culminated in their assault on the regional capital: highly industrialized Bilbao. Nationalists breached the city's fortress defences following heavy artillery and aerial bombardment, while also blockading by sea, which starved the city of supplies (see page 104). Bilbao surrendered on 19 June 1937. Conquest of the north was completed with the capture of Gijón on 22 October 1937. The success of the Nationalist advance was primarily the result of Nationalist air superiority which enormously aided advancing infantry.

> **Technology of the war: warships**
> Naval warfare played a peripheral role in the Spanish Civil War. There were no major sea battles, and most naval engagements were blockade and counter-blockade operations. Nationalist blockades were more successful, but even these were never thorough enough to completely disrupt supplies to the Republic.

Republican divisions: Barcelona, May 1937

The Republican war effort was hampered by internal divisions about the war's conduct. In May 1937, differences in opinion manifested themselves in open conflict in Barcelona as troops from the militias of the extreme left (predominantly the anarchists and left-socialists) fought against militiamen from the more moderate left (socialists and communists). The extreme left believed that far-reaching social reform was being neglected by the moderate left, who dominated the Republican government, and that the war effort was too reliant on conventional tactics. They believed that the Republic should instead use guerrilla tactics and national labour strikes. Divisions culminated in what was effectively a civil war within a civil war in Barcelona in May 1937, resulting in the defeat of far-left extremists. Thereafter, the more moderate left dominated. The prime minister from September 1936, Largo Caballero, was forced to resign. His successor, from May 1937, Dr Juan Negrín, acted to strengthen ties with the Soviet Union and communist militias in Spain, who became an increasingly influential force in the Republican **Popular Army**, which continued to fight conventional battles. Neither Nationalists nor Republicans used guerrilla tactics to any significant degree.

T O K

Terror bombings such as those at Guernica (see Source F) were to be tragically repeated in many future twentieth-century wars, despite international outcry and their arguable failure to impact on the morale of the targeted side. Such examples have encouraged speculation about what, if anything, can be learned from history.

- 'The only thing we learn from history is that we learn nothing from history.' G.W.F. Hegel, 1770–1831.
- 'Those who don't study the past are condemned to repeat it.' G. Santayana, 1863–1952.

In the light of these two quotations, what, if anything, is the value of historical knowledge? Try to use specific historical examples in your discussion. (History, Reason, Emotion, Social Sciences.)

 **KEY TERM**

Popular Army Republican regular army organized in September 1937.

Brunete, July 1937

With Nationalist forces making considerable advances in northern Spain during the summer of 1937, Republicans launched their first major offensive of the war at Brunete, east of Madrid. The objective was to help relieve Madrid's siege.

Initial Republican manoeuvres, in which infantry were supported by artillery, tanks and aircraft, were, in the main, successful; Brunete was captured in two days. Republicans, however, quickly ran into problems. Many of the tanks used to support the infantry were halted by anti-tank weapons. Republicans also lost their dominance of the skies following the arrival of German fighters and bombers from the Condor Legion. Republican troops were subjected to air attack and communications broke down, making it difficult to co-ordinate a renewed offensive. Republicans consequently entrenched themselves but this failed to protect them from air attack. The Nationalists counterattacked and regained Brunete soon afterwards.

Teruel, December 1937 to January 1938

With Nationalist conquest of the north complete by the autumn of 1937, Franco turned his attention again to Madrid. Republicans were determined to divert Nationalist troops away from Madrid by launching another offensive 320 km east near the town of Teruel.

An initially successful Republican offensive captured Teruel and then failed to advance further. A Nationalist counterattack trapped Republican forces inside the town, where they were subjected to heavy artillery and aerial bombardment. After running short of supplies, Republicans abandoned the town to the Nationalists on 22 February 1938.

> **How effective were Republican counter-attacks in 1938?**

The war in 1938: the Nationalist advance into Catalonia

By the beginning of 1938, the majority of Spain was under Nationalist control, with the exception of Madrid, the south-east and Catalonia. The Nationalist Army now numbered 600,000; a third larger than that of the Republicans. Nationalist troops, supported by tanks and aircraft, launched an offensive into Catalonia, taking only six weeks to cut a swathe through Catalonia to reach the Mediterranean Sea. The Republicans sought to halt this advance with a counterattack at the Ebro River.

The Ebro Offensive, July–November 1938

The strategic aim of the Republicans' Ebro offensive was to force the Nationalists to divert troops north and away from Valencia in Catalonia. It was part of Prime Minister Juan Negrín's strategic objective to prolong the war. He believed that a general European war would soon break out between fascist and democratic states into which the Spanish conflict would be subsumed. In such a war, he hoped that Britain and France, who had not helped the Republicans, partly for fear of provoking the outbreak of a broader conflict, might be more amenable to lending assistance to the Republic, or at least that Germany and Italy would lessen aid to Franco as this would be needed to defend their own immediate interests. At any rate, the Spanish conflict would become part of the wider conflict between fascism and democracy which Negrín believed the democratic states would win.

The initial Republican advance across the Ebro River into Nationalist territory progressed rapidly and within a week they had gained nearly 40 km. The advance demonstrated improvements in the organization and discipline of the Popular Army, although the tactical use of tanks, in particular, continued to be poor. It soon became apparent that Republicans could not sustain the momentum of the advance as their troops were slowed by strong Nationalist resistance that was aided enormously by aircraft. Republican troops were slowly pushed back over the next three and a half months until by 16 November they had lost all the territory that they had gained. In retreat, the Popular Army maintained its discipline and organization to a greater extent than it had previously, but the loss of 75,000 troops killed, missing or wounded, as well as huge amounts of equipment, meant that Negrín's hopes of prolonging the conflict were unrealistic.

The war in 1939: the fall of Barcelona and Madrid

← Why did Barcelona and Madrid finally fall to the Nationalists in 1939?

By the beginning of 1939 the war was effectively won by the Nationalists, despite the key cities of Barcelona and Madrid remaining Republican. These cities soon fell to the Nationalists.

Barcelona, February 1939

Nationalists encountered relatively little resistance in their assault on Barcelona. Two million people in the city were cut off from what remained of Republican Spain and demoralized by food shortages and relentless aerial bombardment. Nationalists occupied the city on 26 January, almost without a fight.

SOURCE G

Vicente Rojo, Chief of the General Staff of the Republican forces, writing in 1939, as quoted in *The Spanish Civil War* by G. Ranzato, published by Interlink Books, New York, 1999, page 114.

According to Source G, why did Barcelona fall in January 1939?

On January 26 1939, Barcelona fell to the enemy … resistance was scarce, not to say null … one cannot help but note a tremendous contrast [to] the situation of Madrid in November 1936 and Barcelona in 1936 … what enthusiasm then! What a feverish desire to fight, two years before and what discouragement now! Barcelona was a dead city … it is no exaggeration to say that Barcelona was lost simply because there was no will to resist.

Madrid, February–March 1939

After the fall of Barcelona, Republican resistance rapidly dissipated. The president resigned and went into exile on 6 February. An even more devastating blow came on 27 February when the British and French governments recognized Franco as the legitimate head of the Spanish government. With only 500,000 Republican troops remaining within the Republican zone, Negrín's strategy of prolonging the war was futile. Politicians and military leaders who opposed Negrín's strategy, and his communist-dominated government, rebelled in Madrid on 5 March 1939. The rebels established an anti-communist **junta**, called the National Defence Council, which attempted to open negotiations with Franco for a **conditional surrender**. Another internal civil conflict broke out within the Republican zone, leaving nearly 230 dead and almost 600 wounded; Negrín fled to France. Franco was not interested in overtures for conditional surrender and occupied Madrid on 27 March. Spain was finally fully under Nationalist control.

To what extent were the Nationalists or the Republicans better able to organize the war?

→ # Managing the war

The management of the war involved maintaining a sufficient supply of manpower, weapons and food. Responsibility for the war's management within Nationalist zones lay with the military's Defence Council, which had complete authority over all aspects of life, both civilian and military. In the Republican zones, government remained in the hands of elected politicians whose commitment to democracy sometimes made the organization less effective due to internal divisions and lengthy debate. The failure of the Republicans to be sufficiently supplied with weapons, however, explains their defeat more than their disorganization.

Military personnel

In numerical terms, Nationalist forces were initially at a disadvantage, with forces approximately one-third smaller than those of the Republic, which also controlled most of Spain's small navy and air force. However, the numerical balance of forces was to change significantly as the war progressed. Nationalist forces expanded as they gained control over more territory, while Republican manpower reserves diminished. By the beginning of 1938, the Nationalist Army was approximately one-third larger than that of the Republicans. In early 1939 the Republican Popular Army was half the size of Nationalist forces, which had over a million troops.

Both sides relied heavily on conscription. Initially, the Republic had greater access to manpower since it controlled larger, more densely populated areas of Spain, although this was soon reversed. Nationalist conscripts received better training, which helped to prevent evasion from service; evasion was a significant problem for the Republic.

International troops contributed significant manpower to both sides in the form of pilots, tank commanders, military advisors and ordinary troops. Foreign forces played a particularly important role on the Republican side, participating in the militias and in the International Brigades. In total, approximately 35,000 men fought in the International Brigades until they disbanded in 1938.

In terms of experience and skill of troops, the Nationalists had a clear advantage from the outset with two-thirds of army officers siding with the rebels. The Republic lacked experienced, professional officers. In Nationalist territory, 28 military academies provided basic training for lower ranking commanders; there was no equivalent level of training in the Republican zones.

Militias

A significant proportion of the manpower of both sides came from the militias. On the Republican side, militia units of **labour unions** and leftist political groups formed in the wake of the July 1936 revolt. They were civilian volunteers and organized according to left-wing ideas of equality and freedom of discussion, often rejecting traditional military hierarchies; this was especially true in the radical anarchist militias. Militias were therefore often difficult to command and manage, although this did not necessarily mean they were ill-disciplined and ineffective. Many militia units preferred to operate independently and did not always co-operate with each other or the regular Republican Popular Army. The Republican government attempted to co-ordinate the militias by announcing on 30 September 1936 the incorporation of the militias into the regular army structure, but in reality assimilation did not occur until much later in the war.

What the militias lacked in experience and discipline they made up for in enthusiasm and bravery. Indeed, the military contribution of the Republican militias was crucial. The very survival of the Republic in the early days in many areas was due to the actions of local militias. This was most strikingly illustrated in Madrid and Barcelona in 1936. However, their lack of experience and training all too often showed, as was evident in their failure to halt the advance of the Army of Africa through Extremadura in the early months of the war.

SOURCE H

Excerpt from *Homage to Catalonia* by George Orwell, published by Penguin, London, 1938, pages 28–9. Orwell was a British journalist and writer who fought in Spain as a volunteer.

The essential point of the [militia] system was social equality between officers and men. Everyone from general to private drew the same pay, ate the same food and wore the same clothes, and mingled on terms of complete equality ... in theory at any rate each militia was a democracy and not a hierarchy ... I admit that at first sight the state of affairs at the front horrified me. How on earth could the war be won by an army of this type, it was what everyone was saying at the

 **KEY TERM**

Labour unions
Organizations for workers that negotiate with business owners to improve working conditions.

According to Source H, how were militias organized?

time, and although it was true, it was also unreasonable ... Later it became the fashion to decry the militias, and therefore to pretend that their faults, which were due to the lack of training and weapons, were the result of the egalitarian system.

The Nationalist militias included monarchists, known as the *requetes*, and the paramilitary forces of the fascist Falange. These militias, like those of the Republic, had a strong sense of their own identities, although their right-wing ideologies made them more accepting of military hierarchy. Franco forced their incorporation into the regular military structure from 20 December 1936. This meant that Nationalist militias were more easily controlled than those in Republican zones.

War supplies

War supplies, specifically munitions and technological equipment, were vital for both sides, in both quantity and quality. The limited ability of Spain to produce armaments meant that access to war supplies ultimately came to depend on access to foreign producers.

Domestic production of armaments

Domestic production constituted only a tiny proportion of the armaments used by each side. Access to the industrial and mining regions of the Basque country and the Asturias was central to domestic production, an advantage held by the Nationalists after 1937. Although the Republic continued to control the industrial centre of Barcelona, the lack of raw materials meant that by the end of the war its industrial output was only one-third of what it had been in 1936.

The Republic's ability to produce armaments was also largely hampered by the establishment of **collectives** in many industries in the early days of the war. Many factory workers established collective control over their factories in 1936, which meant that workers decided as a group what and how much was produced. Not only did such fundamental organizational changes frequently result in a fall in production, but it was more difficult for the government to impose central controls over the economy, which was critical for war production. This was in marked contrast to industrial controls in Nationalist territory, where central control over the supply and distribution of war materials was more efficient.

International supply of armaments

Both sides depended overwhelmingly on foreign supplies, access to which was determined by the attitude of foreign powers.

Non-Intervention Agreement

The Republican government looked naturally to the left-wing Popular Front government in France for assistance, and initially it seemed the French Prime Minister, the socialist Léon Blum, was favourable, agreeing on 20 July 1936 to send a shipment of armaments. However, on 9 August 1936 the French government prohibited the export of all war supplies to Spain, prompted by French anxieties that assisting Spain would imperil co-operation between France and Britain, which France regarded as vital to its security interests. This was because by the mid-1930s, the French had become increasingly concerned by German foreign policy and wanted British support against German hostility. Britain disapproved of intervention in Spain largely due to fears that assistance would prolong a war in Spain that might develop into a more general European war. In addition, anti-Republican sentiment was strong in the British government, who believed the Republic was too closely connected to communism, which they vehemently opposed.

The French government, anxious to assist the Spanish Republic but unwilling to intervene directly, proposed an agreement of non-intervention to be signed by all the major European powers. The French hoped that right-wing dictatorships in Europe, such as Germany and Italy, would commit to non-intervention and not supply the Nationalists. This would make the Spanish Civil War a purely Spanish affair and, with the early advantages held by the Republicans, hopefully lead to a Republican victory. The efforts of France and Britain to gain widespread agreement for non-intervention were realized in the Non-Intervention Agreement, which by the end of August 1936 had been signed by 27 European countries, including the Soviet Union, Germany and Italy.

Non-intervention, however, was far from helpful for the Republic. Indeed, it was a great hindrance to their military effectiveness. This was because not all the signatories adhered to the Non-Intervention Agreement. While Britain and France, who might have helped the Republic, remained committed to the principles of non-intervention, Italy and Germany violated the agreement by providing enormous amounts of aid to the Nationalists. Non-intervention therefore left the Republic unable to gain official international assistance, except from the Soviet Union, which also violated its promise not to assist any warring faction in Spain.

International assistance

The Republic relied predominantly on the Soviet Union for munitions and military equipment and the Nationalists on Italy and Germany. In total, the Nationalists received a far greater volume of aid than the Republicans (see Source I, page 102). The quantities of Nationalist aid increased during the course of the war, while Soviet supplies to the Republic diminished (see Source J, page 102). German aircraft were particularly helpful for the Nationalists in allowing them to gain and maintain control of the air after 1937. The quality of the Soviet equipment has been much debated. Soviet-supplied small firearms, such as rifles and machine guns, were of poor quality, with nearly 25 per cent of rifles dating from the 1880s. Many of the Soviet tank and aircraft models, in contrast, were of excellent quality, helping the Republic to achieve air supremacy in the first year of the war.

?

What can be learned from Source I about international involvement in the Spanish Civil War?

SOURCE I

Military equipment supplied to Spain by the USSR, Germany and Italy during the civil war.

Equipment type	Republicans	Nationalists	
	USSR	Germany	Italy
Aircraft of all types	648	621	632
Tanks and armoured vehicles	407	250	150
Artillery units	1,186	700	1,930
Machine guns	20,486	31,000	3,436
Rifles	497,813	157,309	240,747
Ammunition (rounds)	862,000,000	250,000,000	324,900,000
Submarines	0	0	4

?

What can be learned from Source J about how much Soviet assistance was of help to the Republic in the Spanish Civil War?

SOURCE J

Military supplies delivered by the USSR to the Spanish Republican government, October 1936 to January 1974, according to official 1974 Soviet figures.

Equipment type	Period			
	1936–7	1937–8	1938–9	Total
Aircraft of all types	496	152	0	648
Tanks	322	25	0	347
Artillery guns	714	469	3	1,186
Machine guns	12,804	4,910	2,772	20,486
Rifles	337,793	125,020	35,000	497,813

Morale

The maintenance of morale among troops and civilians was particularly crucial during the civil war.

Propaganda and censorship

Propaganda was a weapon used by both sides, and frequently the intended audience was as much international as Spanish. The Republic was keen to exploit the atrocities perpetrated by Nationalist troops in the hopes of gaining international sympathy and consequently assistance. As such, after the bombing of Guernica, eyewitness accounts and images of the horrors of the attack were widely disseminated by the Republic in the international press (see Source K). Sympathy and horror were forthcoming, but material assistance less so.

Nationalist propaganda focused on detailing the chaos, anarchy and terror in Republican zones and described assaults on property and the Catholic Church in order to legitimize the military's revolt (see Source L). Numerous pamphlets were produced purportedly compiled by 'fact-finding' committees detailing atrocities committed by Republican troops.

SOURCE K

A Republican poster appealing to international opinion after the bombing of civilians in Madrid 1937.

¿WHAT ARE YOU DOING

TO PREVENT THIS?

MADRID

MINISTERIO DE PROPAGANDA

According to Source K, why should the international community become involved in the Spanish Civil War?

SOURCE L

Excerpt from 'A Preliminary Official Report on the Atrocities Committed in Southern Spain in July and August, 1936, by the Communist Forces of the Madrid Government', 1936 as quoted in *The Spanish Civil War: A Modern Tragedy* by George R. Esenwein, published by Routledge, London, 2005.

Puente Genil (Province of Cordova)

One hundred and fifty-four citizens were murdered here between July 24 and August 18 by the Communists, who also burnt seven churches, twenty-eight private houses, an almshouse for old men, and the barracks of the Civil Guard. Seventeen of the murdered men were forced to remain with their arms raised above their heads for several hours – a boy of sixteen among them fainted from the pain – and they were then shot dead on the railway line near the station.

According to Source L, what actions were communists accused of by Nationalists?

Both sides vehemently denied allegations of terror. The Nationalists denied, for example, the bombing of Guernica. The head of Franco's foreign press bureau spread the explanation that Guernica had been destroyed by Basque saboteurs and retreating communist troops.

Rationing and food supplies

The ability of each side to access and ensure the fair distribution of food supplies proved more crucial than propaganda in sustaining morale. Nationalists had the advantage from the outset by controlling the major agricultural regions of Spain. The rapid expansion of Nationalist territory added to the volume of food available. The military Defence Council (see page 98), with control of all civilian and military life, strictly controlled food distribution and gave the military priority.

The Republic faced increasing difficulties in accessing sufficient food supplies from its diminishing territories. The Republic's problems of production and distribution were made more difficult by the establishment of agricultural collectives in the early months of the war, largely by anarchist groups keen to achieve profound social reform. By the autumn of 1936, 2500 agricultural collectives had been established, run on the principles of collective ownership by the peasantry. Although agricultural production levels were largely maintained, the existence of these often fiercely independent self-governing communities made the co-ordination of food production more difficult for the Republican government. Some collectives, for example, were prepared to distribute food to their particular militia companies, but not to the regular army. The abolition of money in many of the collectives, where a **barter economy** prevailed, also caused problems in negotiations with the government. The result of this was severely rationed food in Republican-held cities, and soldiers who were often hungry.

The Republic also faced difficulties in transporting essential food supplies to key cities, frequently held under siege by the Nationalists, as was the case with Madrid, Barcelona and Bilbao. In consequence, food shortages and prices became highly inflated. In Barcelona food prices rose 200 per cent during the war.

Why did the Nationalists win the Spanish Civil War?

→ Reasons for defeat and victory

The Nationalists won the war primarily because they benefited from access to superior modern military technology than the Republicans, and in greater quantities. Modern weaponry played a crucial role and in the conflict as the importance of air power demonstrated; it was a key component in all the successful Nationalist campaigns after 1937. It was no coincidence that Nationalist supplies of modern equipment and military successes both increased as the war progressed, while Republican supplies and military performance both diminished. Nationalists were also better able to manage the manpower and supplies demanded during a long civil war through strict central control, while the Republic was more divided. Tactics were less

🔑 **KEY TERM**

Barter economy The exchange of goods or services without the use of money.

significant in determining the outcome of the war. The tactics of both sides were for the most part conventional, using sieges, stalemate and limited trench warfare. There were few examples of stunning and skilful breakthroughs achieved by superb tactical planning.

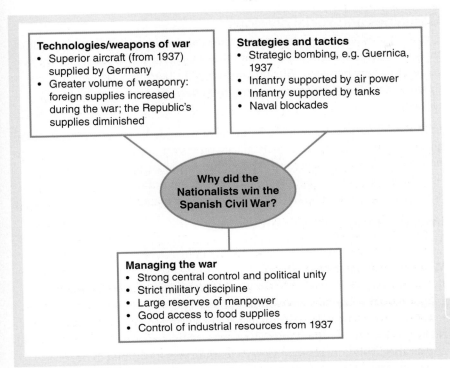

Technologies/weapons of war
- Superior aircraft (from 1937) supplied by Germany
- Greater volume of weaponry: foreign supplies increased during the war; the Republic's supplies diminished

Strategies and tactics
- Strategic bombing, e.g. Guernica, 1937
- Infantry supported by air power
- Infantry supported by tanks
- Naval blockades

Why did the Nationalists win the Spanish Civil War?

Managing the war
- Strong central control and political unity
- Strict military discipline
- Large reserves of manpower
- Good access to food supplies
- Control of industrial resources from 1937

SUMMARY DIAGRAM

The course of the Spanish Civil War

5 The effects of the Spanish Civil War

▶ **Key question:** *To what extent was Spain fundamentally changed by the civil war?*

On the eve of the war, Spain had been in the process of creating a state in accordance with left-wing ideals. Greater political freedom had been allowed for ordinary Spaniards, including women, the social role of the Catholic Church had been minimized in favour of the promotion of a more progressive, secular state, and there were attempts to dismantle the power of the traditional rural landowning class. The experience of civil war disrupted this process, but its impact is hard to generalize, not least because of the very different experiences in the Nationalist and Republican zones.

The social impact of the war

The social and economic impact of the war was substantial. Casualties were high, the economy was devastated, and the legacy of bitterness and mistrust between the sides was long lasting.

Casualties and social divisions

The estimates for those killed during the civil war, including battle casualties, those murdered behind the lines and those killed in the immediate post-war repression, vary between 350,000 and 500,000, about two per cent of Spain's 24 million people. Several hundred thousand were permanently wounded.

In the aftermath of the war, the Nationalist wounded were given preferential access to jobs; there was no such special provision or pensions for those who had been injured fighting for the Republic, perpetuating divisions within Spain. Around 400,000 people initially fled Spain out of fear of the Nationalist government; 250,000 permanently remained outside the country.

Impact of the civil war on women

The experience of women during the civil war varied greatly.

Women in Nationalist Spain

In Nationalist-held areas of Spain women were expected to conform to traditional roles as housewives and mothers. The prominent position given to the Catholic Church in Nationalist zones during the war also served to reinforce this model. There were strict expectations about women's dress and appearance. This conservative view of women was enshrined in decrees passed by the ruling Defence Council. These included:

- the prohibition of divorce and **civil marriage**
- prohibition on mixed-gender classrooms
- education for girls focused on domestic work and motherhood.

KEY TERM

Civil marriage Marriage in which the ceremony is not performed by a religious official.

According to Source M, what actions caused women to be traitors?

SOURCE M

Excerpt from the pamphlet 'Spanish Woman' issued by the Catholic Union of Women of Seville in Abella, quoted in *Spanish Civil War: A Modern Tragedy* by George R. Esenwein, published by Routledge, London, 2005.

While our soldiers and volunteers working for God and our country are sacrificing their lives in the fields of battle, you, the woman of Spain who is dedicating yourself to personal pleasures, to flirting and falling into bad habits, you are: a traitor to your country, a traitor to your faith, contemptible to all and deserving of our repulsion. Spanish woman ... your place ... is in the church and at home ... your dresses should be ... in the modest and retiring style of the moral Christian ... you should devote yourself to assuaging those suffering in the hospitals and homes. Your duty now is not to procure for yourself an easy life, but to educate your children, to sacrifice your pleasures in order to help Spain.

Even with the increased needs of the war economy, women's participation in the war effort in Nationalist zones remained largely confined to traditionally acceptable female spheres such health services and food preparation for public distribution. Paid work, especially for married women, was discouraged, indeed the Labour Charter passed in March 1938 promised to 'liberate' married women from work in workshops and factories.

Women in Republican Spain

Women living within the Republican zones had more freedom. Politically, there was greater theoretical equality with men. In Catalonia, a marriage code was passed which gave women equal rights with men in issues of marriage and divorce. Republican Spain became the first country in Europe where a woman occupied a cabinet position in the national government when Federica Montseny became Minister for Public Health and Assistance in 1936. Other women exercised significant political influence, such as the high-ranking Communist Party member Dolores Ibárruri, who became famed for her speeches and leadership of organizations promoting welfare provision for victims of the war. However, even these women, although occupying a world of politics which was usually the preserve of men, operated within the spheres usually primarily associated with traditional female issues such as welfare provision and public health.

Some women in Republican Spain participated in militias and were referred to as *milicianas*. Republican propaganda posters from early in the war showed male and female volunteers fighting alongside each other. A handful of these women fighters became famous, such as Lina Odena, leader of the communist youth movement, who was killed near Granada. Women's participation in combat was not the norm and in September 1936 the Republican government passed a decree call for women to be withdrawn from combat and banning their admission into the Popular Army.

Women in Republican areas began working in factories and war-related industries, filling the positions of men who were absent fighting. Working women were frequently confronted by hostility from male employees who continued to believe women should remain at home. Most women did remain in the home, struggling to find food for their families.

Economic impact of the war

← **What was the economic impact of the war?**

The Spanish Civil War was hugely destructive, with homes, businesses, agricultural land and industry severely damaged in war zones. Spain also emerged from the war less financially capable of paying for rebuilding.

Destruction

The scale of destruction was immense. Aerial bombardments reduced many towns to rubble and Spain's industrial infrastructure was severely damaged. Industrial production by 1939 was only 25 per cent of 1929 levels. Only half of the Spanish railway stock remained operational and livestock numbers were 33 per cent less than pre-war figures.

Financial difficulties

Spain's financial position was significantly undermined. Spanish gold reserves were spent by the Republican government in their desperation to procure armaments from the Soviet Union. Nationalists amassed huge debts abroad, ending the war owing $700 million for war goods. Most post-war repayments were made in food shipments and industrial raw materials, which represented a considerable drain on the Spanish economy for decades, repayments to Italy continued into the 1960s. In addition, with industrial and agricultural production reduced from pre-war levels and with the labour force losing over half a million men and women, the regeneration of Spanish industry and agriculture was slow.

Was Spain fundamentally changed by civil war?

Political impact of the war

As a result of the Nationalist victory, Franco established a right-wing, conservative dictatorship in Spain which lasted until his death in 1975. Franco's government:

- promoted him as saviour of the nation, creating a cult of personality
- emphasized nationalism and ended regional autonomy
- encouraged economic self-sufficiency
- promoted conservative attitudes and policies towards women and family structures
- re-established the Catholic Church to power and influence.

Franco's power rested on the power of the army, not on his leadership of a political party. Republicans were persecuted and many executed in a terror campaign unleashed immediately after the Nationalist victory. Hundreds of thousands were imprisoned and society was further divided as a result of persecution.

The impact of the civil war on international politics was more limited. Even during the Spanish Civil War, many of the major powers of Europe limited their involvement in the conflict. Spain, for them, remained on the periphery of Europe. They were more concerned with events surrounding an increasingly assertive Germany, which challenged the democratic European powers.

Conclusions

Spain emerged from the civil war a very different nation from that promised by the Republican experiment of the early 1930s. Exhausted, divided and destroyed by years of civil conflict, the scars of the Spanish Civil War were long lasting. Its people were among the first to experience the horrors of modern terror bombing in Europe and the privations of civil war were lengthy. In some ways, however, it was Republican Spain that was the aberration, with Franco's Spain displaying continuity with a more traditional Spain in which the Catholic Church was accorded a prominent place and in which social hierarchy and authoritarian rule were emphasized.

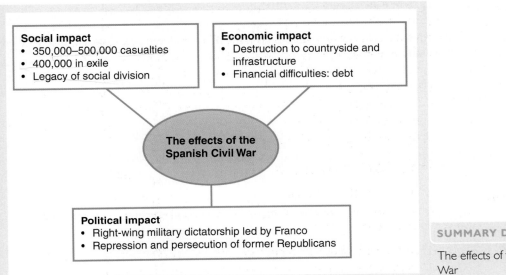

Social impact
- 350,000–500,000 casualties
- 400,000 in exile
- Legacy of social division

Economic impact
- Destruction to countryside and infrastructure
- Financial difficulties: debt

The effects of the Spanish Civil War

Political impact
- Right-wing military dictatorship led by Franco
- Repression and persecution of former Republicans

SUMMARY DIAGRAM

The effects of the Spanish Civil War

Chapter summary

Spanish Civil War 1936–9

The Spanish Civil War began when forces of the conservative right launched a military uprising against the left-wing Republican government in July 1936. The rebels succeeded in establishing substantial, but not total, control over Spain. This meant control of Spain was divided between the rebels, known as the Nationalists, and government forces, known as the Republicans, who then fought for control of the country.

Republican rule in Spain in the early 1930s proved unstable, with the left-wing political parties alternating in power with right-wing groups, each attempting to reform the nation or undo those reforms. Leftists attempted to reduce the power of conservative landowners and the Catholic Church, while rightists undermined these efforts when in power. Agricultural reform has been blamed by many historians as the most important factor leading to a military-led revolt against the Republicans which occurred in 1936.

The victory of the Nationalists in the civil war was not a foregone conclusion. Indeed, in the early months of the war many of the advantages lay with the Republicans. The decisive factor in determining victory was access to supplies of modern weaponry from abroad. In this, the Nationalists held a considerable advantage, which grew as the war progressed. They benefited from consignments of weapons from Italy and Germany, which were not only overall more numerous, but also technically superior to the weapons at the Republic's disposal. The importance of this modern weaponry, especially aircraft, was evident in nearly all campaigns after 1937.

The Spanish Civil War left a legacy of devastation and bitterness in Spain. Republicans were persecuted during Franco's rule, which continued until 1975.

Examination practice

Command term: Evaluate

When a question asks you to evaluate some aspect of twentieth-century warfare, it is asking you to make judgments regarding some issue.

Below are a number of different questions for you to practise using the command term 'evaluate'. For guidance on how to answer exam-style questions, see Chapter 8.

1 Evaluate the importance of technology in the outcome of two twentieth-century wars, each from a different region.

2 Evaluate the significance of guerrilla warfare in two twentieth-century wars, each from a different region.

3 Evaluate the effect of two twentieth-century wars in two different regions on the role and status of women.

4 Evaluate the importance of the involvement of foreign powers during a twentieth-century war you have studied.

5 Evaluate the significance of the mobilization of human and economic resources in the outcome of a twentieth-century war you have studied.

 # Activities

1 The class should divide into groups or pairs with one group representing far-left anarchist and socialist groups in pre-civil war Spain, and the other far-right groups. Prepare for a debate in which you will discuss the extent to which the far left or the far right bears more responsibility for causing the civil war in Spain.

2 Using the information about the course of the war, draw a timeline which includes all the battles between the Nationalists and the Republicans.

3 Draw your own summary diagram in the style of that on page 105 to represent why the Republicans lost the civil war.

4 Choose one of the essay titles listed above and in seven minutes write just an introduction to the title. Share this with a partner or in a group and discuss its strengths and weaknesses.

CHAPTER 3

Second World War in Europe and north Africa 1939–45

The Second World War in Europe was one of the largest and most devastating wars in history and for the main participants was a total war. Starting as a local, limited war between Germany and Poland in September 1939 as the result of the failure of diplomacy, it soon developed into a regional war in Europe while also spreading to Africa. By the end of 1941 the war had become a global one and, at its conclusion in 1945, world politics had altered considerably as a result of the conflict. This chapter will address the following key questions:

★ To what extent was German diplomacy to blame for the outbreak of war in Europe in 1939?

★ Why did diplomacy fail to prevent an outbreak of war in Europe in September 1939?

★ Is it possible to assign blame for the outbreak of the war in Europe?

★ Why was Germany so successful against its foes until mid-1941?

★ What factors contributed to Allied success in Africa and Italy during the Second World War?

★ What was the importance of the war at sea between the Allied and Axis powers?

★ How did the air war affect Allied and Axis nations?

★ What events led to Germany's defeat in the Second World War?

★ Why did Germany lose the Second World War in Europe?

★ How were civilians affected by the Second World War in Europe?

★ How effective were resistance movements in Europe during the Second World War?

★ What were the main results of the war in Europe and how did these lead to a change in world diplomacy?

1 Long-term causes of the Second World War in Europe and north Africa

> ▶ Key question: To what extent was German diplomacy to blame for the outbreak of war in Europe in 1939?

On 1 September 1939, Germany invaded Poland. Two days later, Britain and France, forming what became known as the **Allied Powers**, expanded the conflict by declaring war on Germany. The causes of this war are the subject

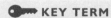 **KEY TERM**

Allied Powers Commonly referred to as the Allies during the Second World War, this group first consisted of Poland, France, Britain and others, with the USSR and the USA joining in 1941.

of continued, vigorous debate. Many historians have simply blamed Germany and its leader, Adolf Hitler, as the instigators of the conflict, and some of these have inaccurately described the Second World War in Europe as 'Hitler's war'. Other historians have seen the Second World War in Europe as a continuation of the First World War and some declare it as an inevitable event that resulted from actions set in motion in nineteenth-century Europe, such as the quest for industrial resources and room for expanding populations. This section looks at the long-term causes of the war.

This is the textbook's bias

To what extent were the long-term causes of the Second World War the result of the decisions reached at the Paris Peace Conference in 1919?

Treaty of Versailles

In 1918, the First World War came to an end as the Central Powers surrendered to the **Grand Alliance**. In mid-1919, the Paris Peace Conference was held in which five peace treaties were imposed on the defeated nations. One of these was the Treaty of Versailles, which focused on Germany. Germany had to agree to the treaty or face invasion.

🔑 KEY TERM

Grand Alliance First World War alliance of Britain, France, Russia, Italy, Japan, the USA and many other countries.

The Treaty of Versailles was perhaps the most important treaty produced at the Paris Peace Conference in 1919. The treaty established the League of Nations but primarily concerned Germany. Some of the key points of the Treaty of Versailles were (see also the map on page 66):

- Germany had to pay reparations to compensate the Allied Powers financially for the war, as well as to punish Germany economically.
- Germany was not allowed to join the League of Nations, ensuring diplomatic isolation.
- Germany lost territory to Denmark, Belgium, France and Poland.
- German territories of Danzig, the Saar and Memel were placed under the control of the League of Nations.
- Germany's army was reduced to 100,000 men with no artillery, tanks or aircraft, and a small navy.
- Demilitarization of the Rhineland. This border region between Germany and Belgium and France had to be free of German soldiers and fortifications.
- Germany was forbidden to merge with Austria.
- Germany's colonies were confiscated and were to be administered primarily by Britain, France and Japan under the League of Nations.

Germans understood that they were being punished for the war but they did not believe they were solely responsible for starting it. The German government reluctantly signed the treaty and followed through with many of its provisions.

How did the Paris Peace Conference treaties help the German economy in the long term?

Other Paris Peace Conference treaties

There were four other treaties forced on the former Central Powers from 1919 to 1920. These divided the former Austro-Hungarian Empire into several smaller states, while granting large parts to existing nations. The argument for creating new national states from this empire was that each nation should have the right to form its own government and live in a state ruled by its own people. This philosophy of self-determination was espoused in US President Woodrow Wilson's **Fourteen Points speech** which was the basis for the Paris Peace Conference discussions. Germans in Austria, however, were forbidden to merge with Germany and there was no major concern that millions of Germans now found themselves in Poland and Czechoslovakia where they would be minorities. Germany explicitly declared its dissatisfaction with its eastern borders with the signing of the Locarno Treaties in 1925. At Locarno, Germany agreed that its borders in western Europe were to never change, but those in the east could be altered through negotiation.

In 1914, there were three major nations in central and eastern Europe: Austria-Hungary, Germany and Russia; the Ottoman Empire held the Middle East. As a result of the First World War, these collapsed. By 1920, there were nine new nations, three reduced ones, and four had expanded (see Source A).

KEY TERM

Fourteen Points speech
Speech by US President Wilson in 1918 which presented 14 separate issues that he believed needed to be enacted to establish world peace.

SOURCE A

Table indicating border changes in Europe as result of First World War.

New	Reduced	Expanded
Finland	Germany	Romania
Estonia	Bulgaria	Yugoslavia (former Serbia)
Latvia	Russia (USSR after 1922)	Greece
Lithuania		Italy
Poland		
Czechoslovakia		
Austria		
Hungary		
Turkey		

According to Source A, how many countries experienced border changes as a result of the First World War?

Although Germany was weakened by the Treaty of Versailles, it remained one of the largest states in Europe, in both population and territory, and was the most industrialized. The new states lacked infrastructure, industrialization and, in some cases, national unity; they remained primarily agricultural and sources of raw material which would be increasingly consumed by German industry in the 1930s. Germany would eventually dominate most of Europe economically by the mid-1930s as a result of the Paris Peace Conference.

Post-war economic problems

In 1921, the total amount of reparations that Germany was required to pay was set at 132 billion gold marks. This amount was to be paid over 42 years. By 1922, Germany asked for a suspension of payments as the government

What was the importance of reparation payments for Germans?

claimed it was unable to make them. This was rejected by France and when payment failed in 1923, France and Belgium occupied the industrialized Ruhr Valley of Germany. For various reasons this led to a period of hyperinflation in Germany when the government printed huge quantities of worthless paper while the cost of living dramatically increased. Negotiations led to the withdrawal of French and Belgium forces in 1924 and a reorganization of Germany's war debt which included huge loans from the USA, helping the economy to quickly recover.

Reparations were seen by the German people as the root of all their economic problems throughout the 1920s, a belief that the German government encouraged even when this was not true. Economic insecurity, political instability and other national hardships were blamed on the need to continue to supply funds to France and Belgium. They also served to constantly remind Germans of their defeat in the First World War and the dictated peace that followed, causing some to call for revenge.

Propoganda

The Great Depression

How did the Great Depression affect Germany?

- US was a major consumer
↓
- GD hits, doesn't Purchase as much
↓
- Economies of Major European countries starts to fall.
↓
- unEmployment rose, banks collapsed, taxes were raised

The USA was the world's largest economy in 1929 when its stock market began a precipitous decline, triggering the Great Depression. As the value of stocks plunged, people were unable to pay for the bank loans they had taken out to invest further in the markets. US banks recalled loans to Germany after 1924, dragging down the German economy, which relied on US investment and purchases of manufactured goods. Without US consumption and investment, Britain, France, Japan and Italy soon joined Germany in a major economic downturn. Unemployment rose swiftly as factories closed and banks collapsed. Most countries created trade barriers by heavily taxing imports to protect their own industries. Britain and France turned to their empires for trade, while Japan sought empire (see page 190). All countries suffered unemployment and many countries created multi-party governments, or coalitions, to manage their state through the crisis.

Conditions in Germany were severe by 1933 with official unemployment at six million, approximately 25 per cent of workers. The various German governments between 1930 and 1933, attempting to rule without parliamentary majorities in a very politically divided country, failed to effectively address the economic situation.

National Socialist German Workers' Party

How was the National Socialist German Workers' Party affected by the Great Depression?

- It was revived because
↳ Other political parties did very little in addressing unemployment
↳ there was a fear

The National Socialist German Workers' Party, often referred to as the Nazi Party, was led by Adolf Hitler. After a failed coup against the provincial government in Bavaria in 1923 and Hitler's subsequent imprisonment until 1924, the Nazi Party was reduced to relative insignificance. Yet the Great Depression caused a revival in the party's fortunes as they gained seats in the German parliament, the *Reichstag*. Part of this was the result of the failure of other political parties in addressing unemployment and also the fear of

communism. The German Communist Party grew in political strength during these years of economic stress, causing many to fear a communist revolution such as the one that had occurred in Russia in 1917, which led to a civil war that killed millions.

Nazi beliefs

The Nazi Party's beliefs included:

- Germany should be self-sufficient and not rely on foreign investment or loans.
- The Treaty of Versailles should be completely undone and territories in Europe that were lost should rejoin the country.
- Germany should expand to include other areas of Europe where Germans lived.
- Germany needed *lebensraum*, or living space, for food production and room to settle more Germans.
- Germans were a master race that was destined to rule over inferior races, including Slavs and other non-Germanic groups.
- Jews, Roma, Africans, the mentally ill, and others were threats to the purity of the German race and needed to be separated from Germans; homosexuals were another threat and needed to be rehabilitated if possible or separated.
- Communism was a threat to German nationalism and independence and must be opposed.

Nazi beliefs changed over time, like those of most political parties, but for the most part they remained anti-communist, anti-Jewish, anti-Versailles and ultra-nationalistic. The Nazi Party was increasingly seen as an alternative to the failing political establishment.

National Socialists into power

By January 1933, the Nazi Party was the largest group in the *Reichstag* although they did not have a majority of seats. In a rapid series of events:

- Hitler was named chancellor by the president.
- New elections were called.
- The Communist Party was blamed for a fire that burned the *Reichstag* building.
- The Communist Party was outlawed and leaders were imprisoned.
- Election returns confirmed the Nazis as the largest party, but without a majority.
- The Catholic Centre Party joined in a coalition with the Nazis.
- The *Reichstag* passed the Enabling Act in March 1933, granting Hitler dictatorial powers for four years without the need to consult or refer to the *Reichstag*.

KEY TERM

Communism A system in which all property of a nation is controlled by the state which represents all citizens; holds that nationalism is a creation by economically privileged classes to divide workers.

Nazi Party consolidation of power

The Nazi Party moved swiftly to consolidate its power by merging with the government itself:

- All other political parties were abolished.
- All governing councils and governors were replaced by party-appointed officials.
- All police forces were merged with the *Schutzstaffel*, a Nazi paramilitary organization known more commonly as the SS.

While the state and party merged, Hitler consolidated his own power by having party rivals executed in 1934. The only institution beyond his control was the German army, which was managed by the conservative nobility. They saw Hitler, who was from Austria and only attained the rank of corporal in the First World War, as a foreigner and a politician who could not be trusted not to involve Germany in a war it could not win. Hitler finally took control of the army in 1938, coinciding with a more aggressive foreign policy.

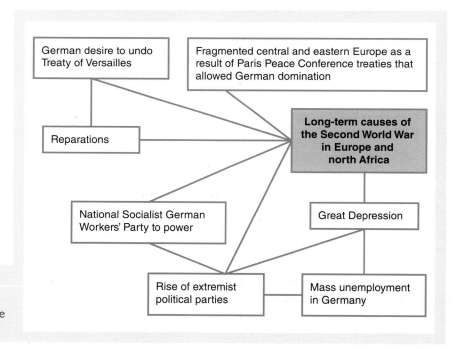

2 Short-term causes of the Second World War in Europe and north Africa

▶ *Key question: Why did diplomacy fail to prevent an outbreak of war in Europe in September 1939?*

After the Nazi Party came to power in Germany, international diplomacy continued to be dominated by Britain and France, often through the League of Nations. Increasingly, however, Germany became more assertive as its economy recovered from the worst effects of the Great Depression, allowing a more aggressive, and successful, foreign policy.

German economic recovery

The Nazi Party aggressively addressed the economic situation in Germany. Under Economics Minister Hjalmar Schacht, the New Plan was created which prevented most imports into the country. All imports had to be approved by the government in order to keep gold and other currencies needed for international trade in the country. Where possible, Germany traded for imports. If Germany needed Romanian oil, then the government negotiated with Romania to discover what German exports Romania needed and a trade occurred. This system meant that by 1935, Germany exported more than it imported and by 1936 was exporting over 500 million more German marks' worth of goods than it brought in from other countries. This meant more hard currency for further investment and imports of items that could not be bartered for, such as iron ore from Sweden. This economic recovery enabled **rearmament** which, according to the government, would allow Germany to conduct a more assertive and successful foreign policy.

> **What factors allowed Germany to economically recover in the 1930s?**

> ○ Exporting more than importing allowed for Germany to have more hard currency.

 **KEY TERM**

Rearmament Rebuilding of a fully equipped military force.

German rearmament

Germany was disarmed after the First World War as a first step towards general disarmament in Europe. This was certainly discussed in the League of Nations' Covenant which called for the reduction of member states' armaments. After many years of research and reports, the World Disarmament Conference met in Geneva, Switzerland, in 1932. France had the largest standing army in Europe with 340,000 men in 1932, and 700,000 more in reserves. France's allies included Poland, Czechoslovakia and Romania, all with substantial forces. Although Germany still had only 100,000 soldiers as stipulated in the Treaty of Versailles, all believed that the German population, more than double that of France, plus its industrial capacity meant that within a brief period of time it could reconstitute its

> **Why did Germany rearm after 1935?**

armed forces and threaten French security. France refused to co-operate with disarmament until Britain and the USA agreed to guarantee its security through an alliance; both countries refused. Germany declared that if France would not limit its military, then it would be forced to arm itself for defence; it then withdrew from the conference and then the League of Nations shortly afterwards. However, Germany's economic condition prevented significant rearmament measures until 1935.

Germany Rearmed itself because France refused to disarm.

Polish–German Non-Aggression Pact 1934

Germany's first major diplomatic success under the leadership of Hitler was a non-aggression treaty made with Poland in 1934. This pact stated that neither Poland nor Germany would attack the other. Poland was the stronger military power in 1934. Germany may have genuinely feared an attack by Poland, especially given Nazi statements that they planned to revise borders and take *lebensraum* in an unspecified place to the east. Poland was pleased not to have to worry about Germany, believing its main enemy to be the USSR since it had defeated Soviet forces to expand Poland in 1920.

Rearmament begins

In 1935, German rearmament, in direct violation of the Treaty of Versailles, began:

- Conscription was reintroduced so that Germany would have an army of 700,000 men and three million soldiers in reserve forces by 1939.
- By 1936, German industry was capable of increased mass weapons production: it could construct 5000 aircraft annually, for example.
- An Anglo-German Naval Agreement was signed, allowing Germany to build more tonnage of ships than allowed in the Treaty of Versailles, but keeping German tonnage 35 per cent of Britain's navy.

While many historians question the quality and equipment of this army, rearmament was accomplished in the midst of the Great Depression when most countries worked to control spending and reduce imports and certainly not build massive, expensive armies. German rearmament appeared as some kind of miracle to most observers, not the least because much of it was built with imported materials and because one of its consequences was practically no unemployment. It is the fear of this army, the fear of war in general, and the fear of the costs of rearmament in the midst of a crushing Great Depression that need to be considered when studying international relations post-1933.

What were the consequences of the failure of the Stresa Front and the Abyssinian Crisis?

→ The Stresa Front and the Abyssinian Crisis 1935–6

With the announcement of German rearmament, Britain, France and Italy, considered the Great Powers at the time, met to condemn it. They agreed to form the **Stresa Front** in 1934 to keep Germany diplomatically isolated and to generally co-ordinate their efforts. Almost immediately diplomatic co-operation was undermined by Britain, which negotiated the Anglo-German Naval Agreement.

The Abyssinian Crisis effectively destroyed co-operation between Britain and France and Italy. Italy invaded Abyssinia (today's Ethiopia), a member of the League of Nations, breaking the League's covenant and negating the concept of **collective security**. Britain and France imposed economic sanctions on Italy which then developed a political and economic relationship with Germany; neither was now isolated. Abyssinia was conquered and the threat of collective security was proven to be a sham. The League failed to protect a member state from attack and ceased to be seen as an effective organization afterwards.

Further alignments

Germany and Italy declared the creation of the Rome–Berlin **Axis** in October 1936. This new diplomatic understanding initially meant little except that Germany was no longer isolated and Italy would not prevent German annexation of Austria as it had in 1934. In November 1936, Germany signed the **Anti-Comintern Pact** with Japan in a symbolic stance against the USSR and a further demonstration that British and French attempts to isolate it had failed. Germany found friendly states through diplomacy, but the economies of many central and eastern European states, such as Yugoslavia and Romania, relied on Germany to purchase their agricultural products and raw materials such as oil and metals. This further enhanced Germany's power in Europe.

German foreign policy success

The reviving German economy, rearmament and diplomacy led to a series of successes for Germany in the late 1930s, undoing many aspects of the Treaty of Versailles, often in co-operation with the victors of the First World War.

The Saar, Rhineland and Austria 1935–8

The Saar was allowed to have a **plebiscite** in 1935 and an overwhelming majority decided to return to Germany instead of joining France. The demilitarized Rhineland was reoccupied by lightly armed German troops in 1936 in violation of the Treaty of Versailles while most of Europe was occupied with the Abyssinian Crisis. France protested, but was unwilling and unable to fight, while Britain was pleased as it seemed to remove another reason for Germany to go to war in the future. After a failed attempt to **annex** Austria in 1934, Germany was more successful in 1938 when German troops, with Italy's approval, moved into the country and a plebiscite confirmed the Austrian people's desire to unify with Germany. This was another violation of the Treaty of Versailles, but with little protest or action on the part of Britain or France.

> 🔑 **KEY TERM**
>
> **Collective security** The concept that a war against one member of the League of Nations is a war against all member states.
>
> **Axis** The alliance in the Second World War that eventually consisted of Germany, Italy, Japan, Slovakia, Hungary, Bulgaria and Romania, as well as several states created in conquered areas.
>
> **Anti-Comintern Pact** Agreement initially between Japan and Germany to work together against Communist International (Comintern), an organization sponsored by the USSR to spread communism.

← **What factors allowed Germany to conduct a successful foreign policy between 1935 and 1938?**

> 🔑 **KEY TERM**
>
> **Plebiscite** A vote by all of a nation's voters on a particular issue.
>
> **Annex** To incorporate a territory into another country.

[handwritten note:] ○ Scared of starting another war, the victors of WWI stood aside while Germany was reviving its economy, rearmament and diplomatic relation while going against the versailles treaty.

11

Sudetenland and the Munich Agreement 1938

In late 1938, Germans living in the Sudetenland of Czechoslovakia, who were discriminated against by their government, demanded annexation to Germany. Britain and France, wanting to avoid war, seized on what they saw as the logical request of Germans wanting the right to live in Germany; other nationalities had been given this right at the Paris Peace Conference (see page 65). In the Munich Agreement, Britain, France, Italy and Germany agreed that Sudetenland should be granted to Germany and it was understood, but not written, that Germany would then respect the territorial integrity of the rest of Czechoslovakia.

Czechoslovakia dismantled 1939

Germany took the Sudetenland in October 1938, while Poland occupied areas it had earlier lost to Czechoslovakia in 1920, when Czechoslovakia had seized it militarily. In November, part of southern Czechoslovakia was seized by Hungary. In March 1939, the Slovak region of Czechoslovakia declared independence, although supported heavily by Germany, while Hungary annexed eastern areas of the country. Germany invaded Czech-dominated regions of Bohemia and Moravia, claiming it was protecting the Czechs from Poland and Hungary. This action by Germany was seen as a violation of the spirit of the Munich Agreement and set world opinion against the German government, especially in Britain and France.

Poland 1939

Germany announced in early 1939 that it wanted to negotiate with Poland to take back at least part of its territory so that Danzig and East Prussia could be reattached to the rest of the country (see the map on page 66); they had been separated from the rest of Germany in 1919 so that Poland would have access to the sea. Of all German requests for territory, this was, ironically perhaps, the most logical of its demands as it had only 20 years before been part of Germany and many of the residents there were Germans. The British and French public, however, were outraged, having been led by their governments to believe that Germany territorial requests ended with the Munich Agreement. Poland very simply stated that it was not interested in negotiating and closed the subject, while Britain and France made a public, verbal declaration of military alliance with Poland in the hope of ending German demands through the threat of war.

Britain and France were now in the midst of a massive rearmament effort as a result of German rearmament. Although they proclaimed an alliance with Poland, both nations refused to arm Poland since they were busy arming themselves. When Poland asked for loans to buy weapons elsewhere, both nations stated that their own financial problems prevented this. They feared that providing weapons to Poland could lead to a war which they hoped to prevent since it would encourage Germany to attack before the new alliance was prepared.

Britain and France negotiate with the USSR

Britain and France made overtures to the USSR at this point, presenting the case that it was in its best interests to help prevent a war between Germany and Poland since Germany was very obviously anti-communist, having exterminated communists in its own country. Britain and France pointed out that a war could be prevented if the USSR would join their anti-German coalition and promise to fight to retain eastern European borders as they were in 1939. The USSR was, quite simply, being asked to fight Germany to preserve borders and states, including much of Poland, that it believed should be part of the USSR since they had been part of the Russian Empire. Poland also refused to allow any Soviet army to cross into its territory to fight even if Poland was invaded by Germany. It seemed that Poland was more afraid of the USSR than of Germany. The Soviets were unwilling to fight Germany only after Poland was conquered since that would mean war with the German military would have to be fought within the USSR itself; this seemed irrational and unfair, and was proof to the Soviets that they were only a tool to be used, not a real alliance partner.

Germany negotiates with the USSR

Meanwhile, Germany began discussions with the USSR. These talks essentially called for Germany and the USSR not to fight each other while allowing Germany to do whatever it wanted diplomatically, and otherwise, with the parts of Europe that had not belonged to the former Russian Empire, which the Soviets hoped to reclaim in the near future. Other parts of the agreement made it clear that the parts of Poland that once belonged to Russia were now to be reabsorbed into the USSR. This document, the Treaty of Non-Aggression between Germany and the USSR, commonly known as the Nazi–Soviet Pact, was announced on 23 August 1939, one week before Germany declared war on Poland on 1 September.

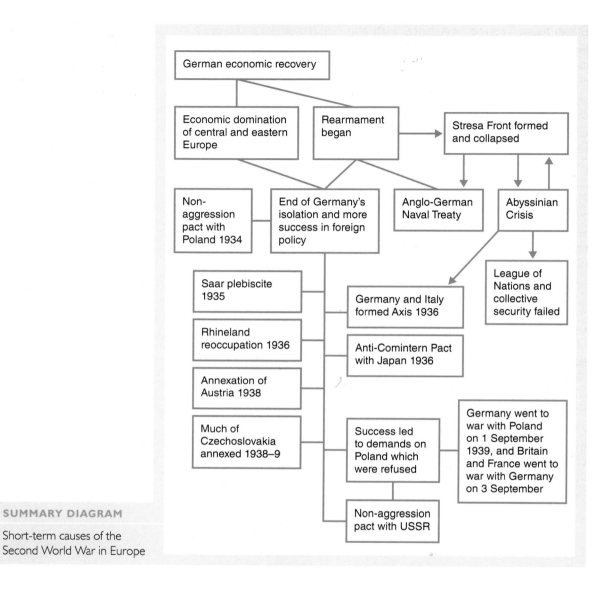

The diagram contains the following boxes and connections:

German economic recovery

Economic domination of central and eastern Europe

Rearmament began

Stresa Front formed and collapsed

Non-aggression pact with Poland 1934

End of Germany's isolation and more success in foreign policy

Anglo-German Naval Treaty

Abyssinian Crisis

Saar plebiscite 1935

Germany and Italy formed Axis 1936

League of Nations and collective security failed

Rhineland reoccupation 1936

Anti-Comintern Pact with Japan 1936

Annexation of Austria 1938

Much of Czechoslovakia annexed 1938–9

Success led to demands on Poland which were refused

Germany went to war with Poland on 1 September 1939, and Britain and France went to war with Germany on 3 September

Non-aggression pact with USSR

3 Key debate

▶ **Key question:** *Is it possible to assign blame for the outbreak of the war in Europe?*

There continues to be significant debate about the causes of the Second World War. While many blame a particular nation or policy, others focus on world economic conditions or the absence of the USA and USSR in international diplomacy. A few viewpoints of historians are presented here.

Appeasement

Appeasement refers to the British policy of settling reasonable differences through negotiation. Many historians have traditionally blamed the policy of appeasement for encouraging Germany to continue to demand more and more territory until Britain and France had to draw a line with Poland. The British, for example, saw it as reasonable that Germany wanted to rebuild its military since it was surrounded by hostile neighbours with huge standing armies. It seemed reasonable that Germany wanted to send troops into the Rhineland, which was actually part of Germany. It made sense, especially when considering the dismemberment of the Austro-Hungarian and Ottoman Empires on the basis of nationalities in 1919, that Germans who wanted to live in Germany should have that right. This meant there was little objection to the absorption of Austria and Czechoslovakia's Sudetenland in 1938 where the majority of the population was German, as long as it was done through negotiation and with British and French permission. It was hoped that by granting Germany its reasonable requests, the need to go to war over these issues would be eliminated.

> **To what extent was appeasement responsible for the outbreak of war in 1939?**

[Handwritten margin note:] The British and France granted Germany the right to:
- rebuild army
- send troops to Rhineland
- absorb Austria and Czechoslovakia Sudetenland.

Appeasement and public opinion

The Munich Agreement was the final, and temporary, triumph of appeasement, giving the public perception at least that Germany would have no further demands for territory. The takeover of the rest of Czechoslovakia caused an abrupt abandonment of appeasement in tacit acknowledgement that this policy had failed or was no longer useful in light of further territorial demands on Poland, however logical the demands seemed. Public opinion in France and Britain demanded this change and governments complied with pledges of assistance for Poland and eventually a formal alliance. Negotiated concessions gave the world, and the British public, the impression that Britain was still a Great Power. In order to maintain Great Power status, British permission had to be given for German foreign policy moves. Once Germany acted on its own, without this permission, Britain's Great Power status was challenged directly. Many recent historians have come to the conclusion that Britain's stance on Poland was primarily the result of a need to defend its status as the arbiter of European diplomacy.

SOURCE B

Excerpt from 'Appeasement' by Paul Kennedy and Talbot Imlay in *The Origins of the Second World War Reconsidered: A.J.P. Taylor and the Historians*, second edition, edited by Gordon Martel, published by Routledge, London, 1999, page 121.

Public opinion's two most significant disruptions of the official policy of appeasing the dictators occurred, first, in late 1935, when the news of the Hoare–Laval pact [to address the Abyssinian Crisis at the expense of Abyssinia] provoked an explosion of discontent against this undermining of League of Nations' principles; and, second (and more importantly), in the spring of 1939, when large segments of British public opinion, including many former supporters

According to Source B what was the effect of public opinion?

For many decades historians have had access to British, French, German, Polish and other nations' documents regarding events in the 1930s that led to the Second World War in Europe and north Africa. Why, then, are historians continuing to debate the causes of the Second World War? (History, Language, and Logic.)

of [British Prime Minister] Chamberlain's appeasement policies, decided that Hitler had to be stopped and urged all manner of embarrassing proposals upon the government: guarantees to east-European states, an alliance with Russia, further rearmament, closer ties with the French, and so on.

Appeasement as weakness

Critics of appeasement state that this policy made Britain and France appear weak to the German government and to its leader in particular. According to this view, Hitler perceived that Britain and France would essentially do anything in order to avoid a war they could not financially afford and which would require them to fight for eastern European states. Hitler's foreign policy agenda, these historians claim, was presented in his book *Mein Kampf* (*My Struggle*) in the early 1920s and in his various speeches. This meant that Hitler had planned the events of 1936 to 1939 very carefully and was fully aware of what he and his government were doing. He wanted war with Poland in 1939 and his government's actions from 1936 onwards put Germany on a course to make this happen. This view is now commonly seen as overly simplistic and not particularly accurate. Hitler seems to have planned for a major Europe conflict in the early 1940s and not in 1939 and there is ample evidence that his foreign policy took advantage of diplomatic opportunities instead of creating them.

Appeasement as delay

Some historians have seen appeasement as a delaying policy by Britain and France. This view holds that Britain and France were not yet prepared for a European war in 1938. Appeasing Germany meant having more time to build fully equipped armies with enough aircraft, tanks and ships to threaten Germany as well as to conduct a successful war if forced into one. Parity with Germany, or even superiority, was achieved by 1939 according to this view and so war could be threatened to prevent further German expansion. It was better to fight in 1939, according to these historians, than wait a few more years when Germany would be more heavily armed.

How significant was Adolf Hitler in causing the outbreak of war in 1939?

The role of Hitler

Hitler as manipulator of events

While appeasement has received much attention from historians, others hold that appeasement had little to do with the outbreak of the Second World War in Europe and that Hitler himself bore this responsibility. In this view, Hitler was a genius with the ability to manipulate Britain, France, the USSR, Czechoslovakia and perhaps even Italy. It is clear that he campaigned for *lebensraum*, the destruction of the clauses of the Treaty of Versailles, and other grand, bombastic ideas, many of which were stated as early as 1923. Several historians, however, have pointed out that Hitler's foreign policy aims were similar, if not identical, to those of previous non-Nazi governments and therefore not particularly unique. Others question to what extent Hitler himself was involved in the government, presenting arguments that Hitler was lazy, often agreed with the last person who presented a proposal regardless of earlier presentations in the same meeting, and actually had few meetings as he spent the majority of his time at his mountain retreat at Berchtesgaden in southern Germany. Debate continues in the discipline of history to the extent to which individuals actually control events or are controlled by them.

Hitler as opportunist

Some historians believe Hitler was simply savvy and cunning enough to take advantage of opportunities as they arose, reacting to events as opposed to controlling them. An example of this would be the reoccupation of the Rhineland, where it is clear that he perceived the British were not opposed to the reoccupation. France, meanwhile, was focused on opposing Italy's invasion of Abyssinia. When Hungary and Poland moved to divide Czechoslovakia, he saw an opportunity to take control of the industrialized portions of the disintegrating state and did so. He may have convinced himself that Britain and France would capitulate over Poland or force Poland into surrendering territory that Germany wanted to reclaim since German claims were even more rational than those regarding Austria or Sudetenland. In this view, he was a successful opportunist until he failed to perceive the importance of public opinion in Britain and France after the occupation of Bohemia and Moravia. He also failed to understand the need for Britain and France to maintain the illusion of Great Power status which allowed them to arbitrate international crises in Europe.

Hitler under pressure to produce

Historians have commented that it is possible that Hitler, buoyed by successes in Austria and Sudetenland, was now under political pressure from the German government or public, perhaps both, to produce something of real importance to them: the return of land of the German Empire; Austria and Sudetenland had never been part of Germany. In this view, his attempts at negotiating, which included threats of military force, were simply ignored by Poland, forcing Germany to follow through with its threats by declaring war on Poland despite a desire to avoid a conflict for which it may not have been fully prepared. Frantic negotiations with the USSR which led to the Nazi–Soviet Pact just before the outbreak of the conflict are presented as supportive evidence of this view as they indicate Germany's desire to prevent a large-scale war which would involve the USSR.

German economic reasons for war

Some historians believe that German rearmament caused too much stress on the German economy. In order for rearmament to continue and expand, more raw materials to build more tanks, aircraft and weapons had to be found. As industry expanded to produce more war-oriented goods, more workers were needed and Germany began to bring in foreigners to fill the demand. With increased war production, fewer consumer goods were being

→ Hitler took advantage of opportunities

. Surrender ↳
 - Rhineland
 - taking parts of Czechoslovakia

→ After successful gain of land, there was pressure from the public and gov to gain more. When he tried to negotiate and failed he declared war.

← **Did Germany's economic needs cause war in 1939?**

produced which meant that Germany was exporting less. With fewer exports, less gold and other strong currencies entered the country that could be used to purchase more raw materials. Fewer consumer goods also meant that Germans had fewer items to spend their wages on and the prices of what was available increased as demand for these items rose, so wages lost their value. In this view, an economic crisis was quickly developing in Germany so that a war was needed to capture territory that contained needed raw materials, as well as foreign gold reserves from conquered nations. War would also justify the need to produce so much for the military, as opposed to consumer goods.

4 The course of the war in Europe 1939 to June 1941

▶ **Key question:** *Why was Germany so successful against its foes until mid-1941?*

According to Source C, which nations remained at war with the Axis in 1942?

SOURCE C

Germany and Axis conquests 1939 to mid-1942.

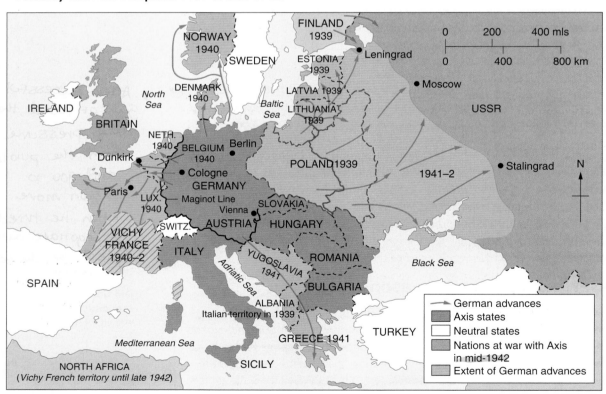

Handwritten margin notes:

Rearmament
↓
more raw material needed for war
↓ Production
more workers needed to work with material
↓ foreigners
more ~~foreigners~~ coming in to fill jobs

Despite various diplomatic efforts to prevent any war in Europe, Germany launched an invasion of Poland on 1 September 1939 to recover territory lost at the end of the First World War. This local conflict would lead to German domination of central, northern, western and south-eastern Europe within two years in a series of short, successful invasions (see Source C).

Invasion of Poland, 1 September 1939

← **What factors contributed to Germany's military success against Poland?**

While the invasion by Germany was not a complete surprise, Poland was not fully prepared. France had successfully convinced Poland not to mobilize its military just before the invasion in order not to provoke Germany into war; France believed negotiations were about to commence to end the crisis.

SOURCE D

German and Polish military forces on 1 September 1939.

Nation	Soldiers	Tanks	Aircraft	Artillery units
Germany	1,500,000	2,400	2,500	9,000
Poland	1,000,000	900	400	4,300

According to Source D, how prepared was Poland's army in September 1939? ?

[handwritten] ↓ Poland was well equipped but they were not prepared to face Germany and it's substantially larger military force.

Polish military strategy

• incorrectly

The Polish army, believing erroneously that Britain and France would attack Germany immediately, rushed its forces to defend the border with Germany instead of moving them to more defensible locations along rivers such as the Vistula and San. There was also the fear that if Germany captured Polish territories, such as the heavily industrialized Upper Silesia, then Britain and France might grant those lands to Germany in order to stop the war; Poland was determined not to cede any territory. Before the war, the Polish military believed it would be able to hold off a German invasion for up to half a year, which would give Britain and France more than enough time to launch a major counterattack; Poland simply had to defend itself until that occurred.

German military strategy

The German military strategy, for which Poland and other countries were not prepared, relied on its superior tanks which were supported by aircraft. German tanks rapidly outflanked enemy troops while aircraft attacked bridges, railways, and enemy positions. Infantry followed to support tanks, encircling enemy forces. This rapid form of warfare was labelled *blitzkrieg*, or lightning warfare, by an American journalist. German armies encircled Poland's troops, cut off their supplies and forced them to surrender. This form of warfare would be repeated during Germany's military offensives across Europe.

[handwritten] → Tanks were incredibly helpful in WWII

Technology of the war: tanks

Tanks, armoured fighting vehicles, were perhaps the most important weapon of much of the war and improved during the conflict. German tanks were superior at first. These were fast, heavily armoured, and were fitted with large guns that could destroy other tanks, fortifications and buildings. German tanks were equipped with radio which allowed communication with other tanks, aircraft and infantry units so that attacks were better co-ordinated than those of their enemies whose tanks often lacked radio in the war's early years. Tanks were Germany's primary weapon, supported by infantry, while in other armies, such as those of France, infantry were supported by tanks.

Tank warfare was the main reason for Germany's rapid success in the early years of the war and partially responsible for Germany's defeat against the USSR after Stalingrad (see page 151). German tanks were eventually challenged on the battlefield by Soviet and US models. All tanks throughout the conflict were constantly improved with larger guns and engines as well as more armour.

Some of the more common and important tanks are listed in the table.

Name	Nation producing	Weight/length with gun	Range	Number produced
Panzer IV	Germany	25.0 tons/7.0 m	200 km	9,200
Panzer V	Germany	45.0 tons/8.6 m	250 km	6,000
T-34	USSR	26.5 tons/6.7 m	400 km	55,000
Sherman	USA	30.0 tons/5.8 m	200 km	50,000

Tanks were widely adapted for various uses. Some were fitted with flamethrowers and others with blades to serve as bulldozers. Most tanks also had machine guns with thousands of rounds as secondary weapons for close combat.

Rapid German advance

Britain and France, the Allies, declared war on Germany on 3 September, although this was meaningless for Poland. France prepared to defend itself, expecting a German attack along its heavily fortified border, while Britain moved parts of its army into position along France's unfortified border with Belgium. There was little effort to help Poland, and within a week German forces had moved 225 km from the border, reaching the outskirts of the capital, Warsaw. On 13 September, Warsaw was surrounded and under constant attack, including an assault on 24 September by over 1100 German bombers. It finally surrendered on 28 September.

End of Polish independence

The USSR, as agreed secretly in the Nazi–Soviet Pact, began the invasion of eastern Poland on 17 September with several hundred thousand troops. The Soviets encountered little resistance since German armies had all but

The supposed "Allies" were more focused on themselves and each other and put little effort into helping Poland

defeated Polish forces. On 22 September, the industrial city of Lwów was captured by the Soviets and various encircled Polish army units surrendered in stages to both Germans and Soviets until 6 October. One hundred and twenty thousand Polish soldiers and the remains of the air force retreated with their government into Romania, refusing to surrender or negotiate with Germany. Most of these were moved to France where Polish army and air units were reorganized to help fight the Germans in other battles. The small Polish navy escaped to Britain, participating in battles throughout the war. A Polish government-in-exile was established in Paris on 30 September. With Poland conquered, it was divided between the USSR and Germany, with the Soviets receiving the larger part. Several Polish **guerrilla resistance movements** were established almost immediately after the fall of Poland, conducting significant military operations throughout the remaining years of the war (see page 171).

Casualties

The war in Poland was quick, but also brutal. It ended with a death toll of civilians unparalleled in modern European history up to that point. Some 65,000 Polish soldiers died, while 660,000 were captured by Germany and the USSR. While it is estimated that between 2000 and 5500 Soviet soldiers died, Germany lost around 16,000; Slovakia, which had joined in the invasion and allied with Germany, had fewer than 100 killed or wounded. It was revealed later in the war that the Soviets executed large numbers of Polish army officers who surrendered, causing difficulties with its allies at the time. The death toll for Polish and German civilians in Poland was enormous, with claims of 150,000–300,000 killed. German aircraft bombed cities such as Warsaw very heavily, accounting for the majority of civilian deaths, but there was also violence among civilian groups. Polish militias hunted down and killed tens of thousands of Polish Germans, while German militias did the same to non-German Polish civilians. Some German army units executed large numbers of civilians as well.

Phoney War 1939–40

Although Britain and France declared war on Germany on 3 September 1939, very little military activity took place until France was invaded in May 1940, leading this period to be called the Phoney War, or fake war, during which no major fighting occurred in western Europe. The French military continued to strengthen its defences, bringing troops from its empire and reinforcing the **Maginot Line** which stretched along the French–German border. The Germans constructed the **Siegfried Line**, primarily anti-tank defences, in the late 1930s in order to protect their border from French attack. German forces now reinforced this barrier while also preparing for offensive operations elsewhere.

The British Empire was in the process of full mobilization, with troops from the Dominions and colonies beginning to arrive in Britain. The British army

Poland was captured yet Polish people were spread all over trying to reorganize and take it back

🔑 **KEY TERM**

Guerrilla resistance movements Groups of fighters who oppose an occupying force using guerrilla tactics such as sabotage and assassination.

Maginot Line A complex system of fortresses and other defences established by France on the French–German border.

Siegfried Line System of anti-tank defences established by Germany on its borders with The Netherlands, Belgium and France.

← Why was there no war to Germany's west in 1939 or early 1940?

Between Sept 1939 – May 1940 (9 months) little fighting took place

KEY TERM

Neutrality Acts A series of US laws that prevented the USA from joining conflicts and from providing weapons for countries at war.

[handwritten margin note, rotated: the increase in military force strengthened by the annexation of Poland]

> What allowed the Soviet army to be successful in its war against Finland?

[handwritten margin note:] After capturing Poland, the USSR became greedy and went into war w/ Finland over land

> What was the significance of Germany's invasion of Denmark and Norway?

[handwritten margin note:] Britain tried to prevent Germany from importing iron ore.

To do this they needed Norway
↓
Germany decided then to take control of Norway

Denmark, needed to get to Norway was overrun as well.

continued building its numbers in France in anticipation of a German attack through Belgium. Both Britain and France increased industrial production of war equipment and the USA altered its **Neutrality Acts** (see page 192) so that both countries could purchase US-produced war goods. This led to increased shipping in the Atlantic, which came under German attack (see page 139). Minor naval clashes began between primarily British and German ships as each began attempts to blockade the other, similar to their actions in the First World War (see page 53). British bombers flew over parts of Germany, dropping leaflets promoting a peaceful resolution to the conflict.

Winter War 1939–40

The USSR moved quickly after the annexation of two-thirds of Poland to reclaim parts of the Russian Empire that had broken away after the First World War. The Soviets demanded territorial concessions from Finland so that the city of Leningrad in Russia, also known as St Petersburg, would be better protected. Finland refused and the USSR began an invasion of the country at the end of November 1939. This attack by hundreds of thousands of troops, with thousands of tanks and aircraft, was met by the small Finnish army. Finnish troops successfully employed guerrilla tactics (see page 3), inflicting heavy losses on the Soviet army. In February 1940, the Soviets tremendously increased the number of soldiers and tanks attacking Finland, leading to a 12 March 1940 peace treaty between the two nations. Finland remained independent, but lost 11 per cent of its territory. In 1940, the USSR annexed Estonia, Latvia and Lithuania, and seized Bessarabia from Romania; all had been parts of the former Russian Empire.

Invasion of Denmark and Norway, April 1940

Britain began mining parts of the North Sea in April 1940, to try to prevent Germany from importing iron ore from Sweden, and made plans to seize the port of Narvik in Norway to further this goal. Germany needed to protect its iron supply and decided to take control of all Norway. This would have the added benefit of putting northern Britain into bombing range and prevent a blockade against German shipping with control of the air over the North Sea.

On 9 April 1940, Denmark was overrun within a few hours with little resistance and was partly used to launch the more important attack on Norway. German aircraft attacked towns, airfields and fortresses while naval vessels landed soldiers; most of Norway was under German control within a week. Only in the north at Narvik was there major, sustained fighting. Two naval battles were fought between British and German ships on 10 and 13 April, with Britain winning both. The land battle, however, continued until June. British, Polish, French and Norwegian troops fought German soldiers for Narvik. By June, Germany controlled the air and Allied soldiers were evacuated; they were desperately needed elsewhere.

Invasion of western Europe, May 1940

← | Why was the German army successful in western Europe in 1940?

Nine months after the declaration of war on Germany by France and Britain, Germany began an attack on its primary enemy in Europe: France. Germany's offensive, named Case Yellow, was launched on 10 May 1940 with the aim of capturing The Netherlands, Belgium, Luxembourg and France. The fight in western Europe, the Western Front, involved a substantial number of troops and equipment (see Source E).

SOURCE E

Table of military forces of nations battling on the Western Front in May 1940.

Nation	Troops	Tanks	Aircraft	Artillery
Germany	3,350,000	2,500	5,000	7,300
France	2,500,000	3,200	1,500	10,700
Britain	240,000	300	1,000	1,300
Netherlands	200,000	<10	150	650
Belgium	650,000	10	<200	1,300

According to Source E, what advantages did Germany have over other nations? ?

While these numbers were impressive for the Allies, their equipment was not as modern as that of Germany and tactics were not as effective. Very fast German tanks, in particular, used radio to co-ordinate attacks and communicate with other parts of the military, while French tanks, lacking radio, were used in small groups to support infantry which were mostly in defensive positions. Germany clearly had superiority in the air and used this dominance to attack bridges, tanks, airfields and cities, preventing enemy movements towards German positions and retreat from advancing German armies.

The Netherlands and Luxembourg fall, May 1940

France, The Netherlands, Belgium and Luxembourg were all attacked on 10 May in an awesome display of German organization and military strength, almost immediately overwhelming their opponents. The Netherlands fell to the German army on 14 May. Germany dropped **paratroops** behind the Dutch army's defences and then destroyed much of the city of Rotterdam with bombers. Belgium was better defended as Belgian forces were joined by three large French armies and a smaller British one. The main fortresses guarding the Belgian border were overrun, some captured or destroyed by German paratroopers, while German aircraft destroyed airfields and aircraft. Luxembourg capitulated almost as soon as the German army entered the country, further exposing Belgian and French borders to German assault. German tanks surged across these borders, protected by their aircraft and followed by hundreds of thousands of infantry.

🔑 KEY TERM

Paratroops Soldiers who jump from planes, usually to establish positions behind enemy armies.

the fall of the Netherlands & Luxembourg exposed French borders

Technology of the war: fighter aircraft

Fighters were small, fast aircraft that normally provided protection for bomber aircraft. Germany, however, successfully adapted fighters to also attack soldiers and tanks from the air, giving them further advantage on the battlefield in the first years of the war. Fighters consumed large amounts of fuel rapidly so that their range was not great. This meant that they could not accompany bomber aircraft on their longer missions and, in consequence, bombers from all nations initially had little protection from the fighters of their enemies, leading to high losses of bomber aircraft. Later in the war, the drop tank, a large fuel container attached to the bottom of the fighter, was employed to extend fighter range so that bombers were better protected. Fighter attacks on tanks, troops, railways, and factories dealt much devastation during the conflict. By the war's end, the jet engine was first introduced by Germany, giving fighter craft great speed which made them hard to destroy by other, slower fighters, but too few were produced to affect the war's outcome.

Some of the more important fighter aircraft are listed in the table.

Name	Nation producing	Range	Armament Number of machine guns/calibre/ rounds per gun[†]	Number produced
Hurricane	Britain	965 km	4/20 mm/60	14,500
Spitfire	Britain	760 km	2/20 mm/60	20,300
P-51 Mustang	USA	2755 km*	6/12.7 mm/400	15,000
Bell P-39 Airacobra	USA	840 km	2/12.7 mm/200	9,500
Focke-Wulf Fw 190	Germany	800 km	2/13 mm/475	20,000
Messerschmitt Bf 109	Germany	850 km	2/13/300	34,000
Yakovlev Yak-9	USSR	1360 km	1/12.7 mm/200	16,800

*Extended range was the result of the addition of drop tanks which carried extra fuel.

[†]Armaments could be altered to include cannon, bombs, rockets and different calibre guns.

Fall of Belgium and France, May–June 1940

The main German assault against France was through the Ardennes Forest, something French military planners believed impassable to tanks, avoiding the Maginot Line along the French–German border. By penetrating the Ardennes Forest, the German army entered northern France and moved towards the English Channel, cutting off the British and French armies that were either in Belgium or heading into it. By 28 May, most of Belgium was under German control and its army surrendered. Surrounded British and French armies retreated to the small port of Dunkirk on the English Channel. From 26 May to 3 June, approximately 330,000 British and French soldiers were evacuated to Britain, while all major equipment had to be left on the beach; over 20,000 French soldiers were captured by the German army.

The way was open for the German army to penetrate deeply into France. French armies continued to fight Germany and Italy after 10 June, when Italy attacked France along its southern border. France's capital, Paris, was captured by Germany on 13 June and nine days later France surrendered. Britain was the only state in Europe at war with Germany until 6 April 1941, when Germany invaded Greece. After France's surrender, Germany administered three-fifths of France. Remaining areas were ostensibly under French government control and known as **Vichy France** until November 1942, when they also came under direct German rule.

Invasion of the Balkan peninsula, 28 October 1940 to 1 June 1941

Albania was occupied and annexed to Italy in April 1939. This gave Italy a base from which to invade Greece on 28 October 1940, in a quest for empire. The invasion was a disaster and Greece soon drove Italian soldiers back into Albania, capturing about 30 per cent of Albania in the process. In March 1941, Italy again attacked Greek troops, trying to drive them out of Albania. This offensive also failed until they were joined in April by German troops, driving the Greek army out of Albania.

In order to invade Greece, Germany first conquered Yugoslavia, assisted by Bulgaria, which joined the Axis on 1 March 1941. The invasion of Yugoslavia began on 6 April 1941 and ended on 17 April. The country was divided between Germany, Italy, Hungary (which had joined the Axis in November 1940, along with Romania) and Bulgaria, with a large portion of it reorganized as the independent state of Croatia, allied to Germany and Italy, as was a Serbian **puppet-state**. A smaller independent state of Montenegro was organized and administered as an Italian puppet-state.

Germany also invaded Greece on 6 April, which was now defended by British troops, capturing Athens, the Greek capital, on 27 April. Britain hurriedly evacuated 50,000 troops to the Greek island of Crete. On 20 May 1941, Crete was invaded by German paratroops and conquered by 1 June.

> ### 🔑 KEY TERM
>
> **Vichy France** The remnant of France that was a German puppet-state between 1940 and late 1942, ruled from the city of Vichy.
>
> **Puppet-state** Government that operates at the will of and for the benefit of another government.

> ← **What was the importance of the Axis invasion of the Balkan peninsula?**

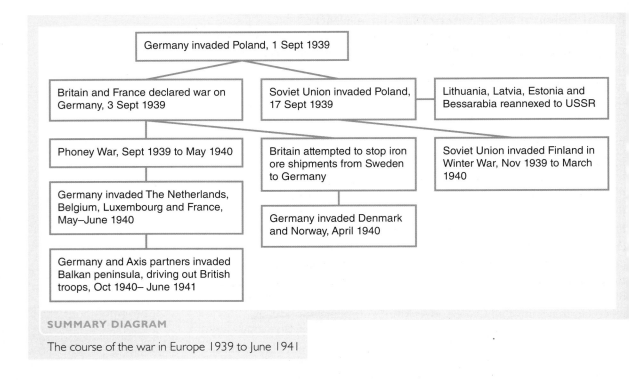

```
Germany invaded Poland, 1 Sept 1939
```

```
Britain and France declared war on
Germany, 3 Sept 1939
```

```
Soviet Union invaded Poland,
17 Sept 1939
```

```
Lithuania, Latvia, Estonia and
Bessarabia reannexed to USSR
```

```
Phoney War, Sept 1939 to May 1940
```

```
Britain attempted to stop iron
ore shipments from Sweden
to Germany
```

```
Soviet Union invaded Finland in
Winter War, Nov 1939 to March
1940
```

```
Germany invaded The Netherlands,
Belgium, Luxembourg and France,
May–June 1940
```

```
Germany invaded Denmark
and Norway, April 1940
```

```
Germany and Axis partners invaded
Balkan peninsula, driving out British
troops, Oct 1940– June 1941
```

SUMMARY DIAGRAM

The course of the war in Europe 1939 to June 1941

(5) The course of the war in Africa and Italy 1940–5

▶ *Key question: What factors contributed to Allied success in Africa and Italy during the Second World War?*

Italy joined the war as a member of the Axis, and therefore as a German ally, in 1940, with an attack on southern France after German armies had essentially defeated the country. Almost immediately 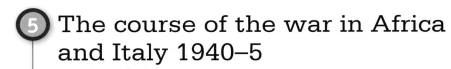there were battles between Britain and Italy in the Mediterranean Sea, on Africa's north coast, and in east Africa, where both Britain and Italy had colonies.

<table>
<tr><td>

What was the most significant result of the war between the Axis and Allied Powers in Africa?

</td><td>

→ Africa 1940–3

Italy had a huge, but poorly defended, empire in east Africa and Libya along the north African coast. As Italy entered the war in 1940 against the Allies, it made moves to attack British territories which were quickly halted before Britain began invading Italian territories.

</td></tr>
</table>

East Africa, January–November 1941

In January 1941, British troops from India and Sudan began a three-pronged invasion of Italy's east African empire. Eritrea was completely conquered by

April 1941 and, by May, most of Abyssinia and Somalia were under British control. The last Italian troops in Abyssinia held out near Lake Tana in the north-west of the region, finally surrendering in November 1941. Italy's east African empire came to an end and the former Emperor of Abyssinia, Haile Selassie, driven out in 1936, was reinstalled as ruler. Eritrea was ruled by the British until 1951, when it was granted to Abyssinia. Somalia was ruled by Britain until 1960, when it became independent.

North Africa 1940–3

Italy desired control of the Suez Canal, which would allow free access to the Italian colonies in east Africa and control oil shipments from the region. Egypt was also desired as it was rich in natural resources and agriculture and had a large, prosperous Italian community. It was hoped that by Italy invading Egypt, Egyptians and resident Italians would revolt against British domination of the government since 1882, assisting the invasion in the process. The revolt never materialized, although an Italian army entered Egypt on 13 September 1940, advancing 70 km within a few days. A British counter-offensive, with primarily Australian and Indian troops, pushed Italian troops out of most of Egypt by mid-December in a series of fierce battles.

Libya, January 1941 to May 1942

In early January 1941, Australian troops from the British army entered the Libyan city of Tobruk; they captured it by the end of the month. Other British forces moved towards the major port of eastern Libya, Benghazi. All eastern Libya was captured by Britain by mid-February. This was the first successful British military operation of any significance in the war up to that point. Germany began to support Italy's north African efforts in mid-February, landing huge numbers of troops and tanks in Libya's western port of Tripoli. By early April 1941, British troops had been forced out of Libya and into Egypt by German and Italian troops. Tobruk was held by Australian troops who were placed under siege.

Britain launched Operation Crusader in November 1941 to recapture eastern Libya and relieve the siege of Tobruk. Tobruk was finally reached on 7 December after a month of heavy fighting. In January 1942, most of eastern Libya was again temporarily under British control. At the end of the month German troops drove the British out of most of the region again, so that by the first week of February, British troops held on to only the easternmost areas of the country. At the end of May, German and Italian troops began another offensive, pushing British troops far back into Egypt.

Germany and Britain continued to fight for control over Lybia

El Alamein, October 1942

At the end of June, the Axis and British battled at El Alamein in Egypt. The Axis was unable to break through the British defensive line with its exhausted troops that were running low on supplies. After a few more attacks at El Alamein, fighting ended and both sides worked to resupply and build forces to dislodge the other in the future. British aircraft and submarines targeted supply convoys of fuel in the Mediterranean that were

SOURCE F

The Second World War in Africa 1941–3.

According to Source F, in what year did the war in north Africa experience the most movement?

bound for Axis troops at El Alamein, preventing any further Axis offensive in Egypt for the time being.

On the evening of 23 October 1942, British troops, accompanied by Polish, Greek and **Free French** forces, launched a massive assault on German positions at El Alamein. In the previous months, Britain had been able to resupply its forces so that its army in Egypt was now twice the size of the Axis army there. With little fuel for tanks and trucks, the Axis army decided to retreat into Libya by 4 November; Egypt and the Suez Canal were not threatened by land forces again for the remainder of the war.

KEY TERM

Free French French troops who escaped the collapse of France in June 1940 and continued to fight with the Allies.

> **The USA joins the European war, 11 December 1941**
> The USA was attacked by Japan on 7 December 1941 (see page 194). Japan was a member of the Axis and therefore an ally of Germany, although there was no co-ordination of war strategy between them. As a consequence, Germany and Italy both declared war against the USA on 11 December. The USA had already participated in the war in Europe by supplying Britain and France with huge quantities of goods, including ships, weapons, ammunition and food. These shipments were the target of German submarines in the Battle of the Atlantic (see page 139). Only at the end of 1942, after building and supplying armies and ships to transport them, was the USA able to field large armies. It did so in north Africa first, while simultaneously fighting Japan in the Pacific. US aircraft joined British efforts in mid-1942 to bomb Germany (see page 145).

North Africa captured by Allies, November 1942 to May 1943

While British and Allied troops slowly pursued retreating Axis forces, a large British and US force began Operation Torch on 8 November, which saw the occupation of French-held Morocco and Algeria by 11 November. Germany moved to occupy Tunisia, held by France up to that point, and Vichy France was itself occupied by German troops as a response to Vichy French forces signing an armistice with Britain and the USA. While German troops battled US and British forces in Tunisia, British troops continued to pursue retreating Italian and German troops in Libya so that by 4 February 1943, the region was clear of any Axis forces. Fierce fighting in Tunisia finally ended on 12 May 1943, when all remaining Axis troops in north Africa surrendered.

[handwritten annotation: British & US forces drive German out of Libya & Tunisia.]

The Italian Front 1943–5

After the fall of north Africa to the Allies, the large Italian island of Sicily was subject to a large amphibious and airborne invasion on 9 July 1943. Sicily was defended by almost 300,000 Axis troops, the vast majority of whom were Italian. The Allies landed almost 500,000 troops during the six-week campaign, conquering the island by 17 August. Around 170,000 Axis troops were killed, wounded or captured during the fighting. During the battle, the Italian king deposed and imprisoned Benito Mussolini, Italy's dictator,

[sidebar] **How critical was the Italian Front to the outcome of the Second World War in Europe?**

reflecting deteriorating support for the war with the Italian population. In addition, in 1943, Axis powers were in retreat on all fronts and Italy hoped either to join the Allies in order to save itself from punishment or to negotiate the best possible terms of surrender.

The Italian peninsula 1943–4

On 3 September, Italy secretly agreed to an armistice with the Allies that would begin on 8 September while Allied troops began landing in the south. Most Italian units quickly surrendered, but German troops did not. Germany moved to take control of the whole Italian peninsula on 8 September 1943, forcing Italian troops to surrender their weapons. The Allied invasion encountered major German resistance, but by November the Allies controlled most of Italy south of Rome. The Gustav Line, a German defensive position spanning the Italian peninsula, proved difficult to breach. All attempts to cross or outflank it failed until May 1944. Rome fell on 5 June and the Germans created a new defensive system, the Gothic Line, which held back Allied troops from 25 August until 17 December 1944.

Final battles in Italy 1945

By December 1944, northern Italy was organized as the Italian Social Republic and led by the former Italian dictator Mussolini, who had been rescued from prison by German troops. This meant that troops from the Kingdom of Italy fought Italian Social Republic troops, so that Italy was essentially fighting a civil war, as well as foreign occupation by German troops. In early 1945, Allied armies slowly captured parts of northern Italy. Italian **communist partisans** captured and killed Mussolini at the end of April and all fighting stopped with the surrender of German forces in Italy on 2 May.

KEY TERM

Communist partisans
Communist guerrilla fighters who fought occupying armies as well as various nationalist groups in many countries during the war.

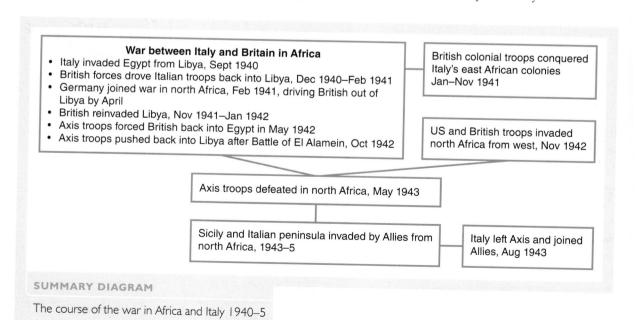

War between Italy and Britain in Africa
- Italy invaded Egypt from Libya, Sept 1940
- British forces drove Italian troops back into Libya, Dec 1940–Feb 1941
- Germany joined war in north Africa, Feb 1941, driving British out of Libya by April
- British reinvaded Libya, Nov 1941–Jan 1942
- Axis troops forced British back into Egypt in May 1942
- Axis troops pushed back into Libya after Battle of El Alamein, Oct 1942

British colonial troops conquered Italy's east African colonies Jan–Nov 1941

US and British troops invaded north Africa from west, Nov 1942

Axis troops defeated in north Africa, May 1943

Sicily and Italian peninsula invaded by Allies from north Africa, 1943–5

Italy left Axis and joined Allies, Aug 1943

SUMMARY DIAGRAM

The course of the war in Africa and Italy 1940–5

6 The course of the war at sea 1939–45

> ▶ *Key question: What was the importance of the war at sea between the Allied and Axis powers?*

At the start of the war in Europe in September 1939, the British and French navies were massive compared to that of Germany. Germany initially feared a naval blockade such as the one the British effectively imposed during the First World War (see page 53). Any notion of blockade ended with the German occupation of Norway (see page 130), which was quickly followed by the fall of much of the rest of continental Europe. Controlling most of Europe meant access to food, supplies and numerous ports.

While Germany constructed massive numbers of modern, long-range submarines, it initially turned to sea **mines** to damage British and French shipping. By April 1940, 128 Allied merchant ships had been sunk by mines laid by German ships, submarines and aircraft.

Battle of the Atlantic 1939–45

The Battle of the Atlantic was the fight between primarily German submarines and aircraft and British and US merchant and war ships. While Britain moved quickly at the war's start to capture or destroy German merchant ships, Germany countered with submarine attacks on British shipping.

By mid-1940, large numbers of German submarines were deployed against increasingly large numbers of merchant ships travelling between the USA and Britain. These ships were carrying food and military equipment through the policy of **cash-and-carry** and the later **Lend–Lease** programme. The submarines were organized into groups called wolf-packs, co-ordinating

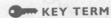

KEY TERM

Mine An explosive device which detonates on contact.

Cash-and-carry Programme of the US government starting in September 1939 which allowed the sale of US-produced war goods to warring nations as long as they paid for items in cash and transported all goods on their own ships.

Lend–Lease US programme begun in March 1941 that lent over $50 billion ($650 billion in today's terms) worth of war supplies to Allied nations.

> **Why did the Battle of the Atlantic last throughout the Second World War?**

Technology of the war: submarines

Submarines were the most effective naval vessels of the Second World War. Submarines were relatively cheap and fast to build compared to larger surface ships that were vulnerable to aircraft. In addition, they required fewer men to operate than surface ships. Germany constructed several types of submarines, also referred to as U-boats, and in great numbers. Using torpedoes, surface ships could be destroyed without the submarine being exposed to attack. German submarines such as the type VII were impressive ships, able to stay submerged for up to 150 km at 230 m below the sea's surface. They carried up to 14 torpedoes and could travel over 15,000 km before refuelling if travelling at moderate speeds of around 19 km/h.

their attacks on convoys of merchant ships by radio, often attacking at night. Submarine attacks were joined by German aircraft when possible, often working in co-operation, so that by mid-1941, 30 per cent of all Allied ships sunk had been attacked by aircraft.

SOURCE G

A destroyer (the smaller ship alone in the rear, right) shepherds freighters across the Atlantic in a convoy during the Battle of the Atlantic on 1 June 1943.

? What information about naval warfare in the Second World War is conveyed by Source G?

KEY TERM

Codes A way of communicating information to prevent an enemy from understanding it.

Cruisers Fast, heavily armed warships that have less armour and fewer weapons than battleships.

Destroyers Fast, lightly armoured ships built specifically to locate and destroy submarines.

Germany's early success

Germany deciphered British naval **codes** early in the war, giving them a strategic advantage as they were able to locate large convoys crossing the Atlantic. This helped the Germans to sink 848 ships by July 1941, with the loss of only 43 submarines. Germany's few surface warships were also active in this period, sinking or capturing approximately 40 enemy ships. These German warships were mostly sunk during the war and were strategically unimportant, as were most large battleships and **cruisers** of all fleets, as they were vulnerable to attack by air (see page 142).

Allied counterattack

a group of merchant vessels sailing together

Britain countered the submarine threat by reintroducing the convoy system that was used during the First World War and by patrolling the sea with aircraft equipped with depth charges (see page 141). Iceland was invaded and occupied by British troops on 10 May 1940 to extend aircraft protection of convoys while Britain rapidly increased its number of **destroyers**. Britain achieved a major breakthrough in 1941 when German naval codes, known as Enigma, were broken, giving Britain knowledge of the location of Germany's submarine groups. British and US aircraft, after the USA joined the war in late 1941, hunted German submarines, flying from bases in the USA, Canada, Greenland, Gibraltar, Britain and Iceland.

Technology of the war: anti-submarine warfare

The Allies used various weapons to destroy enemy submarines:

- Depth charges were bombs that were flung by catapults behind ships such as destroyers and dropped by aircraft. The bomb exploded when it reached a certain depth as determined by a pressure fuse.
- Hedgehog launched many smaller bombs at the same time in front of the ship. The bombs landed in a 30-m wide circle and sank, exploding only when they made contact with something. This made it easier to determine if a submarine, or the ocean floor, had been hit, whereas a depth charge always exploded after a specific, short period whether or not it made contact with anything, making it difficult to know if a submarine had been destroyed.
- ASDIC, or sonar, used sound waves to determine the location of submarines. This helped destroyers and other fast surface ships to chase and destroy these vessels.
- High-frequency direction finding, or HF/DF, used at least two machines to discover the exact location of a German submarine by focusing on German radio signals. These machines, working in tandem, could pinpoint a German radio transmission, allowing Allied ships and aircraft to bomb that location.

Allied victory

The extensive Battle of the Atlantic was eventually dominated by the Allies. This was the result of the convoy system, the use of aircraft, the deciphering of German naval codes, the use of radar and other technologies, and the inability of Germany to counter these measures while maintaining submarine construction. By the end of the war in Europe in May 1945:

- Germany had lost 780 submarines out of 1100 in service and 30,000 out of 40,000 submariners.
- The Allies had lost 175 warships, 3500 merchant vessels and 72,000 sailors.

Technology of war: radar

Radio detection and ranging, commonly known as radar, used radio waves to determine the distance, speed, direction and altitude of various objects such as aircraft, ships and surfaced submarines. Britain was the first nation to effectively use radar. It was used to determine the direction and numbers of German bombers attacking the country after July 1940. Later, radar was installed on Allied ships and aircraft, helping to reduce the threat of German submarines. German submarines were eventually fitted with radar detection devices which indicated when they had been detected by Allied radar, giving them time to go below the water's surface and escape.

What was the
importance of naval
warfare in the
Mediterranean?

→ Mediterranean Sea 1940–3

The Mediterranean Sea was another area of important naval action. With the fall of France in mid-1940, Britain feared that French warships would be turned over to Germany. This could help give the Axis powers control over the Mediterranean, which would allow them easier access to north Africa and potentially oilfields in the Middle East. Britain attacked these French warships while they were at port in France's north African province of Algeria in July 1940, damaging or destroying most of them.

British ships battled the Italian navy in the Mediterranean, culminating in a major defeat for Italy in mid-November 1940 when British aircraft, flying from an **aircraft carrier**, torpedoed three of Italy's six battleships while they were at port at Taranto. This victory by British aircraft clearly illustrated that the era of large surface warships was over, replaced by aircraft and submarines.

Italian and German aircraft and submarines battled British naval vessels that worked to protect troop and supply transports in the Mediterranean for the remainder of the war. British aircraft and submarines did much the same thing, limiting desperately needed supplies for Axis troops in north Africa.

KEY TERM

Aircraft carriers Ships that functioned as floating, armed airfields that launched small bombers and fighters, as well as dive- and torpedo-bombers.

> ### Technology of the war: naval aircraft
> Britain and the USA used a number of aircraft in naval operations. The British Swordfish torpedo bomber was a slow, double-winged biplane that flew low over water, launching a single torpedo. This plane was responsible for some of Britain's most spectacular naval successes in the war, including the destruction of much of Italy's fleet at Taranto. Other aircraft were designed to land on the sea, known as sea-planes, which had boat-like bottoms. Dive-bombers, used also in the land war, were used to drop bombs on naval targets with great accuracy by diving towards the target at great speed before releasing their weapons. Aircraft carriers (see page 195) launched small bombers and fighters, as well as dive- and torpedo-bombers.

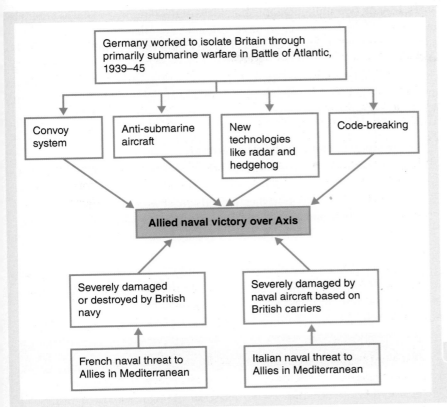

Germany worked to isolate Britain through primarily submarine warfare in Battle of Atlantic, 1939–45

Convoy system

Anti-submarine aircraft

New technologies like radar and hedgehog

Code-breaking

Allied naval victory over Axis

Severely damaged or destroyed by British navy

Severely damaged by naval aircraft based on British carriers

French naval threat to Allies in Mediterranean

Italian naval threat to Allies in Mediterranean

SUMMARY DIAGRAM

The course of the war at sea 1939–45

 # The course of the air war 1939–45

> Key question: *How did the air war affect Allied and Axis nations?*

The Second World War used aircraft unlike any conflict before. Aircraft helped render surface warships almost obsolete (see page 142), could destroy enemy factories and cities, and brought civilians more directly into the war in western Europe. Aircraft were critical to German success in Poland in 1939, as well as for the invasion of other countries in 1940. Bombers allowed countries such as the island nation of Britain, as well as its ally the USA, to participate in the war in Europe when their armies were unable to participate on land.

Britain attacked, July 1940 to July 1941

Germany began bombing Britain by bomber aircraft in mid-July 1940, hoping either to force Britain to negotiate a peace treaty, or to prepare Britain for possible invasion by German armies. Bombing did destroy many urban

To what extent was Germany successful in its bombing campaign against Britain?

143

areas, leaving two million people homeless and killing up to 60,000 others by July 1941. It failed, however, to force Britain to negotiate for peace or adequately reduce Britain's air power to an extent that German ships could safely transport troops to the island. Britain responded to the bombing of its cities by bombing those of Germany (see page 145). After Germany began an invasion of the USSR (see page 149), bombings of Britain became rare events for the remainder of the war.

Technology of the war: bomber aircraft

Bombers were large, but slow, aircraft that dropped various types of bombs on enemy positions or cities below them. Since fighter aircraft had difficulty protecting bombers far from their airfields, most were armed with machine guns to give them some protection from enemy fighters. Throughout the war, bombers were improved so that they were able to carry more bombs and fly at higher altitudes to be less vulnerable. Germany used bombers to great effect when combined with tanks and infantry, while Britain and the USA used bombers to destroy targets deep inside Europe with little or no integration with other aspects of military operations.

Some of the more important larger bomber aircraft are listed in the table.

Name	Producing nation	Range	Load	Number built
Avro Lancaster	Britain	4000 km	Up to 10,000 kg	7,400
Boeing B-17	USA	3200 km	Up to 7800 kg	12,700
Heinkel He177	Germany	5600 km	Up to 6000 kg	1,150
Tupolev TB-3	USSR	2000 km	Up to 2000 kg	800

The USA produced other important bomber aircraft as well (see page 206).

How did the bombing of Germany affect the outcome of the Second World War?

Bombing Germany 1940–5

Britain's first large-scale bombing campaign against Germany began in May 1940 when German industrial sites and railways were targeted while France was being invaded. It was hoped that attacking precious oil supplies, as well as targets in Germany, would slow the invasion of France by having Germany withdraw much of its aircraft from battle to protect its industrial centres. Germany produced no oil, so the destruction of oil supplies had the potential to bring any invasion to halt. British bombers lacked accuracy, partly as a result of having to fly at great altitude to avoid being shot down, and most targets were missed. These initial bomber raids on German targets were largely abandoned until Britain bombed German cities in response to its own urban centres being attacked (see page 143). The British government discovered that only about 30 per cent of all bombs it dropped landed within 8 km of the selected target.

Area bombing 1942–5

Britain created a new policy in which an entire area was selected for destruction, negating the need for precision. By destroying entire industrial areas, including homes, infrastructure, factories, schools and everything else, Britain hoped that suffering, demoralized civilians would compel their government to end the war. It was also hoped that bombing German industrial areas would hamper Germany's invasion of the USSR, which began in mid-1941.

Area bombing raids, also known as strategic bombing, often used hundreds of aircraft attacking at night to avoid German fighters and anti-aircraft artillery as much as possible. Bombing occurred in waves, with the first bombs dropped being designed to destroy roofs, while later bombers delivered incendiary bombs that caused fires in the exposed buildings. The subsequent fires often raged out of control, destroying entire city centres and causing **firestorms**. The first major attack occurred on 3–4 March 1942, when 235 British bombers destroyed much of an industrial complex in Billancourt, France, which took three months to rebuild. The German city of Lübeck was attacked on 28–29 March, destroying or damaging 62 per cent of the city.

> **KEY TERM**
>
> **Firestorms** A fire of such magnitude and intensity that it creates its own wind system, usually as a result of rising heat causing cool air to be pulled towards the fire which provides more oxygen to make the fire more intense.

> How successful was area bombing against Cologne, Germany, according to Source H?

SOURCE H

Cologne, Germany, in ruins from area bombing by 1945.

Expanded area bombing

Operation Millennium, the largest bombing raid up to that point of the war, was launched on 30–31 May 1942. Over 1000 British bombers attacked the German city of Cologne for two-and-a-half hours, destroying 3300 houses and damaging 10,000 more; 36 factories were completely destroyed and 270 others damaged. Area bombing continued to be employed, with US bombers joining the British in 1942, conducting daytime attacks. The largest death toll by area bombing was in Operation Gomorrah by British and US aircraft against Hamburg over a series of nights in late July and early August 1943, which left 45,000 civilians dead, destroying 215,000 houses and 600 factories. Towards the end of the war in February 1945, Dresden was bombed, killing 25,000 people in a single evening. This bombing remains controversial as it was clear by this date that Germany was all but defeated. The bombing of Dresden could serve little military purpose.

Other bombings

While Britain and the USA destroyed targets in Germany, they also bombed other Axis targets including Romania's oilfields and parts of Italy. Germans conducted their own version of area bombing, destroying Soviet cities by air, leading to approximately 500,000 civilian deaths. From German-occupied Crete, Alexandria and the Suez Canal in Egypt were bombed in support of the campaign in north Africa, and Italian and German aircraft repeatedly attacked Malta in the Mediterranean Sea, from 1940 to 1943. None of these attacks had any noticeable long-term effects on the conduct of the war.

Importance of strategic bombing

Although bombers destroyed most German cities, the effect of the bombing continues to be debated by historians today. Just as the bombing of British cities seems to have actually increased civilian morale and support for the government, attacks on German cities also led to more government support. The bombings themselves had little long-term effect on German industrial production as factories were quickly reconstructed or moved away from industrial centres. Hamburg, for example, was largely destroyed in mid-1943, including 600 factories. Within two months industrial production in the city had been largely restored.

Only towards the end of the war, when Allied fighter planes had been improved so that they could protect bombers over most of Germany, did bombers affect Germany's ability to conduct the war. Flying at lower altitudes as the threat of German fighters was reduced, accurate bombing of railways, factories and other targets could be effectively carried out. By the end of 1944, Allied air attacks on Germany's oil installations and railways had crippled the country and, by February 1945, these attacks had all but halted German industry.

Losses

Allied bombing of Germany and other Axis targets during the area bombing campaign resulted in major losses of aircraft, Allied pilots and crews, as well as German and Axis civilians. Allied and Axis losses can be generally summarized as:

- around 600,000 civilians killed and 800,000 wounded in Germany, with 7,500,000 made homeless
- around 500,000 Soviet civilians killed
- 50,000 Italian civilians killed
- 160,000 Allied air crew killed
- 40,000 Allied aircraft destroyed or damaged
- consumed up to 33 per cent of all British war production and 11 per cent of US military spending.

Many historians consider the Allied bombing campaign against Germany and its Axis partners to have been wasteful in terms of production and lives, both Allied and Axis. Many officials during the war, as well as later, believed that bombings by both sides were crimes against humanity. During the Nuremburg Trials at the war's end (see page 157), Germany was not prosecuted for the bombing of Allied, especially British, cities as this would also bring up the fact that the Allies did the same to Germany, killing substantially more German civilians than Germany did in Britain.

> **Technology of the war: rockets**
>
> Small rockets, also known as missiles, were increasingly installed on fighter aircraft towards the end of the Second World War. These rockets delivered bombs to enemy factories, railway locomotives, ships and other targets. They were largely inaccurate and machine guns remained the main fighter weapons. Germany, however, developed larger, more powerful rockets. The V-2 was a missile propelled by liquid fuel that Germany used primarily to attack London and Antwerp. These missiles travelled at 5700 km/h up to 320 km carrying a 1000-kg explosive warhead. Travelling far faster than the speed of sound, they were meant to destroy large areas and cause terror since they struck without warning. Germany launched over 3000 V-2 rockets, killing over 7250 people. Although impressive, they had no impact on the outcome of the war.

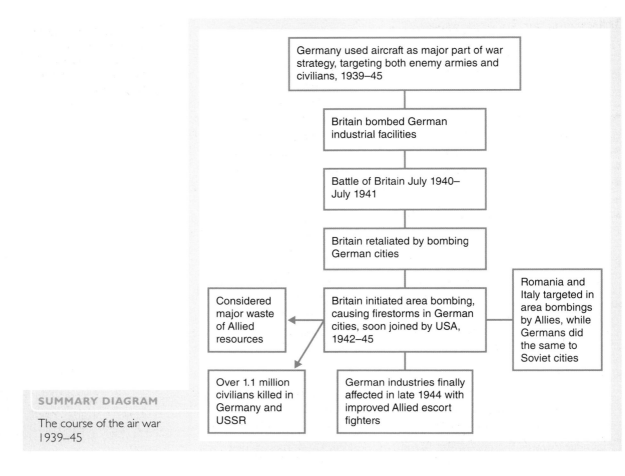

 Main Idea

Examples

(8) The course of the land war in Europe, June 1941 to May 1945

▶ **Key question:** *What events led to Germany's defeat in the Second World War?*

The Second World War in Europe became a global and total war in 1941 with Germany's invasion of the USSR and its declaration of war against the USA. By the end of 1942, Germany controlled much of the USSR's west, including its most valuable farmlands and industrial areas. Yet the USSR was not defeated and increasing war production by all Allied powers, as well as huge sacrifices by Soviet citizens and soldiers, stemmed the German advance in early 1943.

World war in Europe 1941–3

Why was Germany so successful in its invasion of the USSR from mid-1941 until early 1943?

With the fall of France and occupation of the Balkan peninsula (see page 133), Germany controlled much of northern, central, western and south-eastern Europe. Germany and its Axis partners feared the USSR, which had a massive population and growing industrial capacity. This was a threat that Germany intended to eliminate. Germany also planned to use Soviet territory for its own industrial and population needs. The USSR was not well prepared for a war with Germany. It had a large military that was poorly equipped and led and its political leadership believed that the Nazi–Soviet Pact (see page 121) was an agreement that Germany was unlikely to breach.

Operation Barbarossa, 22 June 1941

By June 1941, Germany controlled all central and western Europe. Britain, its only opponent, was bottled up on its home islands and unable to affect Germany's conduct of the war. Germany, for reasons that are not clear, decided to launch the largest invasion in history against the world's largest country: the USSR. On 22 June 1941, Operation Barbarossa began. Three million German troops with over 3500 tanks, 7100 large artillery units and 2000 aircraft moved into the USSR on a 1600-km front, known as the Eastern Front. Finland joined Germany on 25 June to reclaim recently lost territories.

SOURCE 1

Excerpt from a speech broadcast by radio by Vyacheslav Molotov, Foreign Minister of the USSR, to the people of the USSR on 22 June 1941. Located at Fordham University's Modern Internet History Sourcebook www.fordham.edu/Halsall/index.asp.

According to Source 1, how will the USSR achieve victory against Germany?

This is not the first time that our people have had to deal with an attack of an arrogant foe … The Red Army and our whole people will again wage victorious war for the fatherland, for our country, for honour, for liberty. The government of the Soviet Union expresses the firm conviction that the whole population of our country, all workers, peasants and intellectuals, men and women, will conscientiously perform their duties and do their work. Our entire people must now stand solid and united as never before. Each one of us must demand of himself and of others discipline, organization and self-denial worthy of real Soviet patriots, in order to provide for all the needs of the Red Army, Navy and Air Force, to ensure victory over the enemy. The government calls upon you, citizens of the Soviet Union, to rally still more closely around our glorious Bolshevist party, around our Soviet Government, around our great leader and comrade, Stalin. Ours is a righteous cause. The enemy shall be defeated. Victory will be ours.

Rapid German advance

The USSR's military and political leadership was caught completely by surprise, leading to the destruction or capture of huge tracts of territory, factories, airfields, cities and armies. On the first day, 25 per cent of the

USSR's air force was destroyed on the ground, approximately 1600 aircraft. German tanks advanced up to 80 km per day in the first weeks of the battle, encircling Soviet armies and destroying them. By 16 July, the main German army, called Army Group Centre, had advanced 650 km into the USSR, only 325 km from Moscow, the Soviet capital.

After a pause to resupply and reorganize its armies, Germany decided to focus on capturing the Ukrainian region. On 16 September, Army Group South captured Kiev, the region's capital, along with 665,000 Soviet troops. By 30 September, German Army Group South had moved forces towards Moscow to assist Army Group Centre. Other forces moved towards Kharkov, Belgorod and the Crimean peninsula.

Germany's Army Groups North and Centre continued to advance rapidly:

- 1 July: Riga, capital of formerly independent Latvia, captured
- 8 September: Leningrad surrounded and essentially besieged for next three years
- 30 September: German Operation Typhoon launched to capture Moscow with 600,000 Soviet troops captured in first week of campaign
- mid-November: German troops 32 km from Moscow.

[handwritten margin note: Examples of German success in Operation Barbarossa]

Results of Operation Barbarossa

The Soviets managed a massive counterattack on 6 December that prevented Moscow's capture by German forces, marking an end to Operation Barbarossa. The German campaign from 22 June to 6 December 1941 resulted in massive losses for the USSR and also for Germany and its allies (see table below).

Nation	Troops involved	Troops killed	Troops captured	Troops wounded	Aircraft/tanks lost
USSR	Around 8 million	3 million	3.5 million	Unknown	21,200/20,500
Germany and its allies	Around 4 million	250,000	Unknown	500,000	2100/2750

Although the USSR had lost tremendous numbers of soldiers, equipment and territory, it continued to fight. The German government initially believed that the USSR would be defeated by the end of September. This meant that the troops and the German economy were not initially prepared to fight a long war, giving the USSR the opportunity to organize some resistance by the very end of 1941.

[handwritten margin note: Assumption made by Germany]

Soviet resistance

Soviet resistance to the German invasion was a mixed one in the invasion's first months. Many who had suffered from Soviet policies, such as Ukrainians, either welcomed the German invasion or were indifferent. Those supportive of the government escaped the advancing Germans if they could, were captured and executed, or went into hiding to become the basis of

SOURCE J

Soviet soldiers surrendering to German tank crew in the southern USSR.

guerrilla groups that attacked pro-German Soviet citizens or Germans (see page 173). Soon after the invasion, the government understood that it was critical to save as much as possible of its manufacturing and industrial workers from being captured by Germany. A massive evacuation was launched; over 3000 factories were moved from the path of the advancing Germans by the end of 1941 alone, along with millions of people. These factories and workers would be critical to the outcome of the conflict.

> What information does Source J convey about fighting in the USSR at the end of 1941?

German offensives in the USSR 1942

Soviet counterattacks from January to March 1942 against German armies were all defeated, with the loss of almost a million troops. While Germany suffered over 250,000 deaths, it was still able to launch its military operation, named Case Blue, on 28 June 1942 against Stalingrad in the south to capture oilfields. Over a million German troops with 300,000 other Axis troops battled over 2,500,000 Soviet troops. By 9 August, German armies took control of the USSR's most western oilfields, having advanced over 600 km further into Soviet territory in just one month.

Stalingrad

Stalingrad was a major industrial city. Its capture would mean that Germany could stop oil shipments on the Volga that were bound for Soviet factories deep inside the country. In mid-September 1942, German troops occupied the vast majority of the city, although Soviet troops continued to fight, often occupying buildings or trenches just a few metres from German positions. As German troops were bogged down in urban combat, more were sent in to try to destroy Soviet resistance. This diversion of German troops into Stalingrad slowed other offensives to the south.

Operation Uranus, November 1942 to 31 January 1943

Ill-equipped, freezing and exhausted German troops were pinned down in Stalingrad by late November 1942. While Soviet soldiers held small parts of the city tenaciously, inflicting large numbers of casualties on the German military, Soviet armies prepared a counterattack to the north and south of Stalingrad. On 19 November, Operation Uranus began, taking the German military completely by surprise, trapping a large German army within Stalingrad that could no longer receive supplies or retreat, while still fighting for control of the city and suffering from winter conditions. Germans continued to battle for Stalingrad until 31 January 1943, when approximately 100,000 German soldiers surrendered. The Battle of Stalingrad left the city a total ruin and was one of the most destructive battles of the Second World War (see table below).

Nation	Killed	Wounded	Captured	Aircraft lost	Tanks lost	Artillery lost
Germany and Axis partners	750,000 (includes wounded)		~100,000	900	1,500	6,000
USSR	475,000	650,000	Unknown	2,800	4,300	15,700

This was the first major German or Axis defeat of the war in Europe and is considered a turning point of the Second World War between Germany and the USSR.

Soviet offensives, spring 1943

While Operation Uranus was in action against German and Axis troops at Stalingrad, the Soviets also launched attacks against other German and Axis armies. In these battles, the Soviets retook:

- Kursk on 8 February
- Rostov on 14 February
- Kharkov, the USSR's fourth-largest city, on 16 February.

A German counterattack recaptured Kharkov on 15 March and the city of Belgorod 80 km north on 18 March. The Soviets remained in possession of Kursk as warmer weather turned frozen ground into mud, preventing further German advances. By July, both the Soviets and Germans were prepared to continue the war as the ground dried.

Battle of Kursk, July–August 1943

Germany launched Operation Citadel on 5 July 1943, after assembling a large military force in order to drive Soviet armies back from the Kursk region. The Soviets, more confident after earlier successes and better equipped thanks to major industrial production, assembled an even larger force to oppose any German offensive, as well as to launch their own (see table below).

Nation	Soldiers	Tanks	Artillery units	Aircraft
Germany and Axis partners	900,000	2,700	10,000	2,000
USSR	1,300,000	3,400	19,000	2,900

[handwritten note: → USSR has greater advantage in every category]

Germany attacked from both the north and south to the east of Kursk, attempting to encircle the large Soviet army. The northern attack gained little ground and was fought to a standstill by 10 July.

Germany's southern operations were initially more successful. The southern German forces met a massive force of Soviet tanks on 12 July at Prokhorovka in the largest tank battle in history; 850 Soviet tanks battled 600 German ones. While bombers and fighters attacked each other's forces, tanks battled each other at close range. The battle was a mêlée with Soviet tanks ramming German tanks after running out of ammunition. Soviet tank crews, on foot, used grenades and petrol bombs to attack German tanks as well. By the day's end, thousands of German and Soviet dead were scattered around the battlefield, along with 700 destroyed tanks.

[handwritten note: ◦ Chaos]

This battle is considered by many historians as the second turning point of the Second World War in Europe, along with Stalingrad, as Germany was no longer able to mount successful, meaningful offensives; Soviet troops continually advanced against German and other Axis positions for the remainder of the war. While Soviet forces often overwhelmed German forces by sheer numbers and amount of equipment, they also used Germany's strategy of integrating their tanks and aircraft with infantry in rapid encirclements.

[handwritten note: → Countries began to pick up on Germany's tactics making them not as useful as before. It became like fighting fire with fire.]

Renewed Soviet offensives

Operations Kutuzov and Rumyantsev were launched against German troops north and south of Kursk on 12 July, even as the Battle of Kursk was being fought. This led to the capture of hundreds of thousands of German soldiers, as well as the cities of:

- Orel and Belgorod on 5 August
- Briansk on 18 August
- Kharkov on 28 August
- Kiev, the USSR's third largest city, on 6 November.

After July 1943, Germany was unable to initiate major offensive operations on the Eastern Front and for the remainder of the war conducted what at least one historian has referred to as a fighting retreat until its surrender in 1945.

Allied counterattack against the Axis in Europe 1943–45.

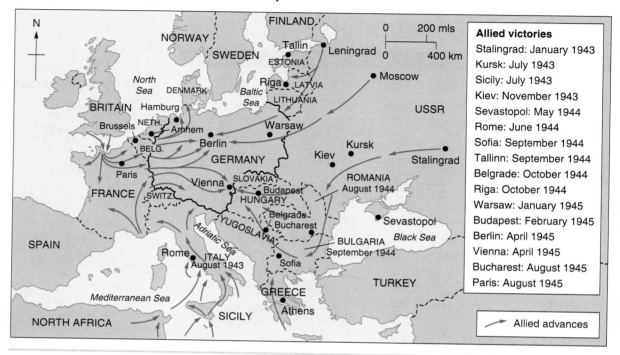

The war in Europe 1944–5

What were the main Allied offensives that led to Germany's defeat in May 1945?

The year 1944 was a critical one for the Allies as they neared victory. The USSR appeared unstoppable on the Eastern Front and in the Balkans, although fighting was still intense, with millions of casualties on both sides. While the Italian Front had stalled, the western Allies opened a Western Front in France.

Soviet offensives 1944–5

According to Source K, on which front did the Allies have the most success against Axis states?

In early 1944, Soviet forces concentrated on removing German armies from Ukraine, although there were offensives on all sections of the front that stretched north to south from Leningrad to the Black Sea. Unable to mount counterattacks, German troops essentially retreated west and south-west, while a large force was trapped on the Crimean peninsula. The main city in Crimea, Sevastopol, was captured by Soviet troops on 9 May 1944.

Operation Bagration, June–July 1944

Operation Bagration was launched by the USSR around the third anniversary of Germany's Operation Barbarossa. In an offensive closely co-ordinated with partisan guerrilla fighters, bomber aircraft, tanks, infantry and artillery, Soviet armies advanced 160 km into German-held territory over a 400-km front in two weeks, capturing 400,000 German troops. By the end of August, Soviet forces controlled eastern Poland as German armies retreated across the Vistula River. There was little movement on the Eastern Front in Poland for the remainder of 1944.

Balkan campaign 1944–5

An attack by the Soviet army in Romania led to the capture of 400,000 German and Axis troops. This led to a rapid series of events:

- 23 August: Romania left the Axis and joined the Allies
- 30 August: Soviet troops seized the Romanian oilfields, Germany's major source of oil
- 8 September: Bulgaria left the Axis, joined the Allies, and began an invasion of Yugoslavia
- 20 October: Belgrade, Yugoslavia's capital, fell to Soviet troops.

Parts of Hungary were entered in September 1944, but fierce fighting by German and Hungarian troops meant that Budapest was only encircled on 26 December, after the rest of the country had been occupied. Fighting ended there on 11 February 1945.

Reason for German defeat: nation's leaving the Axis left Germany vunerable in 2 ways: less troops less supplies

Baltic campaign, 20 June 1944 to January 1945

In June 1944, Soviet troops began a massive attack on German and Finnish troops besieging Leningrad. On 20 and 21 June, Soviet armies moved against the Finns, driving them back from north of the city and allowing in desperately needed supplies. Tallinn, Estonia's German-occupied capital, was captured on 22 September. Riga, capital of Latvia, fell on 15 October and Memel, on the Baltic Sea and German territory, was placed under siege in late October, finally falling to the Soviets at the end of January 1945.

Battle of Berlin, 20 April to 2 May 1945

In January 1945, Soviet forces crossed the Vistula River, trapping a German army in East Prussia. The Oder River was reached at the end of January; here, the Soviets paused briefly to clear the region of German troops.

On 16 April, Soviet troops crossed the Oder River and moved into Germany, driving towards Berlin, the German capital. Hitler, Germany's leader, remained in the city in an underground bunker, directing troops until he killed himself on 29 April. Berlin was finally secured by Soviet forces on 2 May 1945, with 81,000 Soviet and Polish dead and almost 300,000 wounded. Over 100,000 German soldiers may have been killed; with hundreds of thousands surrendered to the Soviets.

The Western Front 1944–5

At the **Tehran Conference** at the end of 1943, the leaders of Britain, the USA and the USSR agreed that a second front against Germany would be opened in the west. In June 1944, British, Canadian and US troops began the invasion of the French Normandy coast, codenamed Operation Overlord, opening this second front. This invasion meant that desperately needed troops for Germany's Eastern Front now remained in western Europe, allowing the Soviets to advance more quickly.

> 🔑 **KEY TERM**
>
> **Tehran Conference**
> Conference held in Tehran, Iran, from 28 November 1943 where the Allies agreed to start a front against Germany in western Europe.

Soviet military forces at the German *Reichstag* during the Battle of Berlin, 1 May 1945.

?

What does Source L indicate about the nature of warfare on the Eastern Front?

The invasion of Normandy, June 1944   ↗ D-day

A massive amphibious assault began on 6 June 1944. Over 4000 Allied ships transported 160,000 British, Canadian and US troops to Normandy in northern France while 1200 warships and bombers bombarded German shore defences. At the end of the day, the Allies had captured all five beaches that had been stormed, with only 3000 dead or captured. By 4 July, a million Allied troops were in France, conducting offensives against Germany.

France and Belgium, August–December 1944

On 15 August, another Allied army landed in southern France during Operation Dragoon, driving out German forces in the region within two weeks. On 25 August, Paris, capital of France, was occupied by the Allies. With minor exceptions, German troops were forced from most of France and Belgium, as well as southern parts of The Netherlands by December 1944.

Battle of the Bulge, December 1944 to January 1945

Germany launched a massive counterattack, the Von Rundstedt Offensive, on Allied positions through the Ardennes Forest starting on 16 December

1944. Known as the Battle of the Bulge by the Allies since it caused a bulge in the front against Germany, the attack was a complete surprise for them. The German offensive ended by early January and by 25 January had lost all territory gained since mid-December. The Battle of the Bulge cost Germany tanks, soldiers and supplies it was unable to replenish, but it did slow the Allied advance along the Western Front.

Final offensives on the Western Front 1945

Allied troops entered Germany at various points in early 1945, fighting intense battles as German troops slowly withdrew further into Germany and across the River Rhine. By March, US troops had crossed the Rhine on **pontoon bridges** and poured into Germany along a 320-km wide front as German troops surrendered in large numbers. The industrialized Ruhr Valley was encircled on 1 April and throughout April major cities were captured as German troops continued to surrender. On 25 April, the Elbe River was crossed. Allied forces on the Western Front did not advance towards Berlin, having agreed earlier that the German capital would be captured by the USSR attacking from the east.

Germany surrenders, May 1945

After Germany's leader, Hitler, killed himself on 29 April 1945, his authority was transferred to Grand Admiral Karl Dönitz. On 4 May, German troops in The Netherlands, Denmark and north-western Germany surrendered. On 7 May, German General Jodl, under orders from Dönitz, signed the German Instrument of surrender in which Germany agreed to cease fighting and **unconditionally surrender** on 8 May 1945, ending the war in Europe. Soon afterwards Dönitz and all members of his cabinet were arrested and all of Germany was occupied. At the war's end, German troops still occupied Norway, most of today's Czech Republic, Austria, and today's Slovenia, northern Italy, part of Estonia and the British Channel Islands.

Post-war trials

German political and military leaders were imprisoned at the war's conclusion and prosecuted for war crimes. From November 1945 to October 1946, the first set of Nuremburg Trials took place in Germany of 24 men, most of whom were found guilty and executed, although a few did receive prison sentences. Further trials at Nuremburg continued until 1949 with 24 more condemned to death and others receiving prison sentences of varying length; 35 were acquitted. Poland tried German officials for the Holocaust (see page 167) at the **Auschwitz** Trials held from November to December 1947; almost all were executed. The Dachau Trials were held at the concentration camp of Dachau by the USA from 1945 to 1948. Over 1600 Germans were tried for war crimes at Dachau, with over 1400 found guilty; 279 were executed and the others received prison sentences. Trials were also held at the concentration camps of Ravensbrück and Bergen-Belsen, and summary executions of former German government officials and military officers were carried out throughout eastern Europe.

 **KEY TERM**

Pontoon bridge
Temporary bridge built on floating supports.

Unconditional surrender
An act of surrender in which you place yourself completely under the control of your opponent.

Auschwitz Germany's largest concentration camp, located in Poland, where over one million people, primarily Jews, were killed during the Second World War.

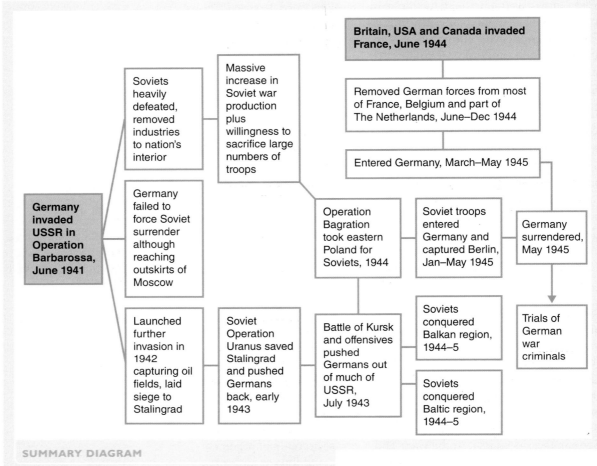

The course of the land war in Europe, June 1941 to May 1945

 Outcomes and conclusions: reasons for German defeat

> ▶ **Key question:** Why did Germany lose the Second World War in Europe?

Historians continue to debate the reasons for Germany's defeat in the Second World War.

To what extent did Germany's Axis partners contribute to the war effort?

Weak Axis partners in Europe

It is commonly acknowledged that Germany's Axis partners contributed little to the overall war effort and probably hindered Germany instead. Evidence for this argument is Italy's failure to conquer Greece without major German assistance, as well as Italy's failed invasion of Egypt. Germany's initial war plans did not even consider Italy, the largest and most capable Axis partner in Europe, and Italy worked to convince Germany not to begin a war against Poland, stating that it was not ready to fight any conflict. Italy had nothing to do with the invasions of Poland, Denmark, Norway, The Netherlands, Belgium or Luxembourg and only attacked France in June 1940 after France had been all but defeated by Germany.

Slovakia, Hungary, Bulgaria and Romania provided over a million troops for the Eastern Front where they assisted German efforts to defeat the USSR. These troops were generally poorly trained and ill-equipped and contributed little to German success. Japan, Germany's Asian Axis partner, never declared war on the USSR, leaving Germany to face practically the entire Soviet army on the Eastern Front.

War production

War production was critical to the outcome of the war (see page 166).

← **How did war production affect the war's outcome?**

German failures

Germany failed to fully mobilize its industry until 1943, partly because the government did not want to inconvenience its citizens and partly because the government was disorganized, with various departments and ministries competing for limited resources and funds. Several historians have noted that Germany produced a wide range of weapons, including several hundred types of aircraft and a large variety of submarines. This meant that time, funds and resources needed in mass production were instead being siphoned off through experimentation. Creating a wide variety of models meant that parts were not interchangeable when breakdowns occurred and it was difficult for armies to stockpile and manage large varieties of parts while also conducting war.

Several historians have pointed out that although Germany conquered much of Europe, these territories were never fully integrated into the German economy. This has become another argument that Germany did not plan for the Second World War since there appeared to be little to no planning for economic exploitation.

Allied economic success

The Allies, in contrast, had practically unlimited resources. The USA and USSR were huge nations with hundreds of millions of people who could fight and work. Both nations were well organized for war production. The USA had long been the world's largest economy, with tremendous infrastructure and manufacturing capability. It was also the world's largest supplier of oil at the time. The USSR had accidentally prepared itself to survive a huge invasion by economically reorganizing itself in the 1930s. During a series of **Five-Year Plans**, the Soviet economy built thousands of factories, expanded mining operations, and moved much of its industry into central Asia, far from potential European threats and closer to the sources of

 **KEY TERM**

Five Year Plans Economic programmes of the USSR which initially focused on mass industrialization.

its raw mineral wealth. This rigid control of the Soviet economy gave the government the ability to rapidly increase war production while allowing Soviet industries to be evacuated from the path of German armies.

Many historians believe that Allied war production was the critical factor in the defeat of the Axis.

Why did Germany's military strategies fail to bring victory?

→ Failed strategy

Historians have long recognized that Germany was successful in its first years of campaigning in Europe as a result of its highly developed *blitzkrieg* tactics (see page 127). Problems arose when adaptations for this were required. Britain was an island and could not easily be invaded, so it was bombed by German aircraft that were designed and trained for working in tandem with land forces. This failed to force Britain's surrender and led directly to the bombing of its own cities in retaliation.

Invasion of USSR

The invasion of the USSR was initially very successful, cutting off and destroying huge Soviet armies. The rapid advance, however, meant that supply lines were over-extended, slowing the German invasion, giving the Soviets time to recover, and giving Polish and Soviet resistance guerrillas ample targets which further affected the German assault. Germany had not planned for a long-term invasion that would go into winter and which would require extensive supplies. Evidence of this is:

- It delayed effort in full war production.
- Germany failed to produce enough trucks and used horses to transport most of its war supplies to the front lines
- German troops fighting deep in the USSR lacked winter gear; many thousands died from exposure.

SOURCE M

According to Source M, how did Germany help Britain to achieve victory?

Excerpt from *The Origins of the Second World War* by A.J.P. Taylor, republished by Penguin Books, London, 1991, page 336.

The British people resolved to defy Hitler, though they lacked the strength to undo his work. He himself came to their aid. His success depended on the isolation of Europe from the rest of the world. He gratuitously destroyed the source of this success. In 1941 he attacked Soviet Russia and declared war on the United States, two World Powers who asked only to be left alone. In this way a real world war began.

Hitler's military decisions

Germany's leader, Hitler, may have been critical in the defeat of Germany against the USSR. He was not only the political leader of Germany, but also the head of all the armed forces. He had little military training or knowledge, yet directed much of Germany's war effort. He seems to have been responsible for the idea of invading France and Belgium through the

Ardennes Forest, which helped to defeat France rapidly in 1940. This made him confident that he was wiser than many of his generals. He refused to allow any form of retreat, even when it was clearly the best way to preserve Germany's armed forces in several important battles, especially Stalingrad and Kursk. With Germany's lower ability than the USSR to produce tanks, aircraft was and other war supplies, these losses were significant, as was the fact that its most experienced troops were killed or captured in these stands. Hitler's decisions were probably, at least in part, determined by National Socialist racial theory which held that Germans were a superior race to other nationalities, including Slavs who formed the majority population in eastern Europe. Generals were often replaced since he could not believe that German defeats could actually come at the hands of the racially inferior, further weakening the military.

SOURCE N

Excerpt from *Hitler's Stalingrad Decisions* by Geoffrey Jukes, published by University of California Press, Berkeley, California, 1985, pages 74–5.

[Hitler's] view of [the generals] as timid and unimaginative is more likely to derive from the ease with which he outwitted them politically after 1933, and their reluctance to support his political use of military power. In the reoccupation of the Rhineland in 1936, and in the invasions of Austria (1938) and Czechoslovakia (1939), he demonstrated that their misgivings were wrong. And in military matters, particularly in adopting new doctrines of tank warfare, in preferring [General] Manstein's plan for the invasion of France to that drawn up by the General Staff in 1940, and in refusing to sanction a general withdrawal on the Moscow front in 1941, his judgment had proved superior to the conventional wisdom of the senior officers.

... Hitler had enlarged the scope of operations [in the Soviet Union] beyond those envisaged in the original Staff plan, and had attempted to compress the time scale by mounting operations against Stalingrad and the Caucasus simultaneously rather than in sequence ... All the dismissals of senior officers were attributed by Hitler to one or the other cause. Underlying it all was an erosion of his self-confidence by the fact that for once military caution and conservatism were proving more correct than the bolder course which ... prevailed in the past ... It led him with increasing frequency to substitute his judgment for theirs, to dismiss them rather than change plans, to interfere with the detailed execution of operations ...

> **Why, according Source N, did Hitler not trust army leaders?**

USSR as the cause of German defeat

> **To what extent was Germany's defeat the result of Soviet strength?**

Many historians have come to believe that although Germany had various weaknesses that made defeat in the long term likely, it was actually the USSR that caused Germany's defeat. Not only did it have a huge population and major industrial capacity located deep inside the country, and covered a vast territory which made it difficult to conquer, it had a nationalistic people and a government willing to sacrifice them. Tens of millions of malnourished women, children and elderly men laboured in factories. Hundreds of thousands of resistance fighters fought the Germans, and other groups, with great tenacity, knowing that they would be executed if captured. Soviet soldiers fought bravely and ferociously, as clearly demonstrated at Stalingrad and Kursk (see pages 151 and 152). It is possible that many of these people participated so fully in the war out of fear of their own government, but it is now understood that probably the vast majority fought for fear of Germany as atrocities became more widely known, and out of a sense of nationalism. It is estimated that 80 per cent of all Germans killed and wounded, as well as captured and destroyed war equipment, were at the hands of the USSR.

According to Source O, how are German arguments countered that state that the war was lost because of its own weakness and not by the success of other nations?

SOURCE O

Excerpt from *Russia's War* by Richard Overy, published by Penguin Books, London, 2010, pages 327–8.

… the Soviet Union ought by rights to have been defeated in the war, but it prevailed triumphantly and comprehensively. Of course, the Soviet Union was not acting alone. Without the division of German energies prompted by the bombing campaign of the Mediterranean theatre the outcome would have been much less certain, perhaps very different. Nonetheless, the bulk of the damage inflicted on German forces was in the eastern campaign – 80 per cent of their battle casualties – and it was here that the overwhelming weight of the [German army] was concentrated until 1944. Nor can the German dimension be ignored. After the war German generals were quick to argue that Hitler's wayward leadership and shortages of equipment made defeat inevitable: Germany lost the war, the Soviet Union did not win it. This view fits ill with the facts. German generals rode to war in 1941 confident that victory was a matter of weeks (eight to ten at most) against the 'ill-educated, half-Asiatic' Russian fighters, and against Soviet commanders 'even less of a threat than … Tsarist Russian generals.' These judgements were almost borne out by events. The defeat of German forces required something German leaders never anticipated: that the Soviet Union would recover its economic strength, reform its armed forces and produce leaders of remarkable quality.

How significant were US and British actions in Germany's defeat, according to some historians?

The role of the USA and Britain in defeating Germany

Some historians have come to the belief not only that the Soviets defeated Germany almost single-handedly, but also that the western Allies, specifically Britain and the USA, played a far less important role than previously assumed. It seems undeniable that US war production assisted the USSR in a substantial way. Bombing Germany, however, produced few results until late in 1944 when Soviet armies were all but on the German border.

While the US, British and Canadian invasions of France in June 1944 certainly pinned down German forces that could have been used against the rapidly advancing USSR, it must be remembered that by this time the Soviets were at the outskirts of Warsaw and only a few hundred kilometres from Berlin. It may be that the most significant result of the western Allied invasion of western Europe was to prevent these areas becoming dominated by the USSR, as happened in most of central and eastern Europe.

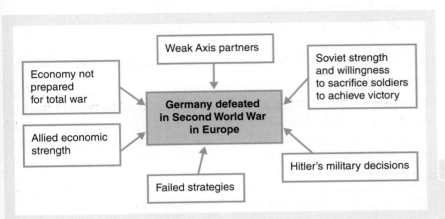

SUMMARY DIAGRAM

Outcomes and conclusions: reasons for German defeat

The home front and occupied Europe

> ▶ **Key question:** *How were civilians affected by the Second World War in Europe?*

The Second World War affected civilians in warring nations on an unprecedented scale. Millions were mobilized for war production, tens of millions were left homeless, and almost every nation rationed food and fuel and produced few consumer goods. Women were critical workers and many in the USSR served as soldiers. Millions of people were imprisoned and millions more were killed. Guerrilla resistance movements fought invaders, and sometimes each other. War production occurred on a massive scale, helping to bring defeat to the Axis nations.

Women in war

Women were affected by the war in different ways, depending on their particular nation's views regarding women. While women joined practically all resistance movements, they participated most fully in war production. Only in the USSR were women allowed to participate as combat troops, while other nations had women performing other roles in the armed forces so that men could be sent to various fronts.

> ← **To what extent did women contribute to their nations' war efforts?**

Germany

The German government resisted calls to increase the participation of women in industrial production at the war's beginning. This was based on the idea that women should be at home raising children and performing domestic duties. Although this was government policy, the German economy in the late 1930s required more workers so that in 1939, 14,600,000 women were working outside the home. This was 37 per cent of all workers, a higher proportion than many other nations in 1939, including Britain. During the war, approximately 250,000 more German women entered the workforce, primarily in agriculture. At no point were women allowed any form of military service.

Instead of recruiting German women into industry, the government turned to foreign workers. By 1943, 20 per cent of all workers in Germany were from other countries. While some of these workers had been specifically recruited, most were forced to come to Germany or were prisoners of war.

Britain

Britain employed millions of women in industry during the war. In early 1941, all women aged 18–60 were required to register with the government in preparation for being conscripted into the industrial workforce. By 1943, 90 per cent of all unmarried and 80 per cent of all married women were in jobs related to the war effort. By the end of the war, 6.5 million British women were employed in factories or shipyards producing war goods. Although women made a significant contribution to Britain's war effort, they continued to face discrimination in terms of wages, which were significantly lower than those of their male counterparts.

Britain also recruited women for non-combat military work. By 1943, 180,000 women were members of the Women's Auxiliary Air Force, working at radar stations, erecting **barrage balloons**, and working with anti-aircraft artillery. Approximately 100,000 women served in a variety of jobs in the Women's Royal Naval Service (WRNS). Women in the WRNS worked mostly as drivers, cleaners and cooks, but some operated small harbour ships and anti-aircraft artillery and worked as mechanics. Over 200,000 women served in the Auxiliary Territorial Service as mechanics, drivers, cleaners and cooks and in other occupations for the military that were all non-combat related. There were 90,000 women serving in the Women's Land Army, which placed women on farms to replace male labourers who had gone into the military. In 1945, 460,000 women were employed in non-combat work for various military services.

USSR

The USSR employed women in greater numbers than any other nation involved in the Second World War. With tens of millions of men conscripted for military service, women, old men and children provided most of the country's workforce. Almost all agricultural labourers were women and so many animals were taken from farms that teams of women pulled farm equipment to till fields.

Over 800,000 women served in the Soviet armed forces during the Second World War. Three military aircraft units were composed entirely of women, including pilots, crews and mechanics. These air units completed over 50,000 missions against Axis targets from 1942 to 1945. Hundreds of thousands of women served in the army as well, where many found success as snipers. By 1945, over 40 per cent of all army doctors were women and many anti-aircraft batteries were manned by women. Many tank crews were entirely composed of women and by the end of the war, 500,000 women remained in uniform, helping to carry out the occupation of Germany.

USA

Large numbers of American women joined the industrial workforce and joined non-combat military units (see page 214).

Rationing

Rationing occurred in all countries participating in the war, but rationing was introduced at varying times and in varying quantities depending on the nation and the year of the war.

How were civilians affected by rationing programmes?

Britain

At the outset of the war in Britain, all oil-based products, such as rubber and fuel, were severely rationed and by January 1940 certain food products were also rationed, such as sugar and butter. Soon this was extended to almost all food products, except fish. In 1942, petrol could no longer be purchased by civilians. Up to 50 per cent of all industry in Britain was devoted to war production, providing few consumer goods for civilian consumption.

USSR

Rationing in the USSR was severe and necessarily so as the most productive agricultural land was quickly seized by German armies in 1941. Peasants who normally farmed were enrolled in military units or conscripted to work in factories to produce war goods. Children and the elderly were granted 700 calories of food daily, while adult factory workers received an average of 1500 calories daily. Men who worked in coalmines received over 4000 calories per day since the entire war effort rested on the fuel from the coal they excavated. With the entire population constantly on the verge of starvation, five million small gardens were established in cities throughout the USSR in parks and on any spare patch of ground. Food remained so scarce in 1944 that one kilogram of bread cost the equivalent of a week's wages in factory work, if purchased illegally.

Italy

Italy was one of the least prepared countries during the Second World War. Rationing began in 1939, even before Italy joined the war in 1940. In 1941, civilians were no longer able to purchase petrol, newspapers were limited to two pages, and each citizen was only allowed either one pair of shoes or a few pieces of clothing annually – but not both. Those living in cities lived on less than 1000 calories daily towards the end of the war.

Germany

Germany began food rationing in late August 1939, just before it invaded Poland. These initial restrictions were mostly minor inconveniences but as the war continued, calorie intake decreased from an average of 3000 daily in 1939 to 2000 daily by 1944. Germans generally ate better than those people in other European countries since food shipments were sent from occupied territories such as Poland, France and the USSR. Germans faced severe shortages of formerly imported products such as fruit and sugar. After early 1943, when Germany increasingly shifted towards full military production, fewer consumer products were available. By the end of 1944, the German economy was in a state of collapse as the transportation system was heavily bombed and fuel supplies for industrial production were destroyed or no longer available.

USA

Rationing occurred in the USA as well (see page 218).

To what extent did the Allies produce more war goods than the Axis nations in Europe?

War production

Many historians believe that Allied war production, particularly by the USA, provided the means to defeat Germany. German war production was substantial, but that of its Axis partners was not conducted on a level to have a significant impact on the war.

The Allies

US military production was critical to the Allied war effort; almost 30 per cent of all British military equipment was made in the USA. Lend–Lease supplies to the USSR demonstrated the importance and scale of US industry for the war effort:

- 400,000 motor vehicles, primarily trucks
- 2000 locomotive engines
- 11,000 locomotive freight cars
- 540,000 tons of locomotive rails
- food supplies capable of feeding the entire Soviet army.

While the USA produced tremendous amounts of war goods, Britain and the USSR also contributed. Britain employed 33 per cent of the adult population for war production and in the USSR there was mass conscription of children, women and the elderly to staff factories that increased production constantly throughout the war, even as workers starved.

the difference

SOURCE P

War production for the Second World War in Europe and north Africa.

	USA*	Britain	USSR	Germany	Italy
Tanks	88,500	30,000	105,000	67,000	2,500
Aircraft	300,000	130,000	145,000	120,000	11,000
Artillery units	257,000	125,000	500,000	160,000	7,200
Trucks	2,400,000	480,000	200,000	345,000	83,000
Machine guns	2,700,000	NA	1,500,000	675,000	NA
Submarine	200	170	NA	1,100	28
Surface warships	1,200	730	NA	42	15
Tons of merchant shipping	34,000,000	6,300,000	NA	NA	1,500,000
Tons of coal	2,100,000,000	1,400,000,000	590,000,000	2,400,000,000	17,000,000
Tons of iron ore	400,000,000	120,000,000	71,000,000	240,000,000	4,000,000
Tons of oil	830,000,000	91,000,000	110,000,000	33,000,000	0
NA, not available.					
*Production for the simultaneous war in Asia and the Pacific.					

The Axis

German production was disorganized in the first years of the war. Private industries competed for contracts and raw materials, and to have various weapon designs approved. In 1942, industry was reorganized, with the government directing all production. This led to increased production and the need for more workers (see page 164). After February 1943, the German economy was officially placed on a war footing for the first time. This led to further government control of production and a severe reduction in non-war production. Germany was by far the most industrialized Axis nation, easily out-producing its allies. Italy's contribution to Axis industrial production, until it joined the Allies in 1943, was the most substantial of any Axis partner with the exception of Japan (see page 219). Romania contributed a significant 25 million tonnes of oil while it was a member of the Axis.

> According to Source P, how did German war production compare to that of Allied nations?

Imprisonment and extermination

← Why did the war lead to the imprisonment and death of many civilians and prisoners of war?

More civilians and troops were imprisoned during the Second World War in Europe than any other conflict in history. While most prisoners survived, tens of millions were killed, many intentionally.

The Holocaust

In the 1930s, Germany enacted laws against its Jewish citizens, about one per cent of the population. State policy became increasingly discriminatory and Jewish-owned businesses and other assets were seized by the state in 1938. Violence against Jews and their property culminated on 9 November 1938 when 100 German Jews were killed, synagogues were destroyed, and homes and businesses looted. The German public reacted negatively to the violence, which limited any further violent display by the government. Naturally, many Jews left the country, moving to France, The Netherlands and elsewhere. At this early stage, government policy was to force Jews to emigrate from the country.

Germany controlled much of Europe, along with its Axis partners, by July 1940. Millions of Jews were located in these territories, causing German policy towards them to evolve. Many Jews in Poland were at first required to live in walled-in areas of cities in eastern Poland. Later, they were moved to an area south of the city of Lublin. The German government continued to be unsure of what to do with these millions of prisoners and even considered sending four million of them to Madagascar just to be rid of them. The invasion of the USSR in June 1941 changed the German government's actions in a fundamental way. Whereas before, Jews were imprisoned and suffered humiliation, starvation and violence, Jews discovered in the USSR were killed out of hand. Special military units were created for this purpose and 500,000 Soviet Jews were killed in the winter of 1941–2 as their areas came under German control.

In 1942, a new, and final, German policy for Jews in Europe was determined. Jews who were capable of work were to be worked to death and those incapable of contributing to war production were to be exterminated. Hundreds of **labour camps** and **death camps** were constructed and are often referred to as concentration camps. Millions of Jews throughout Europe were moved into the camps, along with homosexuals, Roma, those with Arab or African ancestry, Jehovah's Witnesses, criminals, the mentally ill, many Roman Catholic priests and prisoners of war. While it is not known exactly how many people were imprisoned, died or even survived, it is estimated that around six million Jews were killed, around 60 per cent of

What, according to Source Q, would be the result of allowing homosexual Germans?

SOURCE Q

Excerpt from a speech by Heinrich Himmler on 18 February 1937 located in Fordham University's Modern Internet History Sourcebook www.fordham.edu/Halsall/index.asp. Himmler was Chief of German Police and Minister of the Interior from 1943 to 1945 and in charge of establishing the concentration camp system and therefore architect of the Holocaust.

A nation with many children can gain supremacy and mastery of the world. A pure race with few children already has one foot in the grave; in fifty or a hundred years it will be of no significance; in two hundred years it will be extinct. It is essential to realise that if we allow this infection [homosexuality] to continue in Germany without being able to fight it, it will be the end of Germany, of the Germanic world … It is vital we rid ourselves of [homosexuals]; like weeds we must pull them up, throw them on the fire and burn them. This is not out of a spirit of vengeance, but of necessity; these creatures must be exterminated.

Europe's Jewish population. Poland, where millions of Jews lived before the Second World War, lost over 90 per cent of its Jewish population. Over five million non-Jews are estimated to have also died in concentration camps. This destruction of millions of people is known as the Holocaust.

Prisoners of war

Millions of soldiers were captured by both the Axis and Allied forces during the Second World War in Europe. Their fate as prisoners often depended on their nationality and by whom they were captured.

Germany

Allied prisoners of Germany were treated in various ways depending on their nationality. British and US prisoners, for example, were often simply imprisoned and not sent to labour camps. This was the result of National Socialist racial policies that saw the British and white American citizens as racially kin to Germans, if not outright Germans. The only exceptions to this policy were those of Jewish and African descent who were considered racially inferior and sent to concentration camps or killed outright. Conditions for all British and US prisoners worsened towards the end of the war when food rations were reduced and many were forced to march long distances to keep ahead of advancing Allied armies. It is estimated that Germany captured around 250,000 British and US soldiers during the war, with fewer than 10,000 dying.

Germany and its Axis partners treated Soviet prisoners of war poorly. Almost six million Soviet and Polish soldiers were captured during the war, with at least three million dying in prison camps. The vast majority of these prisoners starved or froze to death in appalling conditions, while others were forced into labouring for German war production in concentration camps. After the war ended, Soviet prisoners returned home, where the government punished them for not having fought to their deaths. These men were mostly sent to Soviet prison camps for years after the war.

USSR

Soviet troops captured over three million German soldiers during the war. Until 1943, most prisoners froze or starved to death as the USSR barely had enough food or clothing for its own population. The brutality of the German military towards Soviet citizens, as well as prisoners of war, meant that German prisoners could only expect harsh treatment as well. German prisoners were sent to labour camps to work in Soviet war production factories. It is estimated that 350,000 prisoners of the Soviets died during the war years, with more afterwards since the USSR did not release its prisoners immediately at the end of the war. The last German prisoners were released in 1956. While Germans were the largest nationality of those in Soviet custody, over a million more prisoners were captured by the Soviets, with over 130,000 dying during the war.

Britain, Canada and the USA

Britain was reluctant to keep many German and Axis prisoners in the country, until 1943 when the threat of an invasion was reduced. Earlier, Britain sent the majority of captured enemy soldiers to Canada where they were interned. By the end of the war, Britain had over 600 locations where German prisoners were kept, including old factories and hotels, as well as specially constructed facilities. German prisoners were given the option of remaining in detention or helping with agricultural and construction work, which many accepted. Most German prisoners received the same food rations as British soldiers. Over 500,000 Germans were interned in the USA. As in Britain, prisoners worked in agriculture and other industries.

Internment of foreign nationals

In most countries during the war, many civilians found themselves in countries that were at war with their homelands. In addition, citizens of many countries had their loyalty questioned. Hundreds of thousands of these people, labelled 'enemy aliens', were imprisoned by all nations participating in the war. France arrested and imprisoned all German males at the start of the war, as did Belgium and The Netherlands when they were attacked. The USA imprisoned thousands of Germans and Italians, including US citizens, as well as a large number of US citizens of Japanese descent (see page 221). This pattern was repeated throughout Europe and north Africa. Many thousands of civilian prisoners died during the war through forced labour, diseases such as typhoid, and starvation, although most in the USA, Britain and Egypt fared better. Most lost homes and businesses, and in many cases returned to devastated countries.

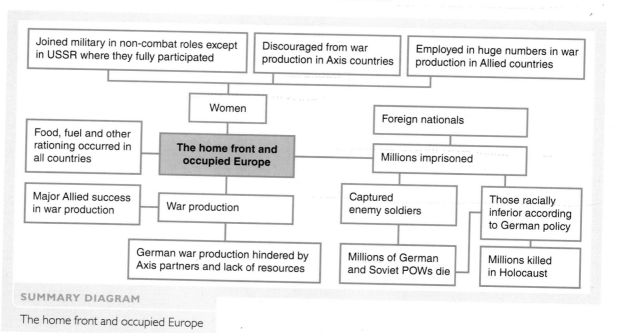

SUMMARY DIAGRAM

The home front and occupied Europe

11 Resistance movements

▶ **Key question:** How effective were resistance movements in Europe during the Second World War?

Throughout Europe there was resistance to foreign occupation and forced labour. Resistance took many forms, including refusal to purchase German-produced goods, hiding Jews, listening to foreign radio stations and spying. Armed resistance movements developed in many countries, especially those occupied by Germany and other Axis powers. These groups used guerrilla tactics to disrupt Axis activities and military operations: sabotaging production, operating spy networks and leading open rebellions with urban fighting in some cases.

Poland

Many anti-German and anti-Soviet resistance movements developed during the war in Poland. These groups provided critical military intelligence which helped the Allies to win the war, as well as severely hindering the passage of German supplies bound for the Eastern Front.

How successful were Polish resistance movements?

Polish Home Army

The largest and most successful Polish resistance group was the Home Army, or *Armia Krajowa* (AK). The AK was allied with the Polish government-in-exile and was the largest, most active of all resistance movements. AK spies provided the Allies with tremendous amounts of secret information on Germany and its military operations. AK units routinely disrupted German supply convoys that crossed Poland on their way to troops in the USSR. Railways were attacked frequently, delaying or destroying desperately needed supplies required by German armies operating further east.

In July 1944, AK-led uprisings began in cities and districts in eastern Poland, assisting Soviet troops. The most spectacular action of the AK was the Warsaw Uprising of 1 August 1944, when AK troops took control of most of Poland's capital without assistance or aid from nearby Soviet troops. After 63 days of heavy fighting, on 2 October, AK troops surrendered. Over 15,000 AK soldiers had been killed, along with 225,000 civilians. What had not been destroyed in the fighting was mostly levelled by the German military.

It is estimated that the AK killed around 150,000 Axis soldiers during the conflict and that up to 900,000 German soldiers remained in Poland to counter the AK, preventing their use against the Allies elsewhere.

ŻOB and ŻZW

In addition to the AK, two Jewish resistance groups were organized in Poland during the war. The Jewish Combat Organization, or *Żydowska Organizacja Bojowa* (ŻOB), and the Jewish Military Union, or *Żydowski*

Związek Wojskowy (ŻZW), were the two most prominent of these resistance groups. The ŻOB was formed by Jewish youths in Warsaw who joined the AK, receiving weapons and becoming an armed force in December 1942. The ŻZW was formed by Jews who had been military officers in the Polish army in November 1939 and, by 1942, the ŻZW had small cells in major cities throughout Poland, including 500 members in Warsaw. The ŻOB, ŻZW, AK and communist guerrillas revolted against Germany's attempt to remove the remaining Jewish population in the **Warsaw Ghetto** in April 1943, when hundreds of resistance fighters were joined by thousands of civilians in a battle against German troops. By the time fighting ended on 16 May, 13,000 had been killed in the ghetto and over 50,000 Jews were captured and sent to the Treblinka death camp, where they were killed.

Why were the Partisans the most successful of Yugoslavia's many resistance groups?

Yugoslavia

Yugoslavia was invaded in April 1941 and then dismantled as its territory was divided into many new puppet-states and annexed to various Axis nations. Never particularly united before the conflict, the former country was in a state of civil war throughout the remainder of the Second World War.

Chetniks

Ultra-nationalist Serbs formed several groups called *Chetniks*. These units, operating mostly independently, fought with and against many other groups throughout the war, including the Italians, Germans, Croats, communist guerrillas and others. Their lack of organization and constantly changing alliances eventually made them vulnerable to other groups who were more successful in gaining control of Yugoslavia towards the end of the war in 1945.

Balli Kombëtar

Balli Kombëtar was an Albanian nationalist group that fought other groups in Yugoslavia in order to bring regions of that country where Albanians lived into an enlarged Albania. They battled *Chetniks*, Croat nationalists and communist groups from both Yugoslavia and within Albania. Greek nationalists who desired expansion of Greece into Albanian-occupied regions were also targeted. *Balli Kombëtar* co-operated with Germany, which armed them, and formed armed units that joined the German military organization.

Independent State of Croatia

Although not a resistance group, Croatia fielded an army of over 50,000 men, as well as military aircraft. Much of this force battled communist partisans, *Chetniks* and others from 1940 until 1945, adding to the chaotic military situation in the Yugoslav region during the war.

Partisans

The National Liberation Army and Partisan Detachments of Yugoslavia, or Partisans, were a large communist resistance movement led by Josip Broz, more commonly known as Tito. These communists conducted guerrilla warfare against all other groups for control of Yugoslavia and were provided with weapons by Britain and the USSR. By 1943, the Partisans had a membership of around 225,000, which meant that Germany had to keep a large military presence in the country, preventing these forces from moving to the Eastern Front where they were desperately needed. In October 1944, the Partisans captured Belgrade, Yugoslavia's capital, and controlled most of the country's east, south and south-west coast. In early 1945, the Partisans numbered at least 800,000 and defeated Croatia's military and German forces remaining in the country. By the time Germany surrendered in early May 1945, the Partisans controlled all Yugoslavia and the easternmost areas of Italy.

France

There were many groups in France that resisted German occupation and the Vichy French government that was associated with Germany. Acts of sabotage against military production, the destruction of war supplies and attacks on railways were some of the activities of French resistance movements. By the end of 1943, there were over 500 attacks on railways every month. French groups provided Britain and the USA with information on German military movements and other essential intelligence that helped the Allies to target specific areas or industries. Disruption of German communications and railways assisted the Allied invasion of France in June 1944, when the French resistance groups numbered around 100,000 members.

> **How did the resistance groups in France help the Allies?**

USSR

Resistance groups were very active in the USSR. While some fought for the government, others fought for independence from the USSR.

> **How effective were resistance groups operating within the USSR?**

Partisans

As German armies moved across the USSR's borders in June 1941, millions of people fled eastward. The Soviet government ordered tens of thousands of men and women to remain behind in order to slow the German advance. These partisans were to disrupt the German military in any way possible, including sniper attacks, sabotage of machinery and infrastructure, and anything else that could be accomplished to slow the invasion. Many of these partisans were Communist Party officials and Jews, who the Germany military would execute automatically if captured, even if they were not members of partisan fighting groups. Others members were Soviet soldiers trapped behind enemy lines.

By the end of 1942, at least 300,000 partisans operated in German-occupied Soviet territory. By 1943, thousands of bombings of Germany's railways in former Soviet territory severely disrupted the flow of supplies to hard-pressed army units. German officers were routinely assassinated, along with civilians who aided them. In 1943 alone, 65,000 trucks and 12,000 bridges were destroyed by partisan units loyal to the USSR. In 1944, with the removal of German forces from Soviet territory, partisan resistance came to an end.

UNO

Ukrainians formed their own partisan nationalist groups. The Ukrainian Nationalist Organization (UNO), formed out of earlier nationalist groups, had 300,000 members in 1943. This group battled Germans and Soviet partisans, working to establish an independent Ukrainian state. Essentially a civil war raged within Ukraine between German troops, Ukrainian nationalists and pro-Soviet communist partisans. Most members of the UNO, and other non-Soviet partisans, were captured and executed by the Soviet military by the end of 1944.

This unlike the others was only concerned w/ their own country

What type of activities did resistance groups engage in during the war?

Other resistance movements

Resistance movements existed in almost every occupied nation in Europe. In Italy, partisans captured and killed the former Italian dictator Mussolini (see page 138). In Denmark, resistance groups were able to remove most of the Jewish population to safety in Sweden. Dutch resistance groups in The Netherlands assassinated those who collaborated with Germany, and organized labour strikes. In Czechoslovakia, German officials were assassinated and factories producing war supplies were sabotaged. In Luxembourg, resistance groups hid Jews and held labour strikes protesting against German policies.

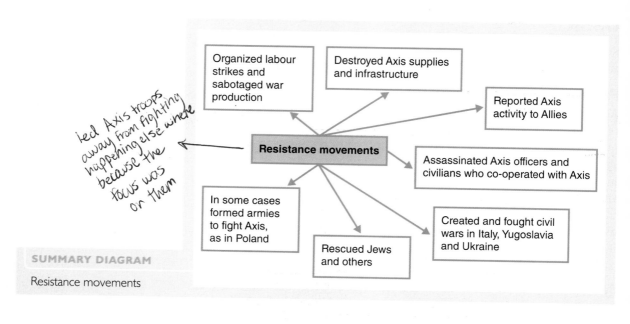

led Axis troops away from fighting where happening else where because the focus was on them

SUMMARY DIAGRAM

Resistance movements

The effects of the Second World War in Europe and north Africa

▶ *Key question: What were the main results of the war in Europe and how did these lead to a change in world diplomacy?*

The Second World War affected all nations involved. Millions were forced to move, or found themselves in new nations. Millions of soldiers were killed, entire cities were bombed into ruins and national infrastructure was destroyed. Borders were moved and the old political order was reduced to relative insignificance with the arrival of two **superpowers**: the USA and the USSR. Soon the world would enter the era of the **Cold War** (see page 181).

Effects on civilians

Civilians throughout Europe were affected by the war. In most countries at war, food was severely rationed, consumer goods were increasingly hard to find, and there was the threat of bombing or invasion.

Death and destruction

Millions of civilians died during the war. An estimated one million civilians died from aerial bombing in Germany and the USSR. Over 11 million people, mostly civilians, died in concentration camps. Unknown thousands died in prison camps as foreign nationals trapped in hostile nations when the war began. Disease, starvation, execution and bad weather killed millions more, while many others died when caught between fighting armies. The Second World War in Europe, especially when coupled with the simultaneous war in Asia, killed more civilians than any known conflict.

Nation	Estimated civilian dead
USSR	16,900,000
China	6,000,000–35,000,000
Poland	6,000,000
Germany	2,000,000
Yugoslavia	1,400,000
Japan (see page 225)	1,000,000
Other nations combined	2,500,000

→ huh?

All but a handful of cities in central and eastern Europe were destroyed. Railways, bridges, dams, roads and factories were heavily damaged throughout the continent and millions were made homeless. Destroyed infrastructure meant that the few who remained in cities faced starvation since food could not easily reach them. In addition, starving millions had no

 **KEY TERM**

Superpowers Nations that have the ability to exert their influence on a global scale.

Cold War The political hostilities in the era 1945–91 between capitalist and communist countries, in particular between the USA and the USSR. The conflict was primarily diplomatic, but serious military confrontation did break out on numerous occasions.

← **Why were civilians so affected by the Second World War in Europe?**

work and therefore no way to purchase anything. An example of the level of destruction faced in Europe is that which occurred in the USSR, where the war destroyed:

- 70,000 villages and 1700 towns
- 32,000 factories
- 64,000 km of railways
- housing for 25 million people.

Many currencies no longer had any value and many had nothing to use for barter, having lost everything in the war. Hunger led to further deaths as people succumbed to illness from weakened immune systems.

Population transfer

During the war millions of civilians were moved to Germany and German-occupied areas of Europe to work in factories to support the German economy. Many of these people died during Allied bombings or were worked to death. As countries were invaded, millions of civilians attempted to flee.

In the USSR, nationalities that either supported Germany or were perceived to be not enthusiastic enough in supporting the war effort were moved from their home regions. Millions of Chechens, Tartars, Koreans, Finns, Poles, Ingush and many other groups were moved to central Asia or into Siberia in the country's north-east; over 40 per cent of these people died during the move or within the next year. Many people who had been moved in Europe and Asia were unable to return home for many years, while others returned soon after the invasion only to be imprisoned, starved, forced into labour, or accused of collaborating with the enemy and suffering, or dying, as a result.

Once the war was concluded, German families who had lived outside Germany, sometimes for hundreds of years, were expelled from some countries they lived in. Germans were forced to leave Poland, whose borders were moved west into Germany, Czechoslovakia, Romania, the USSR and other nations. Poles were moved out of the USSR, and Hungarians fled in large numbers from Romania. Millions moved fearing reprisals or because they wanted to find a better life elsewhere. Surviving Jews mostly left central and eastern Europe, settling in the USA and the British **mandate** of Palestine, which became the self-proclaimed Jewish state of Israel in 1948.

Why did so many soldiers die in the war?

→ Military deaths

The Second World War in Europe killed millions of men who served in their nations' armed forces. While many of these deaths were in combat, many also died of disease or starvation, or from poor weather or even suicide. More soldiers died in this war than in any other in recorded history (see the table in Source R).

SOURCE R

Military deaths during the Second World War in Europe.

Nation	Soldiers mobilized	Military dead	Percentage who died
USSR	20,000,000	8,700,000	43
USA	16,400,000*	292,000[†]	2
Germany	10,800,000	3,250,000	30
Britain	8,850,000[‡]	383,000	4
France	5,000,000	250,000	5
Italy	4,500,000	380,000	8
Poland	1,000,000	600,000	60
Others	5,660,000	445,000	7
Totals	72,210,000	14,300,000	20

*Totals are for soldiers who fought in both Europe and Asia.

[†]Approximately 100,000 were killed in Asia (see page 225).

[‡]Total includes soldiers from Dominions who numbered 4,150,000 of this amount.

> According to Source R, which nations suffered the greatest and least number of military deaths compared to amount of soldiers mobilized?

Many historians believe the massive death toll for soldiers reflects the reality of total warfare (see page 4). Others reject this, stating that many of these deaths were the result of poor strategic planning and the lack of concern for common soldiers. Germany and the USSR are specifically accused of this; for example, German soldiers were not prepared for winter conditions and leaders of both countries were willing to sacrifice as many men as possible to hold Stalingrad (see page 151).

Border changes

> What were the most significant border changes that occurred as a result of the war in Europe?

Several states that were independent before the Second World War were absorbed into other states as a result of the conflict. Many borders were adjusted, with civilian populations moved in order to accommodate these changes, mostly against their will.

Poland

Poland lost most of its eastern regions to the USSR. These areas had been seized from the USSR just after the First World War and were reannexed when the Soviets invaded Poland in 1939. After Germany's defeat, the USSR reoccupied these areas. The Allies compensated Poland for this loss by awarding it much of the German province of East Prussia and the major port city of Danzig, and by moving Poland's western border further into Germany to the Oder and Neisse Rivers. Territorial changes meant that Poland was 20 per cent smaller after the war.

Germany

Germany lost areas it had annexed after 1937, including Austria, Sudetenland and parts of France, as well as its eastern regions to Poland, accounting for 25 per cent of its territory. The resource-rich and industrialized Saar district was placed under French administration. Germany was occupied by the Allies and was temporarily divided into four separately administered zones (see page 183). In time these were consolidated into two zones, one administered by the USA and its economic partners France and Britain, and the other by the USSR. This division led to the creation of two states: West Germany and East Germany.

Others

The USSR moved its borders westward, seizing parts of Finland, and all of Estonia, Latvia and Lithuania in the Baltic. The easternmost section of Czechoslovakia was also taken by the USSR, along with the province of Bessarabia from Romania. Yugoslavia took the Istrian peninsula from Italy.

? According to Source S, which nations were no longer independent after the Second World War?

SOURCE S

Europe at the end of the Second World War indicating areas under Soviet control and new national borders.

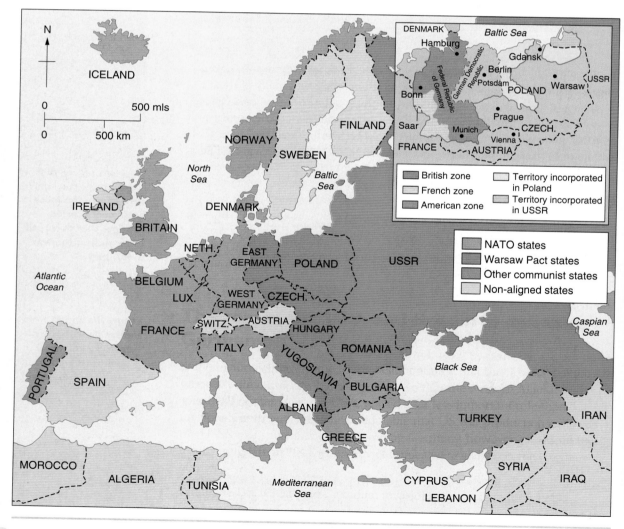

New political realities

Before the Second World War, the USA and the USSR were isolated politically by their own choice. Neither country was particularly interested in being dragged into a European war, especially after the destruction and results of the First World War (see page 61). Yet both were attacked by Axis states in 1941, bringing them into the conflict, making the war in Europe and Asia truly a global conflict instead of regional ones. The quick defeat of France and the impotence of Britain in its fight against Germany were clear demonstrations that neither state was truly capable of functioning as a world power, with the ability to dominate European politics or military actions. Both France and Britain, as well as Germany as it turned out, lacked the raw materials in vast territories, large populations and seemingly unlimited industrial capacity of the USA and USSR.

After the war's conclusion, both the USA and USSR decided that peace was more likely if they remained involved in world diplomacy. This meant that the two superpowers would dominate the post-Second World War era and that all other states, including Britain, France and others, would have to align with one or the other if they hoped to remain significant.

United Nations

Although the League of Nations (see page 33) had failed to prevent the Second World War, the idea remained that an international organization should exist where efforts could be made to prevent further conflicts. The **United Nations** (UN) was initially formed out of the Allied powers that fought the Axis. The first meeting was held in April 1945, just at the end of the war in Europe. The UN differed from the League in several ways, making it seemingly more effective:

- Both the USA and USSR joined.
- All states would have representation in a General Assembly.
- A Security Council of 15 member states would have the ability to undertake peacekeeping missions.
- Five nations would permanently have seats on the Security Council, each with the power to veto any UN decision.
- The UN had the right to authorize the use of military force to prevent further conflict or crimes against humanity.

The UN continued much of the work of the League of Nations in the areas of health care, labour relations, human rights, education and economic development.

Decolonization

The Second World War affected British, French and Italian colonies, leading to many nations gaining independence.

← **How did the Second World War in Europe affect world politics?**

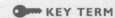 **KEY TERM**

United Nations
International organization whose member states work to resolve crises.

British colonies

Britain's hold over its empire was weakened in many ways during the war. Britain ceased to produce enough goods for its empire to consume and trade for, so increasingly all member states, including Britain, turned to the USA for these products. Britain exhausted its financial resources early in the war by buying raw materials and armaments from primarily the USA, and was heavily indebted to the USA by the war's end. Coupled with these economic difficulties, there was a strong pro-independence movement in India, which at that time included Pakistan and Bangladesh, as well as in many other colonies. Many felt that these areas had earned independence through their contribution to the war.

After mid-1945, Britain's government wanted to **decolonize** because it could no longer afford to maintain its empire and could not afford to militarily suppress rebellions or independence movements. Independence was granted to India in 1947 and Sri Lanka, then called Ceylon, in 1948. In 1948, Britain withdrew from the Mandate of Palestine, which soon was divided by the UN into a Jewish zone ruled by Zionists, and a Palestinian Arab zone of Muslims and Christians. Israel formed from the Jewish zone in 1948 and negotiations continue until today over the creation of a state for Palestinians. Britain left Egypt in 1952 and withdrew from most of its Asian holdings in the same period (see page 229).

French colonies

France was defeated by Germany in 1940 and its hold on its colonies was severely weakened. Its territory in Asia, such as **French Indochina**, was taken by Japan, and its Middle Eastern mandates declared independence or were occupied by Britain. Many under French rule had served in the French military that had helped liberate France from German rule and desired equality which was not forthcoming, leading to political protest and wars of independence. After the war, France attempted to reassert control in Indochina, but was eventually defeated by communist guerrillas (see page 230). In north Africa, independence movements broke out in the 1950s, with Morocco and Tunisia gaining independence in 1956 and Algeria in 1962.

Italian colonies

Italy's east African empire was conquered by British-led forces by the end of 1941. Libya was under British control in mid-1943 and when Italy joined the Allies against Germany in late 1943, Germany seized Albania and other areas under Italian rule on the Adriatic Sea's eastern shore. In 1947, Italy's colonial losses were confirmed in the Treaty of Peace with Italy signed by Italy and the victorious Allied powers:

- Abyssinia, called Ethiopia today, was once again under the control of Emperor Haile Selassie and independent.
- Eritrea was ceded by Britain to Ethiopia in 1951.
- Italian Somaliland was placed under UN control and granted independence, after merging with British Somaliland in 1960.

- Libya became the independent Kingdom of Libya in 1951.
- Albania regained independence with the defeat of Germany in 1945, becoming a communist state allied to the USSR.

The Cold War

How did the Cold War develop between two wartime allies?

Most of Europe was in political chaos at the end of the war. In Germany, most government leaders were either dead or imprisoned. The French government was discredited as a result of France's defeat in war and the collaboration with its German occupiers. The rulers of many states returned from exile to find millions of refugees, destroyed infrastructure and a population on the verge of starvation. In eastern Europe, where devastation was most severe, the USSR established basic administration, creating temporary governments that could oversee some of the dire needs of these states.

The Soviets in eastern Europe

Much of eastern Europe was occupied by the USSR, which had done the bulk of the fighting against Germany. At the **Yalta Conference** in February 1945, the leaders of Britain, the USA and the USSR signed the Declaration on Liberated Europe. This document called for the restoration of democratically elected governments in European states occupied by the Allies. At the **Potsdam Conference** in mid-July 1945, the USA pressed the USSR to implement the agreement, which the Soviets had ignored. They claimed, with good reason, that eastern Europe was unstable as a result of the war. People were starving, German collaborators had to be rooted out, crime had to be suppressed, and people resettled as a result of evacuations of populations during and after the conflict.

Soviet reasoning

The Soviets were certainly interested in maintaining some control over these occupied nations since Germany had invaded their territory in the First and Second World Wars, leading to the death of millions of their citizens in both conflicts. Control of eastern Europe would create a buffer zone to help prevent future attacks. In addition, the creation of Finland, Poland, Czechoslovakia and the expansion of Romania after the First World War was seen by the Soviets, and accurately, as a border of hostile nations to prevent Soviet expansion. This, in effect, meant that the Soviets had been isolated politically and economically. Placing their approved governments in these states after the war would prevent this political and economic isolation, as well as create military allies that it had not had before the war. While it is not clear if the Soviets had determined at the outset to impose communist governments on these states, this was accomplished by 1948 with US and British actions in Germany providing justification (see page 182). States that were **Soviet satellites** included Poland, East Germany, Czechoslovakia, Hungary, Romania, Albania and Bulgaria; Yugoslavia was communist but acted independently after 1948.

KEY TERM

Yalta Conference Meeting of Allied leaders in the USSR in February 1945 where many agreements were made about what the governments and borders of Europe would be after the war's end.

Potsdam Conference Meeting of Allied leaders in Germany in July 1945 where it was decided to divide Germany into four occupation zones, to prosecute war criminals and expel Germans from lands outside Germany, among other issues.

Soviet satellites Nations allied to and dominated by the USSR.

Rising tensions

There were many disputes between the western Allies, specifically the USA, Britain and France, and the Soviets in the war's final months. These included the amount and type of reparations that the USSR would receive as compensation for damage during the war, the fate of Germany after the war, and whether or not the USA should share technical information on the atomic bomb (see page 210). After the war's end, these tensions increased.

The Truman Doctrine, March 1947

British and US actions in Greece and Turkey increased tensions with their former allies by providing clear evidence that they did not intend to allow nations to follow communist ideology, regardless of the desires of the inhabitants of those states. A civil war erupted in Greece at the end of the war in which the constitutional monarchy worked to re-establish itself while being challenged by Greek communists supported by Yugoslavia's now-communist government. Britain provided funds and weapons to Greece, but was so financially stressed that it informed the USA that it would no longer be able to continue its efforts. The USA replaced Britain as the constitutional monarchy's sponsor, sending large quantities of military equipment which helped to crush the communist rebels. Turkey, threatened by the USSR, was also granted substantial aid. The US policy of containment of communism to within the USSR and those states in eastern Europe where it was rapidly becoming established was named the Truman Doctrine after US President Harry Truman.

US economic policy in Europe

It was agreed not only to dismantle Germany industry to prevent future war and provide reparations to the USSR, but to offer little assistance to the German population as well. The USA unilaterally altered this policy in July 1947, without consulting the USSR, by calling for the renewed industrialization of Germany and its economic integration into Europe. Europe suffered after the war from a severely disrupted economic system, of which Germany had been a critical part before September 1939. The USA now believed that the key to preventing the spread of communism to other nations was to alleviate their economic stress. Hungry, impoverished workers were more likely to turn to communism, so the emphasis was now to be that European nations should share resources such as coal, iron and food. This sharing of resources would help to re-establish a functioning economy in western Europe.

The Marshall Plan 1948

The Marshall Plan, named after the **US secretary of state**, was established in mid-1947, but officially launched in April 1948. The USA provided $13 billion (approximately $131 billion in today's currency values) for the economic recovery of Europe over a four-year period. Most of the funds were grants and were used to rebuild infrastructure, mines, factories and cities in western Europe, as well as Greece and Turkey. The USSR and eastern

European states were invited to participate in the Marshall Plan, but the USSR rejected the invitation, requiring its new allies to do the same. The Soviets did not agree with the rebuilding of Germany or allowing the USA to review the economies of either the USSR or its associates and had many other objections. The result of the Marshall Plan was the rapid economic recovery and then growth of states participating in the programme, increasing their trade with each other and the USA. This caused further mistrust between eastern and western Europe, and a growing economic divide.

Berlin Blockade and Airlift 1948

Berlin was Germany's capital and located in the midst of the Soviet-occupied zone. The city was administered by four different nations: France, Britain, the USA and the USSR. The Soviets ruled over half the city, while the other three small zones were merged into one joint western Allied administration, by early 1948, forming an island of western Allied territory in the midst of eastern Germany. The merging of the three zones in Berlin coincided with the merging of the French, British and US zones in western Germany as

According to Source T, which nation controlled the largest area of Germany? ?

SOURCE T

The division of Germany and Berlin into zones after the Second World War.

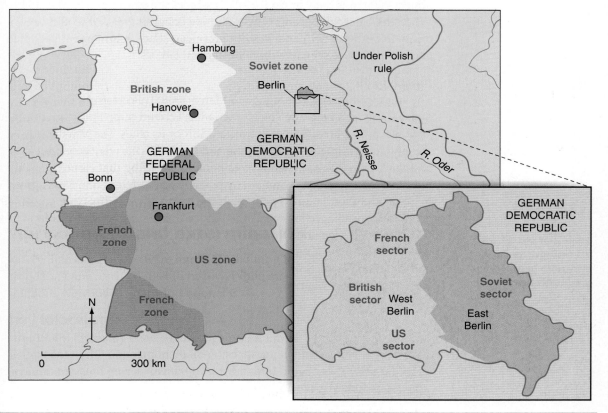

well, despite objections from the USSR. This action, coupled with aid from the Marshall Plan which would be used to rebuild Germany, caused the Soviets to protest by restricting rail and barge traffic to and from Berlin in April 1948. The western Allies introduced a new German currency, despite Soviet protests, in June.

In June, in protest at the unilateral decision to create a new German currency which would help Germany to recover economically, all trains, ships and vehicles were stopped that were travelling from the Soviet-occupied zone going to western Berlin. All food and fuel shipments were stopped, effectively placing the city under siege. The leader of the USSR, Stalin, believed that the USA and its allied partners would not fight the Soviets for the city since they had severely reduced their military strength after 1945. He was apparently not prepared to fight for the city either, believing that the western Allies would either allow the Soviets to take control of the entirety of the city or withdraw the new Germany currency.

Earlier agreements between the former Allies in November 1945 allowed cargo aircraft to reach Berlin through three air corridors. Invoking this agreement, Britain and the USA began the Berlin Airlift on 24 June 1948. By the end of August, 1500 cargo aircraft landed in Berlin daily, delivering over 4500 tons of food and fuel to over two million people; this increased later to almost 9000 tons daily in April 1949. The blockade was ended in May 1949. When the blockade began, many in Europe believed that war would begin again. In both the USA and western European states, rearmament began, to counter what was seen as a more belligerent USSR.

NATO 1949

The Treaty of Brussels was signed in March 1948. This created a military alliance between Belgium, The Netherlands, Luxembourg, France and Britain as they feared a possible attack by the USSR or its allies. The Marshall Plan was still in its implementation phase and these nations were economically and militarily weak and therefore vulnerable. Realizing that alone they did not have the strength to counter any possible Soviet attack, the USA agreed to join with other nations, resulting in the North Atlantic Treaty in April 1949 and a military alliance known as the North Atlantic Treaty Organization (NATO). NATO included the five signatories to the Treaty of Brussels, and added not only the USA, but also Canada, Portugal, Norway, Italy, Iceland and Denmark. The USSR and its allies saw this as a direct threat and formed their own military alliance, although it was only formalized in 1955 as the Warsaw Pact.

COMECON 1949

The USSR countered the Marshall Plan with the formation of the Council for Mutual Economic Assistance (COMECON) in 1949. Western Europe integrated its economy under the auspices of the Marshall Plan. COMECON called for the economic integration of the USSR and its satellite states in a **free-trade** zone. COMECON was not particularly successful but it contributed to the economic separation of eastern and western Europe.

🔑 **KEY TERM**

Free trade Ability to freely trade, usually with low or no taxes on goods crossing national borders.

Conclusion

Perhaps the most important long-term effect of the Second World War was the Cold War. The USA and the USSR, now the world's superpowers, would continue their diplomatic, political and military rivalry for approximately 40 more years. This would cause various small wars, diplomatic crises and an arms race where each competed to have larger numbers of nuclear missiles and other weapons. The Cold War would come to an end with the collapse of the USSR in 1991.

← **Why is the Cold War considered the most important long-term effect of the Second World War?**

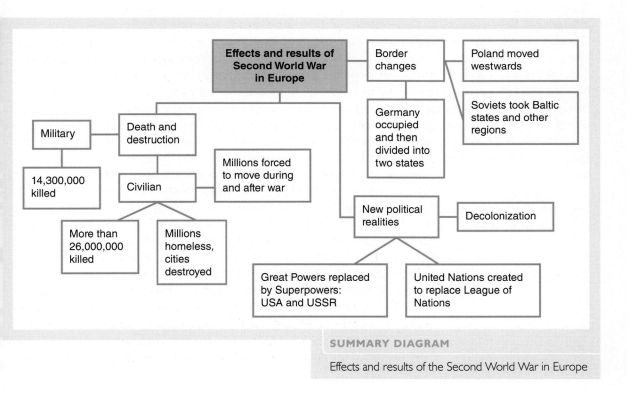

SUMMARY DIAGRAM

Effects and results of the Second World War in Europe

Chapter summary

Second World War in Europe and north Africa 1939–45

The Second World War in Europe was caused in varying degrees by the foreign policy of Germany after 1933, the effects of the Great Depression, failure of the USA and USSR to take a leading role in international diplomacy as superpowers, and the diplomacy of Britain and France. The policy of appeasement failed to curtail German demands or maintain Britain and France as Great Powers. The regional war between Germany and Poland that started on 1 September 1939, despite the British and French declarations of war on Germany on 3 September, failed to erupt into a larger conflict until Germany annexed Denmark and Norway in April 1940.

A massive assault on most of western Europe in May and June 1940 led to a severe reduction in fighting throughout Europe, with the exception of bomber activity which saw Britain and Germany bombed.

Italy's entry into the war in mid-1940 led directly to its defeat in Africa and Greece and the need for Germany to give its ally major assistance.

The attack on the USSR in mid-1941 led to destruction unprecedented in modern European history. The attack was eventually repelled starting in 1943 and Germany was pushed back into its own country and defeated in May 1945.

Victory by the Allied powers was achieved through mass production of war goods, the willingness of Soviet leaders to sacrifice huge numbers of soldiers, and the economic weakness of Germany in comparison to the USA and USSR. Germany contributed to its own defeat with strategic errors and failure to fully mobilize and prepare for total war.

The war in Europe and north Africa led to the death of millions of people, primarily citizens of the USSR, Poland and Germany. More civilians were affected by the war than any other in history. The war destroyed cities and left millions homeless, while providing new opportunities for women.

The Second World War altered the world's balance of power so that former Great Powers were now relatively insignificant. Germany was divided into two zones, other countries lost their independence, and both the USA and USSR left their isolation to dominate the world in a rivalry known as the Cold War. Several nations lost their independence by being absorbed into the USSR, others were dominated politically by the Soviets, and new nations formed from the colonies of Britain and France. The United Nations, a new peace organization, was established to replace the failed League of Nations. The Second World War transformed international politics.

Examination practice

Command term: Discuss

When a question asks you to discuss some aspect of twentieth-century warfare, it is asking you to review arguments and create a conclusion on the basis of the evidence you presented. This will be a common form of question.

Below are a number of different questions for you to practise using the command term 'discuss'. For guidance on how to answer exam-style questions, see Chapter 8.

1 Discuss the relative importance of nationalism in causing war in the twentieth century.

2 Discuss the factors that led to the defeat of nations in wars in the twentieth century.

3 With reference to two twentieth-century wars, each from a different region, discuss the significance of the mobilization of human and economic resources on the outcome of these wars.

4 Discuss changes in conduct of air warfare during the twentieth century.

5 Discuss technological developments in the conduct of two wars during the twentieth century.

 Activities

1 As individuals, or in groups, make a chart or table outlining the strengths and weaknesses of the Axis and Allied powers by year. This will mean that 1939 will have Poland, Britain and France as Allied powers, with Germany and Slovakia as Axis states involved in the conflict, for example. Continue this exercise until you reach the end of the conflict in May 1945.

2 Debate the following positions in class either as individuals or in groups as a connection to history and TOK:

- It was morally acceptable to target civilians in the Second World War.
- Nations that sacrificed more towards victory in the Second World War deserved to be rewarded territory at the war's end.
- It is never acceptable to surrender to an invading military force.

3 Create your own propaganda posters regarding the Second World War in Europe for display in your classroom. Avoid offensive language, symbols or themes.

CHAPTER 4

Second World War in Asia and the Pacific 1941–5

The Second World War is often referred to as two separate world conflicts that shared a certain timeframe and a few of the same participants. The Second World War in Asia and the Pacific Ocean region was fought primarily by Japan, China and the USA with notable participation from The Netherlands, Britain, Australia and others. Starting as a regional war in 1937, it became a conflict of international importance and an example of total war between the Empire of Japan and the USA by the end of 1941. You need to consider the following questions throughout this chapter:

★ To what extent was the Second World in Asia and the Pacific caused by Japanese imperialism?

★ Why was the Empire of Japan not able to maintain its Asian and Pacific empire after initial military success?

★ To what extent was the defeat of the Empire of Japan the result of greater US war production?

★ How did resistance movements affect Japan during the Second World War?

★ What were the short- and long-term effects of the Second World War on Asian and Pacific people?

★ What factors led to Japan's defeat?

1 Causes of the Second World War in Asia and the Pacific

▶ *Key question: To what extent was the Second World in Asia and the Pacific caused by Japanese imperialism?*

On 7/8 December the Empire of Japan, an ally of Germany and other Axis nations (see page 119), launched well-coordinated, massive attacks on military installations of the USA, Britain and other nations throughout Asia and the Pacific Ocean, including Pearl Harbor, the main port for the US Navy's Pacific Fleet. The attack on Pearl Harbor was a great, if temporary, success, disabling or destroying many US warships. This attack led to the USA entering the Second World War which was already taking place in Europe and Africa.

The attack on Pearl Harbor was the culmination of Japanese foreign and military policy that began in the late nineteenth century.

Long-term causes of the Second World War in Asia and the Pacific

← **Why did the Empire of Japan expand in the early twentieth century and with what results?**

Until the mid-nineteenth century, when it started to trade with other countries, Japan was a reclusive nation. Surprised at the technological advancement of the outside world, Japan began to industrialize in the late nineteenth century and constructed a substantial army and navy in the process. Confined to a large group of islands that were poor in raw materials needed for modern technological growth, Japan began to follow European nations in acquiring colonial territories to satisfy its economic needs. A culture of militarism and racial superiority permeated society, was taught in schools, and empowered the military to dominate the nation's political institutions in time.

What information about the Empire of Japan is conveyed by Source A? **?**

SOURCE A

Empire of Japan up to 1940.

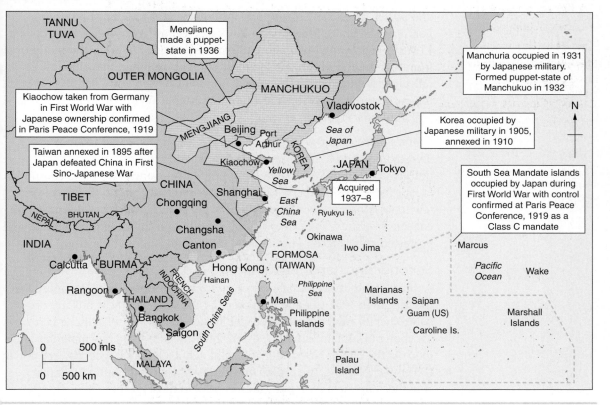

189

Japan expands 1895–1910

Japanese expansion between 1895 and 1910 was rapid and successful. Japan:

- defeated China in 1895 and annexed Formosa, today's Taiwan
- defeated Russia in 1905 and annexed Port Arthur and took control of the South Manchurian Railway, both in China and formerly leased to Russia
- annexed Korea in 1910.

First World War 1914–18

The First World War brought more opportunities. Japan, as one of the Allies:

- seized the German naval base in China at Kiaochow (today's Jiaozhou); this was later returned to China as a result of the 1922 **Washington Naval Conference**
- was awarded former German islands in the form of the **South Sea Mandate**; Japan sent settlers there, who soon outnumbered natives, exploited their natural resources and built fortifications.

Manchurian Crisis 1931–2

Japan suffered extreme economic and social unrest as a result of the Great Depression (see page 114). **Manchuria** was an enormous, underpopulated and poorly defended Chinese province where Japan already had troops guarding the South Manchurian Railway. Needing more resources and land to settle its growing population, the military decided to act without approval from their own government. Japanese soldiers exploded a small bomb on the railway in September 1931, blamed it on the Chinese army, and then seized the entire province within a few months, establishing the puppet-state of Manchukuo in 1932.

China's protests to the League of Nations (see page 33) led to an investigation and a minor reprimand to Japan. Japan responded to this perceived insult by withdrawing from the League and went on to control most of northern China by 1935. This exposed to the world that there were few to no consequences for defying the League's Covenant which called for collective security. The USA was not a member of the League of Nations and protested about Japanese expansion into China, but did little else.

Second Sino-Japanese War 1937–45

A direct result of the Manchurian Crisis was the Second Sino-Japanese War that began in 1937 (see the map on page 189). The Japanese military now controlled its government and using Manchuria as a base, launched an invasion of China in July 1937, ostensibly to secure more raw materials and food. At the end of November 1937, Shanghai, China's largest city, fell and in December, Nanjing, the capital of China, was captured. Although Japan suffered some defeats, it had taken control of most eastern China by 1940. China appealed to the League of Nations in 1937 and barely received a response; Britain and France were preoccupied by events in Europe (see page 120) and could not afford to worry about Asia, even though their colonies were threatened by Japanese expansion. Japan was now the

Washington Naval Conference A conference in 1922 that led to several treaties, limiting the size of the navies of Britain, Japan and the USA, as well as settling other problems.

South Sea Mandate Large numbers of sparsely settled islands in the Pacific Ocean, formerly part of the German Empire.

Manchuria A region in the far north-east of China bordering the then Soviet-controlled territory of Siberia, Mongolia and Korea. Manchuria contained China's largest deposits of coal, iron and gold, huge timber forests and 70 per cent of its heavy industry.

unrivalled power of Asia, with only the USA to contend with in the Pacific Ocean region.

SOURCE B

Japanese troops practising use of bayonets on live Chinese prisoners in Nanjing in 1937.

> What information is conveyed in Source B about the treatment of Chinese prisoners in Nanjing in 1937?

Atrocities against China

Japanese troops committed great atrocities in China during the war. In Shanghai, and many other cities, civilians were bombed by Japanese planes. In Nanjing, approximately 300,000 civilian Chinese were intentionally killed after the city fell to the Japanese army, along with tens of thousands of captured Chinese troops; tens of thousands of women were raped and then also killed. These actions by Japanese troops, in addition to concern about the growing military and economic strength of Japan, alarmed many countries.

War in China continues

Chinese forces, governed from the city of Chongqing, continued to fight and were supplied through French Indochina. Japan successfully invaded this French-held territory in September 1940, provoking a US-imposed **embargo** (see below). Meanwhile, Japan consolidated its hold on major cities in east China and along railway lines. Japan established a puppet government to rule the parts of China it controlled and faced incessant guerrilla attacks at the hands of communist fighters from 1937 to 1945 (see page 223).

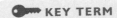 **KEY TERM**

Embargo Ban on trade.

SOURCE C

Excerpt from _A Modern History of Japan: From Tokugawa Times to the Present_ by Andrew Gordon, published by Oxford University Press, Oxford, 2003, pages 206–7.

Over the following months the Japanese army expanded its control by seizing further key cities and railway lines. The military situation then reached a stalemate in the fall of 1938. Japan had committed six hundred thousand troops to the field, but they were barely able to defend the cities and railway lines in the occupied regions. The occupiers had little control over the countryside, and troops faced constant threat of guerrilla attack. Japanese forces murdered civilians as well as soldiers in numerous other incidents throughout the course of the war, especially in North China. Terrorizing the population in this way appears to have been part of a broader, ultimately failed military strategy to 'pacify' the Chinese people ...

Short-term causes of the Second World War in Asia and the Pacific

The USA was concerned about Japan's wars against China since 1931. By the late 1930s, with the outbreak of war in Europe, the USA revised its laws to allow it to respond economically to Japan's expansion.

Friction between the USA and Japan

US President Franklin D. Roosevelt (1933–45) was limited by Neutrality Acts which prevented American involvement in conflicts unless it was itself attacked. In March 1941, the Neutrality Acts were replaced by the Lend–Lease programme which allowed the USA to openly sell weapons and war goods to countries fighting against Germany, Italy and Japan. The USA soon banned all oil exports to Japan, which threatened to bring the Japanese military and all industry to a halt since Japan relied almost exclusively on US oil.

Japan plans attack against the USA

With only two years of oil stockpiles for military operations, Japan decided it had to expand to take control of oilfields in the Dutch East Indies, today's Indonesia, something the USA was likely to resist.

The USA had no desire to see further Japanese expansion, which would threaten its own territories throughout the Pacific Ocean region as well as territories of Britain, The Netherlands and others. The greatest of the US holdings were the Philippines and the Hawaiian Islands. The Philippines held US naval and army bases, along with airfields. They were also located along the route between Japan and the Dutch East Indies, posing a potential obstacle to Japanese military plans. The Hawaiian Islands were located in the middle of the Pacific, providing the USA with a major naval base and multiple airfields at Pearl Harbor, where its Pacific fleet of warships was stationed. Other islands, such as Guam and Wake Island, held airbases as well. Japan had a significant advantage over US naval forces at the time of its attack on Pearl Harbor (see the table below).

Opposing fleets in the Pacific Ocean region in December 1941

Nation	Battleships	Cruisers	Destroyers	Submarines	Carriers/ Aircraft
Imperial Japanese Navy	10	40	100	120	10/440*
US Pacific Fleet	9	20	50	33	3/250*
*Carrier-based aircraft only. Both sides had hundreds of land-based aircraft.					

In order to secure oil supplies in the Dutch East Indies, the Japanese military planned to assault each of these US territories, as well as those of Britain, such as Hong Kong, at approximately the same time. They hoped this would prevent a quick US recovery and counterattack. It was assumed that a severely damaged fleet would take about a year to rebuild, giving Japan ample time to take control of Indonesia and then face US forces. Many in the Japanese military were convinced that if an attack on the US navy was successful and impressive enough, then it was unlikely that Americans, who were assumed to be a weak and comfort-oriented nation, would strike back, because of either fear or sheer laziness.

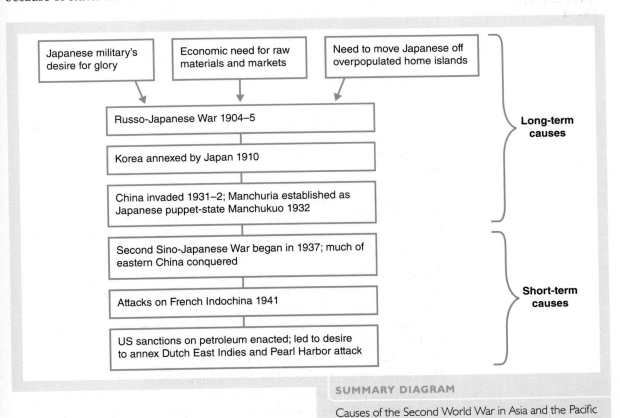

SUMMARY DIAGRAM

Causes of the Second World War in Asia and the Pacific

Course of the war in the Pacific 1941–5

▶ **Key question:** *Why was the Empire of Japan not able to maintain its Asian and Pacific empire after initial military success?*

Japan attacked various targets in December 1941, turning the regional war between Japan and its neighbouring states into a total war which required massive war production and a strategy to defeat the world's most industrialized nation.

Why was the Empire of Japan initially successful in the Second World War in Asia and the Pacific?

War in the Pacific and Asia 1941

Japan's attack on Pearl Harbor at the end of 1941 brought the USA into the Second World War.

Pearl Harbor, 7 December 1941
On 7 December 1941 (8 December in Asia), the US Pacific Fleet was attacked at its base in Pearl Harbor by a large Japanese naval fleet. Six Japanese aircraft carriers launched 353 planes of several types in two waves, attacking US navy ships, airfields, aircraft and other facilities with torpedoes, bombs and machine-gun fire. The attack on the US fleet:

- damaged four battleships and sank four others
- damaged or sank three cruisers, three destroyers and two other naval vessels
- destroyed 188 aircraft
- killed over 2400 people and injured 1200 others.

Japan's losses were minimal:

- 29 aircraft destroyed
- five midget submarines sunk
- 65 men killed.

While the Japanese clearly won the battle, not all their objectives were met since all three US aircraft carriers were at sea on training exercises at the time and therefore survived the attack. Oil- and torpedo-storage facilities also survived the assault. The USA declared war on Japan the next day.

Attacks on US-held territories
On the same day, Japanese forces attacked US and British military positions in the Philippines, Guam and Wake Island.

Philippines, 8 December 1941 to 8 May 1942
The largest US-held territory, the Philippines, was initially attacked on 8 December (7 December in North America). However, the main assault

Technology of the war: aircraft carriers

Aircraft carriers were ships that functioned as floating, armed airfields and were the most important warships of the Second World War in the Pacific Ocean. Fighter, dive-bomber, torpedo-bomber and even bomber aircraft launched from carriers could travel hundreds of kilometres to attack enemy targets. Japanese and US fleets rarely came into visual contact. Battles on the sea were almost exclusively, with notable exceptions, between aircraft and between aircraft and ships.

The largest carriers were fleet carriers which held many aircraft that had longer range capability. They were protected by large numbers of other warships, including battleships, cruisers, destroyers and submarines. Escort carriers were smaller vessels which held fewer aircraft; their primary task was to provide further protection for the carrier fleet. Japan built 16 carriers during the war, while the USA managed to build over 160, the majority of which were used to fight Japan.

Examples of Japanese and US fleet carriers are listed in the table below.

Name	Nation producing	Defensive guns	Range	Number of aircraft
Akagi	Japan	26	19,000 km	60
Enterprise	USA	94	23,150 km	90

there happened about two weeks later when tens of thousands of Japanese troops invaded the main island of Mindanao from various points. Soon US forces, which included tens of thousands of Philippine troops, retreated to the Bataan Peninsula and eventually to the fortified island of Corregidor. On 8 May 1942, US and Philippine forces officially surrendered, although some escaped and conducted guerrilla warfare operations against Japanese targets until the Philippines were reoccupied by US forces later in the war. The capture of the Philippines was one of the USA's largest defeats in history in terms of troop losses, with over 25,000 soldiers killed, 21,000 wounded and 100,000 captured. Japanese losses were relatively light in comparison, with 9000 dead and just over 13,000 wounded.

Guam, 8–10 December 1941

The US-held island of Guam, with its tiny military forces, was attacked 8 and 9 December by air before being invaded by Japanese marine forces on 10 December, the day it surrendered. Guam was a junction for undersea cables linking the USA to the Philippines and other parts of Asia.

Wake Island, 8–23 December 1941

Wake Island, another US-held island that was more fortified than Guam, was attacked by air on 8 December, losing eight of its 12 aircraft on the ground. The first Japanese attempt to land **marines** on the island was fought off by US shore batteries that sank several ships, severely damaging others.

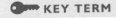 **KEY TERM**

Marines Soldiers trained to invade territories from warships.

Two Japanese aircraft carriers from the Pearl Harbor battle were brought in and the island was stormed and captured on 23 December. Control of Wake Island gave Japanese aircraft the ability to control a large part of the Pacific Ocean.

Attacks on British territories

British colonies and possessions were also targeted by the Empire of Japan. On the same day as the attack on Pearl Harbor, Hong Kong, Singapore and Malaya (today's Malaysia) were attacked.

Malaya and Singapore, 8 December 1941 to 15 February 1942

While Japanese troops poured into Malaya, Japanese bombers flying from Japanese-occupied French Indochina pounded Singapore. By 10 December, the British warships HMS *Prince of Wales* and HMS *Repulse* had been destroyed by Japanese aircraft off Malaya, proving clearly that without protection from aircraft, traditional battleships and cruisers were obsolete.

Malaya was conquered by the end of January, and Singapore, which the British government had claimed to be impregnable, fell on 15 February. With the fall of Singapore, 80,000 British troops were captured with 5000 dead; Japan lost fewer than 2000 men. After the fall of Singapore, Japanese aircraft carriers operated in the Indian Ocean, attacking Britain's Ceylon, today's Sri Lanka, and sinking British aircraft carrier HMS *Hermes*, driving the British fleet out of the Indian Ocean.

Hong Kong, 8–25 December 1941

Hong Kong was attacked eight hours after Pearl Harbor and its small defensive air force was immediately destroyed. The British colony finally surrendered on 25 December after weeks of heavy fighting. Local Chinese continued a low-level guerrilla campaign against the Japanese military throughout the rest of the war, leading to severe Japanese reprisals where entire villages were destroyed.

Attack on Thailand, 8 December 1941

Thailand was also attacked by Japan on 8 December. Controlling Thailand would allow the Japanese military easier access to northern Malaya and Burma (sometimes called Myanmar), a British colony. After a few hours of battling the Japanese, the Thai government agreed to end the fighting, and allow Japanese troops to traverse its territory using its railways, airfields, barracks and ports. In January 1942, Thailand, now in alliance with Japan, declared war on the USA and Britain. There was significant Thai resistance to what amounted to Japanese occupation (see page 224).

Japanese offensives, January 1942

Japan continued military operations in the Philippines, Malaya and Singapore in early 1942, and launched another series of invasions. Burma was invaded from Thailand, naval forces moved against the Dutch East Indies, New Guinea, Rabaul and the Solomon Islands. Seizing the Dutch

East Indies and Burma would secure much needed oil supplies, while capturing New Guinea, Rabaul and the Solomon Islands would be a step towards cutting off Australia from US supplies in preparation for its invasion.

Burma invasion, December 1941 to May 1942

Attacks on Burma were begun in late December 1941, but escalated by mid-January 1942. Burma was quickly overrun by Japanese troops that were eventually joined by sections of Thailand's army. British forces retreated into eastern India. Japan now controlled Burmese oilfields and could benefit from Burma's major rice production. British attacks on Burma to drive out Japanese forces occurred with some success in 1944 and 1945, justified as necessary to protect India, but at the end of the war, Japanese troops were still in Burma fighting.

Dutch East Indies, New Guinea and Rabaul, December 1941 to February 1942

Although parts of the Dutch East Indies had been under attack since 17 December, its main islands were invaded on 10 January with all organized resistance wiped out by the end of March. Parts of New Guinea were soon under Japanese control and the northern Australian city and port, Darwin, came under attack by Japanese aircraft, the first of almost 100 attacks over the next year and a half. Rabaul, to the north-east of New Guinea, was captured from Australian troops after a 23 January marine landing and subsequently built into a major naval station and airbase for over 100,000 Japanese troops. Parts of the Solomon Islands were seized from Australia afterwards, along with further naval stations and airbases. By controlling the thousands of kilometres of airspace, Japan could use its carrier-based aircraft, as well as those flying from airbases, to bomb any enemy ships.

> **Technology and strategy of the war: air power over sea power**
> Battleships, cruisers and other surface ships proved to be vulnerable to attack by aircraft. Although all these ships were outfitted with anti-aircraft guns, these were of limited use in many cases as dive-bomber aircraft, flying at great altitude, were either hard to hit or simply flying so high or fast that artillery could not reach them. While most bombs dropped from this height missed their targets, any hit was usually devastating since the upper decks of ships were not armoured. The best example of this, perhaps, was the destruction of the USS *Arizona*, a US battleship at Pearl Harbor. A bomb dropped from a dive-bomber penetrated into the magazine of the ship and exploded, destroying the ship almost immediately, killing over 1000 men instantly.

Greater Asia Co-prosperity Sphere 1940–5

Japan occupied much of east Asia by 1942, bringing perhaps hundreds of millions of people under Japanese rule. Japan announced in 1940 that their

Second World War in the Pacific and Asia from December 1941 to August 1945. Top map shows Japanese conquests and possessions. Lower map shows the Allies' advances.

? According to Source D, in what years did the Empire of Japan expand and contract the most?

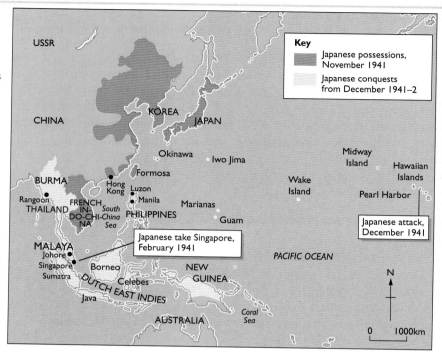

Key
- Japanese possessions, November 1941
- Japanese conquests from December 1941–2

USSR

CHINA

KOREA

JAPAN

Okinawa   Iwo Jima

Midway Island

Hawaiian Islands

BURMA

Formosa

Hong Kong   Luzon

Rangoon

Manila

Wake Island

Pearl Harbor

FRENCH INDO-CHINA   South China Sea

THAILAND

Marianas

PHILIPPINES

Guam

Japanese attack, December 1941

MALAYA

Johore

Singapore

Sumatra   Borneo

NEW GUINEA

PACIFIC OCEAN

N

Japanese take Singapore, February 1941

DUTCH EAST INDIES

Celebes

Java

AUSTRALIA   Coral Sea

0   1000km

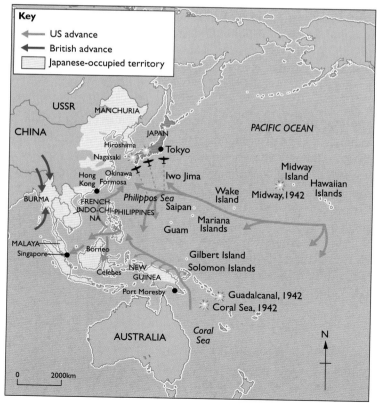

Key
- US advance
- British advance
- Japanese-occupied territory

USSR   MANCHURIA

CHINA

PACIFIC OCEAN

Hiroshima   JAPAN

Nagasaki   Tokyo

Hong Kong   Okinawa   Iwo Jima

BURMA   Formosa

FRENCH INDO-CHINA

Philippos Sea

PHILIPPINES   Saipan

Midway Island

Hawaiian Islands

Midway, 1942

Wake Island

Mariana Islands

MALAYA

Singapore   Borneo

Guam

Gilbert Island

Celebes   NEW GUINEA

Solomon Islands

Port Moresby

Guadalcanal, 1942

Coral Sea, 1942

AUSTRALIA   Coral Sea

N

0   2000km

empire was the **Greater Asia Co-prosperity Sphere** which was meant to free Asia from European and US control. Japan further stated that as the strongest Asian nation, it was obligated to fight for all Asia and help other nationalities establish themselves as independent nations. Puppet governments, similar to those already established in Manchuria and China, were also placed in Burma, the Philippines and others, although Japan pretended they had independence on some level. Long-term plans were made to expand the Co-prosperity Sphere as the Japanese Empire conquered new territories, calling for the settlement of two million Japanese citizens in Australia, for example.

In reality, the Co-prosperity Sphere, while encouraging nationalists to work against European governments, was nothing more than the Japanese Empire in disguise. Conquered territories supplied workers and raw materials for Japanese war industries and non-Japanese were often seen as racially inferior and treated poorly by members of the Japanese armed forces.

> **KEY TERM**
>
> **Greater Asia Co-prosperity Sphere**
> Japanese-created and led organization of puppet-governments established in Japanese-occupied Asian nations that encouraged Asians to oppose European and US rule and to support Japan during the Second World War.

SOURCE E

Excerpt from *A World in Flames: A Short History of the Second World War in Europe and Asia, 1939–1945* by Martin Kitchen, published by Longman, London, 1990, page 327.

The [idea of a] Great East Asia Co-prosperity Sphere ... had first been suggested by Prince Konoye in 1938 when he claimed that the Japanese army in China was not there to conquer the country but to build a new Asia which would be based on high ethical principles and be placed under the benevolent tutelage of Japan. This new order in Asia would provide the necessary guarantees against western materialism, individualism and communism ...

The vast majority of Asians who suffered under Japanese occupation were not taken in by this claptrap. Most found the harsh rule of the Japanese army even more unpleasant than that of the European imperialist powers, and the ideology of the new order was dismissed as transparent hypocrisy. The Japanese had no clear idea what they intended to do with their Empire and did not trouble to work out a programme or ideology for the Greater East Asia Co-prosperity Sphere. They were content to grab raw materials and to follow the dictates of their strategy, but had nothing positive to offer. With their overbearing conviction of their racial superiority there could be no question of co-operation with the lesser breeds ...

> According to Source E, why did the Co-prosperity Sphere fail? **?**

Turning points and Guadalcanal 1942

In 1942, there were three battles against the USA that had major consequences for Japan and its ability to fight the war. These were the Battles of the Coral Sea, Midway and Guadalcanal.

> ← **How did military events in the Pacific in 1942 alter the direction of the Second World War in the Pacific Ocean?**

Battle of the Coral Sea, 4–8 May 1942

In early 1942, Japan moved to capture Port Moresby, New Guinea, which would allow control of the sea around northern Australia and the ability to launch sustained air attacks against Australian targets. The USA had earlier decoded Japanese naval signals and was aware of the invasion plan. Two US carriers, with supporting ships, were moved into the area, to counter the Japanese fleet which included three carriers. Aircraft from the US carrier *Yorktown* attacked and destroyed small naval vessels on 4 May, alerting the Japanese navy that a US fleet was in the area. By 8 May, the USA had lost one of its two carriers; the *Yorktown* was severely damaged, but still floating and hastily sent to Pearl Harbor for repairs. Japan lost only one carrier, but the others were damaged, causing a delay in invading Port Moresby. This delay allowed Australian troops to seize the port, preventing an invasion of Australia for the rest of the war. However, Japanese forces went on to occupy the islands of Rabaul and Guadalcanal in July 1942, which enabled Japan to cut supply lines between the USA and Australia.

Battle of Midway, 4–7 June 1942

In early June 1942, a small Japanese fleet took control over several of the Aleutian Islands, part of the US territory of Alaska. This may have been a diversion for a larger attack on Midway **Atoll**, US-held islands in the Pacific with an airfield about 2100 km from Pearl Harbor, Hawaii. The **IJN** hoped to occupy Midway and lure the US fleet from Hawaii where it was now thoroughly protected by aircraft. The US deciphered Japanese codes and moved to intercept the fleet before it established its own aircraft at Midway.

During the battle from 4 to 7 June, aircraft from four Japanese carriers attacked Midway Atoll and the US carrier *Yorktown*, not realizing there were two other US carriers in the area. Aircraft from Midway Atoll's airfield and from all three US carriers attacked the Japanese carriers and their support ships. In the battle, Japan lost:

- all four carriers
- 240 aircraft
- a cruiser
- 3000 men.

The USA lost:

- one carrier
- 150 aircraft
- a destroyer
- 300 men.

The result of Midway was a turning point of the war in the Pacific. It was the first real victory against the Japanese navy by the USA. After the battle, Japan only had six carriers left in the Pacific and lacked the industrial capacity and resources to quickly rebuild the lost ships (see page 220). The loss of pilots, mechanics, carrier crews and other highly trained naval personnel was significant. Japanese carrier losses prevented the IJN from making any major attacks on US forces for months, allowing the US to begin offensive operations of its own, particularly against Guadalcanal two months later.

🔑 **KEY TERM**

Atoll An island formed from a coral reef.

IJN Imperial Japanese Navy.

Technology of the war: code breaking

Both the Japanese and US militaries used codes to transmit commands and reports. The main Japanese code used for its naval fleet, JN-25 as labelled by the US military, was well-enough understood by US cryptanalysts in May 1942 to affect the outcome of the Battle of Midway. Other codes, such as JN-40, were used by Japanese merchant ships that supplied Japan and its military forces. JN-40 was broken by November 1942, allowing US submarines to severely damage Japan's ability to move supplies, troops and equipment.

US military codes were also broken by the Japanese. However, following a limited, but successful, use of the **Native American** language Choctaw in the First World War as a code, the US Marine Corp recruited hundreds of Navajos, whose language was extraordinarily complex and spoken by very few non-Navajos. These men then created a code based on the Navajo language that required one to hear the code by radio signal and translate the first letters of the Navajo word into English, which were then used to create full English words. Certain military machines or terms were assigned Navajo words, with the Navajo words for iron and fish standing for submarine, for example. This Navajo-derived code was never broken.

 **KEY TERM**

Native Americans
Indigenous inhabitants of the Americas.

Battles at Guadalcanal

Guadalcanal was a strategically important island in the Solomon Islands. A series of battles was held on and around the island starting in August 1942, when US troops landed and soon seized a Japanese airfield. While battles continued on the island between US and Japanese troops and aircraft, both navies battled in the region.

Guadalcanal island, August 1942 to February 1943

Fighting began on 7 August 1942, as US troops landed and quickly seized a Japanese airfield. The US began the operation by landing small numbers of soldiers. It was believed that these troops, supported by nearby warships, would quickly defeat Japan's soldiers, who would be isolated and surrender. Japan, instead, fought tenaciously, landing more troops and war supplies by ship and submarine. By December, the US had been forced to land 60,000 troops who continued to fight Japanese forces until their last soldiers were evacuated by 9 February 1943. This difficult land battle caused the USA to create new strategies when attacking Japanese-held islands (see page 203).

Battle of the Solomon Islands, 24 and 25 August 1942

A Japanese fleet consisting of three carriers and 43 other warships engaged in battle on 24 and 25 August 1942, with a US fleet of three carriers and 16 other ships as Japan moved to support its troops on Guadalcanal. Japan lost a carrier and the USA had one severely damaged, causing both fleets to withdraw from the area. On 15 September, a US carrier was sunk by a torpedo launched from a Japanese submarine, leaving only one carrier to protect US ships in the area.

Technology of the war: submarines

Submarines operated as individual units or in groups, using torpedoes to destroy enemy shipping. Japan's submarines were responsible for some damage to US ships, including sinking two carriers, but did not significantly affect supply or merchant vessels. They never seriously hindered the US navy or its ability to conduct the war.

US submarines at the war's start were older vessels that could not travel far and were armed with defective torpedoes. By 1943, larger vessels took the place of these obsolete models. These could travel great distances and destroy more Japanese shipping with improved torpedoes. Also in 1943, US code breakers deciphered Japan's code for controlling its supply convoys. This meant that they could now be followed by groups of Allied submarines and attacked repeatedly, often at night. By 1944, the US had over 150 submarines hunting Japanese shipping. By the end of the war, submarines had crippled Japan's merchant fleet to the point that it could no longer supply the country with food or raw materials for factories, leading at least one historian to conclude that by submarine warfare alone Japan had been defeated. US submarines were responsible for destroying eight Japanese carriers and a battleship, in addition to their other successes.

Battle of Santa Cruz, October 1942

Japan attempted again to resupply its troops at Guadalcanal at the end of October by sending another large fleet. This resulted in the Battle of Santa Cruz. Two of Japanese carriers were destroyed, but the US navy, with only two carriers operational, suffered more severely in the short term with one carrier destroyed and the other so severely damaged that it could no longer be used without major repairs. This meant that for a period of time the USA had no carriers operational in the entire Pacific Ocean, leaving all naval and marine operations very vulnerable. In the long term, the loss of two more Japanese carriers was a major blow as they were not easily replaced.

Naval Battle of Guadalcanal, November 1942

In mid-November, one of the few battleship engagements of the war took place at the naval battle of Guadalcanal. Japan lost two battleships and three other warships while the USA had nine warships destroyed and one battleship severely damaged. This was Japan's final attempt to resupply its troops on Guadalcanal and led to the decision in December 1942 to evacuate its forces. This was accomplished by early February 1943.

Significance of Guadalcanal

US and Japanese losses at Guadalcanal were significant (see the table opposite).

US and Japanese military losses at Guadalcanal

Nation	Ships sunk	Aircraft destroyed	Troops killed
Japan	38	800	31,000
USA	29	615	7,000

In order to replace these losses, the USA increased its shipbuilding pace, which was already substantial, whereas Japan found it difficult, or impossible, to replace them. Japan moved so many troops to Guadalcanal that it was unable to complete its invasion of New Guinea. This, along with the capture of Guadalcanal by the USA, meant that New Zealand and Australia could be better supplied by US ships, preventing their invasion. While most American historians believe that the Battle of Midway was the turning point of the war, many Japanese historians believe that it was the Battle of Guadalcanal since Japan was beaten on the sea, on land and in the air.

> **Strategy of war: island hopping**
> The USA developed a new offensive strategy as a result of Guadalcanal. Instead of attacking fortified Japanese positions, such as Rabaul, US forces would bypass them. US forces would then capture specific islands, build airfields, install large numbers of aircraft, and use the newly acquired island to destroy any Japanese ships by air that were sent to supply or reinforce fortified positions. In this way, war casualties would be minimized and US aircraft, specifically bombers, could be moved closer and closer to Japan, which then would be bombed into surrender, hopefully eliminating the need for its invasion. This countered the Japanese strategy of garrisoning various islands to create a defensive perimeter to prevent US forces from reaching Japan.

Southern Pacific battles 1943

What was the effect on the US military of the battle for Tarawa?

Guadalcanal caused the US military to be more cautious in the campaigns of 1943. Japanese troops had displayed a determination that surprised US military planners. In all future campaigns, any islands targeted would be overrun by US forces using massed air assault and naval bombardment with thousands of marines and other troops storming beaches.

Operation Cartwheel, June 1943 to August 1945

There were small battles in the area of the Bismarck Sea after Guadalcanal as US forces worked to isolate Rabaul and Japanese forces made efforts to resupply and reinforce it. Operation Cartwheel consisted of:

- US-led forces joined by Australian, Fijian, British and New Zealand troops
- thirteen different offensive operations to isolate Japanese-held islands
- major fighting on Bougainville over a two-year period.

Japanese forces were prevented by this campaign from interfering with the US invasion of the Philippines (see page 207).

Tarawa, 20–23 November 1943

While Operation Cartwheel isolated Rabaul and moved US forces closer to the Philippines, another prong of the offensive against Japan was activated by the US navy. US forces needed an airfield to launch sustained attacks on the Mariana Islands which, along with other US-held islands, would be another stepping stone towards the Japanese home islands. The Japanese military, aware of the value of Tarawa Atoll in any campaign against the Marianas, heavily fortified the islands. Tarawa's main island measured only 2.5 km by 0.5 km and was attacked by the USA with its largest fleet yet assembled on 20 November 1943. The fleet, contrasting sharply with the initial, timid attack on Guadalcanal, contained:

- 17 carriers with 126 support ships, including 12 battleships
- 35,000 marines and army infantry.

They were opposed by less than 5000 Japanese and Koreans, about half of whom were construction workers building the island's defences. US forces met tremendous resistance. On 23 November, only 17 Japanese surrendered; all others died fighting. The USA lost 1700 men, over 700 dying when a ship was torpedoed by a Japanese submarine.

SOURCE F

The bodies of Japanese soldiers killed by US machine-gun attack during the battle at Tarawa Atoll, November 1943.

? What information is conveyed by Source F about the US invasion of Tarawa?

Consequences of Tarawa

A result of Tarawa and other battles in which Japanese troops often fought to the last man, was that the US military wondered what would happen when the Japanese home islands were reached. It was assumed that if Japanese soldiers were willing to die fighting even when it was apparent that their death would have no major impact, then they would certainly do so if Japan itself was invaded. This helped to reinforce the view of many military commanders that Japan should be bombed into surrendering, if possible, before any invasion attempt was made. It seems that the dropping of **atomic bombs** in 1945 (see page 210) was partly the result of these thoughts. Japanese resistance and suicide attacks by **kamikazes** further reinforced these thoughts over the next two years.

The USA defeats Japan 1944–5

US naval and air superiority, already confirmed by 1943, was extended further in battles throughout 1944.

Marshall Islands and Truk, 31 January to 20 February 1944

The Marshall Islands formed part of Japan's outer defensive lines against any invasion from US forces and had been heavily fortified after 1922 when they were granted to Japan as part of the South Sea Mandate. Capturing these islands would bring US forces closer to Saipan, an island within bombing range of parts of Japan. US forces captured Kwajalein Atoll between 31 January and 7 February 1944 as the first stage of these operations. In the fighting, 7780 Japanese troops died and 100 were captured, repeating the pattern established at Tarawa. On 17 February, Eniwetok Atoll was attacked by US forces and captured by 20 February. Only 16 Japanese soldiers surrendered with 2677 Japanese troops dead, giving the US effective control of the Marshalls. Air attacks on other Japanese-held islands continued, however, leaving remaining Japanese garrisons isolated through the remainder of the war, unable to participate or resupply.

Truk, 17–18 February 1944

Truk was a major Japanese naval and airbase in the Caroline Islands. With island hopping, the USA did not need to occupy these islands, but did have to eliminate the Japanese threat housed there so that the Marshall Islands could be captured and then held. A US fleet of 74 warships, including 12 carriers, assaulted IJN forces at Truk on 17 February 1944 for two days, while another force attacked Eniwetok in the Marshalls. Japan lost 15 warships and 270 aircraft along with 32 supply ships, while the USA suffered two ships damaged and 25 aircraft destroyed. Truk was thereafter isolated by sea and after April, when US aircraft destroyed all remaining aircraft and airfields, by air as well.

With US airfields in the Marshall Islands secure and Japanese forces isolated at Truk, US forces moved into the Mariana Islands to the west to secure airfields from which Japan itself could be bombed.

KEY TERM

Atomic bomb A large bomb that uses radioactive material to create an explosion large enough to destroy an entire city.

Kamikazes Japanese pilots who flew aircraft into Allied ships, killing themselves in the process.

What were the major factors that led to the Empire of Japan's defeat in August 1945?

Saipan, 15 June to 9 July 1944

From 15 June until 9 July 1944, the USA battled Japan for Saipan in the Mariana Islands. The struggle was monumental for both sides. Out of 71,000 US troops, almost 3500 were killed. Out of 31,000 Japanese troops on the island, about 24,000 died fighting, 5000 committed suicide, and almost 1000 surrendered or were captured, becoming prisoners of war. Almost 22,000 Japanese settlers on the islands were also killed during the fighting or committed suicide in order to avoid capture and retain their honour. US bombers from Saipan were now able to reach the Philippines, Ryukyu Islands and Japan. In October 1944, 100 B-29 US bomber aircraft attacked the Japanese capital, Tokyo; soon larger numbers of aircraft attacked frequently.

Technology and strategy of the war: bombing Japan

The USA used B-17 bombers for much of the war in the Pacific, bombing Japanese ships and military bases. The B-29 bomber replaced the B-17 in 1944 and by the end of the war 4000 had been produced, many of which were deployed against Axis countries in Europe. It could fly greater distances and had a pressurized cabin which allowed the plane to reach an altitude of over 9000 m, out of the range of most anti-aircraft weapons and Japanese fighters. In order to reach a safe altitude, B-29s reduced their weight by carrying fewer bombs. Bombing from such great heights, where the speed of the aircraft was a factor along with wind speed, was highly inaccurate and ineffective. This led to the idea of burning Japanese cities, where factories and factory workers were located, with incendiary bombs.

This campaign started slowly in December 1944. To make incendiary attacks more accurate, the USA switched to night bombing which allowed B-29s to fly at lower altitudes with greater numbers of bombs. On 10 March 1945, 279 B-29s fire-bombed Tokyo, killing between 80,000 and 100,000 people in one evening and destroying 25 per cent of all buildings. This attack killed as many as the later atomic bomb attacks on Hiroshima and Nagasaki (see page 210). This was followed on 19 March with fire-bombings of Kobe, Nagoya and Osaka, all of which were large, industrial centres. Soon, all cities over 100,000 people had been repeatedly attacked, destroying most food, clothing and medical stockpiles. By the end of the war, many cities were largely abandoned as people feared fire-bombing and 42 cities had at least 50 per cent of their buildings destroyed.

Battle of the Philippine Sea, 19–20 June 1944

While Saipan was being invaded, the IJN moved to support its troops on the island, leading to the Battle of the Philippine Sea from 19 to 20 June 1944. The IJN fleet contained nine carriers and 48 other ships, with 750 aircraft on carriers and from airfields. The US fleet contained 15 carriers with almost 1000 aircraft, and 114 other warships of various types.

The battle was a disaster for Japan as it lost three irreplaceable carriers and 400 aircraft, including its few remaining experienced pilots. The USA suffered one battleship damaged. In the next great naval battle, Japanese carriers could only be used as decoys as they no longer had enough planes or pilots to be effective tools of war.

Mariana Islands, 21 July to 30 September 1944

Battles for Guam and other islands in the Marianas in mid-1944 were similar to early invasions of Japanese-held islands:

- Guam: over 18,000 Japanese killed, 485 captured from 21 July to 10 August
- Tinian: over 8000 Japanese killed, 313 captured from 31 July to 1 August
- Peleliu: over 10,500 Japanese killed, 202 captured from 15 September to 27 November
- Angaur: over 1300 Japanese killed, 59 captured from 17 to 30 September.

US military losses were relatively light compared to Japanese losses and their victories in all these campaigns established complete naval and air superiority over most of the Pacific Ocean.

War in China in 1944

The US established airfields in southern and western China in 1943 allowing B-29 bombers (see page 206) to reach Japan's home islands. In order to capture these airfields and connect Japanese territories in China and French Indochina, Operation Ichi-Go was launched by Japan in April 1944. This was the single largest land invasion of the entire war in Asia with approximately 400,000 Japanese troops backed up by 800 tanks fighting 400,000 Chinese soldiers. Japan captured the targeted airfields, killing up to 200,000 Chinese soldiers and civilians during the attack. This had little effect on the USA's ability to attack Japan since the B-29 bombers were simply flown to Saipan and other airfields.

Philippines invaded, October 1944 to August 1945

While bombing raids against Japan continued from Saipan, US army and naval forces began an invasion of the Philippines. The Philippines supplied rubber to Japanese industry and were on the route of oil tankers moving between the Dutch East Indies and Japan. Control of the archipelago would enable US aircraft and submarines to further damage Japan's economy. The first US landings were made on the island of Leyte on 20 October 1944 and fighting continued there until 31 December. While ground forces fought, one of the largest naval battles in history took place (see below).

Major islands in the Philippines were invaded one after the other while other Japanese garrisons were cut off from their supplies and left behind. The campaign was costly to Japan with over 330,000 troops killed, compared to 14,000 for the Allies. Japan's official surrender of the islands took place on

15 August, 10 months after the initial invasion, but fighting continued as small groups of Japanese troops had no access to radio and were unaware of this. In fact, some Japanese troops were unaware of the surrender of Japan in September 1945 (see page 211) and members of the Japanese imperial family had to be brought to the islands to convince soldiers to surrender. The last Japanese soldier surrendered in 1974.

Battle of Leyte Gulf, 24–26 October 1944

The Battle of Leyte Gulf was fought on 24–26 October 1944, when what remained of the Japanese fleet decided to fight the US fleet in a desperate, but final, attempt to slow the invasion of the Philippines. The US fleet of 34 carriers with 1500 aircraft, and escorted by 177 warships of various types, battled four Japanese carriers with few aircraft, escorted by 65 warships and supported by 300 land-based aircraft. In a series of battles, the USA lost three carriers and a few support ships, while Japan lost all four carriers and 24 other warships, as well as almost all aircraft it sent into the battle. This was the greatest loss of Japanese ships in any single naval engagement. The IJN would make only one more, and equally futile, offensive gesture in April 1945, before completely ceasing operations. The Battle of Leyte Gulf was the first significant use of kamikaze attacks. These suicide flights would wreak havoc on US ships in several future battles.

Iwo Jima, 19 February to 26 March, 1945

The volcanic island of Iwo Jima, with an area of only 21 km², was considered one of the Japanese home islands and was the next Allied target. Radar stations at Iwo Jima gave the Japanese home islands warnings of incoming US bomber raids and fighter aircraft there attacked US bombers. The USA wanted the Iwo Jima airfields for fighters which could then protect B-29 bombers while flying over Japan.

Japan's military repeated its earlier strategy of trying to inflict as much damage on US forces as possible to delay the invasion of Japan itself. Alternatively, a stiff defence might cause the USA to consider a conditional Japanese surrender that would prevent the military occupation of the country and allow the Japanese emperor to remain on the throne. With this in mind, the Japanese army constructed hidden bunkers, installed enormous amounts of artillery, and excavated 18 km of tunnels linking various positions. Over 22,000 Japanese troops were installed on the small island; the US predicted it would be taken within a week.

Iwo Jima was bombed by aircraft regularly after mid-June 1944. On 19 February 1945, the first waves of marines began landing, believing that three days of prior naval bombardment by US warships had destroyed most Japanese installations. Japanese forces inflicted major losses on Allied troops from hidden bunkers linked by tunnels. Flamethrowers, often fitted to tanks, were used to combat these installations, which were often quickly reoccupied as a result of the tunnel network.

Fighting finally ended on 26 March. Out of 22,000 Japanese troops, all but 216 were killed. The USA lost almost 7000 men while 19,000 were wounded out of a force of 70,000. Soon after capture, Iwo Jima was used as a base for US aircraft to attack Japan.

Okinawa, 1 April to 21 June 1945

Okinawa, just south of the main populated islands of Japan but still considered part of the home islands, was within bombing range of most Japanese cities. Its capture would give the USA more airfields from which to bomb all Japan, as well as Japanese military targets stationed in China. It was hoped that by conquering Okinawa, the USA would convince Japan to surrender.

The US-led Allies used 200,000 troops and 1200 ships, including 40 carriers and 18 battleships, for the invasion of Okinawa. Thousands of aircraft flown from carriers and island airfields also participated. They faced around 110,000 Japanese soldiers, tens of thousands of armed civilians, a few thousand aircraft and the remnants of the Japanese navy. The US military estimated it would take about a month to subdue the island, starting on 1 April; 81 days later, the battle ended on 21 June 1945.

As in other island campaigns in the Pacific, most Japanese fought to the death, believing it better to die with honour than surrender. Over 95,000

SOURCE G

US aircraft carrier USS *Bunker Hill* burns after being hit by multiple kamikaze attacks off Okinawa on 11 May 1945.

What information does Source G convey about naval warfare during the Second World War in the Pacific?

Japanese soldiers died during the fighting, along with anywhere from 50,000 to 150,000 civilians who were killed during attacks by each side, or by committing suicide. US ground forces lost 7000 men, with 40,000 others wounded.

Kamikaze attacks on US and Allied warships at Okinawa destroyed around 30 vessels, damaging 370 others. These suicide attacks by 1500 aircraft rarely made it to their targets, but the few that did managed to inflict the greatest losses on the US navy during the entire war, killing 5000 men.

Japan lost almost 8000 desperately needed aircraft and pilots during the battle, making itself more vulnerable to US bombers. The nine remaining Japanese warships were sent on 7 April to attack US ships with little air protection. They were met by 11 US carriers and six battleships; six of the nine Japanese ships were destroyed, the survivors being small destroyers. The impressive IJN was no more after Okinawa.

Consequences of Okinawa

US military planners reasoned that if Japan defended its main populated islands as tenaciously as they had uninhabited Iwo Jima or Okinawa, then fighting on the main islands where millions lived would be even more difficult. Plans were made to land hundreds of thousands of US troops on these main islands but were not needed when two nuclear bombs became available. The US military decided to use them in order to force Japan into an unconditional surrender which they reasoned would save the lives of many US soldiers, as well as millions of Japanese civilians.

6–9 August 1945

The Manhattan Project, started in 1942, was a secret military programme to develop what would be called the atomic bomb. US scientists, co-operating with those in Canada and Britain, raced to develop this weapon before Germany or any other country. In July 1945, after Germany surrendered, the world's first nuclear bomb test was carried out in New Mexico in the USA. The bomb, one of three prepared, produced a mushroom-shaped cloud of superheated gas and debris 12 km high and the shockwave was felt over 160 km away.

Hiroshima, 6 August 1945

Hiroshima was selected as the first target for the second of the three nuclear devices. Hiroshima had been spared major bombing raids so destroying the city would demonstrate to the US government what the bomb was capable of in an urban setting and also make a greater impact on the Japanese government, which still refused unconditional surrender. The bombing of Hiroshima was justified as it had a major military command centre, factories producing war supplies, and an active port.

A US B-29 bomber flew from Tinian Island on 6 August and dropped a 13-kiloton bomb on Hiroshima which entirely destroyed 12 km^2 of the city.

Seventy per cent of the city's buildings were completely destroyed and around 80,000 people died instantly. There were 70,000 people injured, many barely alive and suffering from major burns. Within a few months, the death toll would continue to rise as a result of **radiation sickness** and burns. The total dead from this first use of the atomic bomb was up to 166,000 people.

Japanese conditions for surrender

By radio, US President Harry Truman warned Japan on 9 August that if unconditional surrender was not immediately announced, more atomic bombs would fall on Japanese cities. Japan refused, stating that surrender was possible only with certain conditions:

- no military occupation of Japan's home islands
- only Japanese government to punish war criminals
- the emperor of Japan must be retained.

USSR invades Manchuria

Also on 9 August, the USSR invaded Manchukuo, the Japanese-controlled Chinese province of Manchuria. Over 1.6 million soldiers with 26,000 artillery units, over 5500 tanks and 5300 aircraft invaded in a four-pronged attack, killing tens of thousands of Japanese and Manchurian soldiers and capturing over 600,000 prisoners within days. The rapid collapse of Japan's huge army in Manchuria helped to convince many in Japan's government that unconditional surrender should be declared.

Nagasaki, 9 August 1945

The day the USSR invaded Manchuria was also the day when an atomic bomb was dropped on a second Japanese city. The city of Kokura was originally selected as the target, but it was covered in clouds which would hinder the B-29 bomber's ability to drop the bomb accurately. The plane moved on to the secondary target, Nagasaki, and released its device which exploded 469 m above the ground. The 21-kiloton device killed between 40,000 and 75,000 people instantly, with radiation and burns killing tens of thousands of more by December. The USA prepared more atomic bombs, expecting to have another ready by 19 August and three more for each of the next two months.

Surrender

Also on 9 August, Japan's Emperor Hirohito gave permission for the government to abandon its conditions for surrender and insist on only one: Japan must be allowed to keep Hirohito as Emperor. The USA, informed of this through the neutral government of Switzerland, presented no public objection and Japan surrendered on Hirohito's orders on 15 August 1945. The surrender was formalized by the signing of documents on the USS *Missouri* by Japanese government and army officials on 2 September. Hirohito remained Emperor of Japan until his death in early 1989.

 **KEY TERM**

Radiation sickness A series of illnesses that result from exposure to radiation released in a nuclear explosion, including cancer.

In order to understand why Japanese resistance more or less ended when Emperor Hirohito ordered the surrender, it is necessary to understand the role of the emperor in Japan at the time. The emperor was not just legally the head of all armed forces and the government, but also a divine being, descended from the sun goddess Amaterasu in the Japanese religious system of Shinto. Japanese troops that fought to the death or committed suicide in order to not be captured by US forces in the war did so to preserve their honour and that of the divine emperor in the process. When the emperor ordered an end to fighting, this order was obeyed by almost all groups. Many civilians were relieved as they were hungry, homeless and exhausted; many in the armed forces were also relieved, not willing to die for a lost cause. However, many military officers committed ritual suicide as a way to retain honour in defeat.

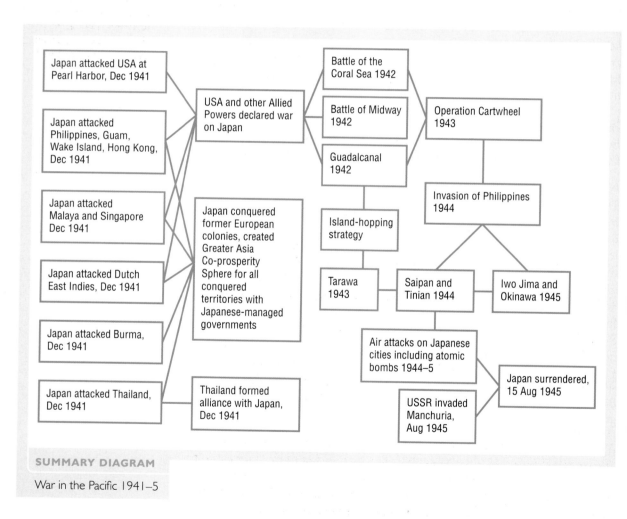

SUMMARY DIAGRAM

War in the Pacific 1941–5

③ The home front

▸ *Key question:* To what extent was the defeat of the Empire of Japan the result of greater US war production?

While armies and fleets battled across Asia and the Pacific, each nation's war effort affected women and other groups. War production was an important aspect of total war and helped to determine the outcome of the Second World War.

Women and minority groups

Women had worked in both the USA and Japan before the war, but their participation in factory work rose significantly during the conflict. While some women were employed against their will, especially by the Japanese army, many millions joined the workforce willingly, altering their lives. Minority groups, especially in the USA, also made significant contributions to the war effort, affecting their lives as well.

← **How were women and minority groups treated during the war and how were their lives changed at the war's conclusion?**

Japan

Japan's government discouraged women from participating in war production, although millions joined the work force in order to earn enough money to feed their families.

Japan's war effort

Japanese women were critical to Japan's war effort. In 1941, the Japanese government forced all men aged 16–40 to enrol in the military and all women between 16 and 25 who were unmarried were drafted into war production industries. Soon, a million women began working in factories, joined by three million schoolchildren and a million conscripted Chinese and Korean workers sent from Japanese-occupied Asia. Japanese government policy discouraged women with families from working in factories until 1943, when the shortage of labour could no longer be ignored; many worked in factories to have enough money to eat. The number of women working outside the home rose to 14 million by 1945, approximately 42 per cent of all workers. Most of these women worked in agriculture and constituted only an increase of a million women more than levels in 1939.

'Comfort women'

The actions of Japanese soldiers raping women in Nanjing in 1937 shocked the world (see page 191). This negative publicity caused the Japanese military to address the sexual needs of their soldiers by creating military operated brothels referred to as 'comfort houses' or 'comfort stations'. Women, often kidnapped, were forced to work as sex slaves in the brothels and were referred to as 'comfort women'. It is believed that over 200,000 women were used in this way.

? According to Source H, why should 'comfort women' be considered slaves?

SOURCE H

Excerpt from *A Modern History of Japan: From Tokugawa Times to the Present* by Andrew Gordon, published by Oxford University Press, Oxford, 2003, pages 224–5.

Another group of war victims received much less public attention at the time or immediately after the war. These were the many thousands of young girls or women who were forced to work in euphemistically named 'comfort stations' near the front lines of battle. About 80 per cent were Koreans, and the remainder included Chinese, Japanese, and a small number of European women. Recruiters told some women they were hired as waitresses or servants. They simply captured others at gunpoint. Once at the front, all the women were forced to serve as prostitutes for Japanese troops … What further distinguished the plight of the 'comfort women' from the common wartime phenomenon of prostitutes selling themselves to soldiers was the hands-on role of Japanese authorities. From cabinet ministers to local commanders, state officials authorized, regulated, and in some cases directly managed the comfort stations.

At the end of the war, the Japanese military destroyed most documents related to the war in an effort to avoid war crimes charges, so exact numbers of sex slaves are not known. The Japanese government denied until 1993 that army brothels had existed in the war and that women had been forced into prostitution. In that year the government issued an official apology.

USA

Women and minorities in the USA participated more fully in war production than in any other nation except the USSR (see page 164). This helped the USA to produce enormous quantities of war goods and affected the lives of groups that had been marginalized before the conflict.

The US war effort

Women were an essential part of the US war effort after 1941, as millions of men joined the armed services. In 1941 over 14.5 million women worked outside the home. By 1945, this number was well over 19 million, constituting 36 per cent of all workers compared to 25 per cent before the war. Women's participation in new, war-related industries was significant, with 91 per cent of new workers being women in 185 war-related factories in Detroit, Michigan, for example. Women had not participated in shipbuilding before the war, but by 1943, 10 per cent of all ship production work was completed by women.

American women in the armed services

Over 300,000 American women joined the military, serving in the US army, navy and marines, serving in almost every capacity except combat. The army established the Women's Army Corps (WAC), while the navy created the Women Accepted for Volunteer Emergency Service (WAVES). The air force, part of the army at the time, created the Women Air Force Service Pilots (WASPs).

SOURCE I

US women workers riveting a wing section for a bomber aircraft during the Second World War in 1943.

What information about the Second World War is conveyed by Source I?

Reasons for joining war effort

American women who became factory employees or joined divisions of the military did so for many reasons. According to historian Allan M. Winkler, many women were tired of the monotony of domestic work where they stayed at home, completing the same tasks repeatedly for years. Others joined out of a sense of nationalism and patriotic duty in order to help win the war. Many joined so they could earn money and therefore enjoy some independence.

Women made a major contribution to the war effort as a group and many remained in factories at the war's end, although they continued to suffer discrimination in terms of pay, types of work that were offered to them, and in not being able to be placed in combat situations in the military for several more decades.

African Americans

African Americans were affected by the Second World War as well. Discrimination against non-whites was law in many states, but was practised throughout the nation. In most US cities, people of African descent lived separately from those of European descent, suffered around 50 per cent unemployment in 1940, and usually found work only in low-level positions. In 1940, there were only 240 African Americans employed in the aircraft industry out of 100,000 workers; most of these were janitors. Seventy-five per cent of all African American women who worked outside the home did so as servants or as field workers on large farms before the Second World War.

Economic opportunities

Many African Americans, and whites, found it ironic that the US government claimed to be fighting to preserve 'freedom', against clearly racist regimes such as the Nazis in Germany while African Americans were clearly, and often legally, second-class citizens in the USA. Nevertheless, African Americans joined the war effort, mostly as a form of economic relief. African Americans joined the workforce in huge numbers which resulted in at least 700,000 African Americans moving into northern and western US cities, mostly from southern states, causing major urban growth (see the table below).

African American population growth in selected US cities from 1940 to 1946

City	Percentage growth
San Francisco	560
Los Angeles	109
Detroit	47

Most African Americans, however, lived in crowded, substandard housing, and experienced discrimination from neighbouring communities. This occasionally led to race riots such as the one that occurred in Detroit in 1943 that left 34 people, mostly African Americans, dead.

African Americans made up eight per cent of all war production workers by 1945 and the numbers employed by the government rose from 60,000 to 200,000 during the war. Increased economic opportunities meant a reduction in African American unemployment and poverty and the entry of many into the middle economic class.

Political developments

With expanded economic opportunities and the irony of fighting a war to liberate other races from oppression, such as the Chinese from Japanese rule, African Americans became more active politically. In 1941, Philip Randolph, head of the Brotherhood of Sleeping Car Porters, the largest African American labour union, called for a massive all-African American march in Washington, DC, the US capital. US President Franklin D. Roosevelt met

Randolph in an effort to persuade him to not conduct a march which he feared would cause race riots. As a result of Randolph's efforts, Roosevelt issued Executive Order 8802 in June 1941 that forbade discrimination on the basis of race or colour for workers in the government or defence industries. The Fair Employment Practices Committee was established to investigate racial discrimination but had limited power.

Military service

The National Association for the Advancement of Colored People (NAACP) was an organization that pressed for racial equality. It successfully pressured the US government to allow African American men to join the military in order to fight the Axis powers, although they were not allowed to fight initially. When allowed to join combat units of the army, which included the air force and marines, they did so in segregated units but not until 1943; they were not allowed in naval combat units. In late 1941, fewer than 100,000 African Americans served in the army, but by the end of 1944, this number was over 700,000. African American soldiers returning from fighting in Asia and Europe at the end of the war were determined to end discrimination, contributing greatly to the **civil rights movement**. Desegregation of the US military took place in 1948 on the order of President Harry Truman.

Hispanic Americans

Hispanic Americans contributed greatly to the war effort by working in factories and in shipbuilding industries. As millions of farmers enrolled in the armed services, agricultural work lacked workers. Hundreds of thousands of Hispanic Americans and Mexican nationals worked on farms throughout the US helping to plant and harvest crops while suffering from discrimination similar to that of African Americans. Tens of thousands of Hispanic Americans joined military services as well, with many moving to urban areas after the war to work in industry as a result of expanded US production.

Native Americans

There were 25,000 Native Americans, many of whom were not allowed to vote in their home states since they were not considered citizens but foreigners, who served in the armed forces, primarily in the army. Unlike African Americans, they were integrated into regular fighting units. Many tribes with a warrior tradition, such as the Crow Nation of Montana, volunteered almost to a man to join the armed services. Navajo code talkers helped the US navy win the war in the Pacific just by speaking their difficult language (see page 201). Men from the Comanche Nation were also code talkers in the Second World War, serving in the US army in Europe. One of the first people to fight their way to the highest point of Iwo Jima, Mount Suribachi, was a Native American from the Pima Nation in Arizona. Although there was discrimination, there seems to have been less discrimination against Native Americans than against most other peoples of non-European descent. It is estimated that 40,000 Native Americans worked

KEY TERM

Civil rights movement
Political movement in the USA that worked for equal rights for all citizens.

🗝️ **KEY TERM**

Reservations Territories within the USA operated with varying levels of autonomy by and for Native Americans.

in war industries, causing many to leave **reservations** for the first time. After the war, most did not return to the reservations and they assimilated with people in the cities, losing much of their traditional culture in the process.

Rationing

Both Japan and the USA reduced the amount of consumer goods available during the war. This was to conserve scarce supplies of metals, petroleum and food, but also to use factories for producing war goods.

Japan

Japan imposed a strict system of rationing in 1941. While many products were rationed, such as clothing, metal objects and fuel, it was food rationing that affected Japan the most. Strict food rationing was critical since Japan imported much of its food supply. Chemicals needed for fertilizers were instead used in war production, so that Japanese fields grew fewer crops. Submarine and air attack destroyed most shipping by 1943, preventing imports of desperately needed food. Japan's annual rice supply was halved between 1941 and 1945. Hungry workers were often absent from factory work as they went to the countryside to barter directly with farmers for more food. Malnourishment led to weakened immune systems and therefore more illness, causing people to be absent from factories involved in war production. By the end of the war, many millions were starving.

SOURCE J

Excerpt from 'Need, greed and protest in Japan's black market, 1938–1949' by Owen Griffiths in _Journal of Social History_, Vol. 35, published by George Mason University Press, Virginia, 2002.

As food became the central preoccupation for most urban Japanese, new forms of protest began to seep through the cracks of government censorship with one of the most common phrases being 'empty bellies can't fight a war.' As if to demonstrate this, millions of Japanese embarked on regular trips to the countryside to buy or barter food directly from farmers, frequently calling in sick at their work to make the journey. This practice, called kaidashi _(going out to buy), quickly became part of the language of the black market, although it has been mistakenly enshrined in historical memory as a post-war phenomenon. Farmers, for their part, obliged urban dwellers by withholding or hoarding part of their crop and selling it at many times the official price. Not only did this practice fan the fires of wartime inflation but it thoroughly undermined the rationing and distribution system for staple foods. Ironically, like the day labourers whose stock soared during wartime, farmers also found that they were on top of the traditional rural/urban split and, for a time, enjoyed the power that food production brought with it._

?

According to Source J, what was the effect of farmers hoarding food in Japan during the war?

JSA

A system of strict rationing was introduced in 1942 in conjunction with war production. All factories that had produced cars now switched over to military equipment, so no cars were produced at all until after the war. Tyres, which depended on imported rubber that was no longer available (most rubber came from Japanese-occupied south-east Asia), could no longer be purchased even after synthetic rubber, made from petroleum, became more common. In order to preserve petroleum for the war effort, leisure travel and races were banned. Food was rationed, with consumers having to present ration books when making purchases to prevent hoarding and over-consumption. The USA produced enormous quantities of food and rationing allowed the USA to supply food to other Allied nations, especially Britain which relied on food imports.

War production

← **What was the importance of war production to the outcome of the conflict?**

In many ways, the Second World War, in both Europe and Asia, is a prime example of total war. Never in history had factories produced war goods on such a scale or mobilized so many millions of workers while simultaneously mobilizing millions of men to fight for victory. Production was perhaps the most important element in final victory for the USA.

Japanese war production

The ability to produce large quantities of ships, planes, arms, ammunition and other war goods was critical to the conflict's outcome. Japan did produce large numbers of aircraft and ships, but not on the scale of the USA (see the table below). Japanese industry lacked raw materials and was a main reason for going to war in the first place (see page 189). When sources of metal, oil

War production in Japan and the USA

Production and raw materials between 1941 and 1945	Japan	USA*
Aircraft (all types)	76,000	300,000
Aircraft carriers (all types)	16	163
All other warships	241	1,028
Trucks	165,000	2,400,000
Tanks	2,500	88,500
Atomic bombs	0	3
Coal (tonnes)	185,000,000	2,100,000,000
Iron ore (tonnes)	21,000,000	400,000,000
Petroleum (tonnes)	5,000,000	830,000,000

*Production numbers include products for war in Europe, north Africa, Asia and the Pacific.

and other needed products were located, they had to be sent to Japanese factories by ships which were vulnerable to submarine and air attack. Japanese shipping was never adequately organized to efficiently ship needed supplies either. Moreover, the government never organized industry to maximize production or use workers efficiently or gave priority to certain industries over others; women were discouraged from work although factories lacked workers. This severely affected the nation's ability to supply its army and navy. Throughout the war, Japan lacked fuel and metals of all sorts, and later its production facilities, and entire cities, were destroyed by US bomber aircraft. Production by both nations, however, was on a scale not seen in any earlier conflict.

US war production

The USA was the world's most industrialized country and its largest producer of petroleum. It had little need to import raw materials and it had a large population that was quickly organized to produce war goods. There were few qualms about employing millions of women in factories, compared to some other nations, and the USA's production increased each month throughout the conflict. Production was also unhindered by bombing or other aspects of total war that affected Japan and other nations since no Axis state could reach it with their aircraft.

While the USA battled Japan, it also battled Germany and Italy, as well as the puppet-states they created, with over 16 million men in the armed forces by 1945. The USA also supplied millions of soldiers in Britain, the USA, Australia, France and other countries and helped to feed Allied civilian populations. While it is impossible to break down US industrial production figures to determine which items went to fight Japan or were sent to Europe, it is safe to conclude that most naval vessels were used against Japan; tanks were used primarily against the Axis in Europe and north Africa. US production in the war was on a tremendous and unprecedented scale so that by 1945 over 66,000,000 men and women were employed in the war industry.

US production was so great that Japan would never have been able to counter it effectively, even if it had unhindered access to raw materials. Many historians argue that US production was the crucial factor in US success against Japan.

To what extent did the treatment of prisoners by both the USA and Japan depend on their nationality?

Prisoners of war

During the course of the war, both the USA and Japan took many prisoners, both military and civilian.

Japan

Japan treated prisoners harshly by providing little health care, food or clothing. Prisoners were subjected to torture, heavy labour, medical experimentation and executions. It is not known how many Chinese soldiers and citizens were imprisoned by the Japanese military during the war, but massacres of both are well documented, such as the one that occurred at Nanjing (see page 191). At the end of the war, only 56 Chinese people remained imprisoned by Japan; it is widely believed that hundreds of thousands of captured Chinese soldiers were killed through execution or starvation. Approximately 80,000 British, US and other Allied troops survived the war, most suffering from malnutrition.

Japanese Americans

Before the outbreak of the war in December 1941, there were approximately 127,000 Japanese Americans. The attack on Pearl Harbor led to accusations that Japanese Americans could not be trusted and there were calls for their expulsion from the USA.

US President Roosevelt signed Executive Order 9066 in February 1942, forcing all Japanese Americans living on the US Pacific coast to move to prison camps for fear they would help Japan if it launched an invasion of the USA; 110,000 people were imprisoned. While some were released from the camps in 1943 and others in 1944, the majority remained until early in 1945. It is estimated that Japanese Americans incurred financial losses of over $400 million as a result of imprisonment, mostly through losing homes and businesses while in the camps. This was the worst violation of civil rights in the USA during the war. It was officially acknowledged in 1988, when compensation was provided to those former prisoners still living.

China and the USSR

Millions of Japanese soldiers and civilians were in China when the war came to an end. Many soldiers committed suicide, but the majority surrendered to Chinese government troops and other Allied Powers. Around 150 Japanese officers were charged with war crimes and executed after trials by the Chinese government. Unknown numbers captured by the USSR and communists were also executed. Most soldiers, however, were repatriated to Japan slowly, some returning years later. Japanese troops captured by the USSR in Manchuria and other northern regions were imprisoned in harsh conditions. Many died through abuse and starvation, while others were worked to death. Those that survived were returned to Japan by 1956.

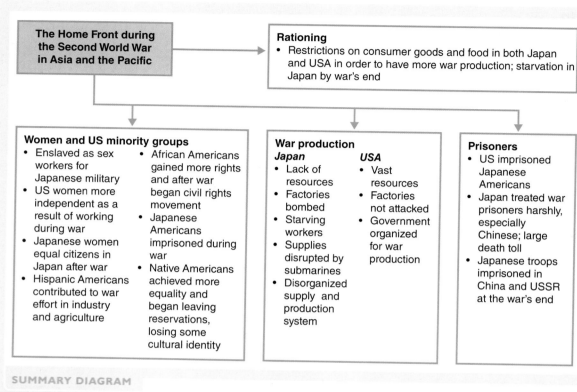

SUMMARY DIAGRAM

The home front

4 Resistance movements

> ▶ *Key question:* How did resistance movements affect Japan during the Second World War?

Throughout Asia, there was resistance to Japanese occupation and forced labour. Resistance took many forms, especially armed resistance. These groups usually used guerrilla tactics (see page 3) to disrupt Japanese military operations as well as sabotaging production, operating spy networks and leading open rebellions.

→ Chinese resistance

Resistance groups in China were formed as early as 1931, after Japan invaded Manchuria and later established Manchukuo. Guerrilla units, primarily directed by the **Chinese Communist Party** (CCP), were active until 1945, inflicting considerable damage on Japanese forces and forcing Japan to abandon large areas of the countryside.

 KEY TERM

Chinese Communist Party The communist party of China, established in 1921.

What was the importance of Chinese resistance movements during the Second World War?

Resistance in Manchuria

At least nine separate resistance groups fought Japan in Manchuria from 1931 to 1942. These groups numbered a total of at least 300,000 men and occasionally worked together, often fighting conventional land battles with troops from both Japan and Manchukuo. Japan kept several hundred thousand troops in Manchuria to combat rebels and, by the end of 1938, Japan estimated that there were only 10,000 resistance fighters left. Most of the rebel groups were eventually merged to form the Northeast Anti-Japanese United Army (NAJUA) which was operated by communists in alliance with the CCP. NAJUA was eventually driven out of Manchuria by Japan and into the USSR in 1942. NAJUA formed part of the Soviet army that attacked Japanese forces in Asia in August 1945.

Resistance in China

Resistance in China began as soon as Japan attacked in July 1937. The Chinese government began a war of attrition in August to delay advancing Japanese troops, buying time for civilians and parts of the army to retreat, along with war equipment and factories, into China's interior. Dams were destroyed to flood areas, while bridges, railways and roads were demolished to prevent Japanese troops from using them. The USSR supplied China with large quantities of weapons, hoping that Japan would become bogged down and not able to mount an attack on them. The CCP's forces, which had battled the Chinese government for over a decade in a civil war before 1937, now merged their forces with the government, temporarily forming two armies that worked together with other government forces of China.

These forces operated until 1941 when the CCP and Chinese government ceased co-operation and renewed the civil war, attacking each other as well as the forces of Japan. CCP opted to use guerrilla warfare with some success, causing Japanese troops to garrison cities but abandon much of the countryside, where assassinations of Japanese officers and Chinese people who co-operated with Japan were routine. Communist forces increased in number throughout the war, rising from around 30,000 in 1937 to over 900,000, including both men and women, by 1945. The damage inflicted by Chinese guerrillas on Japan, and vice versa, remains unknown but Japan did station over a million soldiers in China throughout the war in order to maintain some control over captured territory.

Other resistance movements

Philippines

Around 250,000 people in the Philippines joined a myriad of resistance movements against Japanese occupation, fighting both Japanese soldiers and Filipinos who co-operated with Japan. It is estimated that there were 277 separate guerrilla units, many of which co-operated with each other in ever-changing coalitions. Many of these groups were based on individual islands. While some groups were communist in nature, others were US and

← **How successful were guerrilla movements in defeating Japanese forces?**

Filipino soldiers who escaped capture in 1942 when Japan forced the US military to surrender at Corregidor (see page 194). Many guerrilla units co-ordinated their efforts with US military assistance, including intelligence reports passed to them by radio; they were often supplied by submarines. Resistance was so successful on many islands that Japan controlled only 12 of 48 provinces.

Thailand

Khabuan Kan Seri Thai, or Seri Thai Movement, was formed in early 1942 when the Thai Prime Minister Plaek Phibunsongkhram made an alliance with Japan and declared war on the USA and Britain. Seri Thai was supported by major government officials, including Queen Ramphaiphanni, as well as Thailand's ambassador to the USA. Seri Thai grew into a major force as Japanese troops essentially occupied the country and abused its citizens, conscripting many for forced labour. Seri Thai rescued Allied pilots shot down over Thailand, operated a small air force, unlike any other resistance movement of the Second World War, and in June 1944, helped overthrow Plaek Phibunsongkhram, who was replaced by a Seri Thai member.

Smaller resistance movements

Resistance movements operated in almost all areas occupied by Japan. The Korean Liberation Army amalgamated many smaller resistance groups and co-operated with the Chinese government against Japan, but had limited success, similar to resistance movements in Hong Kong. Communist groups were active against Japan and former colonial powers, including:

- the Malayan People's Anti-Japanese Army in Malaya
- *Việt Nam Độc Lập Đồng Minh Hội*, known as the Viet Minh, in Vietnam
- the Anti-Fascist People's Freedom League in Burma.

These groups conducted guerrilla campaigns that did not kill large numbers of Japanese soldiers or co-operating civilians, but did force Japan to station large numbers of soldiers in these areas to retain control and to prevent the spread of guerrillas. This tied down large numbers of soldiers needed elsewhere, consuming valuable supplies.

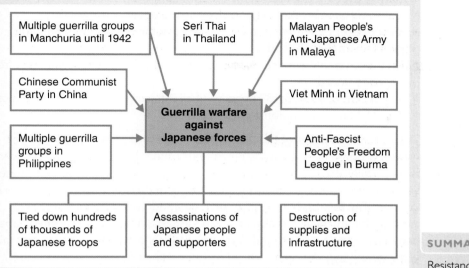

5 The effects of the Second World War in Asia and the Pacific

▶ **Key question:** *What were the short- and long-term effects of the Second World War on Asian and Pacific people?*

The war destroyed millions of lives, many cities and governments. It also led to the formation of new governments, new states and further conflict.

Death and destruction

The death toll of people, both military and civilian, was enormous in Asia and on the Pacific islands. While Japan was severely damaged through US fire-bombing, it was the war in China that caused the most deaths.

> **What were the most significant losses for each of nations involved in the Second World War in Asia and the Pacific?**

Japan

Japan suffered greatly and lost an empire despite having had up to 5.5 million men in the military during the war. At the war's conclusion, according to historian John Dower, Japan had:

- 1,740,000 armed forces dead and 4.5 million injured or ill
- a million dead civilians
- 4.5 million injured or ill armed forces
- 66 major cities heavily bombed with 40 per cent of all urban areas destroyed

- Tokyo's pre-war population of seven million was only two million at the war's end as many had fled the city or were dead
- 30 per cent of all urban populations were homeless, with nine million people homeless in total
- 3.5 million members of the armed forces and three million civilians were stranded outside Japan
- 80 per cent of all ships, 33 per cent of all industrial machinery and 25 per cent of all railway equipment was destroyed.

The war left hundreds of thousands of orphans and homeless children, as well as widows, maimed soldiers with no families left alive, and others who were socially stigmatized in a culture that had never had to deal with these issues before; they were neglected by society and government, sometimes for decades. The repatriation of 6.5 million Japanese to the home islands was complicated by the fact that many were diseased, many were children, Japan had no housing for them, and there was little food available. It took several years for the majority to return, while hundreds of thousands disappeared, were made to work as forced labourers, or were killed by disease or violence. Around a million Koreans were repatriated to Korea over many years, having been brought to Japan as labourers during the war; 400,000 remained.

China

Much of China was destroyed in the initial invasion by Japan in 1937, including major damage to its largest city, Shanghai, and the capital of the time, Nanjing. Many villages, towns and cities were either razed or heavily damaged in bombing raids and battles during the eight-year war. Around 1.3 million Chinese government soldiers died battling Japan, with around two million wounded. China suffered large numbers of civilian deaths; 17 million dead is commonly cited.

US forces and other civilian dead

Just over 100,000 men in the US military died during the war with Japan, with around 250,000 wounded. US civilians did die, but numbered no more than 2000. The Philippines, a colony of the USA, was heavily damaged in the war. In Manila, 100,000 people died during fighting which destroyed most of the city as well. Some historians estimate that a million civilians in the Philippines died during the war. Other civilian war dead include:

- Burma: 250,000
- Dutch East Indies: approximately 3.5 million
- French Indochina: approximately one million
- Korea: approximately 400,000
- Malaya: 100,000
- Portuguese Timor: 70,000
- Singapore: 50,000.

Japan, China and Korea

There were many difficulties that needed to be resolved at the end of the war. Millions were starving, new governments were formed and wars broke out. Resistance movements that had pressed Japan throughout the conflict now called for the independence of their homelands instead of being returned to the USA and European states.

← **How were Japan, China and Korea politically affected by the Allied victory in the Second World War?**

Occupied Japan

On 2 September 1945, US troops began landing in Japan. It had been several weeks since Japan's surrender and the Japanese army and various government offices busied themselves destroying documents that could be used against the leadership for war crimes charges.

War crimes

Soon war crimes trials were conducted for a number of government and military officials, across Asia and the Pacific, leading to prison terms and execution. Among the war crimes were the imprisonment and torture of local populations and enemy soldiers. There were 200,000 government officials who were expelled from the government as a result of their connection to the war.

Japan's new government

A new constitution was written in 1946 by the USA, to be enacted in mid-1947 by a new US-approved Japanese government. The new constitution kept the emperor as head of state, but limited his powers to being a state symbol that was no longer divine. Freedom of religion, speech, press and political association were included in the document. It also banned discrimination on the basis of gender, race, social status or family origin. The constitution also stated clearly that Japan would never again settle its problems through war. By all accounts, the vast majority of Japanese citizens were pleased with the document which continues to be followed until today.

Japan's recovery

Although the USA at first meant Japan to pay war reparations, this was dropped when it was determined that it was more important to rebuild Japan's economy. Japan suffered massive price inflation, continued hunger and mass unemployment for years after the war. Ironically, it was war that revived the Japanese economy. With the outbreak of the **Korean War** in 1950, the US government placed billions of dollars worth of orders with Japanese industries as production costs were low and it would reduce the expense of shipping war goods from the USA. This led to a 300 per cent increase in exports and a 70 per cent increase in production for the country. By 1952, Japan was economically and politically stable. In April 1952, Japan became fully independent when US occupation ended.

KEY TERM

Korean War A military conflict between communist northern Korea and non-communist southern Korea which in the context of the Cold War attracted significant international involvement. It was fought between 1950 and 1953.

? According to Source K, how did the Korean War affect Japan?

SOURCE K

Excerpt from *A Modern History of Japan: From Tokugawa Times to the Present* by Andrew Gordon, published by Oxford University Press, Oxford, 2003, page 241.

*This tragedy across the straits [the Korean War] conferred great fortune on Japan. With the war came a surge of American military procurement orders placed with Japanese industries, which were located conveniently close to the front. In the years 1951–53, war procurements amounted to about two billion dollars, or roughly 60 per cent of all Japan's exports. Japanese leaders tastelessly celebrated what Prime Minister Yoshida called a 'gift of the gods' and businessmen dubbed 'blessed rain from heaven.' From 1949 to 1951 exports nearly tripled, and production rose nearly 70 per cent. Corporations began to show profits for the first time since the surrender, and they responded with a surge of investment in new plants and equipment. The **gross national product** began to increase at double-digit rates. Japan's recovery was underway.*

With reforms in place and the economy on the mend, and with the Korean War placing great demands on American military resources, pressures in Washington [the US capital] mounted to end the occupation. The end came sooner than many had anticipated; in 1945, some top officials in the United States had spoken of the need to occupy Japan for two decades, or even a century. As it turned out, the era of formal occupation lasted just under seven years.

🔑 KEY TERM

Gross national product
All economic activity of a nation, which includes production, exports and imports.

China

The USSR's capture and occupation of Manchuria greatly affected the Chinese Communist Party (CCP). Not only were Japanese troops and the Manchukuo government captured, but their weapons were given to the CCP. Manchukuo's troops, several hundred thousand, were integrated quickly into the CCP's own Red Army which worked to protect northern China, where they were based, from China's government forces (see Chapter 5).

SOURCE L

Excerpt from *Modern China: The Fall and Rise of a Great Power, 1850 to the Present* by Jonathan Fenby, published by HarperCollins, New York, 2008, pages 327–8.

… Two days before Hirohito surrendered, the Communists [CCP] rejected an instruction from [Chinese President General Chiang Kai-shek] for their forces not to advance into territory formerly held by the invaders. Instead, they sent in troops to link up with the Soviets, and brought back units that had been sheltering in Siberia. The new invaders handed them 100,000 guns from Japanese stores, and 200,000 Manchukuo troops were recruited.

? According to Source L, what were the results of the USSR's invasion of Manchuria?

Korea

Korea was returned to nominal independence at the end of the war in August 1945. Korea's institutions and culture had been heavily suppressed after it was annexed by Japan in 1910 and hundreds of thousands of

Japanese people had been settled there as well. With all these difficulties to overcome, the newly formed United Nations (see page 179) divided the peninsula into northern and southern zones. The northern zone was to be administered by the USSR, which had fought Japan in Korea just at the end of the war, and the USA, which had never fought in Korea, would administer the southern zone. The Soviets established a communist administration in the north, while the south developed democratic institutions and an economy based on capitalism. In 1950, the northern zone, now named North Korea, invaded what was then known as South Korea for various reasons, becoming one of the largest conflicts of the Cold War. The war would leave millions of Koreans dead and the peninsula divided almost exactly as it was before the conflict.

Decolonization

The **Atlantic Charter** was signed by the USA, Britain and eventually all the Allies during the Second World War. The Charter stated, among other things, that all people had the right to self-determination. The Charter was soon quoted by people in Asia who had been first under European and US rule and then governed by Japan. One of the difficulties for the USA, Britain, France and The Netherlands, all of whom stood to lose vast and valuable territories if they followed through with self-determination, was loss of prestige and the politics of the Cold War. It was difficult for nations to relinquish their grip on their Asian territories as these were symbols of empire and glory, and while not all were importantly economically, some were, such as Singapore, Hong Kong and the petroleum-producing oilfields of the Dutch East Indies.

How successful were former European and Japanese colonies in achieving independence after the Second World War in Asia and the Pacific?

 **KEY TERM**

Atlantic Charter A declaration of goals of Allied nations in the Second World War.

SOURCE M

Excerpt from *Empires on the Pacific: World War II and the Struggle for the Mastery of Asia* by Robert Smith Thompson, published by Basic Books, New York, 2001, page 377.

Throughout East Asia, the old order had receded and a new order had taken its place. When the Japanese surrendered, the Union Jack rose again over Hong Kong and Mark Young, the prewar governor now emaciated from his imprisonment, returned to Government House. But Man-Kan Lu, leader of the Legislative Council, made clear that henceforth the resident Chinese would receive just and equitable treatment.

On September 5, 1945, British reoccupation forces, headed by Lord Mountbatten, landed at Singapore, but they found a largely Chinese local population unwilling again to accept colonialism. Lee Kuan Yew, formerly a brilliant student at Cambridge University and later prime minister of independent Singapore, stated in a talk given in 1961 that 'My colleagues and I are of that generation of young men who went through the Second World War and the Japanese occupation and emerged determined that no one – neither the Japanese nor the British – had the right to push and kick us around.'

According to Source M, how did the Second World War affect relations between Britain and some of its colonies in Asia?

Decolonization in south-eastern Asia and the Pacific Ocean region.

① Philippines from USA in 1946

② Malaysia in stages from Britain from 1946 until 1963 when Singapore formed a separate nation

③ Burma from Britain in 1948

④ Dutch East Indies as Indonesia declared independence in 1945 and was recognized by The Netherlands in 1949

⑤ Laos with autonomy from France in 1949 and full independence in 1953

⑥ Cambodia in 1953 from France

⑦ Vietnam declared itself independence from France in 1945 and then fought France until 1954 which led to two states, one in the North and the other in the South; united Vietnam formed in 1976 at the end of the Vietnam War when all foreign troops left the country and North Vietnam conquered South Vietnam

⑧ Nauru from joint British, Australian and New Zealand supervision in 1968

⑨ Portuguese Timor from Portugal in 1974 and from Indonesia in 2002

⑩ Papua New Guinea from Australia rule in 1975

⑪ Solomon Islands from Britain in 1978

⑫ Kiribati from Britain in 1978

⑬ Brunei from Britain in 1984

⑭ Federated States of Micronesia from the USA in 1986

⑮ Palau from the USA in 1993

⑯ Hong Kong from Britain and given back to China in 1997

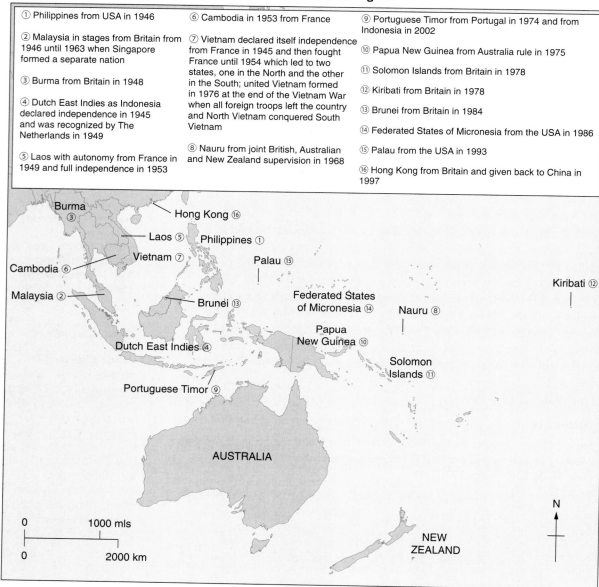

What information is conveyed by Source N about decolonization?

There was also the issue of the Cold War in which the USA and its allies and the USSR competed to promote their form of government and economic system. For many Asian groups, communism was a legitimate alternative as they had fought colonial powers and Japan. It helped that these communist groups had deviated somewhat from the Soviet version of communism since they often had nationalist ambitions as well. There was fear among colonial powers that if self-determination was allowed, then many newly independent states would become communist and be allied with the USSR.

Independence was granted to these states over a long period of time, often as the result of wars of independence.

Some territories either held before the Second World War or captured from Japan that are not independent today include several islands and archipelagos in the Pacific Ocean. Among these are New Caledonia, Guam and American Samoa.

Effects and results of Second World War in Asia and the Pacific

Death and destruction:
- 2.74 million dead Japanese, including soldiers
- Most Japanese and Chinese cities and industries heavily damaged
- At least 18 million dead Chinese civilians and soldiers
- 100,000 US war dead
- At least six million civilian deaths in other parts of Asia and the Pacific

Political effects on Japan, China, Korea:
- China erupted into civil war and became a communist state in 1949
- Korea divided between USSR and USA with Korean War between divisions 1950–3
- Japan occupied by USA, 1945–52
  - Demilitarized
  - Economy restored
  - Democratic government
  - Few punished for war

Independence movements of former European and Japanese colonies:
- Philippines from USA, 1946
- Malaysia, Singapore, Burma from Britain, 1946–63
- Dutch East Indies from The Netherlands, 1949
- Laos, Cambodia, Vietnam from France, 1949–76
- Various island nations, 1968–93

SUMMARY DIAGRAM

Effects and results of the Second World War in Asia and the Pacific

---

6 Key debate

▶ *Key question: What factors led to Japan's defeat?*

Japan's invasion of China in 1937 was seemingly successful. Huge swathes of territory were conquered from the poorly led and equipped Chinese government's army. Yet, the Chinese government and its military, although weakened, survived by retreating into the interior of the country, far from the reach of Japanese aircraft and troops. In the face of relentless communist guerrilla attacks and the possibility of counterattack by Chinese government forces, Japan stationed millions of men there to retain control, preventing their use elsewhere. There seems to have been no plan to counter the possibility of sustained Chinese resistance. Yet, the IJN, not tied down in

China, was able to launch a startling and rapid invasion of the Pacific, handing the US navy its greatest defeat at Pearl Harbor while invading many other areas at the same time with divisions of the army. By mid-1942, the Empire of Japan stretched thousands of miles and contained hundreds of millions of people.

According to Source O, what was the importance of China during the Second World War?

SOURCE O

Excerpt from *Modern China: The Fall and Rise of a Great Power, 1850 to the Present* by Jonathan Fenby, published by HarperCollins, New York, 2008, page 289.

Though China could not beat the enemy, the fact that the enemy could not beat it meant that up to a million [Japanese] troops and a large air force were tied down for eight years, with the associated cost in material resources and planning skills. The strain on Japan of the China Front thus made it an important piece in the jigsaw of the Second World War, as [US President] Roosevelt always appreciated, even if [British Prime Minister] Churchill complained about the attention paid by the Americans to a country he dismissed as 'four hundred million pigtails'.

Economic problems

Japan failed, however, to organize its war industry fully and only towards the end of the war began to enlist women in war production. Instead of having other Asian peoples join them in a true Greater Asia Co-prosperity Sphere where the various nationalities would work together to prevent European and US domination, the Japanese government, instead, exploited and abused them, causing widespread resistance. This resistance meant that China and other areas had to be occupied with vast military forces that consumed war supplies and petroleum that were desperately needed in the battle against the USA, and prevented or delayed raw materials needed for Japanese industry to fight the war.

According to Source P, why did Japan lose the war against the USA?

SOURCE P

Excerpt from *War in the Pacific: Pearl Harbor to Tokyo Bay* edited by Bernard C. Nalty, published by Salamander Books, London, 1991, page 291.

Japan's industrial infrastructure proved too fragile to sustain modern warfare. Stockpiles, especially of oil, could be replenished only through conquest, and the very act of conquering drew upon these reserves. Handicapped by industries that produced just 3.5 per cent of the world's manufactures, compared to 32.2 per cent for the United States, plagued by shortages of essential materials, the Japanese had no strategy, a shortcoming masked by tactical successes like the devastation … at Pearl Harbor and the conquest of Malaya. Instead of clearly defining a strategic objective and marshalling the resources needed to achieve it, Japan devoutly believed that the warrior spirit would prevail, that Americans lacked courage and resolve and would accept a negotiated settlement leaving the Japanese in control of Asia and the western Pacific.

Codes and submarines

The Japanese military suffered greatly after US code breakers decrypted naval and other codes. This allowed the USA to counter the move by the IJN to occupy Midway and destroy four critical carriers in the process. Submarine warfare was extremely effective in destroying Japanese shipping after the decryption of codes for Japan's merchant fleet. Once the IJN lost its aircraft carriers, the rest of the ships could be destroyed by air attack, and most were. Once ships travelling to and from Japan with supplies and troops were destroyed, the resource-poor Japanese home islands, which could not produce enough food to feed the population, were essentially already defeated and in time could have been starved into submission by the USA.

SOURCE Q

Excerpt from *The Pacific War: Japan Versus the Allies* by Alan J. Levine, published by Praeger, Connecticut, 1995, pages 86–7.

In 1944 the submarine war reached a climax. There were fierce battles against convoys. In February, Jack sank four out of five tankers in a single convoy in the South China Sea. In June and July, Tang achieved a record, exceeded once later in the war, of 10 ships sunk on a single patrol. From February to May, the submarines wreaked great destruction on convoys carrying troops to the Marianas and New Guinea. The submarines were numerous enough to carry on the war against the convoys while strongly supporting the fleet; they sank two of the three enemy carriers destroyed in the Battle of the Philippine Sea in June. Submarines also carried supplies to the Filipino guerrillas … Submarines increasingly operated from advanced bases, especially at Guam and the Admiralty Islands, while the American advance across the Pacific crowded Japan's shipping toward the coast of Asia. By the summer of 1944, they were shutting down many shipping routes.

According to Source Q, what was the importance of submarine warfare in the US campaign against Japan?

US production

Japan simply did not have the organization, resources, population and governing philosophy towards conquered peoples to allow it success when facing a large, industrial nation like the USA. The USA began preparing to fight a long-term war by mid-1941 with the **Victory Programme** when it was not even involved in a war. It was also the world's largest producing and consuming nation for decades before 1941, and had vast resources such as metals and petroleum, as well as an enormous number of people working in industry. Its factories, employing anyone who could work, practically buried Japan with their production during the war. While Japan struggled to build 16 carriers of all types, for example, the USA produced over 160. The US government was relatively efficient in its organization of the war effort by rationing food, making sure critical industries received whatever supplies were needed, and managing the economy so that the entire system functioned as smoothly as possible.

KEY TERM

Victory Programme US government initiative to increase the size of its armed forces in mid-1941 although it was not at war with any country.

In 1945, most US citizens believed that the USA was right to destroy the cities of Hiroshima and Nagasaki with atomic bombs, believing this ended the war faster and saved US soldiers' lives. How ethically defensible was this belief? (Ethics and Logic.)

T
O
K

US strategy

US strategy also led to success. Island hopping simply cut off Japanese-held islands so that many costly battles became unnecessary. Instead of invading China or the Dutch East Indies where Japan had vast armies tied down consuming its precious supplies, US strategy to bomb Japan into surrender saved the lives of US troops, although at great cost to Japan. Attacks by US submarines had effectively ended the movement of war goods, raw materials, soldiers and food to and from Japan, an action which would likely have starved Japan into submission all by itself. The loss of cities, workers, ports, ships and infrastructure ensured Japanese defeat. The dropping of two atomic bombs, the Soviet invasion of Manchuria and the destruction of the majority of Japan's cities by B-29 bombers all led to Japan's surrender, which was simply a formal recognition of defeat that was already a reality.

Chapter summary

Second World War in Asia and the Pacific 1941–5

The Second World War in Asia and the Pacific began in stages starting early in the twentieth century as Japan acquired parts of Asia. These military successes, coupled with economic need and population pressure, led to further conflicts including the invasion of China in 1937. In order to secure access to petroleum in the Dutch East Indies, Japan chose to attack the USA to delay or prevent any US attempt to halt its expansion, leading to a total war.

While the USA was temporarily unable to respond as a result of the attack on Pearl Harbor, it soon was able to counter Japan's expansion with a massive increase in war production and the creation of a huge navy and air force. These developments, plus the breaking of Japanese codes, the destruction of Japanese shipping using submarines and the strategy of island hopping, allowed the USA to start destroying Japanese cities and industry in late 1944. Further territorial gains by the USA in 1945, as well as the tying up of huge Japanese armies in Asia which consumed war supplies needed to fight the USA, meant that Japan was already defeated. Japan continued to fight, however, even as most of its urban areas were devastated by US bomber aircraft. The invasion of Manchuria by the USSR and the dropping of two atomic bombs on Japan forced the Emperor of Japan, Hirohito, to surrender on 15 August 1945.

Examination practice

Command term: Examine

When a question asks you to examine some aspect of twentieth-century warfare, it is asking you to analyse the strengths and weaknesses of various arguments and conclude with your own supported opinion.

Below are a number of different questions for you to practise using the command term 'examine'. For guidance on how to answer exam-style questions, see Chapter 8.

1 Examine the success of guerrilla warfare in two twentieth-century wars.

2 Examine the causes of two twentieth-century civil wars, each from a different region.

3 Examine the long-term causes of two twentieth-century wars, each from a different region.

4 Examine the political repercussions of a twentieth-century conflict.

5 Examine the use of naval warfare in two wars in the twentieth century.

Activities

1 Create a board game that requires knowledge of the events, people and places discussed in this chapter. This game may be based on board games you are already familiar with, or perhaps one of your own creation. The following are a few example questions for such a game:

   • Name the Emperor of Japan. Answer: Hirohito.
   • What product did the USA no longer have access to during the Second World War that had to be created synthetically? Answer: Rubber.
   • What was the importance of Saipan to the USA? Answer: Japan was now in B-29 bomber range.

2 Japan was given a new constitution by the USA that became effective in mid 1947. Create a constitution for Japan, China or any nation that became independent after the Second World War. With your class, discuss what should be in your constitution. Place the ideas you have in order of their importance, compromising as necessary. Be sure to address issues of gender, religion, minorities and whatever freedoms the class decides are actual rights.

3 Debate: should the USA have used nuclear bombs on Japan during the war? The class should divide, with one group supporting the use of the bombs and the other stating that this was wrong. Be sure to make historical arguments based on evidence when possible.

4 Once the debate has been concluded, you should consider having those who were against the use of the nuclear bombs argue that Japan was correct in expanding its empire throughout the first half of the twentieth century, while the other half of the group debates against this notion.

CHAPTER 5

Chinese Civil War 1927–37 and 1945–9

China was in a state of civil conflict for much of the first half of the twentieth century. The most significant and prolonged clash arose between the authoritarian ruling Nationalist Party and the Chinese Communist Party (CCP). The civil war between them, like many civil conflicts, had a strong international dimension. The eventual outcome was a Communist victory which alongside the experience of years of civil war fundamentally changed China politically, economically and socially. The war also had a profound impact on international politics during the era of the Cold War.

The following key questions will be addressed in the chapter:

★ To what extent was the Chinese Civil War the product of social inequality within Chinese society?

★ How did the Second Sino-Japanese War of 1937–45 contribute to the outbreak of the Chinese Civil War?

★ Why did the CCP win the Chinese Civil War?

★ To what extent did the civil war transform Chinese society?

1 The long-term causes of the Chinese Civil War

▶ *Key question:* To what extent was the Chinese Civil War the result of social inequality within China?

KEY TERM

Guomindang The Chinese Nationalist Party. It can also be transliterated to Kuomintang (KMT).

Second Sino-Japanese War Military conflict, primarily between Japan and China, 1937–45. It became one of the Asian theatres of the Second World War of 1939–45.

Civil conflict between the Nationalists, also referred to as the **Guomindang** (GMD), and the Chinese Communist Party (CCP) took place in two main phases, the first between 1927 and 1937, the second more intense period of fighting between 1945 and 1949. In the intervening period, an uneasy co-operation existed as both nominally worked together to counter the Japanese invasion and occupation of China during the **Second Sino-Japanese War**.

The civil war had its long-term roots in profound social inequalities within Chinese society. These alone, however, were not decisive in bringing about conflict. Ideological differences between the Nationalists and the CCP which made compromise impossible were vital, as was the context of political instability within China in the first half of the twentieth century.

The socioeconomic conditions in China, c.1900–37

← To what extent did social inequalities contribute to civil unrest between the Communists and the Nationalists?

Significant inequalities existed in Chinese society in the early twentieth century in both rural and urban areas. These created the conditions necessary for civil conflict.

Rural poverty

China was predominantly rural; 85 per cent of the population were peasants even in the 1930s. Agricultural life continued as it had for centuries with little evidence of mechanization in the methods of production. Living conditions were basic, with no running water or electricity and mud-track roads limiting travel and communication. Although there was huge geographical and climatic variation in the different provinces of China, most of the peasantry lived on the edge of subsistence; it only took a bad harvest to bring about catastrophic famine. Particularly severe famine occurred in northern China's Gansu and Shaanxi Provinces in 1920–1 where drought contributed to 500,000 deaths, and in north-west China in 1927 where natural disasters led to over three million deaths from famine.

The vast majority of peasants did not own their own land, but rented it from wealthy landlords who usually charged very high rents. In Hunan Province, which was not untypical, these rents frequently constituted 70 per cent of the value of the crops produced, leaving very little money on which the peasant family could survive. Landlords were, understandably, usually unpopular.

SOURCE A

China's rural economy remained basic, relying on traditional practices with virtually no evidence of mechanization. This photo is from about 1905.

What can be learned from Source A about rural China in c.1900?

Urban poverty

China's urban population remained tiny even in the 1930s, with approximately 4.5 per cent of the population living in towns of over 100,000 inhabitants. In large part this was a consequence of China's small industrial sector which constituted less than 10 per cent of China's gross domestic product (GDP). The majority of the industrial regions were located along China's eastern coastline, the largest being Shanghai, where approximately 40 per cent of China's industrial capacity was located by the end of the 1930s.

Industrial growth

China's industrial sector was expanding in the 1920s and 1930s, stimulated by:

- an increase in foreign investment
- the development of new techniques in fabric, glass and steel manufacture.

This expansion brought about an increase in the urban population as peasants migrated to the cities. By the 1920s Shanghai already had a population of over 1.5 million.

Living and working conditions

The living and working conditions of the urban workforce were in the main abysmal. There was a huge polarization in wealth between employers and workers. For the workers, low wages, the lack of any social security and relatively high unemployment meant many were forced to live in slum conditions on the outskirts of the cities. In Shanghai, deaths in the slums from disease and hunger were not uncommon, with municipal sanitation teams collecting as many as 20,000 dead bodies from the streets each year, the majority of whom were children.

Trade unions

Attempts were made to organize the urban workforce into trade unions in order that they might more effectively campaign for an improvement to their living and working conditions. However, the organization of the workforce proved difficult. In part this was because many workers remained scattered in small handicraft-style workshops and so were difficult to co-ordinate, and because the vast majority were illiterate. Difficulties remained in reaching the growing numbers who were concentrated in the newer larger textile and steel factories. The majority of these workers were newly arrived from the countryside, poor and desperate for work, and easily threatened by employers.

Despite these difficulties there was growth in union membership and union activity, in particular strike action in the 1920s. In Shanghai, for example, the CCP succeeded in bringing workers together into the Central Shanghai General Union, whose membership had increased to 821,000 by March 1927, compared to just 43,000 in June 1925. The number of unionized workers, and their potential power to affect real change, however, remained minimal in this period.

Political fragmentation in China 1912–27

Political fragmentation and instability characterized Chinese politics between 1912 and 1927. Central authority, which had been exercised by the Imperial Qing dynasty since 1644, collapsed with the abdication of Pu Yi, the last emperor, on 12 February 1912. The revolution of 1911–12 which brought this about was primarily a military revolt, in large part inspired by the ideals of the reformist Nationalist Party.

However, the ideals of the reformers were not permitted to guide the republic for long. The general Yuan Shikai used his military power to establish himself as a dictator. His death in 1916 created a power vacuum at the centre of government and the fragmentation of political power in China through the rise of regional **warlords,** influential landlords and military men who used their power to establish themselves as independent dictators in their regions.

In 1923, the Nationalist Party was substantially reorganized with the assistance of advisors from the USSR, which was keen to develop political influence in China. The Soviets helped to establish the Military Academy at Whampoa, near Canton, in May 1924, to train Nationalist Party members for future attempts to retake power in China. The Soviets insisted that the Nationalists co-operate with the small CCP which had been formed in 1912. In consequence, despite their ideological differences, the Nationalists and the Communists worked together from 1924 in the (First) **United Front** alliance to try to eliminate the power of the warlords.

The Northern Expedition

The CCP and the Nationalists jointly launched a military campaign in 1926 known as the **Northern Expedition** to defeat the warlords and to reunify China. This campaign was largely successful. Through a combination of military defeat and negotiation, the majority of the warlords ceased to exercise independent power, and the Nationalist Party emerged as the ruling party in China by late 1927. However, fundamental differences between the CCP and the Nationalists quickly surfaced, leading to the outbreak of conflict between them.

Ideological differences

The ideological differences between the Nationalist Party and the CCP were fundamental to the outbreak of hostilities between them in 1927. In this context, the United Front alliance was an expediency which would never have been anything other than temporary.

The ideology of the Nationalist Party

The formal political ideology of the Nationalist Party was to create a modern, unified and independent China. To achieve this, 'Three Principles of the People' were identified in the 'Manifesto of the First National Congress of the Nationalist Party' in January 1930. These were:

← **How did the Nationalist Party rise to power by 1927?**

KEY TERM

Warlords Wealthy, powerful individuals whose control of private armies enabled them to establish themselves as virtual dictators in the regions of China following the collapse of imperial rule.

United Front An alliance between the Nationalist Party and the CCP between 1924 and 1927 which was revived between 1936 and 1945.

Northern Expedition A military expedition undertaken by the Nationalists and the Communists to reunify China by defeating the warlords between 1926 and 1927.

← **To what extent did ideological differences between the CCP and the Nationalists contribute to conflict between them?**

1 Nationalism. The objectives were to:
   - eliminate foreign influence in China
   - bring about the reunification of China
   - ensure equality between all ethnic groups within Chinese territory.
2 Popular sovereignty, notably the participation of ordinary Chinese in elections.
3 The 'principle of the people's livelihood'. This aimed to improve the welfare of the people through a variety of measures including:
   - some redistribution of land to landless peasantry
   - the supply of credit by the government to peasants without capital through the establishment of rural banks
   - a degree of state support for the relief of the sick, old and disabled
   - the nationalization of key industries like banking and railways, although otherwise encouraging the development of private businesses.

Main Goals of GMD

These principles were based on the thinking of Sun Yatsen, who had established the Nationalist Party in 1912.

Appeal of the Nationalist Party's ideology

Nationalist Party ideology had a clear appeal. Nationalism was popular. Many Chinese, particularly the growing middle classes, were keen to see an end to what was widely regarded as the exploitation of China's economic assets by imperialist powers, frequently termed foreign devils. Britain, France and Japan had substantial influence, especially in China's prosperous eastern port cities. Foreign powers had the right to set their own taxes and trade tariffs and implement their own laws in areas known as **foreign concessions** or **foreign enclaves** in many of these cities. In Shanghai, for example, there existed the International Settlement which by the 1920s encompassed nearly three-quarters of a million people, including 30,000 non-Chinese, and operated as an independent city outside Chinese law.

The objective of introducing democracy was also popular, especially to the growing numbers of economically prosperous and educated middle-class Chinese who had been denied a political voice during centuries of authoritarian imperial rule and the warlord era.

CCP did

The social reform agenda of the Nationalist Party potentially held appeal to the peasantry. The Nationalist Party, however, did not actively cultivate a significant peasant base, and remained predominantly an urban, middle-class movement.

However, when the Nationalist Party found itself in a position of power in China, it failed to deliver on many of these principles (see page 245).

The ideology of the CCP

The CCP, which was established in Shanghai in July 1921, shared some ideological aims with the Nationalist Party, but ultimately proposed a very different type of Chinese society.

n common with the Nationalists, the CCP espoused nationalism. They were n favour of eradicating the foreign concessions and building on the defeat of he warlords to achieve political reunification. Both parties also shared a lesire to relieve the conditions of the peasantry, although the context in which they hoped to achieve this was very different.

The greatest ideological difference between the Nationalists and the Communists was that the CCP advocated a profound restructuring of society n accordance with Marxist principles. This meant the elimination of the property ownership and privilege of the **bourgeois classes.** This would be achieved through class warfare which would be carried out by a revolution of he ordinary people, guided by the CCP. Property would become collectively owned. Political power would, at least initially, reside in the CCP as the guiding and organizing force in the revolution. The CCP ultimately sought absolute power since this was the only way in which it was believed a communist revolution could be achieved.

The ideology of the CCP as developed under the leadership of **Mao Zedong**, however, diverged significantly from traditional **Marxism**. Mao's interpretation of Marxism became known as Mao Zedong Thought, and was largely inspired by his concern to make Marxism fit within the specific Chinese context, which in many ways was totally unsuited to communist revolution. Marx predicted that class revolution would be successful only when led by the **proletariat** within a highly industrialized society. China, however, was predominantly rural with only a tiny proletariat. Mao Zedong Thought proposed that this was not a problem and could be overcome. The key differences between Mao Zedong Thought or Maoism and traditional Marxism are shown in the table below.

KEY TERM

Bourgeois classes A term used to refer to a social class characterized by their ownership of property. It is largely synonymous with the middle classes.

Mao Zedong Leader of the CCP and ruler of China between 1949 and his death in 1976.

Marxism Marxism is also often referred to as communism. It is an economic and sociopolitical theory which identifies progress in history as coming about through class conflict and revolution, with the ultimate goal being the establishment of a society without government, private property or hierarchy. It is named after the originator of the theory, Karl Marx (1818–83).

Proletariat The working classes in an industrialized society.

Marxism and Maoism compared

	Marxism	Maoism
Similarities	Revolution was to be achieved through class struggle against the propertied classes whose possessions would be removed and redistributed more fairly in society	
	In the initial stages of revolution the Communist Party would rule as a dictatorship, guiding the people through the first stages of communist revolution	
	Anti-imperialistic, since empires were seen as exploitative	
Differences	The agents of the revolution would be the proletariat: communist revolution could only succeed in an industrialized nation	The agents of the revolution would be the peasantry
	No private ownership of land, property or the means of production – everything was to be held in common, or nationalized (owned by the state), until this was possible	Communist revolution could succeed in a predominantly rural society
	Internationalist in outlook, it encouraged workers to unite beyond the confines of national boundaries	Initially redistributed land could be owned by the peasantry since this would encourage their support
	During the early days of the revolution the collective leadership of the Communist Party would rule. Eventually there would be no need for government at all.	Encouraged nationalism
		The adulation of Mao as the single leader was encouraged rather than collective leadership by the CCP

What was the nature
of the early conflicts
between the
Nationalists and the
CCP?

Early clashes between the Nationalists and the CCP 1927–34

Tensions between the CCP and the Nationalists became increasingly apparent during the Northern Expedition. The CCP used the Northern Expedition to spread its message to the peasantry in the areas through which its army passed, which increased the concerns of the Nationalists that the United Front was giving the CCP the opportunity to grow in strength.

The White Terror in Shanghai, April 1927

On 12 April 1927 the criminal organization the **Green Gang** launched a series of attacks on CCP headquarters, known Communists and ranks of workers protesting in Shanghai. These assaults were sanctioned by Chiang Kai-shek, the leader of the Nationalists since 1926. Nationalist forces in Shanghai, under the command of the strongly anti-Communist General Ba Chongxi, therefore did nothing to oppose the violence. Communist estimates suggested at least 5000 were killed (police estimates were much lower at 400 killed). The massacre devastated the CCP organization in Shanghai, which was its birthplace and where it had built up its most substantial following among the urban workers.

Communist counterattacks, August–December 1927

The CCP launched two main counterattacks against the Nationalists in 1927 in reprisal for the massacre in Shanghai. The first, known as the Autumn Harvest Uprising, took place in Hunan Province between August and September 1927. Mao was involved in the campaign which consisted of a series of skirmishes between CCP forces, largely composed of peasants who operated a guerrilla-style campaign in the countryside, and Nationalist troops. The much smaller and comparatively ill-disciplined, ill-equipped CCP guerrillas were easily defeated by the Nationalists. The same fate befell the CCP's second action against the Nationalists in Canton in December 1927, when thousands of Communists were killed in Nationalist counterattacks.

The Communists at Jiangxi 1928–34

Many of the Communists who survived the Nationalist attacks gravitated towards the comparative safety of more isolated countryside areas. There they regrouped, gaining the support of the local peasantry primarily through their land-reform policies (see page 247), to establish rural base areas. Such bases existed in many rural areas, but the one that was to become the most significant was in Jiangxi province in south-east China. It was here that Mao and remaining guerrillas joined with surviving Communists following the defeat of the Autumn Harvest Uprising. The Jiangxi base, which became known as the Jiangxi **Soviet**, also became the home of other high-ranking members of the CCP and their Soviet advisors after the White Terror forced them from their Shanghai headquarters.

Nationalist campaigns against the CCP 1930–4

By 1928 the Nationalist Party had established itself as the ruling party of China under the leadership of Chiang Kai-Shek, officially titled Chairman of the National Government. It was keen to use its position of relative power to continue assaults on the CCP. These attacks took the form of a series of military encirclement campaigns which aimed to destroy Communist rural bases by surrounding them, cutting off their supply lines and subjecting them to a series of artillery and infantry-led assaults.

The first of these encirclement campaigns against the Jiangxi Soviet began in November 1930. Communist forces, outnumbered and with much inferior weaponry, countered the Nationalists with guerrilla tactics, ambushing Nationalist reinforcements and exploiting gaps between units of troops in the Nationalist encirclement lines to raid Nationalist territory and to prevent the Nationalists units from linking up. The first four encirclement campaigns, between November 1930 and March 1933, resulted in defensive victories for the CCP since it repeatedly succeeded in repulsing the Nationalist advances. However, the guerrillas were unable to break the encirclement completely and with supplies diminishing due to the continued blockade, the CCP's position was increasingly precarious.

The fifth encirclement campaign

The Nationalists finally succeeded in taking the Jiangxi Soviet in the fifth encirclement campaign between September 1933 and October 1934. In this campaign, Chiang Kai-Shek deployed half a million troops, thereby reducing the frequency and size of breaks between units in the Nationalist line. This denied Communist guerrillas the opportunity to divide Nationalist troops. The massively outnumbered Communist forces faced little prospect of success.

The CCP leadership, heavily influenced by Soviet advisors and their supporters, decided to launch a counterattack using concentrated forces in a conventional style battle at Guangchang in April 1934. CCP troops were outnumbered and outgunned by Nationalist forces and it was clear that further long-term defence of Jiangxi was impossible. The CCP prepared to evacuate the base as their only chance of survival.

The Long March 1934–5

In October 1934 approximately 90,000 of the Communists encircled by the Nationalists at Jiangxi set out on what became the legendary Long March. With the Nationalists in pursuit, the tortuous retreat would eventually take the Communists over 9000 km, through 11 provinces, 18 mountain ranges and across 24 rivers, before they reached Yanan Province in north China. There they established a new base area. Only 20,000 of those who set out on the Long March survived.

Although the retreating Communists tried to avoid clashes with the Nationalists, battles did take place between their forces and the Nationalists.

One of the most celebrated and controversial of these clashes occurred at Luding Bridge over the Dadu River in May 1935. Here CCP forces fought against troops under the command of the warlord Liu Wenhui, who was allied to the Nationalists. In Communist mythology the battle of Luding Bridge was an epic struggle in which the Communists overcame superior forces at Luding Bridge through courage and skill. However, more recent accounts based on eyewitness evidence from Chinese living near Luding Bridge at the time of the alleged battle have denied the ferocity of the battle, some denying that it took place at all.

The Nationalists in government 1928–37

To what extent was Nationalist rule unpopular?

The problems that confronted the ruling Nationalist Party in the late 1920s were substantial. However, there was much that was promising about their rule, and it would be incorrect to see the civil war as resulting primarily from the collapse of a decayed and weak regime.

Politics

The Nationalist Party strengthened the central power of the Chinese state. The regional autonomy of the warlords was considerably reduced through a combination of military suppression and negotiation; Chiang made a number of alliances with powerful warlords such as Yan Xishan in Shanxi and Zhang Xueliang in Manchuria. The Nationalists also succeeded through negotiations in reducing the number of foreign concessions from 33 to 13. In consequence, by 1928 many of the most densely populated and economically significant portions of China were unified under Nationalist rule.

The regime was authoritarian, with power residing within the Nationalist Party, primarily with Chiang Kai-Shek and his key advisors. Many senior posts were held by military men, trained at the élite Whampoa Military Academy, including Chiang himself. Another of the Whampoa cadets, Dai Li, became head of the newly established Investigation and Statistical Bureau, a substantial security organization consisting of a network of spies and secret police to track and eliminate political opponents of the Nationalists. Their methods included arrest without trial, interrogation and execution.

Economy

Economically, the **Nanjing Decade** was a period of modernization and growth. The GDP growth rate was strong at around nine per cent a year and visible signs of this growth included:

- new railway track being constructed (nearly 5000 km)
- the opening of the first commercial airlines in China.

This growth increased support for the Nationalists from the powerful commercial élites. Foreign investment in China was encouraged during this period, such as investment from Italian companies in the early days of aircraft production.

KEY TERM

Nanjing Decade The period of Nationalist rule between 1927/8 and 1937. During this period the Nationalist Party's headquarters were in the city of Nanjing.

Foreign influence led to cultural changes in the cities, with Western styles being embraced in fashion, architecture and film. The Nationalists also sought to influence culture directly through the launch of the **New Life Movement,** which aimed to inculcate a strong moral code and respect for authority. Politically it encouraged a respect for community and obedience which it was hoped would strengthen the authority of the Nationalists.

 **KEY TERM**

New Life Movement
A cultural movement introduced by the Nationalists in the 1930s to encourage moral values and obedience to the state.

Nationalist failings

The successes of the Nanjing Decade were to some extent illusory, obscuring fundamental problems and weaknesses with the regime. The extension of state control was less secure than it appeared. In part this was due to the fact that reduction in warlord power had often been achieved through negotiated settlements with warlords rather than complete military subjugation. In these negotiations the warlords were allowed to retain some considerable regional independence in return for promises of loyalty to the regime, which often turned out to be nominal.

Although the Nationalists succeeded in establishing themselves as an authoritarian government, in some ways this undermined their support base. Many of the well-educated élites, who had hoped that the Nationalists would introduce greater democracy, were disappointed by their failure to do so. This disappointment was accentuated by the corruption which ran through the leadership of the party. An example of this was Chiang's promotion and reliance on the advice of close family members such as his wealthy in-laws, the Soongs (his brother-in-law, T.V. Soong, was Chiang's main financial advisor). Dissatisfaction with Chiang's leadership was increased by heavy taxation and loans imposed particularly on the urban areas.

Another significant failing of the Nationalist government in the 1930s was the lack of attention it paid to peasant suffering. Chiang's regime was committed to the maintenance of the existing social hierarchy which meant supporting landlords, and the government failed to deliver the social reforms promised in the Three Principles of the People (see page 239). The continued hardships of the peasantry created a reservoir of dissatisfaction which was to be effectively exploited by the CCP to build up their own power base.

Overall, despite significant flaws beneath the surface of an increasingly modern and prosperous China, the Nationalist regime had arguably made a promising start. This regime might well have survived had they not been confronted, almost at the same moment, by two opponents who presented extraordinary problems: the Japanese and the Communists.

Japan's occupation of Manchuria

Japan's invasion of Manchuria in 1931 was part of its policy of imperial expansion. Japan quickly asserted authority over the region, establishing the puppet-state of Manchukuo in 1932. From this base, Japan began to extend its control. By 1933, Japanese troops had entered areas north of Beijing and Inner Mongolia which were beyond the boundaries of Manchuria.

The Nationalist response

The response of Chiang's regime to the growing Japanese threat was widely condemned as weak. Chiang appealed to the League of Nations to act against Japan's invasion, but the League's investigation of the event was slow and ineffectual and only resulted in **diplomatic sanctions** being imposed against Japan. Chiang's forces did not put up substantial military resistance to Japan, but instead reluctantly acknowledged the independence of Manchukuo and agreed to a demilitarized zone between Beijing and the Great Wall in the Treaty of Tanggu in May 1933.

Chiang's apparent weakness did have a strategy. He was mindful that the military advantage in early 1933 lay very much with the modernized Japanese army, and that the best hopes for eventual Chinese victory lay in his belief that Japan could not possibly hold all the territory it wished to possess in China and eventually the Japanese would overstretch themselves, becoming more vulnerable to attack. Chiang's strategy, frequently referred to as *trading space for time* was, however, widely perceived as an excuse, appearing as a weakness to a Chinese population fearful of Japanese occupation.

What really damaged Chiang's prestige and undermined his support base was that simultaneous to his policy of offering concessions to the Japanese, he pursued an actively aggressive policy towards the CCP (see page 243). Many in China were opposed to his prioritization of the pursuit of fellow Chinese over a foreign invader. For Chiang this made sense since he regarded the Communists as the more dangerous enemy, stating that the Japanese were a disease of the skin, the Communists a disease of the heart.

Opposition to Chiang's policy

The strength of opposition to Chiang's policy became evident in the demonstrations which broke out in cities across China in 1935. In what became known as the 9 December Movement, students demonstrated against the Japanese invasions and denounced Chiang's response. The seriousness of opposition was exemplified in the Xi'an incident of 1936 when Chiang was forced to discontinue his prioritization of attacks on the CCP. The dramatic event occurred following Chiang's order to Zhang Xueliang, a former warlord based in Manchuria, that he organize the deployment of Nationalist troops against the CCP's Yanan base. Instead of assaulting the CCP, Zhang Xueliang's troops actually turned against Chiang, detaining him at Xi'an in December 1936. Chiang's release was only permitted once he agreed to work with the CCP, in a revival of the United Front alliance (see page 239), to fight Japanese troops. The revival of the United Front was welcomed by the CCP, which needed to restore its strength after continual Nationalist attacks.

🔑 **KEY TERM**

Diplomatic sanctions
The punishment of a country by the severing of normal relations.

Communist strategies of survival and growth at Yanan 1935–47

In what ways did the CCP increase their strength between 1935 and 1947?

The prospects for the continued survival of the CCP looked bleak in 1935. By the time they arrived at the comparative isolation and safety of Yanan after the Long March, CCP numbers were massively reduced and they stood little immediate prospect of success against the Nationalists. The fact that intensified civil conflict between them was later possible, and indeed, resulted in a CCP victory, owes much to the skilful strategies of the CCP. During this period there was a substantial growth in CCP membership (see Source B), and even these figures do not acknowledge the many Communist supporters who did not join the party.

SOURCE B

CCP membership 1936–45.

Year	CCP membership
1936	22,000
1937	40,000
1941	700,000
1945	1,200,000

What can be learned from Source B about the strength of the CCP?

Communist land reform policies

Central to the policy of survival and growth during the Yanan years was the establishment of a strong peasant support base. This was achieved largely through land reform. When the CCP, led by their Red Army's military units, moved into a village, they established local committees of ordinary peasants to help implement this policy. Land was confiscated from local landlords, and divided into plots which were allocated to the local peasantry. This appealed to peasants who for centuries had been denied their own land and had been exploited by their landlords.

Land reform and the establishment of peasant committees was not the only change implemented by the CCP. Their emphasis on the abolition of traditional customs, including arranged marriage and **foot binding**, helped to gain further support. The behaviour of the Red Army, which was used as much as a tool of political indoctrination as for military purposes, also helped to increase the appeal of the CCP. Mao insisted on a strict code of conduct among Red Army troops in order not to alienate local populations who were normally abused by the armies of warlords and the Nationalists.

KEY TERM

Foot binding The traditional practice of binding the feet of women from when they were children in order to keep feet dainty in size. It caused substantial physical discomfort.

The CCP use of terror and coercion

The establishment of Communist control in an area was frequently characterized by terror and coercion. The greatest victims of CCP terror were landlords and wealthy peasants. CCP officials encouraged the local peasantry to enact vengeance on their local landlords. Peasant gangs would hunt down landlords, who were then often dragged before assembled villagers where they were verbally and physically assaulted. The killing of landlords was common. Some who were denounced were not even exploitative landlords but simply unpopular individuals (see Source C). This created an atmosphere of terror in which compliance, for fear of denunciation, made it easier for the CCP to assert its authority.

? What does Source C show about the nature of the CCP's land reform policy?

SOURCE C

Wang Fucheng, a Communist Party activist who helped to implement land reform in Houhua village, describing his memories to the historian Peter J. Seybolt in the 1990s. Quoted in Peter J. Seybolt, *Throwing the Emperor from His Horse: Portrait of a Village Leader in China, 1923–1995*, published by Westview Press, Boulder, Colorado, 1996, pages 35–6.

During land reform I was not a Party member, but I was an activist working for the Party ... I criticized the landlords, telling them to confess that their property came from us. I led people to their houses and brought their furniture to our office to be distributed to poor peasants. Sometimes we would go to the landlords' houses at night and beat them. Wang Zengduo was the only person from this village who was killed during land reform. He wasn't really a landlord ... he was really just a rich peasant. We called him a landlord because people hated him ... We struggled against Wang Zengduo's widow ... we hung her from a big tree with a rope tied to her hands behind her body. Most people taking part were women and children. They beat her to find where she had hidden the family property.

Communist anti-Japanese policies

A further policy adopted by the CCP was their strong anti-Japanese stance. At Yanan, they established the Anti-Japanese University in order to train recruits for war against Japan, which was promoted as a patriotic duty. Communist forces initiated a series of guerrilla campaigns against Japan following the occupation of Manchuria from 1931. The willingness of the CCP to participate in the establishment of the United Front alliance against the Japanese from 1936, although largely due to self-interest, contrasted with Chiang's reluctance to do so. The anti-Japanese stance of the CCP was particularly powerful in attracting recruits, as the steep rise in membership following the Japanese invasions showed (see Source B, page 247).

The CCP at Yanan

Many young, enthusiastic idealists were drawn to Yanan due to the reputation of the CCP leadership for idealistic and selfless dedication to the goal of furthering the common good of all Chinese through the application of the communist message.

It was at Yanan that Mao was accepted as undisputed leader and his ideological vision finally emerged triumphant within the party hierarchy. (In the 1920s Mao's interpretation of Marxism had been less favoured by the high officials within the CCP, who tended towards a more traditionalist interpretation of Marxism, see page 241.) At Yanan the image of Mao as a great thinker was encouraged. He wrote prolifically and gave lectures on communist doctrine.

The Communists in Yanan were depicted as living simply, often in caves, fully dedicated to their cause. While elements of this picture were certainly true, it was also idealized. In reality, many CCP leaders, including Mao, lived quite differently, often in mansions that had been abandoned by wealthy Yanan residents when the Communists arrived. Many followed Mao's teachings as a result of terror, exemplified by the later Rectification Campaign of 1942–4 during which those who criticized Mao Zedong Thought were punished and expelled from the party.

Conclusion

Social inequalities within Chinese society played a significant role in the outbreak of hostilities between the Nationalists and the CCP in the period 1927–37. They provided an audience for the CCP's message of social revolution from among the peasantry and pro-reformers who were alienated by the Nationalist failure to implement reform. The more affluent in Chinese society saw the CCP agenda as a direct threat and looked for protection to the Nationalists.

However, social inequalities were not enough alone to cause hostilities. The Nationalists and the CCP might potentially have agreed on an agenda to alleviate these problems. This was impossible because the rivalry between the Nationalists and the Communists was about more than social injustice. There were fundamental ideological differences between their visions for China that made compromise impossible. In addition, opportunity existed for civil conflict, not least because of political instability in China after the collapse of imperial rule and the implosion of a strong central authority, which made it easier for both parties to build up support bases sufficient to enable them to engage in armed conflict.

The Japanese occupation of Manchuria further facilitated the opportunity for civil conflict since it was exploited by the CCP to gain supporters. The ability of the CCP to survive repeated Nationalist onslaughts at a time when Communist strength was clearly inferior was also vital in sustaining civil conflict.

> **To what extent was the Chinese Civil War the product of social inequality within Chinese society?**

Cause	Description	How contributed to civil war
Socioeconomic causes: the rural situation	• 85% of population peasants in the 1930s • Extreme poverty of the peasantry: unable to own land, exploited by landlords, affected by famine • Wealth and privilege of landlords	• The peasantry were a potential audience for the CCP message • The substantial numbers of peasantry made them a potentially powerful group • Landlords identified with the Nationalists
Socioeconomic causes: the urban situation	• Small but growing number of urban working class • Poverty and poor conditions of urban workers: overcrowded housing, low wages, exploited by employers	• The urban workers were a potential audience for the CCP message • The urban middle classes identified with the Nationalists
Ideological causes	• Profound ideological differences between the Nationalists and the CCP	• Made long-term compromise impossible between the CCP and the Nationalists
Political causes: the political situation	• Political fragmentation: collapse of imperial authority, the warlord era • Significant reunification under the Nationalists from 1927	• Political fragmentation made it easier for both to build up support bases
Japanese invasion and occupation	• Invasion of Manchuria in 1931 • Occupation of Manchuria (Manchukuo)	• Nationalist failure to prevent the Japanese occupation was exploited by the CCP to increase Communist popularity
Nationalist attacks on the CCP	• White Terror (1927) • Encirclement Campaigns (1930–4) • Long March (1934–5)	• Triggered actual conflict between the CCP and the Nationalists
CCP strategies of survival	• Building rural base areas, e.g. Jiangxi Soviet • Use of guerrilla tactics during encirclement campaigns • Long March • Propaganda and policies at Yanan	• Enabled the CCP to survive Nationalist assaults despite the superior strength of the Nationalists

SUMMARY DIAGRAM

The long-term causes of the Chinese Civil War

 # The short-term causes of the Chinese Civil War

▶ Key question: How did the Second Sino-Japanese War of 1937–45 contribute to the outbreak of the Chinese Civil War?

The Second Sino-Japanese War broke out in July 1937. It saw the Japanese rapidly extend their territorial control in China through brutal military conquest. During this period of foreign invasion the civil hostilities between

he Nationalists and the CCP largely ceased as both focused on combating
he Japanese. But animosities between the Nationalists and the Communists
emained, and in the wake of the Japanese surrender in August 1945, civil
onflict broke out on a larger scale.

The Second Sino-Japanese War 1937–45

More substantial conflict broke out between the CCP and the Nationalists
ollowing the end of the Second Sino-Japanese War in 1945. In large part this
vas due to the impact that the Japanese invasion, and subsequent
occupation of much of China, had on both parties. The CCP was
trengthened, having used the opportunity provided by the war to enlarge its
reas of control in the countryside of northern China. The Nationalists
merged militarily stronger due to the assistance they had received from the
JSA, but politically weaker due to criticisms of their policies which had been
unable to prevent the Japanese occupation.

The early months of the Sino-Japanese War,
August–November 1937

The Sino-Japanese War broke out following a clash between Chinese and
apanese troops near the Marco Polo bridge close to the border of Japanese-
eld territory in northern China on 7 July 1937. The skirmish quickly
scalated and by August, Japan had invaded China's largest city, Shanghai.
Shanghai was taken by Japanese forces by the end of October, with the
Chinese suffering 250,000 casualties.

The Japanese advance west, November 1937 to
October 1938

After the fall of Shanghai, Japanese troops rapidly advanced westwards,
aking the capital, Nanjing, in December 1937. The capture of the city was
ccompanied by devastating violence in what has become known as the
Rape of Nanjing. In this slaughter, as many as 300,000 of the civilian
opulation were murdered, and tens of thousands raped and tortured by
apanese troops.

he Japanese conquest and occupation was frequently brutal. In the face of
ne Japanese advance the Nationalist government moved China's capital to
Chongqing in October 1938. To Chiang this represented a strategic
vithdrawal but many in China felt that the Nationalists had abandoned
nem by retreating beyond the immediate reach of Japan's military,
veakening support across China for the Nationalists.

The increase in CCP strength 1937–45

the Japanese invasions were a disaster militarily and politically for Chiang,
ney represented an opportunity for the CCP. The size of CCP-controlled
erritory in northern China grew considerably from their base area at Yanan.
n large part this was made possible by the isolation of the Nationalists in

---

To what extent did the Second Sino-Japanese War weaken the Nationalists and strengthen the CCP?

T O K

In 2001 the Japanese authorities approved a new school history textbook which provoked demonstrations in North and South Korea and China from those angered by the book's treatment of the actions of Japanese troops in the Second World War. The Chinese, for example, objected to the textbook's minimal treatment of the Rape of Nanjing, denying that it was a massacre.

- Can you think of the presentation of any other historical events which have caused controversy?
- Does this suggest that we can never be certain of the truth about historical events?

(History, Reason, Language, Emotion, Ethics.)

What does Source D show about the nature of the Japanese invasion, 1937–45?

SOURCE D

The Second Sino-Japanese War 1937–45.

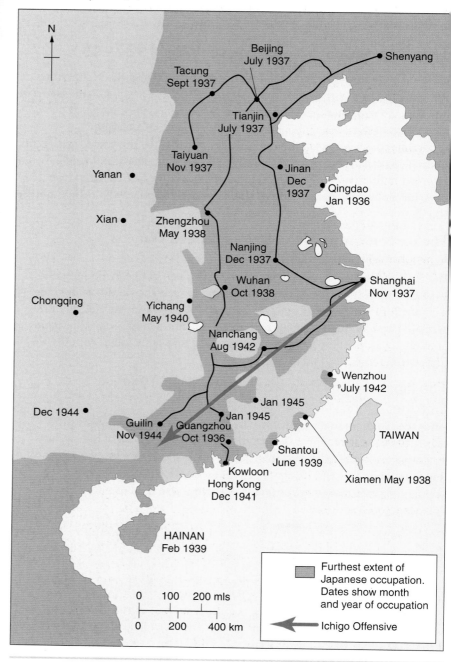

Chongqing and their preoccupation with the fight against the Japanese. In addition, the Japanese occupying forces in northern China were primarily concerned with holding the cities and railway lines, leaving the countryside largely to the CCP. The Communists exploited this development by enacting land reforms that appealed to peasants, thereby expanding their base areas, which became known as the liberated areas.

There were several important Communist attacks against the Japanese military. One such assault was the Hundred Regiments Campaign in July and August 1940, when Communist guerrillas destroyed railways to important coalmines in Jingxing. Red Army guerrilla units continually harassed and sabotaged Japanese troops and supply lines in the countryside. However, such attacks were regarded by the communists as secondary to the consolidation and extension of the liberated areas in the countryside.

The Communists continued to operate, officially at least, as part of the United Front alliance against Japan, although there were difficulties. These culminated in January 1941 when Nationalist troops attacked the Communist 4th Route Army, killing 3000 for disobeying the United Front agreement that Red Army troops would not operate south of the Yangtze River. This incident, however, strengthened CCP propaganda vilifying Chiang for prioritizing attacks on fellow Chinese rather than fighting Japan.

The success of the CCP in gaining strength and supporters in this period can in part be seen in the increase in membership to the CCP (see page 247). The size of the Red Army also grew from approximately 22,000 troops in 1936 to 910,000 in 1945. Additional strength was provided by the Communist militias to which the majority of male peasants were expected to give their services.

US intervention

By the end of 1941, Japan occupied Manchuria, much of northern China and the eastern coast and had penetrated inland in central China to the region of Wuhan. The Nationalist government, at Chongqing, was subjected to relentless aerial bombardment and was finding it increasingly difficult to maintain crucial supplies, especially after the occupation of Burma by Japan in 1942 cut crucial supply routes. The Nationalists were helped, however, by the assistance they received from the USA following its declaration of war against Japan in December 1941, after the Japanese attack on Pearl Harbor (see page 194). In particular, US air power assisted in transporting vital supplies over the Himalayas. However, the relationship between the Nationalists and their US allies was uneasy. The US commanding officer in the China–India–Burma theatre, Joseph Stilwell, came to regard Chiang's military leadership as incompetent, corrupt and cowardly.

Why CCP strengthened

- *countryside left open to take*
- *attack on 4th Route Army made GMD look bad*
- *Nationalist moving to Chongqing made them look weak*

Renewed Japanese offensive 1944

Japan launched a major new offensive to sweep southwards in May 1944, codenamed the Ichigo Offensive (see page 252). By September Japan occupied all of southern and eastern China. The Nationalists had lost over half a million troops and were more isolated than ever at Chongqing. Chiang's position was further weakened because Nationalist military incompetence was widely blamed for Japan's military success.

How did the Japanese surrender contribute to the civil war?

Japanese surrender, August 1945

The Second Sino-Japanese War, and Second World War, came to an abrupt end when two atomic bombs were dropped on the Japanese cities of Hiroshima and Nagasaki by the USA on 6 and 9 August 1945, respectively.

The formal Japanese surrender came on 2 September 1945. Japan's subsequent rapid withdrawal from China created the opportunity for renewed civil conflict between the Nationalists and the CCP. Both parties raced to fill the power vacuum left by the departing Japanese troops, who had been instructed to give their surrender to the nearest Chinese troops in the region, whether they were Nationalist or CCP forces. Territory was not the only potential prize. Both groups were keen to capture Japanese weapons, which were particularly important for the CCP, which lacked modern weaponry.

The end of the Sino-Japanese War set the stage for a renewed and intensified civil war. Not only had the war strengthened both parties in military terms, but the conclusion of the war set the stage for a race for control of territory between the CCP and the Nationalists which provided the impetus for an immediate resumption of civil conflict. By the end of August 1945, despite the fact that officially a truce existed between the two sides, clashes had already begun for control.

The impact of the Second Sino-Japanese War, 1937–45	
Main events of the war: Rapid Japanese advance and occupation of most of China including: • Capture of Shanghai (July 1937). • Massacre at Nanjing (December 1937). • Nationalist capital relocated to Chongqing (October 1938). • Capture of Wuhan City (1941). • Ichigo Offensive (1944). • Japanese surrender after USA dropped atomic bombs on Japan (August 1945)	

Increase in CCP strength during the war:	*Increase in Nationalist strength during the war:*
• Enlargement in size of the Communist-controlled territory in north China • Increase in CCP membership • Growth in size of Red Army and Communist militias • Captured Japanese weaponry • Strengthened Nationalist credentials and popularity • Presence of Soviet troops in Manchuria potentially of assistance to the CCP	• Increase in military strength and access to modern weaponry due to supplies from USA • Increase in size of the Nationalist army *Decrease in Nationalist strength during the war:* • Reputation damaged by accusations that military incompetence failed to prevent the Japanese advance and occupation • Economic pressures, e.g. inflation and high taxes due to the war were unpopular

When civil hostilities between the Nationalists and the CCP resumed after the Japanese surrender they were more intense than they had been before, since both sides were more capable of sustained conflict

The Japanese surrender in 1945 created a power vacuum which both sides rushed to try to fill

SUMMARY DIAGRAM

The short-term causes of the Chinese Civil War

③ The course of the Chinese Civil War

▶ *Key question: Why did the CCP win the Chinese Civil War?*

A Communist victory in the civil war was not a foregone conclusion. Indeed, in 1945 the Nationalists appeared as the stronger side. As the war progressed, however, the CCP was increasingly assisted by problems which weakened the Nationalists, although ultimately the Communists brought about their own victory. This was due to the CCP's skilful management of the demands of the war, which involved the maintenance of essential supplies, the gaining of popular support, and above all, the formulation of successful military strategies and tactics.

The civil war in 1945: competition for control of northern China

At the time of the Japanese surrender in September 1945, the Nationalists appeared to hold significant advantages. Nationalist forces:

- outnumbered the Red Army three to one
- had more military equipment, in particular airpower.

In contrast, Communist troops were desperately short of modern military technology, especially artillery, and had no airpower. Most of their weapons were captured from the Nationalists and Japanese. The Communists did, however, possess several strong potential assets (see below).

Territorial control

In terms of territorial control, the Nationalists also seemed to hold a considerable advantage. The CCP had very little presence in southern and eastern China, so the Nationalists faced little resistance in establishing control in these regions. However, in northern China the CCP was in a stronger position. By August 1945 they had substantially expanded their areas of control beyond their base at Yanan to include over 19 Communist base areas encompassing a population of 95.5 million. This put them in a strong position to take control of the formerly Japanese-occupied regions of Shandong and the resource-rich Manchuria.

The presence of Soviet troops in Manchuria, where they had been involved in the struggle against the Japanese in the closing months of the Second Sino-Japanese War, was potentially advantageous to the Communists. The CCP had reason to hope for, potentially substantial, assistance from the USSR as a fellow Communist power. Soviet troops in Manchuria might act to facilitate the establishment of Communist control in the region, including access to the Japanese arms depots. The Soviets might also provide additional personnel and weapons which could be easily transported over the border into Manchuria. Support from the USSR, however, was not guaranteed, but as relations worsened between the Soviets and the USA as the Cold War began, it seemed more likely.

The Nationalists hoped for support from their wartime ally, the USA. Chiang had some reason to be optimistic that this would be provided since in the context of the Cold War the USA's anti-communism stance encouraged them to take action to help prevent the spread of communism. However, in August 1945 the extreme tensions of the Cold War had not yet manifested themselves and there were signs that US aid might not be forthcoming. Indeed, relations between the Nationalists and the USA during the Second World War had frequently been strained and there was evidence that the USA's preferred outcome for China in August 1945 was for a peace agreement between the Nationalists and the CCP.

The race to control northern China

The CCP's strategic priority in the wake of the Japanese surrender was to expand its territorial control in northern China. Initially it made significant progress, particularly in the countryside, but it was less successful in gaining control of the cities. This was largely because of the rapid advance of Nationalist troops into northern China. The Nationalists made use of US naval and air transport to move their forces swiftly to the region. By the end of August, they had taken control of 17 key cities, including Beijing, Tianjin and Datong, and the majority of the railways in north China. They also captured approximately 179,000 km² of territory within the Communist-liberated areas.

SOURCE E

The main battles in the Chinese Civil War 1945–9.

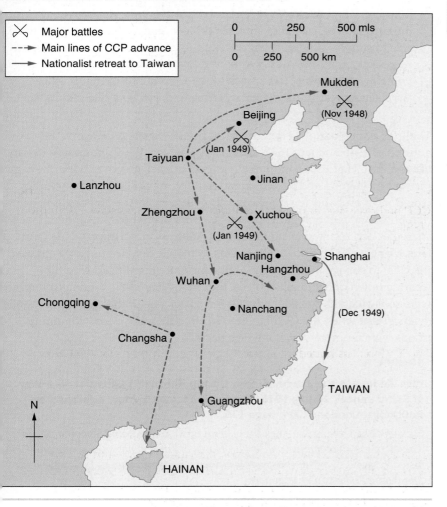

What can be learned from Source E about the fighting in the Chinese Civil War?

In response to the strength of Nationalist control of the cities in northern China, the CCP's strategy shifted in early autumn 1945. The CCP moved away from efforts to extend territorial control towards the defence of existing territory and guerrilla-style operations known as **mobile defence**.

Mobile defence A military strategy that uses the guerrilla tactics of sabotage and ambush to weaken the enemy by disrupting supply lines and inflicting casualties. It does not prioritize the enlargement of territorial control.

Small arms Firearms that can be carried by hand, such as rifles, pistols and small machine guns.

> **Strategy and tactics: mobile defence**
>
> The strategy of mobile defence was focused not on gaining new territory or engaging in conventional-style battles, but on weakening the enemy through ambush and sabotage in order to inflict casualties and disrupt supply lines. The strategy was designed not to bring about a swift victory, but to wear down the enemy slowly. It was influenced by guerrilla-warfare tactics, but tended to deploy troops in larger-scale units more consistent with conventional armies than small bands of guerrilla fighters. Knowledge of the local terrain and support from the local population were vital prerequisites for the successful utilization of a mobile defence strategy; troops needed to be able to survive without having to return to a base camp in order to launch successful ambushes. The weapons required for mobile defence were primarily **small arms**. This played to the Communist strengths, since they lacked larger-scale modern military technology such as artillery and aircraft.

The CCP adopted mobile defence as its primary strategy between the autumn of 1945 and late 1947. It arguably enabled the Communists to win the civil war. Had they continued to pursue offensive, conventional strategies focused on gaining and holding new territory, in particular the cities, they would most probably have been swiftly overcome by the Nationalists, whose numerical and technological advantages were overwhelming. Indeed, such strategies had resulted in significant CCP defeats in northern China (and later Manchuria) in 1945–6. The switch to mobile defence not only enabled the CCP to survive in these years, but contributed significantly to the wearing down of Nationalist forces. Indeed, by late 1947 Nationalist forces were so weakened, considerably but not solely, due to the strategy of mobile defence, that when the CCP reverted to attacks on the cities, Communist troops were far more successful (see page 261).

SOURCE F

What can be learned from Source F about CCP strategy in the civil war?

Mao Zedong in the article 'Smash Chiang Kai-shek's Offensive by a War of Self-defence', 20 July 1946. Quoted in M. Lynch, *Mao*, published by Routledge, London, 2004, page 136.

For defeating Chiang Kai-shek the general method of fighting is mobile warfare. Therefore the abandonment of certain places or cities is not only unavoidable but also necessary ... we must cooperate closely with the masses of the people and win over all who can be won over.

The race to control Manchuria

In October 1945, the CCP shifted its offensive priorities to Manchuria. Neither the CCP nor the Nationalists had a troop presence in the region, which had been dominated by the Japanese during the war. Manchuria's substantial resources made it a valuable prize and the Communists had reason to hope that the Soviet presence there would help them to obtain power.

The Soviet occupation of Manchuria did assist the CCP, although not as much as they had hoped. The Soviets:

- gave the CCP access to Japanese arms depots in the region, such as that at Shenyang which contained over 100,000 guns and artillery pieces
- transferred the 200,000 Chinese troops of the Manchukuo regime, who had surrendered to the Soviets, to the CCP, thereby substantially enlarging their forces
- presented Nationalist troops from entering some of the key cities in the region.

However, the Soviets were not entirely helpful to the CCP in Manchuria. From November 1946 the Soviet leader, Joseph Stalin, whose relations with Mao had always been strained, instructed that the Chinese Communists must leave the key cities in Manchuria, weakening their urban bases. In addition, the Soviets dismantled industrial machinery worth over $858 million from Manchuria for use in the USSR.

In response to the CCP's focus on Manchuria, Chiang deployed an increasing number of troops to the region. By September 1945, 150,000 Nationalist troops, including large groups of élite US-trained divisions, had been sent there. The first major confrontation with the Red Army came at the Shanhaiguan Pass on 15–16 November 1945. In this conventional-style battle, the Red Army was decisively beaten. Thereafter Nationalist forces made rapid progress in Manchuria, taking many of the key cities.

Despite this success, Chiang's decision to deploy significant troops to Manchuria may have contributed to his overall defeat. This was because it diverted troops from northern China before the Nationalists had fully secured the region, adding to the overextension of their forces, which made them vulnerable to Communist attacks. This was certainly the criticism levelled at Chiang's strategy by the US Army Chief of Plans and Operations in China from 1945, General Albert C. Wedemeyer.

The Chinese Civil War in 1946: the failure to achieve a decisive result

← Which side had the military advantage in 1946?

In early 1946, the Nationalists made further territorial gains, dominating the majority of urban centres in northern China and Manchuria, while continuing to control southern and eastern China. The CCP's strength lay in its control of the countryside in the north. It would take good fortune and skilful strategy to convert this strength into overall victory, but there were signs in 1946 that this was precisely what the CCP might be able to do.

Communist advance and retreat in Manchuria, January–June 1946

In Manchuria, the last Soviet troops finally left in May 1946. Their withdrawal was marked by a significant, but brief, extension of CCP control as its troops swiftly moved into many of the key cities. However, the advance of the CCP was short-lived. It took Nationalist troops only weeks to take almost every key city in the region. The Communists were forced into a northerly retreat, bombarded for much of the way by Nationalist air attacks. By June it seemed likely that the Communists would have to abandon their last urban stronghold in Manchuria, the city of Harbin.

The truce in Manchuria, June–October 1946

In June 1946 a ceasefire in Manchuria was agreed between the Nationalists and the CCP. This truce was arranged primarily by the USA. The timing of the truce, however, was extremely fortuitous for the CCP, who made use of the respite to strengthen its forces (see below). Chiang's agreement to the truce forced the Nationalists to halt what was a successful advance in Manchuria. Although Chiang came to regret his acceptance of the truce, seeing it as fundamental to his ultimate defeat, he did have reasonable political and military grounds for his decision at the time. These included:

- The USA put enormous pressure on him to agree to a truce.
- His Manchurian forces were overstretched and would benefit from respite to reorganize.
- He believed that a brief truce would not affect his longer-term chances of victory, given the hugely superior position of the Nationalists.

Fighting resumes

The truce lasted only four months, with fighting breaking out in Manchuria again in October 1946. However, renewed Nationalist assaults on the city of Harbin failed to dislodge the CCP, which had spent the four months of ceasefire building up the city's defences, fully utilizing its 800,000-strong population to provide manpower, resources and funding. During this time, the CCP had also received crucial aid from the Soviets. The historians Chang and Halliday have shown that more than 2000 wagonloads of equipment, the majority of it captured Japanese weapons from the Second World War, came over the border from Korea on railways which the Soviets had also assisted in repairing. The equipment included desperately needed heavy artillery, machine guns and rifles.

The respite also enabled CCP military commander Lin Biao to reorganize, train and re-equip troops. He effectively transformed the small guerrilla detachments into more professional, larger-scale units that could successfully use artillery and engage the enemy in large-scale battles in conventional warfare. The results of this transformation of the Red Army were apparent in the success of a surprise attack on the Nationalists camped to the south of the Sungari River in the winter of 1946–7. Although the substantial CCP force of 400,000 failed to take the key railway junction at Siping, it inflicted considerable casualties on the Nationalists and was able to capture vast amounts of Nationalist weaponry. By the end of 1946, the situation in Manchuria was inconclusive. Although the Nationalists continued to hold the majority of the cities, they had failed to dislodge the CCP from the countryside.

The Chinese Civil War in 1947: the highpoint of Nationalist success

← **How likely were prospects of a Nationalist victory in 1947?**

The Nationalist advance in central and northern China, May–December 1947

The lack of a decisive victory in northern China and Manchuria encouraged Chiang to launch a new offensive in May 1947, called the Strongpoint Offensive. In this, the Nationalists focused on trying to secure the key cities in the central and eastern provinces of Shandong, Shanxi and Shaanxi. Their troops initially made rapid advances, forcing the CCP out of almost all the key cities in these regions. Nationalist garrisons were then stationed in these cities to defend them from possible CCP counterattacks. In March 1947, Nationalist troops achieved the hugely important symbolic, but strategically less significant, capture of the CCP base at Yanan.

In many ways, however, the achievements of the Strongpoint Offensive were illusory. Its focus on the cities meant that Nationalists did not prioritize the destruction of the CCP in rural areas, allowing the mobile defence operations by the Red Army to continue. The focus on holding key cities across multiple provinces without securing the countryside ultimately left Nationalist forces overextended and vulnerable to ambush, siege and sabotage. This urban strategic focus reflected long-standing Nationalist priorities and their relative neglect of building support in the rural areas.

Communist counterattacks in central and northern China, November–December 1947

From late 1947, CCP strategy shifted towards large-scale assaults on urban centres, an approach which had previously been avoided. But by late 1947, the CCP was in a stronger position not only because they had increased their stockpiles of weapons, but because the Nationalists were in many ways weaker. Nationalist forces were thinly spread out in garrison duties in the major towns throughout China, where their supplies and reinforcements were frequently disrupted by CCP attacks. The city of Shijiazhuang in Hebei province was the first major city the CCP successfully captured, doing so on 12 November 1947. This was followed by the capture of the key Manchurian city of Siping in the winter of 1947.

Why were the
Communists able to
make significant gains
in 1948?

The civil war in 1948: the Communist advance

CCP campaigns of 1948–9 transformed its growing advantage into actual victory. Its urban offensives brought about an end to the war sooner than would have occurred had the strategy of mobile defence been continued.

The Communist Manchuria Campaign, October–November 1948

In Manchuria, the CCP's assaults on the cities achieved significant success. They began with the destruction of the Nationalist base at Jinzhou on 15 October 1948. This was followed by the capture of Changchun on 26 October after a devastating siege of the city which resulted in over a quarter of a million deaths, largely from starvation; the Red Army had prevented even civilians from leaving the besieged city. The surrender of the city of Shenyang on 2 November 1948 finally left Manchuria firmly under the control of the CCP.

The Huai-hai Campaign, November 1948–January 1949

The CCP's Huai-hai Campaign from November 1948 to January 1949 continued the strategic focus on cities, this time in China's central provinces. The main focus was the city of Xuchou, a key junction on the Longhai railway (see the map on page 257). CCP troops attacked Nationalist troops *en route* to Xuchou to prevent reinforcements from reaching the city. They then encircled Xuzhou, destroying the villages on its outskirts in a 30-km radius. The Red Army then besieged the city through the winter. Without adequate food or supplies Nationalist troops deserted in increasing numbers. They were encouraged by Communist propaganda which promised food to defectors. With the Nationalist units in the city weakened, the Red Army launched an assault making full use of their new artillery power, capturing the city four days later in January 1949.

The Pingjin Campaign, November 1948 to January 1949

CCP control of central China was assured by the Pingjin campaign, which ran simultaneously to the Huai-hai campaign. Red Army attacks and increased use of artillery decimated Nationalist troops, enabling them to take the cities of Xinbaoan and Zhangjiakou, followed by Taiyuan in 15 January 1949 (see the map on page 257). The culmination of the campaign came with the decision of the Nationalist commander, Fu Zuoyi, to surrender Beijing on 16 January 1949. Chiang attempted to initiate peace talks, proposing that the USA and USSR act as mediators. Stalin advised Mao to engage in talks, but Mao refused. With the Nationalists clearly on the brink of defeat, he was determined to pursue the war to a decisive Communist victory.

What control did the
Communists establish
over China in 1949?

The Chinese Civil War in 1949: the Communists achieve victory

By 1949, a complete CCP victory seemed to be a foregone conclusion. Its strategies, coupled with problems for the Nationalists, brought a swift victory.

The Red Army advance into southern China

With the CCP in control of north-eastern, north and central China, its objective in 1949 was the territory south of the Yangzi River. In contrast to the heavy fighting that had taken place in northern and central China, Nationalist forces put up only minimal resistance when the Red Army began to march south. The city of Nanjing was taken by the CCP in April, Shanghai and Wuhan were taken in May, Xian and Changsha in August, and Chongqing and Xiamen in November 1949.

Chiang, and what remained of the Nationalist forces, fled to Taiwan, still asserting that they represented the legitimate government of China. The reality on the Chinese mainland, however, was that the CCP now ruled China. Only the outlying and separatist regions of Tibet and Xinjiang remained outside their control; areas which had never been controlled by the Nationalists. Mao proclaimed the establishment of the Communist People's Republic of China (PRC) from the walls of the Forbidden City, the palace of the Chinese emperors, in Beijing in October 1949.

Managing the war

Given the demands of a lengthy civil war, the effective management of manpower, weapons and supplies was essential. Ultimately the CCP met these demands more effectively than the Nationalists.

← To what extent did the CCP manage the war more effectively than the Nationalists?

Military personnel

Nationalist troops significantly outnumbered the Red Army during the early years of the war. In August 1945, the Nationalist army consisted of 2.7 million men, approximately three times the size of the Red Army. By June 1946, the proportions were similar, with Red Army troop numbers at 1.27 million and the Nationalists at 4.3 million. However, the CCP could also call on a militia force of some 2.2 million even in August 1945, although this primarily consisted of untrained and ill-equipped peasants and so was arguably of much lesser military value.

As the war progressed and greater amounts of territory, and hence potential recruits, came under Communist control, numerical superiority swung in favour of the CCP. The CCP's growing numerical advantage was evident in its ability to launch the huge Huai-hai and Pingjin campaigns simultaneously in November 1948 to January 1949 (see page 262).

The significance of the advantage conferred by troop numbers, however, was not decisive. The Nationalists failed to win the war in its earlier stages despite having a substantial numerical advantage. Communist military strategies, such as the adoption of mobile defence tactics, were able to nullify numerical advantage alone.

Conscripts and defectors

Both armies relied extensively, although not exclusively, on conscripts. In July 1947, Chiang issued a general mobilization bill giving the Nationalists unrestricted powers of conscription throughout China. Recruitment gangs were sent into the countryside to obtain troops, and their methods were often brutal. Reluctant, often malnourished, conscripts were not infrequently tied together with ropes to prevent them escaping. The Communists too, relied heavily on conscripted peasants. The historians Chang and Halliday estimate that in the Pingjin Campaign of 1948 alone 1.5 million peasants were conscripted.

The ranks of the Red Army were enlarged by Nationalist defectors and prisoners. Defections were actively encouraged by the Communists through promises of good treatment and nutrition, which appealed to many Nationalist troops who were frequently short of food. In 1948 Mao insisted that all captured prisoners should be assimilated into the CCP's forces, including large numbers captured following fighting in Shandong. The swift increase in manpower this provided enabled the Communists to attack Xuzhou during the Huai-Hai Campaign before Chiang had the opportunity to reinforce the defences or to bring in reinforcements. Although the use of former enemy troops was a risk, the CCP's willingness to execute those suspected of duplicity created an atmosphere of terror which minimized the potential dangers.

Matériel

The supply of weapons and food to troops was crucial to military success. Neither side manufactured significant armaments and so both relied on foreign supplies and captured weaponry. Overall, despite early Nationalist advantages in access to modern armaments, the CCP showed itself better able to sustain vital support and supplies throughout the war.

The supply of armaments to the Nationalists

The Nationalists relied for the majority of their weapons on armaments sold to them by the USA. The USA gave $2 billion in aid between 1945 and 1949. This US assistance included artillery, firearms, ammunition and air power. The US Secretary of State Dean Acheson expressed the view in August 1949 that the extent of assistance provided by the USA should have been enough to ensure a Nationalist victory, and the fact that this had not occurred was due to the tactical incompetence and corruption of the Nationalists themselves (see Source G).

However, there are claims that US support for the Nationalists was less valuable both in monetary terms and in military effectiveness than is often supposed. The $2 billion value of American assistance included *all* US supplies to China rather than just military aid, which actually constituted $798 million. Some historians, like Freda Utley, have argued that further deductions to this figure should be made to take into account items and costs which were never of any effective military value to the Nationalists. She presents the figure of $360 million of *effective* military supplies provided by the USA to the Nationalists. This is still higher than the $225 million the Nationalists claimed to have received.

SOURCE G

US Secretary of State, Dean Acheson, in an official statement on 5 August 1949.

The reasons for the failures of the Chinese National Government ... do not stem from any inadequacy of American aid. Our military observers on the spot have reported that the Nationalist armies did not lose a single battle during the crucial year of 1948 through lack of arms or ammunition. The fact was that the decay which our observers had detected in [the Nationalist leadership] early in the war had fatally sapped the powers of resistance of the Nationalists. Its leaders had proved incapable of meeting the crisis confronting them, its troops had lost the will to fight, and its Government had lost popular support.

What reasons does Source G give for why the Nationalists lost the civil war?

loss of momentum

Many of the US supplies also arguably arrived too late to be of maximum assistance to the Nationalists. The Americans, keen to broker peace talks in China (see page 260), actually imposed an embargo on arms sales to China between 1946 and July 1947. This embargo limited the ability of the Nationalists to obtain weaponry at a crucial stage in the war when they were still dominant over the Red Army and stood a greater chance of defeating the Communists than later on. There were delays even after the embargo was lifted. Many supplies did not arrive until early 1949, by which time the CCP's territorial control of China was almost complete.

The supply of armaments to the CCP

Like the Nationalists, the CCP relied heavily on armaments manufactured abroad. Most of their weapons were captured, initially from the Japanese and, later, from the Nationalists themselves (see page 259). In the early months of the war in the wake of the Japanese surrender, the Communists were able to access huge stockpiles of Japanese weapons in northern China and Manchuria. Russian assistance eased the transfer of 900 Japanese aircraft, 700 tanks and almost 4000 artillery pieces, and nearly 12,000 machine guns to the Communists, many of them from Korea. The Russians also provided training for Chinese commanders at Russian military training schools. However, there is little evidence that the Soviets transferred arms directly from the USSR. The US ambassador to China, John Stuart Leighton, wrote on 29 October 1947 that there was 'little if any evidence of material assistance from Moscow'. Captured Nationalist weapons later constituted the majority of Communist armaments. These were obtained through attacks and raids on depots and from deserters. The CCP always lacked airpower and armoured vehicles, which the Nationalists possessed in superior numbers. Knowledge of this deficit informed the choice of CCP tactics; conventional battles were initially avoided and mobile defence was prioritized, in which small arms and artillery were most crucial.

By the final years of the civil war, the CCP had substantially closed the gap in armaments between itself and the Nationalists. This equalization was evident in the CCP's ability in 1948 to launch decisive urban campaigns, for which heavy artillery was a prerequisite.

Sustaining civilian support

The ability to sustain the support of the civilian population is crucial in civil war in order to raise and supply troops. Both the CCP and Nationalists attempted to do this using a variety of means including propaganda and popular policies and, when these failed, terror and coercion.

Communist propaganda and policies

Communist propaganda and the patriotic songs which were taught to villagers emphasized that they were fighting a people's war in order to bring about profound and lasting social change to ordinary Chinese people.

Communist social reform policies, such as land redistribution (see page 247), were successful in gaining civilian support, particularly among the peasantry. The modification of the land reform campaign begun during the war against the Japanese continued. Consequently, official policy was that moderate landlords should not be targeted since Mao was keen not to alienate them by excessive confiscations and violence. However, in reality the extreme violence of class warfare which accompanied land reform frequently continued at a local level.

SOURCE H

What does Source H suggest about how the Communists gained control in the countryside?

Trial of a landlord by the Red Army 1949.

SOURCE I

The special correspondent Kongxin Zhan yu Quanxin Zhan writing in *Guancha* (*The Observer Newspaper*), 8 May 1948.

Because the Communist armies have changed production relations and social and economic organization in the liberated areas, they have been able to establish the new social order they need. Grain requisitions, military conscription and self-defence can therefore be carried out with a high degree of effectiveness. There is no need to use excessive military force to defend the villages and towns they control.

According to Source J, what helped the CCP to perform well in the civil war?

As the CCP took control of urban centres later in the war, it implemented policies to improve the lives of urban populations in an effort to gain supporters. Mao's insistence on the disciplined and respectful behaviour of Red Army troops while carrying out these reforms also helped to project a favourable image of the Communists (see Source J).

SOURCE J

Excerpt from the novel *Wild Swans: Three Daughters of China* by Jung Chang, HarperCollins, London, 1991, pages 150–2. This excerpt is based on her mother's experiences in the civil war, particularly relating to the Red Army's entry into the city of Jinzhou in 1948.

It was Communist policy not to execute anyone who laid down their arms, and to treat prisoners well. This would help win over the ordinary soldiers, most of whom came from poor peasant families … most [soldiers] willingly stayed and joined the Communist army … The first priority after the battle was clearing up, most of which was done by Communist soldiers … the most immediate problem was food. The new government urged the peasants to come and sell food in the city and encouraged them to do so by setting prices at twice what they were in the countryside … another good thing that captured the goodwill of the locals was the discipline of the Communist soldiers. Not only was there no looting or rape, but many went out of their way to demonstrate exemplary behaviour. This was in sharp contrast to the Nationalist troops.

What does this source show about how the Communists gained people's support in the civil war?

Nationalist propaganda and policies

Nationalist propaganda focused on the social revolution that would be unleashed by a Communist government, a frightening prospect to the urban commercial and business élites. However, the Nationalists struggled to halt the disenchantment with Nationalist control that was growing even among their traditional supporters due to increasing hardships in the cities, notably the rising rate of inflation and food shortages. Popular discontent was exacerbated by the widespread perception that corruption was rife among Nationalist officials. Many came to believe that the Nationalists had had their chance at reforming China and had failed.

Terror and coercion

Communists and Nationalists also coerced the civilian population into assisting them. Both sides relied on conscripts (see page 263). Both imposed

What can be learned from Source K about attitudes towards the Nationalists in the civil war?

SOURCE K

Excerpt from a speech on 13 January 1946 by Professor Zhang Xiruo, Head of the Department of Politics at the Southwest Associated University, Kumin, China. He was a non-partisan.

China is suffering because political power has been monopolized by an extremely reactionary and exceedingly despotic political faction, demonstrated by a group of stupid, ignorant ignoramuses. This conglomeration is the Nationalists. I do not say that the Nationalists have always been such a body. It has developed into such a body, and today thinks only of its own interests. It shouts high-minded slogans such as 'for the nation and the people'. It professes to 'bring happiness to the nation and welfare to the people'. But these are mere words, and it really plunges the nation into ruin and the people into misery.

KEY TERM

Corvée Forced labour tax.

Yuan A unit of currency in China.

considerable economic demands on civilians. Inhabitants in Nationalist and CCP zones were forced to pay very high taxes. In Communist zones the practice of taking ever larger volumes of food in grain tax from the local peasantry had been common even before the civil war. The CCP also insisted the peasantry perform **corvée** labour, a labour tax of unpaid work. Peasants were forced to carry out repair work on roads and bridges and to transport food and ammunition. Communist campaigns were also set up urging the local population to donate materials such as firewood, food and jewellery. Many volunteered goods in these campaigns more from fear than genuine willingness.

CCP access to food supplies

The Communists seized enormous provisions of food from their countryside base areas to supply their armies. To this end, food was requisitioned from every household. This ready access to food from the countryside enabled the Communists to pursue the strategy of mobile defence since their troops could effectively live off the land around their countryside bases, a strategy which proved vital to their eventual victory (see page 258).

Nationalist access to food supplies

Nationalist troops, without access to large countryside areas, were far more severely affected by food shortages. Their bases in the cities made them dependent for food supplies on the railways, which were frequently cut by Communist troops. This resulted in food shortages in the cities. The foodstuffs that were available were subject to massive inflation, as currency values ran out of control, worsened by the Nationalist reliance on large foreign loans and the practice of printing large amounts of paper money. In 1940, 100 **yuan** would have bought one pig, by 1946 only one egg. The situation was exacerbated by the corruption of Nationalist officials who hoarded food to sell for profit. Conscripted Nationalist soldiers not infrequently went hungry. Short of rations, they were sometimes only given mugs of congee, the water in which rice had been boiled.

These shortages and inflationary pressures contributed to a decline in morale in Nationalist-held areas. Demonstrations against the shortages and corruption became more frequent and contributed to a large number of conversions to the Communist cause, particularly among students. Such growing animosity towards Chiang's regime contributed to the virtual implosion of Nationalist authority in southern China in 1949, with the key cities surrendering to the CCP within a few months and with very little resistance (see page 262).

SOURCE L

An excerpt from *I Stayed in China* **by William Sewell, published by Allen & Unwin, London, 1966. Sewell was a British biology teacher at the West China Union University in 1947.**

The economic situation was beginning to dominate everything ... and the well-being of the people was indicated by the price and availability of rice. A teacher eats about a bushel of rice every month ... In 1939 it cost two Chinese dollars a bushel ... [by 1941] it had risen to $45 ... in 1947 it had risen to $50,000 a bushel, but already by the spring of the following year it was $110,000. Paper money was almost worthless; we were most of us millionaires but quite unable to cope ... Rice was frequently hard to get. The military men, who were becoming richer while the others got poorer, were buying it up, storing it, and then selling again only when the price was much higher.

What can be learned from Source L about the problems confronting the Nationalists during the Chinese Civil War?

Conclusion

Communist victory in the civil war was not a foregone conclusion. Indeed, in 1945 it seemed that the odds were stacked against them. That the Communists were able to overcome these odds was primarily due to their strategic and tactical decisions, in particular the strategy of mobile defence which nullified the considerable initial military advantages of the Nationalists and wore down the Nationalist army.

The US government was clear in blaming Nationalist strategic incompetence and corruption for their defeat. However, while mistakes were certainly made, and less than optimal strategies pursued, many Nationalist strategies were based on sound, albeit conventional, military reasoning and usually resulted in significant, if ultimately superficial, gains. The fact that Chiang's forces were defeated was due more to Communist skill than Nationalist errors.

CCP management of the war, in particular its emphasis on the importance of establishing control of the countryside, was crucial in facilitating their victory. This was because mobile warfare was only really possible in a context where the troops could be supported and supplied by the local population. However, while CCP management of the war was fundamental to its chances of victory, it took strategic and tactical skill to exploit these potential advantages and translate them into military victory.

← **Why did the Communists win the civil war?**

How useful is Source M as
evidence of the reasons why
the Communists won the
civil war?

SOURCE M

An excerpt from 'Smash Chiang Kai-Shek's Offensive by a War of Self-defence', an article by Mao Zedong, 20 July 1946. Quoted in M. Lynch, *Mao,* **published by Routledge, London, 2004, page 128.**

Although Chiang Kai-shek has US aid, the feelings of the people are against him, the morale of his troops is low, and his economy is in difficulty. As for us, although we have no foreign aid, the feelings of the people are with us, the morale of our troops is high and we can handle our economy.

The main developments in the (second phase of) civil war	
1945 **Focus: north China** • Nationalists gained control of cities • CCP dominated the countryside	**1947** **Focus: central and northern China** • Nationalist advance, gained majority of cities • CCP in retreat (lost Yanan) but retained countryside bases
1946 **Focus: Manchuria** • Nationalists gained control of cities • CCP retreated from cities but dominated the countryside Truce (June–October)	**1948** **Focus: central and northern China and Manchuria** • Nationalists in retreat (losing many key cities) • CCP launched successful attacks on cities
	1949 **Focus: southern China** • Nationalists in retreat • CCP gained huge amounts of territory and ultimate victory

	Nationalists	**CCP**
Strategies and tactics	• Prioritized taking and holding urban centres, e.g. Strongpoint Offensive (1947) • Favoured conventional-style battles	• Prioritized maintaining rural bases between 1945 and 1947 • Used the mobile defence strategy between 1945 and late 1947 • Shifted to strategy of attacking urban centres from late 1947
Military personnel	• Initially outnumbered the CCP (3 to 1), but later lost this numerical advantage • Conscripts used frequently	• Initially outnumbered by the Nationalists, but later gained the numerical advantage • Conscripts used frequently
Weaponry	• Benefited from access to US armaments supplies • US supplies perhaps not as helpful as has been claimed	• Benefited from captured Japanese weaponry, with access facilitated by the USSR • Used captured Nationalist weaponry
Civilian support	• Propaganda • Use of coercion: for taxes, recruits	• Popular policies: land reform, social reform • Propaganda • Use of coercion: for food supplies, recruits
Access to food supplies	• Food shortages and hunger a significant problem • Relied on rail and air transportation of food into the cities which was frequently sabotaged	• No significant food shortages • Food accessed (often forcibly) from rural base areas to supply troops

SUMMARY DIAGRAM

The course of the Chinese Civil War

4 The effects of the Chinese Civil War

▶ *Key question:* To what extent did the civil war transform Chinese society?

The experience of the civil war had a profound effect on Chinese society. This was brought about not just by the destruction and dislocation caused by civil conflict, but also through the actions of Communists who sought to implement profound social and economic change.

The socioeconomic impact of the civil war

The Civil War caused substantial social change in terms of casualties, the nature of the social structure and opportunities for women. Economically, the war combined with the effects of almost a century of intermittent conflict in China to create profound economic problems.

← To what extent did the civil war lead to socioeconomic change?

Casualties

Estimates of the number of deaths caused by the Chinese Civil War, including deaths from famine and destruction that accompanied the war, vary considerably. They range from four to six million for the years 1945–9 alone, not including the casualties caused by conflict in the period 1927–37. In the three major campaigns of 1948–9 alone, the Nationalists lost over 1.5 million men and the CCP a quarter of a million. The scale of deaths, however, pales in comparison to the number of Chinese who were killed in the Second Sino-Japanese War: three million combat casualties and 18 million civilian deaths due to famine and conflict.

The civil war's impact on social structure

Communist policies in the areas under their control during the civil war led to fundamental changes in the structure of society. A substantial change was that landlords were removed from their position of power and persecuted by local peasantry. These changes affected territory encompassing some 160 million people, and it is probable that some 16 million people were persecuted to some degree during this period. Indeed, at least one million landlords were killed during the period 1945–9.

Communist land reform policies meant that peasants found that they owned land for the first time. Although this redistribution of land to peasant ownership clearly contravened the principles of communism, which was against individual land ownership in whatever form, it was regarded as an expedient measure in order to appeal to the peasants during the civil war. Once the Communists had secured power, there was a move towards creating **co-operative farms** and then **collective farms** in the 1950s.

KEY TERM

Co-operative farms Farms in which individual plots of land continued to be individually owned but were managed and worked collectively by their owners.

Collective farms Farms in which land was not individually owned but was managed by to the collective.

The impact of the war on women

The experience of a woman during the civil war was incredibly diverse. It depended on her social status, whether she resided in a rural or urban area and within Communist- or Nationalist-controlled territory. Traditionally women were regarded as inferior to men and had few legal rights. Foot binding was common until the early twentieth century, as were arranged marriages. Women were largely confined to the domestic duties of child-bearing and maintaining the household. Overall, the civil war period witnessed an improvement in the legal status and educational and political opportunities for women, but this affected only the minority. In practice for the majority of women little changed, and if anything life became harder.

Women in Nationalist zones

During the Nanjing Decade there was some expansion in legal rights and opportunities for women. The legal status of women, particularly in marriage and divorce, was improved in the Civil Code of 1930:

- Arranged marriages without the consent of the woman were prohibited.
- Wives were able to initiate divorce proceedings.
- Daughters were given equal inheritance rights to sons.

A labour law in 1931 stipulated that women should be paid the same rate of pay as men for the same work.

In practice, however, these legal changes often brought no real change to women's lives, especially in remote rural communities where traditional customs and attitudes continued to prevail.

Educational opportunities

There was an increase in educational opportunities for women. By 1935 over 6000 colleges and universities admitted women, who largely went on to pursue traditional female careers in education, nursing and the civil service. Distinct differences in ideas about male and female roles in society persisted, and women were still expected to fulfil a more domestic role within the home. For poorer women, unable to access education, very little changed at all.

Women in the Communist zones

In CCP-controlled zones there was, in theory at least, a greater acceptance of sexual equality.

- Women were encouraged to participate in CCP committees and even serve as officials.
- Arranged marriages were strongly discouraged, even before the Nationalist Civil Code outlawed the practice.
- Women were regarded as being as legitimate a source of manual labour as men. Women played a more active role in manual work in the fields than had previously been expected of them, especially as many men had been conscripted into the Red Army.

Some women served in the Red Army and Communist militias. The Special Company of the 2nd Independent Division of the Chinese Red Army, for example, was a female-only unit.

Women also played a significant role in catering to the needs of the Red Army, making clothes, nursing the wounded and transporting supplies. In many ways, the life of women in Communist-controlled zones actually became harder since they were expected to continue their domestic duties while also taking on new roles.

After the CCP's victory, new laws enshrined greater legal rights for women. The Marriage Law of 1 May 1950:

* abolished arranged marriages
* granted husband and wife the right to seek divorce on equal terms
* guaranteed equality in the management and inheritance of family property
* stipulated that a husband could not apply for divorce if his wife was pregnant, and could only do so one year after the birth of the child.

However, once again, social customs and poverty frequently meant that little often changed in reality for the majority of Chinese women.

The economic impact of the war

The civil war had a devastating and profound impact on the Chinese economy. Industrial production, only a tiny proportion of the Chinese economy before the war, was further weakened due to:

* the destruction caused to urban centres by civil conflict and the Second Sino-Japanese War
* the Soviet removal of much of Manchuria's best industrial infrastructure in 1945–6 (see page 259).

Years of civil conflict also destroyed and disrupted significant areas of agricultural land, not least because many of the male peasantry needed to work the land were conscripted into the armies of both sides. In Communist-controlled areas the disruption associated with land reform created upheaval which was disruptive to crop yields. Years of conflict also had a detrimental impact on the currency, with inflation rising rapidly (see page 268).

The Communists introduced many economic and social reforms, although the implementation of more genuinely communist principles was largely delayed until after they had consolidated power. In the early months after their victory, the CCP focused on smaller scale social and economic reform to ameliorate some of the worst hardships and corruptions experienced by the population due to years of warfare, such as ending inflation and eliminating the thriving black market.

The political impact of the war

The Chinese Civil War brought about profound political change with the establishment of communist rule, although in some ways its authoritarianism was part of a long tradition of such rule in China. In international politics, the establishment of a communist state in China intensified the rivalries of the Cold War.

Communist rule in China

The CCP's victory in the war meant the imposition of single-party dictatorship; the CCP held all power. Mao, the head of the party, was referred to as Chairman Mao, and rapidly became revered as an iconic figure Small party committees were established throughout China to discuss local issues and to elect delegates to sit in higher committees. By the 1950s there were over one million local CCP committees.

The persecution of political opponents

The persecution of political opponents and class enemies had been a feature of communism during the war and was extended after the CCP victory. All other political organizations were banned and in October 1950 a campaign was launched to suppress all counter-revolutionaries. The vagueness of what constituted a counter-revolutionary encouraged the settling of personal scores, creating an atmosphere of fear and compliance. Indeed, a surveillance society was actively promoted, with Order Keeping Committees established in factories and schools to monitor neighbours and colleagues. In this campaign approximately 28,000 were executed in Shangdong province alone.

Further campaigns of terror were launched in 1951 and 1952, including the Three-Antis Campaign in late 1951 and the Five-Antis Campaign in January 1952. Both targeted those perceived as guilty of financial corruption and were essentially aimed against private businessmen of property, who the Communists regarded as class enemies.

The reunification of China

By the end of the civil war China was more unified than it had been in decades. Mao sought outright authority and Red Army troops were sent to establish control over the more remote regions in the west: Tibet and Xinjiang. These regions had been outside the effective control of the Nationalists, despite Chiang's efforts to incorporate them, and they retained their own distinct ethnic and religious identities.

The treatment of Tibet was particularly brutal. Red Army troops were sent to Tibet in 1950 as part of the **Reunification Campaigns**. In order to promote Tibetan assimilation into mainland China, Tibet was renamed Xizang and was forcibly incorporated into China. The public practice of Tibet's form of Buddhism, *lama,* was prohibited and the teaching of the Tibetan language and history forbidden in schools. There was a national uprising in Tibet in 1959, but this was suppressed with estimates of 87,000 killed.

KEY TERM

Reunification Campaigns
China's military campaigns to annex Tibet and Xinjiang to China.

Communist and Nationalist rivalries 1949–58

The legitimacy of the Communist People's Republic of China (PRC) was challenged by Chiang Kai-Shek and his supporters. From Taiwan, where they had fled at the end of the civil war, they maintained that their government, the Republic of China (ROC), represented the legitimate Chinese government, a claim that continues to the present day. In the context of the Cold War, most Western countries and the United Nations recognized the Taiwanese government as China's legitimate government until the 1970s.

From Taiwan, Chiang remained committed to the re-establishment of Nationalist authority over mainland China. In consequence, periodic military clashes between the PRC and the ROC arose in the 1950s. These focused on the islands in the **Taiwanese Strait**. The ROC established troops and fortifications on the islands of Matsu and Quemoy, situated just off the coast of mainland China. The PRC responded by shelling the islands and declaring that Taiwan must be 'liberated' in August 1954. This was the First Taiwan Strait Crisis. In the Cold War context, the conflict threatened to enlarge and escalate. Many in the USA regarded it as essential to ensure Taiwan did not become communist. American forces were therefore authorized by Congress to defend Taiwan. This proved unnecessary as the PRC ceased shelling in May 1955. The uneasy coexistence between the PRC and ROC again flared into military confrontation in the Second Taiwan Strait Crisis in 1958, with similar results.

 **KEY TERM**

Taiwanese Strait The channel of sea separating mainland China and Taiwan.

The impact of the civil war on international politics

The Chinese Civil War served to intensify the Cold War. From the US perspective, the CCP's victory was further evidence of the danger of the global spread of communism. In consequence, the USA became more determined to act to resist its spread. It was a common perception in the USA in the 1950s that not enough had been done to help the Nationalists.

When war broke out in Korea between the communists in the north and non-communists in the south, the USA adopted a hardline attitude, pushing the United Nations to give military assistance to the south; the bulk of forces sent to the Korean War were US troops. In addition, US President Dwight Eisenhower, Truman's successor, pledged to stand firm against communism. This was evident in:

- the Formosa Resolution in 1955 which authorized US troops to be sent to defend Taiwan in the First Taiwan Strait Crisis
- increasing US commitment to assist the non-communist regime in Vietnam against communist insurgents there.

The Vietnam War was the most dramatic and tragic example of how the 'loss' of China to communism would haunt US presidents and contribute to a more interventionist foreign policy, which in turn served to further escalate Cold War tensions.

Social structure
- The power and privilege of landlords was removed
- Land was redistributed to the peasantry
- In the 1950s co-operative and collective style farms were introduced, ending peasant ownership of land

Economics
- Limited industrial production was weakened by disruption and damage caused by war
- The implementation of communist economic principles was largely delayed until after a period of political consolidation

Women
- Variation in experience
- Some greater legal rights (particularly in marriage) and more educational opportunities
- Communist ideology promoted, theoretically, greater equality
- For most women little changed as traditional attitudes persisted and daily realities meant new opportunities were difficult to access

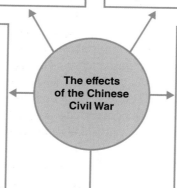

The effects of the Chinese Civil War

Politics
- A single-party Communist state established with Chairman Mao as the leader
- Military campaign to achieve reunification of China, including the assimilation of Tibet
- The Nationalists (based in Taiwan) continued to maintain they were the legitimate government of China, leading to military clashes in the Taiwanese Straits in the 1950s

International relations
- Intensified fears about the spread of communism
- Contributed to the USA's increasingly interventionist stance against the spread of communism e.g. US involvement in the Korean War and the Vietnam War

SUMMARY DIAGRAM

The effects of the Chinese Civil War

Chapter summary

The Chinese Civil War 1927–37 and 1945–9

Violent clashes between the ruling Nationalist Party and the Chinese Communist Party (CCP) began in 1927 and continued, with brief interludes of uneasy co-operation, until 1949 when the CCP achieved victory at the end of the civil war. The most decisive phase of the civil war occurred between 1945 and 1949.

The rivalry between the parties was rooted in profound and incompatible ideological differences in their vision for China. However, ideological difference was not enough to bring about armed conflict on a significant scale. For this, both parties required supporters and the ability to wage military conflict. In this the Communists were helped by the social inequalities and injustices in Chinese society, which helped to create an audience for their radical message of social reform. The lack of complete central control, following decades of political fragmentation, also helped the Communists as it assisted them in being able to build up base areas in the relative isolation of the countryside during the 1920s and 1930s.

The event which transformed the violent clashes into a more intense and sustained conflict was the Second Sino-Japanese War and Japanese occupation of China between 1937 and 1945. This had the effect of strengthening the military capacity of both the Nationalists and the Communists. When the Japanese surrendered and vacated China abruptly in August 1945, the Communists and the Nationalists rushed to fill the power vacuum. This triggered the most intense phase of their conflict in a civil war which lasted until 1949.

Communist victory was ultimately achieved despite the initial military superiority of the Nationalists. The Communists were able to largely negate the initial Nationalist advantage through their skilful use of tactics, in particular the strategy of mobile defence. The Nationalists lacked any real rural bases, something which left them potentially vulnerable to isolation and siege in their urban bases.

The experience of years of civil war and of Communist policies profoundly changed China socially and economically. As class warfare was unleashed, the traditional privileged classes, notably the landlords and the urban élites, had their wealth and power removed, often forcibly. Certainly the peasantry benefited initially, gaining land for the first time. However, the authoritarian Communist government also used terror and coercion against ordinary people. Campaigns were launched against counter-revolutionaries and the outlying regions were forcefully assimilated, as the Communist leadership sought to establish a unified, centralized Communist state.

Examination practice

Command term: To what extent

When a question asks you to address 'to what extent' about an aspect of twentieth-century warfare, it is asking you to determine how much something is true or false. This usually means that you should have a clear answer that will likely state that something is 'to no extent', 'to some extent' or 'to a great extent' true or false. This is a very common form of question.

Below are a number of different questions for you to practise using the command term 'to what extent'. For guidance on how to answer exam-style questions, see Chapter 8.

1 To what extent did technology affect the outcome of two twentieth-century wars, each from a different region?

2 To what extent were women affected by the outcome of two twentieth-century wars?

3 To what extent were twentieth-century wars caused by the same issues?

4 To what extent did naval warfare change during the twentieth century?

5 To what extent did two twentieth-century wars lead to territorial changes?

 # Activities

1 Work in groups of three. One person chooses and states a cause of the Chinese Civil War, such as 'peasant poverty'. The second person then explains two reasons why this contributed to causing the war. Finally the third person explains two reasons why this cause on its own was not sufficient to bring about civil war.

2 Draw a timeline from 1927 to 1949 that includes all the significant clashes between the Nationalists and the CCP that took place during the civil war.

3 For each of the individuals below list the ways in which their life was affected, both positively and negatively, by the civil war and rate how much overall they benefited with a score from 0 to 5 (with 5 being they benefited most):

- a female peasant
- a landlord
- a student living in Shanghai.

- a male peasant
- a businessman

CHAPTER 6

Nicaraguan Revolution 1976–9

The Nicaraguan Revolution was a conflict that involved a limited guerrilla campaign linked to a major political challenge to the single-party state system of Nicaragua. Since the revolution was primarily the result of a growing political challenge, its starting point is difficult to pinpoint. Indeed, many historians believe the real Nicaraguan Revolution was actually achieved after rebels took power in 1979, as major reforms transformed the country and led to a larger conflict that lasted for a decade.

You need to consider the following questions throughout this chapter:

★ What were the main causes of the Nicaraguan Revolution?
★ Why did Somoza fall from power in mid-1979?
★ To what extent did the revolution affect Nicaraguan politics, economics and society?

1 The causes of the Nicaraguan Revolution

▶ **Key question:** What were the main causes of the Nicaraguan Revolution?

In the 1970s, the Nicaraguan Revolution erupted when the ruling family, the Somozas, faced a guerrilla campaign (see page 3) and political revolt from groups who were unhappy about how the country was being run. Most Nicaraguans lived in dire poverty and the political system had been dominated by one family for decades. Its economic and political development had remained limited, despite the involvement of other countries due to Nicaragua's strategically important location in the region. This section will first examine how these long-term problems led to the revolution, before exploring the short-term causes of why it occurred when it did.

Long-term causes of the revolution

> What factors allowed the Somoza family to establish a dictatorship?

Nicaragua became independent in 1838 and, except for a few brief periods, was politically stable until the 1890s when a series of revolts and civil wars plagued the country. The USA, interested in possibly constructing a canal across the country to connect the Atlantic and Pacific Oceans, before finally deciding to construct one through Panama instead, deployed troops to stabilize the country's political systems in 1909. Continued revolts led to the creation of the National Guard by the USA in 1927. The organization, which functioned as both police and army for Nicaragua, was led by Anastasio Somoza García, known as Somoza Senior, who overthrew the government in 1936. He was then elected president in December 1936, with only 100 votes cast against him, with his term beginning in January 1937.

Somoza dictatorship

Somoza Senior placed family members in leading government positions and used the National Guard to manage elections which kept him in power. While consolidating his authority, he cultivated close ties with the USA. Nicaragua, for example, was one of the first countries to declare war on the Axis Powers in the Second World War after the USA was attacked by Japan on 7 December 1941. The Nicaraguan government seized German and Italian property during this war and accommodated war refugees. Nicaragua joined the United Nations at the end of the Second World War and always supported the US political position. During the Cold War (see page 181), Nicaragua co-operated fully with US efforts against the spread of communist-friendly regimes. Somoza Senior helped in a 1954 invasion of Guatemala and Nicaragua was a staging area for the **Bay of Pigs** attack on Cuba by Cuban exiles in 1961.

Dynasty formed

Somoza Senior served as president from 1 January 1937 until 1 May 1947. After a brief interlude, he returned to the presidency in 1950. He had two sons that he carefully groomed to help him control Nicaragua and rule it after his death. Luis Anastasio Somoza Debayle (Luis Somoza) was expected to follow his father as president. The second son, Anastasio Somoza Debayle, commonly referred to only as Somoza, was groomed to command the National Guard, the power behind the Somoza dynasty. Somoza Senior had the constitution changed in 1955 to allow him to run for president again, prompting Rigoberto López Pérez, an outraged poet, to assassinate him in 1956. He was immediately replaced by his son Luis.

Luis Somoza served as president of Nicaragua from 1956 until 1963 and instituted some reforms, such as allowing limited political opposition. While confirming his brother as head of the National Guard, he transitioned the family from **direct rule** to **indirect rule** by having René Schick elected president. Schick was controlled by the Somozas until his death in 1966. In April 1967, Luis died and by the end of the year, Somoza, his younger brother, became president in an election managed by the National Guard which he commanded. He made his half brother, José Somoza, the new head of the National Guard.

Minor opposition

The Somoza dynasty had little effective opposition through the majority of its rule. Those who rebelled against the government were usually jailed for a year or so, often under house arrest, and then pardoned; a few were exiled. While there were **human rights violations** on occasion, the National Guard

KEY TERM

Bay of Pigs A US-supported attack on Cuba by Cuban exiles in 1961 in which the exiles were heavily defeated.

Direct rule Ruling a country from a position of authority.

Indirect rule Ruling a country unofficially through others.

Human rights violations Torture, illegal imprisonment, rape, executions and similar crimes.

and the government rarely bothered the majority rural population. Although poor, they were also religious and dependent on work found on large agricultural estates owned by the Somoza family or other wealthy landowners. They were not part of the political system, had no time to oppose the government, and were mostly illiterate with no ability to organize any form of opposition. They were also easy to intimidate by the National Guard if that need arose, which it rarely did.

While the Somoza family ruled through their political party, the Nationalist Liberal Party (PLN), other parties did exist, such as the Conservative Party of Nicaragua. These parties were tolerated as long as they co-operated with the Somoza dynasty.

Economics
Nicaragua had very uneven economic development, with the vast majority of the population living in poverty, while the ruling family used its position to increasingly control the economy.

Somozan wealth
The Somoza family not only controlled the political and military institutions of Nicaragua, they also controlled the economy. Somoza Senior, with control of the presidency and National Guard, used the government's institutions to buy the best farmlands in the country. He also seized land which had never been officially registered to owners and land granted to former rebels in the early 1930s as part of peace agreements. Italian and German property seized in the Second World War was sold cheaply to Somoza.

Using government money, he built infrastructure such as roads, bridges and electricity stations for his vast land holdings which were intensely cultivated by poor peasants working for minimal wages. National Guardsmen often cleared forests from his lands and planted his fields.

By the late 1930s, the Somozas owned coffee, cotton and beef cattle plantations. They were able to dominate the beef export market by having the government charge export taxes on products of other exporters. Somoza Senior's economic empire consisted of:

- sugar mills
- alcohol distilleries
- 51 cattle ranches
- 46 coffee plantations
- a shipping company
- a national airline (*Líneas Aéreas de Nicaragua*)
- a huge container port on the Pacific Ocean named Puerto Somoza.

He also:

- became Director of the Pacific Railroad Company which transported all his products and equipment for free

- received personal financial gifts from US companies to develop gold mines, cut forests and develop rubber plantations
- prohibited companies other than his own from importing products into Nicaragua
- purchased vast properties in the USA and Canada.

The National Guard, another Somoza family holding:

- managed the country's health services
- controlled all radio broadcasts
- operated prisons, national railways and the postal system
- produced and sold liquor and weapons
- controlled borders, thereby managing imports and exports.

According to Source A, what led to the downfall of the Somoza family in 1979?

SOURCE A

Excerpt from *The Military and the State in Latin America* by Alain Rouquié, published by University of California Press, Berkeley, 1987, page 159.

Electricity, hospitals, railroads, and water companies were state companies in which the clan took care to place near or distant relatives, thus furthering the business interests of the group by putting public enterprises at the service of the private interests of the [Somoza Senior] dictatorship. This confusion between the state and the interests of the family gave a certain foundation to the humorous claim of the last Somoza that since the time of his father Nicaragua had been a 'socialist state.' In fact it was precisely the insatiable cupidity [desire for wealth] of the Somocista dynasty that produced its defeat.

Under the presidency of Somoza, son of Somoza Senior, family control over the economy expanded. During his rule, half of all registered land in Nicaragua was owned by the family, approximately 75,000 km². By the mid-1970s, it was estimated that the Somozas owned 346 companies and Somoza was known as one of the world's wealthiest people.

Rural Nicaraguan economy

While the Somozas controlled the economy and government, the majority of Nicaraguans lived in extreme poverty. The United Nations Economic Commission for Latin America reported in 1972 that:

- 67 per cent of the rural population could not read or write
- 59 per cent of homes had no electricity
- 26 per cent of urban homes were connected to sewage treatment systems
- 54 per cent of homes had no access to safe drinking water
- 69 per cent of rural homes had dirt floors.

The **World Health Organization** reported that Nicaragua had the second highest incidents of diseases like typhoid in the Americas and that malnutrition caused the death of half of all children who died under the age of five. The **Inter-American Development Bank** reported in 1972 that from 1960 to 1972 the gross national product had risen by 7.1 per cent, meaning

KEY TERM

World Health Organization International body that works to prevent disease and promotes health.

Inter-American Development Bank Central and South American organization that works to alleviate poverty and promote economic development.

hat the poor did not benefit from this massive economic growth. The growing gap between the wealthy, led by the Somozas, and the poor, primarily rural population would be a key factor in gathering national support for opposition to Somoza after 1974.

Opposition and revolt before 1972

While the majority of the population may have supported the Somoza family for a variety of reasons, there were some who openly challenged them. Since it was impossible to work through the governmental system to create change, they worked outside the system with varying success. Opponents were usually treated lightly as they were from the small group of wealthy and better-educated élite and therefore often related to the Somozas or their political allies. Harsh punishments would have potentially caused further dissent.

Chamorro

In Managua, the capital, the government allowed *La Prensa*, the newspaper with the largest circulation in the country, to be published although it was owned and operated by the biggest political opponent of the regime: Pedro Joaquín Chamorro Cardenal (Chamorro). Chamorro attempted a minor rebellion against the state in 1954 which led to a year in prison and a year of house arrest. After Somoza Senior was assassinated, Chamorro was sent to prison again for six months along with many others who opposed the government, although they had nothing to do with the murder. He fled to Costa Rica in 1957 and visited Cuba after the rise of **Fidel Castro** in 1959. Chamorro returned to Nicaragua in 1959 and attempted another rebellion with 100 youths he had recruited. After 15 days of fighting and running, the rebels surrendered. Although a few died in battles, most were sentenced to prison and freed a year later. Chamorro returned to *La Prensa* in 1969 and continued his attacks on the regime through the newspaper.

Frente Sandinista de Liberación Nacional (FSLN)

The FSLN (Sandinista National Liberation Front) began in 1961, adding Sandinista to the name in 1963 in remembrance of Sandino, popular leader of a rebellion in the 1920s and 1930s. The founders of the FSLN, usually known as the Sandinistas, were inspired by the writings of **Marx** and **Lenin**, as well as Castro's success against the dictatorial regime of Cuba. In the first years, although inspired by **socialism** and communism, they did not clearly communicate their philosophy, perhaps to retain cohesion in the group where not everyone could agree on which governmental system to follow. They could agree, however, that the Somoza regime needed to be removed and that the way to do it was to mobilize rural, impoverished peasants. Sixty members crossed from Honduras into Nicaragua in 1962 with the intention of taking control of a small area before expanding their territory. The National Guard quickly killed about 20 Sandinistas in fighting and captured almost all the rest; a few made it back to Honduras. The group was presumed extinct by the government since there was no more activity for the next few years.

KEY TERM

Fidel Castro Guerrilla fighter who overthrew a dictatorship in Cuba in 1959 and gradually introduced a communist form of government, allying with the USSR during the Cold War.

Marx Wrote the Communist Manifesto and other writings which formed the basis of communism.

Lenin Russian Marxist who led a revolution in Russia in 1917, establishing a communist state which became the USSR.

Socialism Political and economic system in which a nation's resources and means of production are controlled by the government to prevent extremes in wealth and poverty.

FSLN goals

In December 1966, 35 Sandinistas crossed again into Nicaragua in order to fight the National Guard in small, quick battles. By August 1967, 20 rebels were dead and most of the rest had fled to Cuba. It seems that a major problem for the Sandinistas was the peasants themselves. They feared National Guard retaliation and did not understand Sandinista goals. To them, Sandinistas were outsiders and they preferred to trust the National Guard who they knew and who rarely bothered them. In 1969, Sandinistas finally published their overall goals. Some of these were to:

- improve the status of women and minorities
- seize major estates from the wealthy and redistribute them to the peasants
- seize major wealth, redistributing it to the population as a whole
- improve health care and education
- improve human rights and freedom of the individual
- establish a revolutionary government to accomplish all the above.

FSLN expansion

Sandinistas received military training primarily in Cuba and in 1972 tried to restart their rebellion in Nicaragua's north. Again, peasants distrusted them and assisted the National Guard in locating them. Many Sandinista leaders were killed, but their fight caught the attention of Catholic youth in a district of Managua, Nicaragua's capital. The youth group created a commune of sorts, living around the church of a sympathetic priest where they studied Christian teachings in the morning, went to university in the day, and discussed Marxism in the evenings. A Sandinista visited in late 1972 to meet the group and in 1973 the students left the commune to join the underground movement. It was not the peasantry where opposition to Somoza could be found, but in urban, generally affluent youth who were disturbed by corruption and lack of democracy. The earthquake of 1972 helped push them to join the rebels.

To what extent was the Managua earthquake of 1972 the main short-term cause of Nicaraguan Revolution?

Short-term causes of the revolution

Opposition to Somoza expanded greatly after 1972 as a result of corruption after an earthquake destroyed much of Nicaragua's capital. Business leaders, the Catholic Church and guerrilla rebels began to oppose the regime separately and gradually. While the rural poor continued to remain uninvolved until the late 1970s, opposition in the cities expanded greatly as a reaction to increased awareness of corruption and the murder of a major opposition leader.

Managua earthquake 1972

On 23 December 1972, a major earthquake levelled 80 per cent of Managua, Nicaragua's capital, killing 10,000 people and leaving the majority of the population homeless.

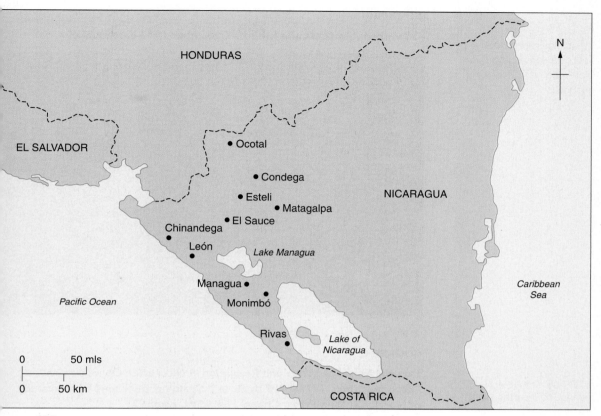

map of Nicaragua

undreds of millions of dollars of emergency aid flowed into the country, rimarily from the USA, to rebuild the city. Most of the money was directed y Somoza into his family's businesses which received most rebuilding ontracts. Buildings and businesses owned by the Somoza family and their llies were built first and then housing for the wealthy. High import taxes ere placed on construction materials needed by rival construction ompanies. Hitherto, Somoza had had very little vocal opposition other than ne minor and ineffectual opposition of Chamorro and the FSLN. Now the rban middle classes, both **Liberals** and **Conservatives**, began to see the resident's greed as threatening their economic existence.

1any business owners belonged to the Superior Council of Private Initiative COSIP) and in March 1974, they organized a large gathering of private usinessman. They issued a public statement accusing Somoza of corruption n the use of earthquake relief funds. Chamorro was able, in this new olitical climate of opposition to Somoza, to organize the *Unión Democrática e Liberacion* (Democratic Union of Liberation or UDEL), a coalition of seven olitical parties and labour unions.

KEY TERM

Liberals Political groups mainly concerned with free trade and economic development.

Conservatives Political groups dominated by major landowners that desired a closer relationship between the government and the Catholic Church.

COSIP Nicaraguan group of businessmen opposed to Somozan domination of the economic system in the mid-1970s.

SOURCE B

Downtown Managua after the 23 December 1972 earthquake.

SOURCE C

Excerpt from *Capitalists and Revolution in Nicaragua: Opposition and Accommodation, 1979–1993* by Rose J. Spalding, published by University of North Carolina Press, Chapel Hill, 1994, page 52.

In the aftermath of the December 1972 earthquake in Managua, the Somoza regime's capacity for self-indulgence and indifference to national needs was starkly revealed. The imposition of a series of new emergency taxes, combined with the unrelieved suffering resulting from the earthquake, the accelerated theft of relief assistance by officials, and open profiteering by Somoza family members, led private sector leaders to adopt a more critical attitude toward regime mismanagement and corruption. The rebuilding process triggered the expansion of Somoza family businesses into growth industries – construction, real estate, and banking – that had traditionally been the province of the dominant economic groups. Direct economic threat merged with a smouldering sense of moral disdain to prompt elite intervention.

Christmas Party Raid

The Sandinistas had been forgotten by almost everyone and it was assumed, wrongly, that the organization had come to an end in 1972. On 27 December 1974, at a Christmas party for the US ambassador to Nicaragua, a small group of Sandinistas, including 10 men and three women, took the Nicaraguan foreign minister and Somoza's brother-in-law hostage, as well as many wealthy businessmen. Roman Catholic Archbishop Miguel Obando y Bravo negotiated with the rebels over a two-day period, leading to the government agreeing with Sandinista demands:

14 Sandinista rebels to be released from prison

$1 million in cash

publication in national newspapers of an FSLN-composed statement on Somoza

a flight to Cuba.

As soon as the rebels had been flown to Cuba, the National Guard began an aggressive campaign to root out Sandinista rebels wherever they could find them. This renewed campaign almost destroyed the Sandinistas, who were few in number, and splintered the survivors.

Sandinista fragmentation

There was dissension within the surviving Sandinista leadership regarding the Christmas Party Raid, which some saw as a great success and others as a strategic mistake. The three Sandinista factions competed for followers and support from Cuba.

Proletarian Faction

The Proletarian Faction, led by Jaime Wheelock, believed that instead of carrying out spectacular, but counter-productive, raids, the Sandinistas should be working to educate people about Marxist principles which would eventually lead to a change in the system. This group opposed working with other political parties and the Catholic Church as they were seen as contributing to Nicaragua's poverty and corruption.

Prolonged Popular War

The Prolonged Popular War group were strongly Marxist. They believed that a guerrilla war in the countryside against the National Guard and major estate owners would lead to governmental change.

Terceristas

The Terceristas were the largest faction. They believed that the best way to remove the governing system, specifically the Somoza dynasty, was to build alliances with all groups. This included working with business owners and even the Catholic Church.

National Guard actions 1975–6

Somoza ordered the National Guard to crush the Sandinistas in early 1975. The Christmas Party Raid had raised the profile of the Sandinistas and that, coupled with the COSIP statement and the formation of the UDEL, led to a crackdown. The press was heavily censored and opposition leaders were threatened with prison and torture. The National Guard conducted anti-guerrilla operations against the Prolonged Popular War in the northern mountains, killing the majority of its leadership. Peasant farms and villages

were destroyed in the north and east, driving thousands of peasants away so
that the Sandinistas would have no local support or access to food.
Hundreds of peasants were tortured and killed in order to get information
on Sandinista movements. Hundreds disappeared by the end of 1975,
probably killed, and mass graves were discovered by Catholic missionaries.

The Catholic Church sent a protest to the government about human rights
violations in early 1976. The National Guard was accused of killing 200
peasants who were unaffiliated with rebel groups. While some priests
claimed the number was actually around 400, the National Guard did not
deny killing the peasants and simply responded that the victims had worked
with the rebel guerrillas. The Catholic Church would increasingly criticize the
government over its actions.

Sandinista factions based in Nicaragua were practically wiped out by
National Guard actions; Terceristas leaders were saved by being mostly in
Cuba. Other members were in hiding in Nicaragua or in Costa Rica.

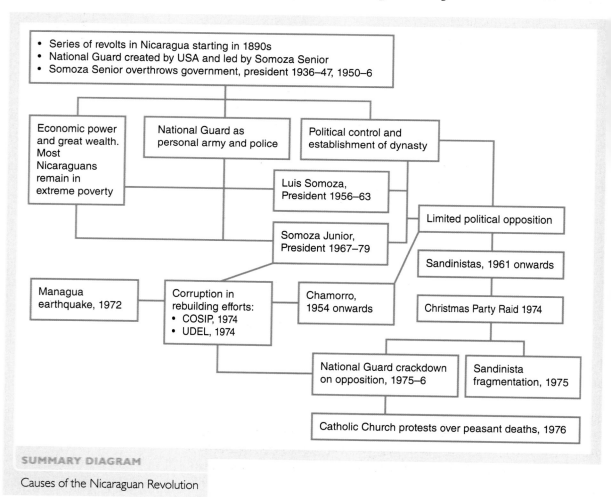

Causes of the Nicaraguan Revolution

The course of the Nicaraguan Revolution

▶ *Key question:* Why did Somoza fall from power in mid-1979?

Until early 1979, it was unclear if Somoza would be removed or continue to the end of his term in office. While he had little support politically, this mattered little when he controlled the National Guard and the majority of the economy, and was supported by the USA. US support, however, was questioned by a new US president and other Nicaraguan groups organized against him, siding with the Sandinistas to force change on the Nicaraguan government and people.

The year of coalitions and committees 1977

Jimmy Carter became the US president in 1977. The US government soon announced that its support should no longer be considered automatic and that it was concerned about corruption, human rights and democracy, specifically mentioning Nicaragua as a case in point. This encouraged those in opposition to Somoza, while he disregarded these statements as meaningless. He believed that he would maintain US support in the face of Marxist-leaning rebels since the world was still in the midst of the Cold War.

← **Why did groups opposed to Somoza form coalitions starting in 1977?**

Terceristas build alliances

The Terceristas made contact with various business leaders and landowners in early 1977, encouraged by the growing US dissatisfaction with Somoza. Many of the Terceristas themselves were related to these economic classes, making connections easier. This approach was the idea of Sergio Ramírez and Humberto Ortega. Ramírez was a well-known writer and Ortega was a Sandinista who had lived in exile in Costa Rica. Both men, members of the Sandinistas (Ramírez's membership was kept secret), created a plan for bringing in non-Marxists to expand the appeal of the group to help achieve their overall goals. This plan had three tenets:

- The future political system would allow multiple political parties.
- The economy would consist of both private and government-owned businesses, a mixed economy.
- The nation would not be aligned with any other international power, meaning neither the USA nor the USSR.

On the basis of these tenets, several business leaders, lawyers and others discussed the formation of an anti-Somoza coalition with the Terceristas (see page 287). Ortega cemented the growing relationship by stating that these educated men should fill most governmental positions in the future since they were the most qualified.

Constitutional law re-established 1977

On 25 July 1977, Somoza had a heart attack and went to the USA for medical treatment. He soon returned to Nicaragua, confined to his house while he recovered. Shortly afterwards, he ended the extreme measures put in place after the Christmas Party Raid, and re-established constitutional law which included freedom of the press. Immediately, critics of the regime publically published a demand for Somoza's resignation and for a new head of the National Guard that was not related to him; his half-brother José remained the Director of the National Guard.

Renewed Sandinista attacks

In October 1977, Terceristas decided that a series of spectacular attacks on National Guard positions might incite a general rebellion against the Somoza government. The attacks on two National Guard barracks were failures as participating Sandinistas were killed, captured or retreated into Costa Rica; no national rebellion occurred. Many in Nicaragua, primarily youth, were impressed by these bold actions in the face of the overwhelming power of the National Guard. The government believed, however, that the Sandinistas were of no consequence as there were fewer than 200 Sandinistas in all three factions.

Los Doce

Twelve members of the new coalition of Sandinistas, business leaders, lawyers, intellectuals and priests against Somoza established themselves in San José, the capital of Costa Rica, just after the failed July 1977 attacks. They began working in October 1977 to create an alternative political structure for Nicaragua.

The group, soon known as *Los Doce*, The Twelve, decided:

- Sandinistas would be part of any future Nicaraguan government.
- Political affiliations of *Los Doce* members would be kept secret to present a united front to the world.
- It was important to convince the USA and neighbouring states that their goal was not to form a Marxist state in Nicaragua.
- The focus of their international efforts should be Somoza's corruption, the single-party state system and human rights violations in Nicaragua.

Committee of National Dialogue

Archbishop Manuel Obando y Bravo, who negotiated with the Sandinistas during the Christmas Party Raid, created the Committee of National Dialogue just as the *Los Doce* group began to function. He feared Sandinista guerrilla actions would eventually lead to a civil war since they might eventually be joined by growing numbers of people dissatisfied with the Somoza regime. He also believed Somoza and his family had become a problem and labelled them the cause of Nicaragua's crisis. The committee was soon led by Alfonso Robelo Callejas (Robelo), the president of COSIP (see page 285). The Committee unofficially came to the conclusion that the Somoza family needed to be transitioned from power. Their general ideas were:

- Somoza should agree not to run for president again after his term expired in 1981.
- There should be free elections at the end of 1980.
- The president's half-brother, José Somoza, should be removed from being head of the National Guard.
- A slow, but sure, change in government would prevent civil war and not disrupt the country's economy.

The committee met with Somoza in December 1977. He agreed to continue discussions with them about the possibilities of a transition, but no talks could take place before local elections scheduled for February 1978; he may have feared that any concessions would have led to more effective opposition. The US ambassador to Nicaragua also came to the conclusion that Nicaragua needed to transition from Somoza, but the US State Department was divided. Some in the US government wanted Somoza removed from power, while others believed he should remain since he was a Cold War ally and friendly to US businesses.

The Somoza regime loses support 1978–9

Political opposition gained momentum in 1978. Somoza's main political opponent was killed, new coalitions of opponents were formed and international pressure became increasingly important.

> **To what extent was Somoza's loss of support related to the assassination of political opposition leader Chamorro?**

Assassination of Chamorro

Chamorro was the most famous opposition leader in Nicaragua and seen as the probable successor to Somoza, if Somoza would allow free elections in 1980. He was head of the newspaper *La Prensa*, and his reporters continually investigated and exposed corruption in both the government and the Somoza family. He had formed the UDEL opposition alliance (see page 285). On 10 January 1978, he was shot around 20 times by three gunmen as he drove to work. He died and tens of thousands of people escorted his body to his home. People believed he was killed because of his opposition to Somoza. Chamorro's funeral was attended by 10,000 people, while about 50,000 people rampaged through the streets in anger, attacking businesses and destroying cars and buses. The construction workers' union began a strike on 23 January to protest at the government's supposed involvement in Chamorro's death and on 24 January COSIP members joined the strike, which lasted for several weeks.

Government denials and eroding support

The government soon caught the men who confessed to killing Chamorro for $15,000 per man. This was paid for by a US physician after *La Prensa* published negative articles about him and his business. The government charged them with murder. No one was sure what to believe, and a rumour began that Somoza's oldest son, Anastasio, might have ordered the killing or was associated with the US physician. What was certain is that the initial reaction to the murder demonstrated that people believed Somoza was capable of having opposition killed, that they were tired of his presidency, and that they wanted a change in Nicaragua's government. Since Chamorro was seen by many as the probable replacement for Somoza in any future governing system, his death required them to look elsewhere for political leadership in a potential post-Somoza Nicaragua.

Chamorro's death caused the Committee of National Dialogue to cancel its talks with Somoza. Groups that had called earlier for a transition government to remove the Somoza dynasty now called for its immediate replacement. The assassination seemed to many to indicate that the old system of lightly punishing opposition had ended. Now one might simply be shot, even if the government claimed that they had nothing to do with the assassination. In the least, the assassination proved that the one thing that the Somoza family had always provided, public order, was now gone. Not being able to prevent the assassination damaged the government's reputation.

SOURCE D

Excerpt from *Nicaragua Divided: La Prensa and the Chamorro Legacy*, by Patricia Taylor Edmisten, published by University of West Florida Press, Pensacola, 1990, page 7.

It was as if the assassination was the last straw for the people. The upper class, hoping for a peaceful change, had been waiting for pressure from Washington that would have persuaded Somoza to step down. These wealthy people, who might have disagreed with many of Pedro Joaquín's [Chamorro's] ideas, still had a deep respect for him. They viewed his murder as a terrifying omen that their country was now beyond the brink, and if it was to reclaim any dignity and autonomy, they would have to join the cause to bring down ... Somoza. These people, too, had experienced economic losses due to his incursions into their own business fields. He had interests in many Nicaraguan concerns, and his power was such that he pressured people to do business with him or suffer the consequences. Additionally, the upper class believed that if [Somoza] stayed in power and a more democratic president were not found, the Communists would surely gain control.

With Chamorro's assassination, the small middle class lost all hope. He had fought for them. He believed that their enterprises were crucial to the economic health of the nation. He praised their hard work and saw the dignity in their struggle to provide for their families.

*The poor also loved Pedro Joaquín. He had visited them in their **barrios** and had inspired them to fight for their rights ...*

? According to Source D, why were so many people affected by Chamorro's assassination?

🔑 **KEY TERM**

Barrios Spanish word for a crowded, low-income city district.

Outbreaks of violence

February was an active month for rebellions in the country. The National Guard attempted to disperse a crowd of Native Americans in Monimbó who had left a religious service honouring Chamorro. The people fought back with the few weapons they owned and Sandinistas soon arrived to help co-ordinate the resistance. The number of dead was perhaps 200, primarily Native Americans. Soon there were attacks by youths on the National Guard in León, Chinandega and Managua itself. The Sandinista response was to create a 40-member group that could respond quickly to any disturbances so that it could take control and instigate more youth to join. Members of this fast response team were sent to the poor sections of various cities throughout the country.

Appeasing the USA 1978

The US government under President Carter believed that the solution to Nicaragua's political problems was to withhold military and other aid so that Somoza would free prisoners, end repressive actions against political opposition and follow the constitution. Somoza believed that he could withstand national unrest if he could keep the US government as his ally. He asked the US ambassador in February 1977, what he could do to satisfy the USA. The ambassador suggested that perhaps he should step down at the end of 1980 when his term as president ended. Somoza agreed, aware that President Carter, also facing elections in 1980, might be out of office by then. The next US president might be more amenable to Somoza remaining in office. Somoza announced to the nation in a public gathering attended by 50,000 on 27 February that he would not continue as president after the end of his term. Political opponents were dissatisfied because they wanted him to leave immediately. They believed that over the next three years he would use his power to select a puppet president that would allow him to control the country. In those three years, Somoza would also have time to deal with all his political opponents.

Central America's growing involvement 1978

Nicaragua's ruling regime was of interest to other Central and South American leaders. While some were sympathetic to Somoza's political opposition, others wanted to replace Nicaragua as the US's main ally in the region.

Costa Rica

In 1978, Costa Rica, the only truly democratic state in Central America, elected a new president who was sympathetic to calls by Nicaraguans for Somoza to step down. Whereas Costa Rica earlier worked to prevent Sandinistas from using it as a base of operations, the new president decided not to interfere with growing Sandinista activity in the country. Camps were established by the rebels in northern areas along the Nicaraguan border, and planes carrying supplies, including weapons and ammunition, were allowed to operate in Costa Rican airspace, using beaches and remote farms for air strips.

Venezuela

The President of Venezuela, Carlos Andrés Pérez, had been a friend of Chamorro and now came out in support of ending the dictatorship in Nicaragua, if not directly supporting the Sandinistas. Pérez hosted a meeting with US President Carter in March 1978, and suggested that force was needed to remove Somoza. It was hoped that the USA would order Somoza to step aside and then there would be a transition period that would eventually lead to a multi-party democracy.

Panama

Pérez also worked to convince Panama's leader, General Omar Torrijos, that Somoza needed to be removed. President Carter visited Panama in June, and Torrijos told Carter much the same thing that Pérez had said. Torrijos ran a regime that was similar to that of Somoza, but he disliked him as he found him arrogant. He also wanted to replace Somoza as the main US ally in Central America. Torrijos was friendly with a cousin of Somoza, Luis Pallais, and he gave him a verbal message to communicate to Somoza:

- The US government wants a new leader in Nicaragua.
- Somoza should resign after creating a **national unity government**.
- Somoza should go into exile.

When Somoza received this message from his cousin, he was outraged. He simply could not believe that the USA wanted him replaced and decided to make gestures to address what he believed were the main US concerns in the country:

- Amnesty was granted for many political prisoners.
- Members of *Los Doce* could return to Nicaragua from exile.
- The electoral system would be reformed.
- The **Organization of American States** (OAS) Human Rights Commission could come to Nicaragua and inspect the country for any violations of human rights.

After the reforms announcement, Somoza began a tour of the USA looking for political support, but did not see Carter himself. Carter instead sent Somoza a letter on 30 June 1978, explaining that he looked forward to the implementation of recent promises regarding human rights. Somoza believed this was evidence that the USA would continue to support him.

Frente Amplio de Opposición (FAO)

Los Doce returned from exile in Costa Rica on 5 July 1978, with tens of thousands of cheering people lining Managua's main street from the airport. By the end of August, *Los Doce* and 15 other political parties and labour unions created the FAO (Broad Opposition Front). COSIP was not officially part of the FAO, but its former president Robelo, now leading his own political party, the Nicaraguan Democratic Movement, indirectly represented COSIP; he became a leader of the FAO.

On 21 August, FAO announced a 16-point plan regarding the end of Somoza's rule. This included plans for the end to Somoza's control over the National Guard and the creation of a united government on Somoza's departure. Catholic bishops also called on Somoza to resign in a letter at about the same time, adding further pressure on the regime.

End of the Somoza regime 1978–9

It was clear to many people that Somoza and his family had to end their monopoly on power. While more and more groups required that the regime end immediately, others, particularly the US government, wanted a slow, smooth transition to a new government. Many feared that a sudden change would lead to a Sandinista takeover which they believed would lead to some form of communist system.

Seizure of the National Palace

On 22 August 1978, 25 Sandinistas, dressed as National Guardsmen, seized the National Palace where the **Nicaraguan Congress** was in session and where the Ministers of Finance and of the Interior had their offices. Approximately 1500 government employees were busy going about their various tasks that morning. The entire building was under Sandinista control within 20 minutes and Somoza's cousin Luis Pallais, his nephew and the Minister of the Interior were among the captives, along with almost all the members of the Nicaraguan Congress. Sandinistas asked that Archbishop Obando come to the Palace to receive their list of demands. The leader of the Sandinista raid, Edén Pastora, explained to reporters that he was not a communist as the government would have people believe, but was a practising Catholic and that Cuba was not behind the raid as the government stated. The demands were:

- the release of 83 prisoners
- $10 million in cash
- publication of a series of Sandinista statements.

On the second day of the siege, 300 people were released, mostly women and children, but 1200 remained under Sandinista control.

Negotiations led to 50 prisoners being released (the other 33 were not in prison) and $500,000 being delivered. Sandinista statements were published in a Somoza-owned newspaper and filled six pages. These included:

- a demand to abolish the National Guard
- a call to create a national army after Somoza
- criticism of various political groups for negotiating with Somoza to achieve his departure.

On 24 August, planes from the governments of Venezuela and Panama arrived to collect the rebels and former prisoners. Sandinistas left the palace with a few prize hostages, including Pallais, escorted by Archbishop Obando; they were cheered by thousands of well-wishers lining the road to the

Why did Somoza leave Nicaragua in July 1979?

🔑 **KEY TERM**

Nicaraguan Congress
Parliament dominated by supporters of the Somoza family and co-operative minor opposition parties until 1979.

airport. The Sandinista raid had the immediate effect of energizing the population against Somoza, making the efforts of more moderate opposition groups seem timid or somehow not anti-Somoza enough to many.

National unrest, late 1978

On 25 August, the FAO announced a **general strike** to show that they remained politically relevant after the daring Sandinista raid. At about the same time, disaffected youths, not affiliated with the Sandinistas, battled National Guard troops in the northern city of Matagalpa for five days. A few weeks later, the government arrested the leaders of the FAO-sponsored strike and of several political parties, and then hundreds of others that it believed were behind recent disturbances. As the government made arrests, the Sandinistas launched simultaneous assaults on National Guard positions all over the country. The attacks were simple: Guard positions were briefly assaulted and the Sandinistas quickly retreated. In some cities, local people continued fighting the National Guard after the Sandinistas departed.

The National Guard responded to these attacks with major force, killing 63 rebels and several hundred civilians, even bombing buildings by air and crossing briefly into Costa Rica to attack Sandinista camps. Around 200 Sandinistas sought asylum at Central and South American embassies in Managua as a result of National Guard actions. As dramatic as the Sandinistas had been, the vast majority were now either dead or leaving the country for exile. They were soon joined by hundreds of Nicaraguan youth, inspired especially by the raid on the National Palace. They crossed the border into Costa Rica into Sandinista training camps.

International mediation, October 1978

The USA called on the OAS to help find a solution to the crisis after coming to the conclusion that its earlier emphasis on human rights had achieved little. Somoza was visited by a US ambassador who told him he should consider resigning and that US policy was now to plan for a post-Somoza government. The US change in policy was the result of concern about the growing support for the Marxist-affiliated Sandinistas. It was also realized that Somoza had few supporters outside the National Guard. Somoza had alienated the Catholic Church, all political parties and most business owners. The USA sought moderate politicians who would have broad-based appeal to replace Somoza, fearing a potential Sandinista government that would oppose US policies in the midst of the Cold War. Somoza, under pressure, accepted an OAS committee to help resolve the crisis. The committee was composed of representatives of three nations: the USA, Guatemala and the Dominican Republic. While negotiations occurred, the USA requested that Venezuela, Costa Rica and Panama curtail their support for Sandinista guerrillas and they complied.

In October 1978, the committee began its work in Managua. It confirmed that practically everyone in Nicaragua was opposed to Somoza and his family. While the Sandinistas were not involved in discussions, the FAO became central to them as they represented most political parties, labour unions and many business leaders. The FAO presented a modified version of its earlier 16-point plan. It called for Somoza to leave the government immediately, and the creation of a unity government of three people supported by a council composed of two representatives from each group in the FAO; two representatives could also come from Somoza's National Liberation Party. In the plan, the National Guard would be reorganized but not dissolved. The *Los Doce* group withdrew from the FAO, opposing the inclusion of Somoza's political party and retention of the National Guard. On 6 November, Somoza rejected the FAO offer, stating that he would remain in power until his term was over, but that perhaps some of the more popular opposition parties could name ministers in his cabinet in the meantime. He stated clearly to mediators that he was not prepared to resign.

Mediation fails, January 1979

The OAS committee insisted on a plebiscite in Nicaragua to allow people to vote on whether they wanted Somoza to remain in power or for him to resign and go into exile. Somoza made various counterproposals and eventually talks ended in mid-January 1979. It was clear to the OAS mediators that Somoza had no intention of allowing a plebiscite. It was also clear to US President Carter, Venezuela's President Pérez and others that Somoza had no intention of stepping aside. He continued to insist on US support, giving the alternative of a communist Nicaragua if the Sandinistas, or their allies, came to power. The USA cut off military and other aid to Nicaragua in response to failed mediation and Somoza turned to Israel and Guatemala to keep his forces supplied, purchasing primarily rifles and ammunition.

Failure of four months of OAS efforts to diffuse the crisis meant that moderates, which included the Catholic Church, the FAO and others, had to choose between Somoza and the growing Sandinista movement. Most were surprised that the USA seemed incapable or unwilling to force a solution considering the political stakes, but the US government under Carter refused to force changes in the governance of other nations.

Sandinista unity and attacks

While negotiations were conducted, and failing, Sandinistas resupplied and reorganized. In December 1978, they announced from Cuba that the three Sandinista factions (see page 287) were once again united and working together. Three representatives from each faction created the **National Directorate** to lead and co-ordinate Sandinista policy and activities. Meanwhile, the flow of weapons, primarily rifles and ammunition, increased. Cuba was the main supplier of these materials, shipping them through Panama to Sandinista camps in Costa Rica. By June 1979, Cuba sent weapons directly to the Sandinistas in Costa Rica as Panama came under US pressure to cease the flow of arms.

 **KEY TERM**

National Directorate
Governing group of the Sandinistas which included members from all factions.

Sandinista guerrilla warfare 1979

The Sandinista guerrillas in Costa Rica came to be called the Southern Front, while rebels who had been part of the Prolonged War Faction based themselves in Honduras forming the Northern Front. The Northern Front was a much smaller group, but was the first to strike. On 7 April, hundreds of guerrilla fighters moved to seize the city of Estelí, while also launching attacks on National Guard positions in León, Condega, Chinandega, Ocotal and El Sauce. Most of the citizens fled Estelí, expecting a National Guard assault. Within two days the National Guard had 1000 troops in position, supported by a tank and aircraft. After surrounding the town and cutting off its water and electricity, the National Guard fought the guerrillas street by street. Artillery helped to level part of the city and a few days later, the guerrillas escaped at night. The heavy-handed tactics of the Guard brought much criticism internationally. Nicaraguans were shocked at the level of destruction inflicted on the town just to defeat a few hundred rebels.

Small battles erupted across the north and west of Nicaragua from April to June, and while not on the scale of the attack on Estelí, there was much destruction. On 11 June, during fighting in the industrial areas of Managua, National Guard tanks destroyed the building of *La Prensa*, the opposition newspaper. Around this time, Somoza sent his best National Guard troops to the southern border, which the Sandinistas were crossing to attack Guard outposts and border control stations. At least 130 Sandinistas were killed while making no headway into Nicaragua. It is estimated that the Sandinistas had only 1500 guerrilla fighters, both men and women, on the Southern Front, making these casualties significant.

Junta of National Reconstruction

Mexico cut relations with Nicaragua in May 1979, following Costa Rica which had done so in late 1978 as a result of Nicaraguan attacks across its border. This added international pressure and these states called for opposition leaders to form a provisional government to lead a post-Somoza Nicaragua.

In response, leaders of the FAO, *Los Doce* and the Sandistas, in exile in the Costa Rican capital San José, formed a provisional government call the Junta of National Reconstruction. The members of this Junta were:

- Robelo: former leader of COSIP and leader of FAO, clearly a moderate who would appeal to the business community who might fear the Marxism of most Sandinistas.
- Violeta Barrios de Chamorro: Chamorro's widow, who would appeal to those who had thought of her husband as a replacement for Somoza, but also the leading economic classes of which her family was a member.
- Sergio Ramírez: a well-known writer, made more famous by being a member of the popular *Los Doce*. He was also a secret member of the Sandinistas, so as to not alarm other members of *Los Doce* or the Junta

who might think the Sandinistas had too much representation. This was especially important when Daniel Ortega was added to the group.

- Daniel Ortega: a member of the National Directorate and brother of Humberto Ortega who was a member of *Los Doce*; he openly represented the Sandinistas.
- Moisés Hassan: a famous academic who was a university leader as well as founder of the United People's Movement (MPU). The MPU helped to co-ordinate student groups and labour strikes, often in support of the Sandinistas. Hassan was another secret Sandinista, giving the Sandinistas three out of the five seats on the Junta.

The new government-in-exile was announced to Nicaraguans on 17 June by radio from Costa Rica.

SOURCE E

Excerpt from a speech by Father Miguel D'Escoto, foreign minister-designate of the Junta for National Reconstruction to the Organization of America States' foreign ministers' meeting on 22 June 1979, quoted in *Nicaragua: Dictatorship and Revolution*, published by the Latin American Press Bureau, London, 1979, page 37.

Americans should not forget that the sacred right to rebel against tyrannical regimes is included among the inalienable rights of the individuals and of peoples listed in the first paragraph of the United States' Declaration of Independence.

On the other hand, all of us, I believe, know that the Western Judeo-Christian tradition also clearly recognises this right.

Loyal to this tradition, the bishops of Nicaragua published a pastoral letter scarcely two weeks ago, recognising the moral legitimacy of the Sandinista revolt.

Those who want to prevent the success of the noble and heroic struggles of the Sandinistas are wasting their time. They lose credibility when they falsely make reference to humanitarian and Christian values in order to defend their unjust and anti-democratic intentions.

According to Source E, why is the Sandinista guerrilla morally and legally correct?

Final US attempts to remove Somoza

The USA suddenly became more active as events moved quickly, deciding to treat Somoza less gently and without involving other nations. The new US ambassador to Nicaragua, Lawrence Pezzullo, met Somoza and presented him with an ultimatum on 18 June:

- You will resign in a dignified manner.
- You will help form a unity government of representatives from all political parties, including the Sandinistas as well as Archbishop Obando, Robelo and Pastora.
- You will allow the OAS to organize national elections.
- You will appoint a new leader of the National Guard that is not a relative.
- You can come live in the USA if you do all the above.

- If you do not, expect to be completely cut off and suffer sanctions.
- You have one day to make a decision.

Somoza responds
Somoza responded one hour before the deadline on 19 June:

- The US ultimatum is not appreciated or respectful.
- I will resign if the OAS can create a stable transition of power.
- I must have a promise to not be extradited from the USA to any other country in case of future trials.
- The entire Somoza family must receive visas to live in permanent exile in the USA.

Junta announces future plans
Also on 19 June, the Junta announced many of its intentions and plans for Nicaragua. They were:

- All property owned by the Somoza family would be confiscated.
- Nicaragua would not be allied to any other country, including the USA or the USSR.
- There would be a social and economic reconstruction programme to address mass poverty and illiteracy.
- Nicaragua would be a multi-party state with complete freedom of speech and religion.
- Nicaragua would honour all its foreign debt.
- The National Guard would be dissolved and a new army created where most members of the Guard would find jobs if they left the Guard immediately.

OAS resolution
On 23 June, the OAS passed a resolution calling for Somoza to be replaced with an interim government, but refused US pressure to organize and support an international police force to help with the transition. The OAS resolution also demanded a ceasefire by all groups and an arms embargo. The OAS and the USA were, however, becoming irrelevant as events in Nicaragua were moving faster than anticipated.

Increasing insurrection, June–July 1979
The battles between the Sandinistas and National Guard had not only damaged cities throughout the country, but also exhausted the population, many of whom had fled to other areas. On 17 June, National Guard troops abandoned all of León, the second largest city in Nicaragua. On 24 June, Masaya, near Managua, was captured by the Sandinistas when it too was abandoned by the National Guard. Diriamba was captured by the city's youth, not the Sandinistas, after they drove out the National Guard, demonstrating, that many people supported the Sandinista effort, but were now willing to take matters into their own hands. A national strike was called by businesses and labour unions, while foreigners fled the country in

SOURCE F

Young Sandinista soldiers in the streets of Masaya, June 1979.

What information about the Sandinistas is conveyed by Source F?

anticipation of a major battle in and around Managua. While it appeared to many that the Sandinistas were winning the war, the reality was that the National Guard not only controlled the vast majority of the country, they also inflicted heavy defeats on the guerrillas. The National Guard numbered about 10,000 men by the end of June 1979 as the government recruited more members.

The Sandinista Southern Front

While battles in the north continued, the larger Southern Front faced Somoza's best Guard troops. Three hundred guerrillas were killed in the battle for Peñas Blancas on the Costa Rican border and 100 more died when attempting to reach Rivas, a leading city between Costa Rica and Managua. This was a loss of more than 25 per cent of the Southern Front's forces. Pastora, one of the Southern Front leaders, sent a message to US President Carter through a former Costa Rican president asking for the USA to get Somoza to remove National Guard forces opposing him. Pastora was not a Marxist and was the most moderate member of the Sandinista leadership. He explained clearly to Carter that he was very popular and if he could take control of Managua, he could prevent a takeover of the country by more radical Sandinistas. The USA refused, hoping for a stalemate between the two sides so that it could then manage the transition itself to form a government that it felt most comfortable with.

Somoza departs, 17 July

The five-member Junta was approved by the USA, which wanted a stable transition, on 15 July after they announced the names of 12 individuals who would serve as ministers in the cabinet of the transition government. The cabinet integrated Sandinistas, former National Guard officers, members of *Los Doce* and others. This alleviated US concerns that the future of Nicaragua would be dominated by the Marxist-leaning Sandinistas. On the same day, Somoza agreed to replace his half-brother who led the National Guard with Federico Mejía, who was promoted to general and Director of the National Guard, as well as military Chief-of-Staff. It was expected that Mejía would offer Pastora the position of Director or Chief-of-Staff after the departure of Somoza. Most National Guard officers were retired by Somoza's dying government at the same time. Earlier, on 12 July, Somoza selected Francisco Urcuyo Maliaño (Urcuyo), the lower house speaker of the Nicaraguan Congress, as the temporary transitional president for whenever Somoza left the country.

? According to Source G, what seemed to be most important to Somoza as he departed Nicaragua?

SOURCE G

Excerpt from _Death of Somoza_ by Claribel Alegría and Darwin Flakoll, published by Curbstone Press, Connecticut, 1996, page 10.

After delivering his resignation to Congress, Somoza canceled his televised farewell address to the nation and disappeared into his supposedly impregnable 'bunker' atop the low hill of Tiscapa, a few blocks from the hotel. Here he finished packing, leaving unmade beds and items of clothing scattered about the presidential bedroom, while Urcuyo Maliaño was sworn in and adorned with the presidential sash at 0152 hours in the morning. At 0430 hours Somoza climbed into a helicopter and was flown to Las Mercedes airport on the outskirts of Managua, where three getaway planes were awaiting him and members of his entourage. Top military and civilian officials of the crumbling regime boarded [two aircraft] and took off in a northerly direction. In the baggage compartment of [one aircraft], surrounded by a jumble of bags and suitcases, were two zinc coffins containing the remains of the dictator's father, Anastasio Somoza García, and his elder brother, Luis Somoza, both of whom had preceded Anastasio II in the presidency.

At the last moment, eight gaily-colored parrots from the dictator's private zoo were loaded incongruously, into his plane … and the craft took off at 0510 hours, bringing an end to the Somoza dynasty's 43-year reign in Nicaragua.

Urcuyo's government, 17 July

Somoza's resignation was announced to Congress at 1a.m. on 17 July when Urcuyo read the resignation letter to them and then made a speech that called on all factions to meet with him to create a new government. This completely ignored the US plan that had been carefully negotiated between Somoza, the Junta and various Central American countries. The US ambassador, Pezzullo, believed it meant that Urcuyo intended to complete

he remainder of Somoza's term of office, which would end in late 1980.
ezzullo told Urcuyo after the speech that he wanted him to contact the
andinistas and the National Guard to work towards integration of the two
rces, as worked out in earlier negotiations, and to invite the Junta to come
 Managua as planned. Urcuyo simply answered: 'No'. Somoza, meanwhile,
ft Nicaragua with his family for his house in Florida before moving to
araguay. Many National Guardsmen panicked when they realized the root
 their support was gone and many began trying to flee the country for fear
 reprisals by their countrymen.

ater in the morning on 17 July, US Ambassador Pezzullo met Urcuyo and
formed him that he needed to resign and be replaced by Archbishop
bando, who would shortly afterwards turn over power to the Junta. Urcuyo
fused, stating that that would violate the nation's constitution and that he
ad no intention of having anything to do with a group that he considered
 be communist. After Pezzullo's departure, Urcuyo named new cabinet
inisters and formed a government, refusing to believe he had little support
 the country and that the National Guard's strength was dissolving. The
ational Guard informed him that they were running out of ammunition
id had little fuel for their vehicles.

ational Guard collapses and Urcuyo flees, 18 July

he National Guard continued to prevent the Southern Front of the
andinistas from entering the country, but disintegrated elsewhere, allowing
e Sandinistas to gain control over other cities, helped by excited teenagers.
y 18 July, the National Guard was falling apart as officers fled to Honduras
 went into hiding with their troops. National Guard Director Mejía
tempted to arrange a ceasefire with the Sandinistas, but the rebel
adership demanded unconditional surrender, something Mejía refused. In
der to prevent a military takeover by the Sandinistas, and then the
nplementation of a Marxist state by its more radical members, the President
 Costa Rica flew the five-member Junta to León to establish the transition
overnment. It was hoped that with this group in the country, it would
ssume leadership of the political scene and place the Sandinista guerrillas
nder its control. Urcuyo was finally aware that he could not remain
icaraguan president as the Managua airport came under Sandinista attack
id the National Guard disappeared from the city. The Guatemalan air force
racuated him, his family and the newly named government ministers. Mejía
scaped on the last flight out of Nicaragua of a National Guard plane at
awn of 19 July. The government of Urcuyo had lasted almost two days.

ational Guard ends

n 19 July, National Guard troops in Managua surrendered to the **Red
ross**, as commanded by the highest ranking officer left in the city, the head
 the traffic police. Thousands of troops were sent to part of the airport
hich was declared a special Red Cross zone, while others surrendered
emselves and their weapons to the Red Cross at hospitals, schools and

 **KEY TERM**

Red Cross International
organization that provides
emergency medical services.

other locations. Officers were sent to the Venezuelan Embassy by Red Cross officials where they would be safe from potential reprisals by Sandinistas and their allied youth. The 1000 National Guardsmen who had defended the southern border so successfully, now retreated to San Juan del Sur and seized boats in the harbour to take them to El Salvador. Around 2000 Guard fled to Honduras, many on foot, abandoning their homes and possessions out of fear for their lives. On 20 July, the Junta arrived in Managua on top of a fire engine, cheered by tens of thousands of people. Many wondered if the revolution had finished or was just beginning.

Victory achieved

How were the Sandinistas, perhaps the smallest of Nicaragua's political groups, able to take control of Nicaragua in mid-1979?

SOURCE H

Excerpt quoting Humberto Ortega in *Caribbean Revolutions and Revolutionary Theory: An Assessment of Cuba, Nicaragua and Grenada* by Brian Meeks, published by University of the West Indies Press, Barbados, 2001, page 84.

The truth is that we always took the masses into account, but more in terms of their supporting the guerrillas, so that the guerrillas as such could defeat the National Guard. This isn't what actually happened. What happened is that it was the guerrillas who provided support for the masses so that they could defeat the enemy by means of insurrection.

According to Source H, what did the Sandinista guerrillas accomplish during the revolution?

Sandinistas were firmly in power by the end of 1979, if not by mid-July. While the Sandinistas claimed victory, victory was not achieved by force of arms. The Sandinistas were a relatively small group that had few weapons other than rifles, often lacking ammunition, proper training or combat experience. They were daring, for sure, carrying out the spectacular Christmas Party Raid and seizing the National Palace. At no point, however, did they ever come close to having the same numbers or armed strength of the National Guard.

The Somoza regime lost practically all support by organized groups in the country by early 1979, if not in 1978. The regime was not under major military pressure from the Sandinistas, but was under pressure from business leaders in urban centres, from the Catholic Church, which most people held in high regard, and from the USA. All these groups feared the *possibility* of the Sandinistas overthrowing the established order with violence, which they certainly tried to do but with very limited success, especially in the south. In order to prevent a civil war, Somoza was pushed into leaving the country by the USA, Nicaraguan political groups and even neighbouring states. Yet the departure of Somoza, which was demanded by practically everyone with a political voice, caused the entire system to collapse. The only armed group, the Sandinistas, was then able to seize power through its manipulation of the Junta on which it secretly had a majority. After proclaiming victory, the Sandinistas could then create a real revolution for the country in terms of social, economic and political changes.

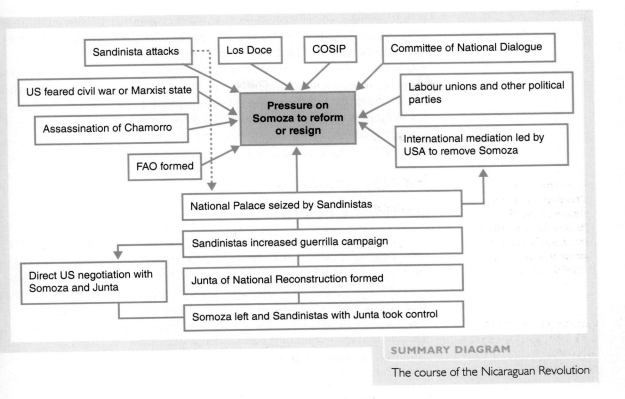

SUMMARY DIAGRAM

The course of the Nicaraguan Revolution

③ The effects of the Nicaraguan Revolution

▶ *Key question: To what extent did the revolution affect Nicaraguan politics, economics and society?*

The Sandinistas began major political and economic changes in the country almost immediately, dominating the Junta and other governmental bodies until they ruled openly. Social changes were also implemented and the status of women was affected as a result. Many historians argue that the real revolution in Nicaragua began with the departure of Somoza and the implementation of these changes.

Deaths

The most violent period of the Nicaraguan Revolution was from September 1978 until the collapse of the National Guard and its surrender on 19 July 1979. While estimates vary, perhaps 600 Sandinistas were killed in this year of violence and somewhere between 200 and 300 National Guards. Fighting between the groups killed between 9000 and 50,000 civilians according to

> **What were some possible reasons for the low death toll in the revolution that ended in Nicaragua in 1979?**

various sources. The smaller of these numbers is argued by those authors who believe that the relatively small types of weapons used could not have led to a high death toll. These weapons were rifles, grenades and so forth. Advocates of the higher death toll indicate that this was the result of attacks by National Guard tanks and planes on civilian populations. Regardless of the civilian death toll, the total number of combatants was small; the Sandinistas never had more than 3000 fighters, and the National Guard numbered 10,000 at its greatest strength. Civilians were simply caught between these two groups, mostly in 1979. Somoza was eventually killed by a pro-Sandinista group in 1979 in Paraguay, where he had moved after a brief stay in the USA.

How was the Catholic Church affected by the Sandinista government?

Catholic Church

Archbishop Obando had been a prominent opponent of Somoza after 1974 at the height of corruption and scandal as a result of the Managua earthquake rebuilding efforts (see page 284). He was the mediator between rebel groups during the Christmas Party Raid and the seizure of the National Palace by Sandinistas. Marxism opposed religion generally since it was seen as a fabricated system to control the masses. This necessarily meant that Marxists, and their communist and socialist derivatives, opposed the Catholic Church and vice versa. Nevertheless, by 1979 Obando went so far as to accept the military campaigns of the Sandinistas as necessary in order to rid the country of Somoza and his regime. He also supported the Sandinistas by explaining to Nicaraguans that they should not necessarily fear socialism. But by the early 1980s, he was in opposition to the Sandinista government, which supported **liberation theology** and therefore interfered with the Catholic Church.

Several Catholic priests were members of the Sandinista movement, and they supported liberation theology. This set of beliefs was quite complex but did emphasize the practice of religion instead of religious belief. It also promoted the idea that the structure of the Catholic Church, where all authority emanated from the Pope, to cardinals and archbishops, to bishops to priests and from there to everyone else, was essentially backwards. Where there were few or no priests, Catholics who believed in liberation theology believed that regular people, such as peasants, could conduct their own religious services, including mass, on their own without the need for a priest. Obando and the Catholic Church as a whole condemned these views, seeing in them influences from Marxism.

In order to limit Marxist influence on Catholics, Obando forbade any Catholic priest from participating in the government and eventually expelled a prominent priest who was a member of the government from his **religious order**. Pope John Paul II visited Nicaragua in 1983 to shore up support for Catholics and the Catholic Church at a time when the Sandinistas were moving closer to communist nations diplomatically. Obando, who became a cardinal in 1985, continued to be a popular leader with most Nicaraguans, speaking out against Sandinista human rights violations and various injustices as he saw them. He remains head of the Catholic Church in Nicaragua today.

Domestic affairs

Major changes occurred in Nicaragua almost immediately after Somoza left the country in July 1979. These changes affected all social and economic classes in the country and even led to further fighting over a 10-year period.

← How effective were Sandinista policies in addressing the needs of Nicaragua's citizens?

Governance

Almost immediately it was clear that the Junta for National Reconstruction was being sidelined, with the Sandinista's National Directorate making most of the decisions. Agreements worked out in Costa Rica just before the fall of Somoza about how the government would operate, were simply ignored. The Sandinistas, for example, moved into properties owned by Somoza and his allies, including government buildings, and used them for their own purposes, such as a party headquarters. These properties technically belonged to the government and not just the Sandinistas, who were supposed to be only part of the ruling coalition. The Sandinistas also assumed the responsibility of building a new army, the Sandinista Popular Army, with much help from Cuba, again ignoring the Junta and its minister of defence. They also formed Defence Committees, which were groups organized in neighbourhoods, districts and regions throughout the country that could try to get people involved in Sandinista activities. This move made them a party with mass support that could mobilize tens of thousands of people in a brief period of time for any action that the Sandinistas desired.

Chamorro and Robelo resigned from the five-member Junta in April 1980, protesting Sandinista domination of the government in violation of agreements arranged in mid-July 1979. The main violation was the refusal of the Sandinistas to set dates or structures for new elections, while taking more and more control of government institutions. Sandinistas found two co-operative Conservative politicians to join the Junta and others to join the **Consultative Council**, but in reality the Sandinistas had a majority in both bodies and managed the state. Elections were finally organized and held in 1984, with the Sandinista FSLN party garnering 67 per cent of the vote, electing Daniel Ortega as president of Nicaragua. In 1990, a coalition of parties would unseat Ortega, with Chamorro becoming the first elected woman leader in North or South America.

 **KEY TERM**

Consultative Council
Group that gives advice to a government.

Economics

The Marxist leanings of the Sandinistas emerged very quickly in terms of economic policy:

- All foreign trade and banks were nationalized.
- All insurance companies and mining companies, as well as mines, were nationalized.
- Only the government could export agricultural products.

- All Somoza family property was seized by the state, including businesses, vast amounts of agricultural land, houses and cars.

Up to 30 per cent of business owners fled the country with their money within weeks of the Sandinista takeover, fearing the confiscation of their property. Remaining business owners were unwilling to import new merchandise to sell or invest in their businesses for fear that they too would have their property seized. COSIP, the association of business owners, now referred to as COSEP after a name change, protested government seizures, stating that they violated the plan that the Junta had outlined in Costa Rica in mid-July. At the end of September, the Sandinistas held a large gathering of their members, forming the Sandinista Assembly, a group with 27 representatives from each of the three factions. They created a document that explained that they did want to establish a Marxist state, but gradually. This alarmed the business community and many foreign nations. Within a year, 40 per cent of the nation's economy was under the control of the Sandinista-dominated government.

Agricultural reform

All land owned by Somoza and his allies was confiscated. This included one-quarter of all farmland in the nation. By 1984, the Sandinistas had confiscated 2.75 million acres of land from those that it said had co-operated with the Somoza regime. This was one-third of all farmland. Larger farms were turned into state enterprises, usually employing the same farm workers that had toiled for the large landowners; most of these workers saw little difference between the old system and the new since the government dictated what was planted. In 1983–4, the government changed this policy of large state farms and began to distribute lands to small groups of peasants who worked in co-operatives, or even to individuals, to counteract the **Contras** (see page 311). This gave one-third of the rural population their own land to farm. Support for the Contras often came from peasants who wanted to have their own land and from farmers who feared the Sandinista government would seize their property.

Human rights violations

While the economy was being addressed by Sandinistas, human rights violations took place. The Nicaraguan Permanent Commission for Human Rights, which had documented Somoza's National Guard's violations against the Sandinistas, now documented the Sandinistas' violations. Many former National Guardsmen were imprisoned and put on trial for collaboration with the Somoza regime, along with some members of their families and others that the Sandinistas thought might have been associated with the National Guards. It is estimated that about 7500 people, mostly men, were imprisoned by the Sandinistas. Hundreds of others disappeared after being arrested, and were never seen again. In at least some areas, mass graves were found, including some near the city of Granada. Hundreds may have been executed and buried this way. Within three months of coming to power, the Sandinistas abolished the Permanent Commission for Human

Rights. The Sandinista-dominated government also worked to limit freedom of speech by censoring the press and limiting public debate on their policies and programmes.

Literacy

Using university and secondary school students, as well as Nicaraguan, Cuban and Costa Rican teachers, the Sandinista-dominated government began the National Literacy Crusade. This effort was meant to eradicate illiteracy in Nicaragua. It was estimated that just over 50 per cent of the population was unable to read and write in March 1980. The government announced in August that the campaign had concluded; illiteracy was now just under 13 per cent of the population, a remarkable result. Over 90,000 people taught over 400,000 people to read. Within the next 10 years, over 1.6 million people were taught to read and write through continued education efforts in rural districts. The government mass printed inexpensive books, including the writings of Sandino and other Sandinista-approved authors, adding a political dimension to the education campaign. The campaign brought many educated people from the urban areas into the impoverished rural villages for the first time, making an impression on many about living conditions for the poor. Nicaragua's efforts to eradicate illiteracy were acknowledged by the United Nations.

Women

Before 1979, the condition of women in Nicaragua was poor:

- 93 per cent of rural women were illiterate
- 20 per cent of girls attended secondary school (most of these lived in urban areas)
- 75 per cent of women with children were not married
- 48 per cent of all households had women as the primary income earners
- over 10 per cent of all children died in infancy as a result of malnutrition
- rural women had practically no health care or education.

Under Somoza, by law a husband could take the salary of his wife and had legal control over any children. Men could also divorce women if women committed adultery in the marriage, but there were no such laws penalizing men for the same act. Women were culturally expected to be subservient and, other than farm work, they were primarily servants, except in the small middle and upper economic classes. Women had practically no legal rights and were neglected by the state.

Improvements for women after the revolution

Sandinistas, perhaps because of their Marxist background which promoted social and economic equality for all people, welcomed women in the movement for the most part. Approximately 30 per cent of all Sandinista members were women by mid-1979. Women fought in guerrilla units, some forming all-women battalions, as well as working as organizers, operating communication systems and serving as officers, even over men. After the

Sandinistas came to power, campaigns to promote literacy and improve health care affected women all over the country, leading to longer and healthier lives for them and their children. The Junta, just after the fall of Somoza, announced the equality of men and women as law. Other laws forbade media to promote women as objects of desire, allowed maternity leave, divorce by women from their husbands, and full equality for all children regardless of whether or not their parents were married. Husbands were no longer allowed to collect the salaries of their wives.

Women in Nicaragua in the 1980s were able to leave the traditional roles of farming and being servants. The small numbers of middle and upper economic class women were soon joined by growing numbers of women from rural areas who joined in improving the status of women throughout the country:

- 60 per cent of all those teaching peasants to read were women
- over 75 per cent of the people working to improve health care in rural regions were women
- over 30 per cent of all management positions in the government were held by women by 1987
- 30 per cent of leadership positions in the Sandinista organization were held by women by 1987
- women comprised 37 per cent of workers in industry, although less than 20 per cent were able to rise to management status in private business.

While women's lives improved remarkably under the Sandinistas, they were still paid less than men and faced discrimination that was illegal but still tolerated, as in many other countries. Some of the government's initial enthusiasm and special programmes were tempered or put on hold during the war with the Contras (see page 311), which sapped the state's economic resources. The Sandinista government apparently did not wish to cause potential social divisions while unity was needed during the war.

What was Nicaragua's relationship with Cuba and the USA after Somoza's fall in mid-1979?

Foreign affairs

A week after Somoza fled Nicaragua, the Sandinistas accepted Cuban assistance. Hundreds of teachers, doctors, nurses and engineers arrived, with numbers reaching into the thousands in a few months. Cuba also sent military advisors and personnel. Nicaraguan university students suddenly received scholarships to study in Cuba and over 1500 Nicaraguan school children were sent to special schools set up for them. Over 1000 Cuban teachers moved into rural areas where no teachers were present, helping to establish a mass literacy campaign. While the Sandinistas claimed they were grateful for Panama's help during the revolution, Panama was soon ignored as relations with communist Cuba grew stronger, a relationship which dismayed the US government. There was a fear that the Sandinistas would assist rebel groups in other Central American states, such as in El Salvador. Military aid was sent from the Sandinistas to Marxist-leaning rebels in El Salvador starting in mid-1980, confirming US fears.

Rising tensions with the USA

Many Sandinista leaders verbally attacked the USA in speeches, blaming the USA for inflicting Somoza and his regime on them. They believed that the USA was responsible for Nicaragua's poverty and it should compensate them with grants and loans. The US State Department, fearing the growing influence of Cuba, asked the US Congress for $75 million in emergency aid in November 1979, most of which would be a loan. After many months, the US government finally approved the aid, which stipulated that the US president could cancel the loan at any moment and demand full repayment. There was also a warning that it would be cancelled if the Sandinistas assisted rebel groups in any other nation. Meanwhile Cuba poured thousands of people into the country to help in concrete ways. When the Sandinistas failed to follow through with a promise to have national elections (see page 307), the USA ended its financial support for the new government.

SOURCE I

Excerpt from *Jimmy Carter: Foreign Policy and Post-presidential Years*, edited by Herbert D. Rosenbaum and Alexej Ugrinsky, published by Greenwood Press, Westport, Connecticut, 1994, page 82.

Carter's idealism was neither ephemeral [temporary] nor unrealistic. His was not, despite the rhetoric, an absolute human rights standard, which would have been destructive of certain other US interests linked to the predominant authoritarian regimes, some of whom were key allies. He nonetheless did give more weight to human rights than any other president.

Some allies lost their military assistance because of their violations. The only alternative for military governments like Argentina and Guatemala was to hold fair elections and leave power, which they refused to do at the time. Anastazio Somoza declined to hold elections in 1978, and the loss of US assistance was crucial. Then the Sandinistas promised to hold fair elections before taking power in July 1979, and were therefore initially recognized by the Carter government. When it became clear by April of the following year that they were only consolidating the power of the Sandinista Front and limiting the human rights of other civilian groups that had been participating in the Junta, Carter ended the US assistance that had initially been so generous. The Sandinistas showed no signs of holding fair elections soon.

> According to Source I, why did the USA withdraw assistance from Nicaragua twice?

Contras

Rebel groups opposing the Sandinista regime were formed in Nicaragua soon after the departure of Somoza. These groups are known collectively as the Contras. The various Contra groups were composed of peasants who resisted Sandinista attempts to nationalize their farmlands, ex-National Guardsmen, anti-Sandinista business owners in Nicaragua and Native Americans among others. What all these groups had in common was that they opposed the Sandinistas for various reasons, including their Marxist

> **What was the importance of the Contra movement?**

leanings, their dependency on and friendliness to Cuba, as well as human rights violations. Contras had bases in Honduras and Costa Rica and the groups rarely worked together, despite attempts by the US government to unite them. One of the more famous commanders was Edén Pastora, the non-Marxist Sandinista who seized the National Palace in 1978 but later left the group in protest at its policies.

Nicaraguan Civil War

The Contras fought the Sandinista government of Nicaragua in the Nicaraguan Civil War from 1979 to 1990. During its first years, US President Ronald Reagan channelled arms, money and supplies to Contra groups in order to counteract growing Soviet and Cuban involvement in Nicaragua. The **Reagan Doctrine** essentially called for pushing communist and communist-leaning governments out of power as a method of opposing the USSR during the final years of the Cold War. This was done partly through funding anti-communist guerrilla groups, such as the Contras. Contra groups received significant assistance from President Reagan until 1984 when the US Congress forbade any further assistance as a result of major human rights violations being perpetrated by Contra guerrillas. While fighting Sandinistas, Contras often targeted civilians in terror campaigns involving torture, rape, burning of crops and executions.

International Court of Justice ruling and the Iran–Contra Affair

The USA escalated its conflict with Nicaragua's government by placing sea mines in its ports and an embargo on all Nicaraguan products, severely affecting the economy. Nicaragua took the USA to the **International Court of Justice** (ICJ), which ruled in Nicaragua's favour while also ordering the USA to pay to Nicaragua for damages inflicted on the country. US involvement in Nicaragua was not only embarrassing diplomatically as a result of the ICJ's decision, but caused a major political scandal in the USA, the Iran–Contra Affair, that tarnished Ronald Reagan's presidency. Essentially, Reagan's officials continued supplying the Contras despite Congress's law. This was accomplished by secretly selling weapons to Iran and sending the profits of these sales to the Contras to purchase arms. This violated an arms embargo the USA had earlier imposed on Iran as well as Congress's earlier decision.

End of civil war

The war caused 500,000 Nicaraguans to flee the country, villages to be destroyed, thousands killed and wounded, and economic privation for everyone involved. By the late 1980s, the Contras and the Sandinista government were exhausted from the conflict. The Contras were poorly led, no longer well-supplied and under international pressure to end the conflict. They were also extremely unpopular because of human rights violations, corruption and trafficking of drugs. In 1990, Violetta Chamorro was elected as President of Nicaragua (see page 307). As a result, Contra groups disbanded and returned to Nicaragua in a general amnesty.

 **KEY TERM**

Reagan Doctrine Policy of US President Ronald Reagan to remove governments friendly to the USSR, which included the arming and funding of rebel groups.

International Court of Justice Court that deals with disputes between nations, located at The Hague, The Netherlands.

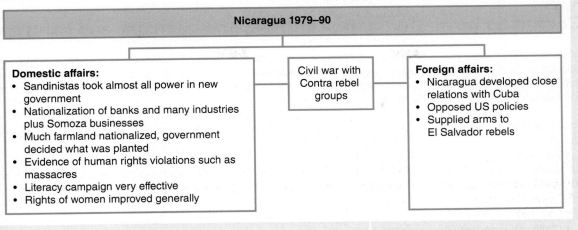

SUMMARY DIAGRAM

The effects of the Nicaraguan Revolution

Chapter summary

The Nicaraguan Revolution 1976–9

Nicaragua's Somozan dictatorship was established on 1 January 1937 and continued for 42 years. The Somoza family produced three presidents, all of whom added to the family's wealth, eventually dominating the country not just politically, but also economically. While the few wealthy people in the country benefited from massive economic growth through agricultural exports, the rural masses lived in abject poverty. Illiteracy, poor health care and other maladies affected the majority of the population as a result of being ignored by the corrupt, centralized government.

Opposition was successfully suppressed in the 1960s, including minor rebellions by Sandinistas and Chamorro. This all changed in 1972 when an earthquake levelled the capital city. International financial assistance flowed into Nicaragua and directly into businesses of the Somoza family, alienating other businessmen. The Catholic Church joined COSIP and other groups in criticizing the Somoza regime, while

Sandinistas resurrected themselves before being crushed in 1975 by the National Guard, which was operated by the Somoza family. The election of US President Carter meant that Somoza no longer had unlimited US support, encouraging opposition groups who began to work together to build national and international pressure to remove Somoza. These groups joined the Sandinistas, now armed with Cuban weapons and supported by Costa Rica and Panama, and attacked the National Guard, energizing the population to resist Somoza. Fearing a civil war and the creation of a Marxist state, the USA helped push Somoza out of office and into exile, arranging a coalition government to take its place.

This coalition, the Junta, was soon supplanted by the Sandinistas, who aligned the state with communist nations, nationalized property and supported rebels in El Salvador. The takeover of the government by Sandinistas led to a civil war with Contra rebel groups that ended in 1990. Between 1980 and 1990, the Sandinista effected much social and economic change, including improved health care, education and women's rights, while suppressing freedom of speech and committing human rights violations.

Examination practice

Command term: Compare, contrast, and compare and contrast

When a question asks you to compare *and* contrast some aspect of twentieth-century warfare, it is asking you to discuss similarities and differences between them. Questions that require you to *only* compare aspects of war ask that you explain and analyse the similarities. Questions that require you to *only* contrast aspects of war ask that you explain and analyse the differences.

This means that questions with the command term 'compare and contrast', or just 'contrast' or just 'compare', will always require you to use at least two wars in your essay.

Below are a number of different questions for you to practise using the command terms 'compare', 'compare and contrast' and 'contrast'. For guidance on how to answer exam-style questions, see Chapter 8.

1 With reference to two wars, each from a different region, compare and contrast the importance of militarism in causing war in the twentieth century.

2 Compare and contrast the role of technology in achieving victory in two twentieth-century wars you have studied.

3 Compare and contrast the significance of human and economic resources in two twentieth-century wars.

4 With reference to two twentieth-century wars, each from a different region, compare and contrast the use of naval warfare.

5 Compare and contrast the causes of two wars in the twentieth century.

6 With reference to two twentieth-century wars you have studied, contrast the role of foreign powers in the conduct of these wars.

7 Contrast the role of women in two twentieth-century wars in two different regions.

8 Compare the causes of two wars in the twentieth century that you have studied.

9 With reference to two twentieth-century wars, each from a different region, contrast the most significant factors that led to victory.

10 Contrast the importance of technology to the conduct of two twentieth-century wars.

Activities

1 As individuals, or in groups, create a timeline of Nicaragua's history as discussed in this chapter. Begin with the creation of the National Guard in 1927 and end with the election of President Chamorro in 1990. Plan carefully as there are many events in the 1970s which will require proper spacing. Also:

- Expand your timeline by including pictures and biographies of groups and individuals mentioned.
- Connect your extra material to your timeline with coloured wool or string to give yourself more room to work.

2 As individuals, or in groups, make a chart to discuss the strengths and weaknesses of political groups mentioned throughout this chapter. This could include the Catholic Church, the Somoza regime, the Sandinistas, COSIP/COSEP, the US government, FAO, Los Doce, Cuba and so forth. You may wish to put restrictions on your chart such as confining the period of time being discussed, such as September 1978 to June 1979. Once you have completed your chart, make separate rankings for each of these categories, justifying your answers:

- political power
- military power
- economic power
- moral authority.

Which of these categories is the most important? Which group covered the largest number of these categories? Did the group exercise their full abilities? Why? Why not? You should create your own discussion questions with your chart.

3 Divide your class into groups, answering the following questions in either bullet-points or narrative form. Each group should photocopy their responses and distribute to other members of the class for discussion and to be kept for examination preparation in the future.

- Was Nicaragua better off under the Somoza or Sandinista regime?
- Were the political moderates who opposed Somoza ineffective because they were not prepared to use violence?
- Was political reform possible in Nicaragua without the violence of Sandinista guerrillas?
- If guerrilla warfare was not particularly effective against the National Guard, how did the Sandinistas come to power?
- Could it be argued that the Nicaraguan Revolution was actually the work of the USA and Central American countries?

CHAPTER 7

Making thematic connections between twentieth-century wars

In the examination of Topic 11 'Causes and effects of twentieth-century wars', there will be thematic questions asking you to use examples from more than war, or to make connections between them. For example, you might be asked about the impact of wars on the role and status of women, the role of guerrilla warfare or technology in the outcome of wars, the importance of ideology in causing wars or the significance of the home front, among others. To help you make these types of connections, this chapter starts by looking at similarities and differences in the causes of the First and Second World Wars before going on to compare practices and results of twentieth-century warfare more generally – drawing on examples from the wars covered in detail in Chapters 1–6 of this book. You need to consider the following questions throughout this chapter:

★ How similar were the causes of the First and Second World Wars?

★ To what extent did methods of warfare develop during the twentieth century?

★ What were the common effects of twentieth-century warfare?

1 Comparing and contrasting the causes of the First and Second World Wars

> ▶ **Key question:** How similar were the causes of the First and Second World Wars?

Both the First and Second World Wars were arguably caused by some of the same factors, including:

- imperialism
- militarism
- the role of individual nations.

> **For more detail on imperialism as a cause of the First and Second World Wars see Chapters 1 (pages 14–17), 3 (pages 114–26) and 4 (pages 189–93).**

Imperialism

Imperialism is essentially the quest for territorial expansion and all the benefits that it supposedly brings the state that possesses an empire, such as more resources, markets and national pride.

First World War

Imperialism exacerbated tensions between European powers in the years directly preceding the First World War. Imperialism was a factor in:

- Germany building a powerful navy, stating that it did so partly to protect its expanding overseas territory and trade – this increased tension between it and the other Great Powers
- Germany provoking two crises in Morocco, in 1905 and 1911, in order to place pressure on France and Britain and perhaps gain a port on the Atlantic
- Austria annexing Bosnia-Herzegovina in 1908, causing tension with Russia and Serbia
- several Balkan wars in 1912 and 1913 leading to enlarged states, such as Serbia and Greece, causing tensions among the major powers in Europe.

Tensions over territory were not the only factor, and imperialism is closely connected to the concepts of nationalism and militarism. All European countries had or wanted empire, believed that empire brought economic wealth and political prestige, was a reflection of national pride, and should be defended with armies and fleets of ships.

Second World War

The Second World War, arguably, was about imperialism as well. Germany, the USSR, Italy and Japan wished to expand their territory.

Germany and the USSR

Germany expanded in 1938 by annexing Austria, with little international protest or apparent interest, and then Sudetenland, Czechoslovakia, with international approval. German expansion in 1939 to include much of the rest of Czechoslovakia and demands for territory in Poland, which had formerly been parts of Germany, provoked a war.

The USSR, too, desired to expand to include European territories that had formerly been part of the Russian Empire and, with that in mind, made the so-called Nazi–Soviet Pact which allowed that to happen. This agreement meant that Germany did not believe it would fight initially with the USSR, could conquer Poland quickly with Soviet assistance, and that any war with Poland would be a short one which would preclude its receiving help from Britain or France. It also meant that the USSR could retake parts of Russia's former empire: Finland, Estonia, Latvia, Lithuania, much of Poland and part of Romania. This desire for expansion on the part of Germany and the USSR helped the Second World War to occur in Europe.

Italy

Italy's quest for empire led to the Abyssinian Crisis, which in turn made the League of Nations an irrelevance in international diplomacy, removed Germany from international diplomatic isolation by collapsing the Stresa Front, and eventually caused the Second World War events in Africa.

Japan

Japan's quest for empire and the resources that came with it led to war with the USA in the Pacific. Japan's attack on the US navy at Pearl Harbor, Hawaii in December 1941 made the Second World War a truly world war in which all the world major powers were involved with conflict spread around the planet.

France and Britain

French and British imperialism also had a role to play in causing the Second World War. Some historians have argued that the Second World War was about these nations fighting to maintain their status as the world's leading states in the face of challenges by Germany, Italy and Japan. In this way, imperialism was a factor in the outbreak of war in Europe in 1939 because France and Britain were trying to maintain empire.

For more detail on militarism as a cause of the First and Second World Wars see Chapters 1 (pages 19–25), 3 (pages 117–20) and 4 (pages 189–93).

→ Militarism

In the years prior to both world wars, there were major efforts at building, or maintaining, large armies and navies by most powers. The construction of powerful military forces was seen then and now not only as protection from attack, but also as a way of forcing other countries to respond to foreign policy issues. Militaries were useful tools for diplomacy. For example:

- In 1905, Germany was able to force France to replace its foreign minister and to attend a conference over the future of Morocco by threatening to attack France's borders.
- In 1934, Italy threatened Germany when it attempted to annex Austria, preventing this from happening.
- In 1935, Britain and France placed economic sanctions on Italy as a result of the Abyssinian Crisis, afraid to do more for fear of a war in the Mediterranean.
- In 1935, Germany claimed that it needed to rearm since it was surrounded by large, unfriendly armies in France and Poland.

For more detail on the role of individual nations as a cause of the First and Second World Wars see Chapters 1 (pages 32–4), 3 (pages 122–6) and 4 (pages 188–93).

→ The role of individual nations

Many historians have specifically blamed Germany for both world wars. This is an easy argument to make, if a bit simplistic:

- Germany declared war on France and Russia in 1914 when the only other war declared was a limited one between Austria-Hungary and Serbia.
- Germany invaded Poland in 1939, provoking a larger conflict with Poland's allies France and Britain.

Other historians have pointed out that the First World War could be blamed on Serbia for arranging assassins to kill Archduke Franz Ferdinand, on Russia for mobilizing its military against Austria-Hungary knowing it would probably provoke a German response, on Austria-Hungary for demanding war with Serbia with little regard to overall consequences, and so forth. Others try not to blame specific nations, but systems and structures that made war a likelihood instead of just a possibility, including the Schlieffen Plan of Germany, imperialism, economic rivalries including competition for resources and markets, and much more.

The Second World War has been blamed on a flawed Treaty of Versailles which either punished Germany too much or not enough, on Germany's leader, Hitler, who has often been depicted as some sort of genius, on the Great Depression and world economic conditions, or even on Poland which refused to negotiate with Germany over borders. The possibilities are many, some of which are discussed in Chapter 2.

 # Comparing and contrasting the practices of different wars

▶ *Key question: To what extent did methods of warfare develop during the twentieth century?*

The twentieth century experienced many types of warfare, including total warfare for the first time. In this section, we will consider the similarities and differences of the technology and strategies used and the types of war employed in the wars covered in this book.

How the wars were fought: technology and strategy

← **To what extent were twentieth-century wars fought differently?**

The wars were fought quite differently from each other with different strategies, but there were also similarities, as summarized in the table below.

War strategies and technology compared

	First World War	Second World War	Spanish Civil War	Chinese Civil War	Nicaraguan Revolution
Where primarily fought?	• Practically simultaneous fighting on Western, Eastern, Italian and Ottoman Fronts from 1914 • Relatively minor battles in Africa and Asia-Pacific region • Naval warfare primarily in and around Europe	The European war began in stages, with Germany invading: • Poland, September 1939 • Denmark and Norway, April 1940 • The Netherlands, Belgium, Luxembourg and France, May 1940 • Greece and Yugoslavia, April 1941 • USSR, June 1941. The Asia/Pacific war began with Japan attacking the USA, December 1941	Spain	China	Nicaragua

continued

War strategies and technology compared (continued)

	First World War	Second World War	Spanish Civil War	Chinese Civil War	Nicaraguan Revolution
How primarily fought?	• Trench warfare and variations of it fought on the Western and Italian Fronts and in Gallipoli • Mobile warfare on Eastern Front • Guerrilla warfare in Africa	• Mobile warfare in Europe • Naval warfare in the Pacific • Aerial bombardment in Europe and Asia	• Mobile warfare • Trench warfare • Guerrilla warfare	• Guerrilla warfare • Mobile warfare	Guerrilla warfare
Technology and strategy of the war: naval warfare	• Battleships • Submarines • Strategy: blockades and convoys	• Aircraft carriers and aircraft • Submarines • Strategy: blockades and island-hopping	• Minor role for navy	• Minor role for navy	N/A
Technology and strategy of the war: land war	• Machine guns and artillery • Tanks • Strategy: attrition	• Tanks supported by major air power and infantry • Strategy: rapid movement and encirclement	• Limited use of tanks • Artillery and small arms • Strategy: infantry supported by tanks and aircraft	• Limited use of tanks • Mostly smaller arms • Strategy: mobile defence	• Small arms • Strategy: constant small attacks to gain political attention
Technology and strategy of the war: aircraft	• Zeppelins and small biplanes • Strategy: reconnaissance, bombing, attacking enemy fighters	• Fighters and large bombers • Strategy: support tanks and infantry • Strategy: protect and destroy enemy ships • Strategy: bomb cities	• Fighters and bombers • Strategy: support tanks and infantry • Strategy: bomb cities	• Limited use of fighters and bombers • Support tanks and infantry	N/A
Effect on civilians	• Starvation in Central Powers • Millions made homeless in eastern Europe, hundreds of thousands in western Europe	• Civilians often the primary target such as in bombing cities, with more civilians dying than soldiers • Tens of millions made homeless • Millions imprisoned, with many of these dying • Mass starvation in much of Europe and Asia	• Civilians often targeted • Millions made homeless • Mass starvation	• Civilians often targeted by artillery and aircraft • Millions made homeless	Limited effect on civilians generally

What were the main types of warfare employed during the twentieth century?

→ # Types of warfare

Many types of warfare were practised during the twentieth century and most wars saw the use of more than one type. (See the introduction for a description of the different types of warfare.)

Total warfare

Both world wars are considered total wars for various reasons. They involved:

• the world's most important military, economic and political powers

- reorganization of the economies of the main countries involved in the conflict in order to sustain their involvement
- mass production of weapons, transport ships and general war supplies
- expanded governmental powers to limit civilian rights such as freedom of speech and press, as well as to enforce rationing
- major loss of life, although by far more died in the Second World War
- fighting across the world, especially during the Second World War.

Other types of warfare

Both world wars involved other types of warfare as well as total war, and the other wars covered in this book are also examples of different types of war, as shown in the table below.

Types of war compared

Type of warfare	First World War	Second World War	Spanish Civil War	Chinese Civil War	Nicaraguan Revolution
Civil war	• The Arab Revolt within the Ottoman Empire (see page 50) • The Russian Civil War (see page 70)	• Civil war in Yugoslavia between multiple groups (see page 172) • Allied Italy fighting Axis northern Italy (see page 138) • Various groups fighting each other in China (see page 222) • Various groups fighting each other in the Philippines (see page 223)	Nationalists fighting Republicans	Chinese Communist Party fighting Nationalists	Sandinistas fighting National Guard
Guerrilla warfare	• Fought in Africa between German and British-led forces (see page 51) • Fought in Middle East by Arab forces against the Ottomans (see page 50)	• Used in Poland by several groups against Germany (see page 171) • Used in the USSR primarily by communist partisans against Germany and collaborators (see page 173) • Used in the Philippines by various groups against each other and Japan (see page 223) • Used in China primarily by Communists against Japan (see page 222)	Used by both sides	Used primarily by Chinese Communist Party against Nationalists	Used by Sandinistas against government and National Guard
Limited warfare	• Japan: limited effort needed to capture German territories in Asia and Pacific • China, Portugal, Brazil: limited contribution to overall Allied effort in economic and military terms	• France: limited to primary participation in world conflict from September 1939 to June 1940 (see page 133) • Mexico, Nicaragua, Brazil: very limited involvement economically or militarily • Limited war between USSR and Finland (see page 130)	• Limited to Spain • Little international involvement	• Limited to China; much of western China uninvolved • Little international involvement	• Limited to Nicaragua • Limited civilian casualties or war damage

3 Comparing and contrasting the effects of different wars

▶ *Key question: What were the common effects of twentieth-century warfare?*

Wars affected people and their governments throughout the twentieth century. These produced various results including the formation of international peace organizations, treaties, new countries and social changes. Some of these are shown in the table below.

Effects of different wars compared

Results of wars	First World War	Second World War	Spanish Civil War	Chinese Civil War	Nicaraguan Revolution
Peace settlements	Paris Peace Conference created treaties: • Versailles for Germany • Trianon for Hungary • St Germain-en-Laye for Austria • Neuilly-sur-Seine for Bulgaria • Sevres for Ottoman Empire	No major peace treaties, just post-war settlements mostly based on wartime conferences at Yalta and Potsdam	No formal treaty	No formal treaty	No formal treaty
Collective security	Attempted with the creation of League of Nations	• United Nations created to work towards peaceful resolution of conflicts, but no formal collective security arrangement • NATO and Warsaw Pact alliances created	N/A	N/A	N/A
Territorial changes	• New nations created • German colonies made into mostly British and French mandates	• Germany divided • Poland's borders moved • USSR expanded into eastern Europe • Decolonization followed war	N/A	China regained Manchuria and control over western regions	N/A
Political repercussions	• Communist state established in Russia/USSR • Republics formed in central and eastern Europe	• Great Powers replaced by Superpowers • Cold War began • More states became communist	Conservative dictatorship established, replacing republican government	Most of China became a communist state	• Somozan dictatorship replaced by Marxist-leaning Sandinista government • Civil war erupted

continued

Results of wars	First World War	Second World War	Spanish Civil War	Chinese Civil War	Nicaraguan Revolution
Economic impact	• Destruction of much of industrial areas of Belgium and France • Britain and France owed huge financial debt to USA • Germany required to make war reparations • USSR repudiated Russian national debt • Hyperinflation and economic chaos in new European states	• Severely disrupted European economy • US Marshall Plan • COMECON • Formation of western European trade zones which eventually led to the European Union	Destruction of major industrial cities	• Government took control of all industry • Old agricultural system replaced with peasant, communal control of farmlands	Nationalization of much industry and farmland
Social impact	Women gained right to vote after war production work, with many remaining in industry	• Women became more economically independent and politically active • Mass extermination of various religious and social groups in Europe • Minority groups in USA gained political rights • Soviet women proved that women can successfully serve in combat roles which was extended eventually to many other states	Women's and workers' rights curtailed	• Destruction of economic upper classes through government policy and violence • Women made equal citizens	• Women made equal to men • Major campaigns to eradicate illiteracy • Efforts made to improve lives of peasants

CHAPTER 8

Examination guidance

IB History Paper 2 requires you to write two essays, each from a different topic. Now that you have studied Topic 11: Causes and effects of twentieth-century wars, you have the knowledge to address the questions on the examination. This chapter is designed to help you:

★ understand the different types of questions

★ select an appropriate question

★ make a historical argument using evidence

★ outline and write your essay

★ involve historiography appropriately.

 ## Preparing for Paper 2 examination questions

It is important that you understand the structure and demands of the Paper 2 examination. This section specifically focuses on Topic 11: Causes and effects of twentieth-century wars.

Types of questions

There will be two possible questions for you to answer for each topic. You are to answer only one of these questions in Topic 11 and a second question for the other topic you have studied. Questions for Topic 11 may address:

● one war
● two or more wars
● two wars from two different regions
● some aspect of wars of the twentieth century generally

Command terms

A key to success is to understand the demands of the question. IB History questions use key terms and phrases known as command terms. Common command terms are listed in the following table, with a brief definition of each. Many of these command terms have also been explained briefly at the end of chapters in this book. Examples of questions using some of the more common command terms may be found in the Introduction of this book.

Command term	Description	Where found in this book
Compare	Discuss the similarities of conflicts, referring to both conflicts throughout your answer and not treating each conflict separately. You should not give an overview of each war and should focus on the most important similarities, rather than every tiny detail	Page 314
Compare and contrast	Discuss the similarities and differences of conflicts, referring to both conflicts throughout your answer and not treating each conflict separately. You should not give an overview of each war and should focus on the most important similarities and differences, rather than every tiny detail	Page 314
Contrast	Discuss the differences of conflicts, referring to both conflicts throughout your answer and not treating each conflict separately. You should not give an overview of each war and should focus on the most important differences, rather than every tiny detail	Page 314
Discuss	Review various arguments regarding a conflict or conflicts and conclude with an argument supported by evidence	Page 187
Evaluate	Make a judgement based on how strong or weak evidence may be	Page 110
Examine	Analyse the strengths and weakness of various arguments with a concluding opinion	Page 235
To what extent	Determine the extent to which something is true or false, with answers usually being 'to no extent', 'to some extent' or 'to a great extent'	Page 278

Answering questions

You will have five minutes of reading time at the start of your examination. It is during this time that you should review the questions in the two or more topics you have studied, including Topic 11. You should be able to answer at least two to four questions. Once you have identified which ones you are able to address, choose the Topic 11 question for which you have the most knowledge and for which you fully understand its demands. Many students have great knowledge regarding a conflict or conflicts, but they may not understand fully what the question wants them to do. If you find the wording of a question confusing, consider addressing another question if you feel more comfortable doing so.

Once you have chosen your question for Topic 11, you may look at your other topic of study to repeat this exercise. Once you have made a decision on your second question for Paper 2, return to your Topic 11 question and begin to think about how you will address it, waiting for the end of the reading time.

Marks

All questions on Paper 2 are worth 15 points each for a total of 30 possible points for this paper. Your goal is to achieve marks in the upper mark bands, or range of grades. In order to attain the highest mark band (13–15), your essays should include:

- answers that very clearly address the demands of the question and are well structured and clear

- correct, relevant historical knowledge used appropriately to support your argument
- evidence that is critically analysed
- historical events that are placed in their context
- evaluation of different perspectives.

Timing your writing

You will have 1 hour and 30 minutes to complete both Paper 2 essays. This breaks down to 45 minutes per essay on average.

Part of your writing time, however, should be spent preparing a basic outline which will help you keep your answer structured and focused. You should spend perhaps five minutes on this. An example of a good outline to a question is shown on page 327.

Defining your terms

It is important that you define the terms you use in the introduction of your essay. For example, if your question asks you:

- about guerrilla warfare, be sure to explain your interpretation of that form of war
- to discuss two wars from two different regions, make sure you clearly identify the regions and name the wars. If you wish to address the Second World War as two wars in two different regions, then make that clear in your introduction.

Information that you may wish to use in defining a conflict may be the dates, form or forms of warfare employed, and the nation or region in which it occurred. An example of how terms are well defined in an introduction is shown in the sample essay on page 328.

Making an argument

Your essays should make an argument, not just repeat details of a conflict or conflicts.

Your argument is likely to be stated explicitly in your essay's introduction and conclusion with the supportive evidence discussed in the essay's body. To strengthen your argument, you may wish to acknowledge historians that you agree with, preferably by naming them and either summarizing their remarks or quoting them. You may even have enough knowledge on the issue being examined that you are able to discuss opposing historians' viewpoints and why you disagree with their conclusions. This historical debate in which evidence is interpreted differently is called historiography and if it is used wisely and correctly, it can help you achieve marks in the upper mark band.

② Examination answer

This section gives a high-level sample answer with examination advice and comments. You can apply this guidance and the comments when answering different questions on this topic.

Question

With reference to two wars, each from a different region, explain the role of imperialism in causing war.

First, you will need to decide which two wars you wish to address, making sure they are from two different regions. You decide to focus on the First World War in Europe, and the Second World War in Asia and the Pacific, as your two wars. A sample outline for this is given below.

P1 (Paragraph): Name conflicts, state argument: imperialism primary cause of these conflicts

P2: Imperialism defined
• Connect to economic policy
• Connect to militarism
  – Means to achieve empire and foreign policy goals
  – Example of British and French military expansion
  – Leads to economic pressures to use army

P3: European imperialism before WW1 regarding Germany
• Moroccan crises 1905, 1911
  – Military threat to achieve end result
  – Army and navy threat to Britain and France lead to closer relations
  – Leads to larger war in 1914

P4: Balkan imperialism issues
• Russia expands influence
  – Allied to Serbia
• Bosnia annexed to Austria-Hungary (A-H)
• 1912–13 Balkan Wars
  – Serbia expands
  – Limited by A-H creating Albania
• Serb nationalist kills future A-H emperor in response to A-H actions

- Leads to WW1

P5: Japanese imperialism before WW2
- Port Arthur, Korea, Kiaochow, S. Seas Mandate
- Manchurian Crisis
- War with China, French Indochina
- US oil embargo
- Dutch East Indies and war with USA

P6: Other arguments
- Emperor Wilhelm's encouraging A-H in war against Serbia
- Schlieffen Plan
- Japan's racial superiority

P7: Counter-arguments and conclusion
- Bethmann-Hollweg's aims with September Programme
- Schlieffen possible only with militarism that came out of imperialism
- Japan's racial belief justified imperialism
- Conclusion: imperialism has profound role in causing the conflicts

Sample answer

The introduction states the conflicts that will be used as examples and indicates their regions.

The argument is clearly stated in the introduction.

Imperialism and associated terms are defined and then explored with further definitions and examples. Links are made between the terms and the two conflicts being discussed.

The First World War in Europe and the Second World War in Asia/Pacific occurred for similar reasons, although there are also notable differences between them. The primary cause of both conflicts was imperialism, the idea that states needed to expand and control large territories, with its associated economic and military elements, while most other causes for these conflicts advocated by historians are actually related to imperialism as well.

Both the First World War (WW1) and Second World War in Asia and the Pacific (WW2) were caused to a large degree by imperialism. Imperialism was the desire to increase territory under a state's control for national pride, space to settle a nation's excess population, and to gain new sources of raw materials and markets. In order to acquire and maintain an empire, large armies and navies were required, leading to militarism, partly defined as a belief that military threats and force were acceptable ways to achieve foreign policy aims while constantly increasing the size and power of the military to this end. In the years before the outbreak of both of these conflicts, there was a rapid increase in the size of armies and navies that seemed to make war more likely. Britain's army, for example, went from fewer than 300,000 to over 700,000 troops from 1900 to 1914, while France's military doubled to over one million men. In order to end the huge economic burden of a large military, an opposing military had to be destroyed so that a nation could reduce its own military's size, thus adding pressure to have war. Before WW1, there were many diplomatic conflicts over empire between European states which involved militarism, and Japan, before WW2 in Asia and the Pacific, followed an imperialistic, expansionist policy that often involved its vast, and expanding, military.

An example of imperialistic tensions in pre-WW1 Europe, often involving military threats, includes Germany's desire to limit French control of Morocco and even gain territory for itself which resulted in two crises in 1905 and 1911. Germany threatened to use its army to force French concessions in 1905 with limited success and implied it would go to war in 1911, eventually gaining French Congo, over 275,000 sq km of Africa. The effect of German imperialism, which included the maintenance of a large military that threatened France and the building of a powerful navy which threatened Britain, was to bring France and Britain closer together with an informal military arrangement. This made France more confident in opposing German demands so that in August 1914, when presented with an ultimatum from Germany or face invasion, France rejected German demands and had war declared upon it. This started WW1 in Europe which had just days before begun as a limited conflict between Austria-Hungary and Serbia.

> There is an example of imperialism in pre-First World War Europe presented and a clear connection made with the outbreak of war in 1914.

While Germany's imperialism threatened Britain and France, the imperialistic policies of various states in south-eastern Europe in the Balkan peninsula also increased tensions in Europe before WW1. Russia worked to extend its influence in the region at the expense of the failing Ottoman Empire, supporting its informal ally Serbia. Russia's main imperialistic goal was to obtain access to the Mediterranean Sea from its Black Sea ports which would allow it further military, and therefore diplomatic, influence in the region. In 1908, Serbia's desire to expand into Bosnia was intentionally

> A second example of imperialism in pre-First World War Europe is presented and a clear connection made with the outbreak of war in 1914.

destroyed by Austria-Hungary's annexation of the province. Russia was unable to prevent this event because of its own military weakness at the time, but by 1912, it was able to wield more influence. In 1912 and 1913, Serbia greatly expanded in a series of wars at the Ottoman Empire's expense which was tantamount to Russia extending its influence in the region. Austria-Hungary worked to limit Serbia's gains, creating Albania along Serbia's newly-won coast to prevent the expanded state from having access to the sea, thereby hindering its economic development. Serbian nationalists in Bosnia killed the future emperor of Austria-Hungary in 1914, partly in response to Austria-Hungary's limiting Serbia's growth, giving Austria-Hungary the excuse it wanted to invade and destroy the expanding Serbia, something Russia mobilized its army to prevent. This provoked Germany to declare war on Russia and its ally France in order to protect its own ally Austria-Hungary, causing the First World War. Russian, Serbian and Austro-Hungarian imperialistic policies in the Balkans played a large role in causing WW1.

Japan's policy of imperialism, like those of European states earlier in the century, led directly to WW2 in the Pacific. Japan steadily expanded at the expense of neighbouring states between 1905 and 1940, annexing Port Arthur from Russia in 1905, Korea in 1910, Kiaochow naval base from China in 1914, taking over the South Seas Mandate for the League of Nations in 1919, invading and controlling Manchuria from China by 1932, conquering large parts of China starting in 1937 and invading French Indochina in 1940. This constant expansion of territory was justified for economic reasons, much as Germany justified its demands in Europe earlier, since Japan's home islands lacked coal and most metals, and Japan had to import food to feed itself. The acquisition of more territory was meant to alleviate these problems. Instead, it led to an embargo on oil from the USA in 1940 after the invasion of French Indochina. Japan decided that the best course of action was not to end its war in China or French Indochina, but to expand even further to include territories that produced oil. Believing that the USA would intervene militarily to prevent further growth to Japan's empire, Japan attacked the USA to destroy its navy so that the oil-producing Dutch East Indies could be absorbed before the USA could prepare a

There is an example of Japan's imperialistic policy with clear connection made with the outbreak of war with the USA in 1941 which addresses the second region the question requires.

military response. This attack on the US navy at Pearl Harbor in December 1941 initiated WW2 in Asia and the Pacific.

Although imperialism's role in causing both conflicts is certainly important, many historians claim that there were other issues involved. Some have blamed Germany's Emperor Wilhelm II who encouraged Austria-Hungary to pursue an aggressive stance against Serbia after the Austrian heir's assassination in mid-1914. Others have blamed Germany's Schlieffen Plan, a military programme that was inflexible and worked to prevent the possibility of a two-front war. The Schlieffen Plan guaranteed that there would be a large European war if Russia ever mobilized against Germany or its ally, as it did in August 1914, even when Russia and Austria-Hungary were negotiating over Serbia's future. Japan's conflicts with its neighbours from 1905 to 1941 may have been partly caused by Japan's belief in its racial superiority over other Asian people which gave them the right, and responsibility, to remove European colonial powers from the region so they could rule it themselves.

Wilhelm II's encouragement to Austria-Hungary was the result of his desire for war to achieve imperialistic aims, partly laid out in the September Programme in 1914 which included an expanded German state at the expense of its neighbours, as well as expansion of its own African colonial territory at the expense of France and others. The Schlieffen Plan certainly expanded a conflict rapidly, but it was the result of having a large, powerful military that was needed to push through Germany's foreign policy demands, which were primarily imperialistic. Japan's belief in racial superiority was an excuse to claim empire and nothing more. Imperialism, therefore, had a profound role in causing both the First World War in Europe and the Second World War in Asia and the Pacific.

Evidence is presented that there is awareness of other arguments for the causes of both conflicts.

Explanation as to why other arguments are not as central to the argument presented in the essay.

Examination question answered in the essay's final sentence.

This essay is clearly focused on the question and indicates there is great awareness of the demands of the question. There is consistent use of historical knowledge that is used as evidence to support the argument. There is clear understanding of historical processes and awareness that there may be other approaches to answering the question. The essay is structured, uses analysis and its argument is consistent throughout. While the essay tends to focus more on the First World War, it clearly indicates that the Second World War conflict was much more straightforward, involving fewer participants and complications.

Examination practice

Below are questions for Topic 11: Causes and effects of twentieth-century wars. Advice on answering the different types of questions may be found at the end of Chapters 2–6.

1 Evaluate the effectiveness of guerrilla warfare in two twentieth-century conflicts.

2 Examine the extent to which two twentieth-century conflicts, each from a different region, were total wars.

3 To what extent did technology affect the outcome of twentieth-century one war that you studied?

4 Compare the importance of foreign involvement in two twentieth-century conflicts, each chosen from a different region.

5 'Peace treaties do not often lead to peace.' With reference to twentieth-century wars, to what extent is this statement true?

6 Compare and contrast the results of two twentieth-century wars, each from a different region.

7 Contrast the causes of two twentieth-century wars, each from a different region.

8 Discuss the importance of naval and air warfare in two twentieth-century conflicts, each from a different region.

9 To what extent did one war in the twentieth-century affect civilians?

10 Discuss the most important form of warfare employed in a twentieth-century war that you have studied.

Glossary

Aircraft carriers Ships that functioned as floating, armed airfields that launched small bombers and fighters, as well as dive- and torpedo-bombers.

Allied Powers Commonly referred to as the Allies during the Second World War, this group first consisted of Poland, France, Britain and others, with the USSR and the USA joining in 1941.

Allies In the First World War, an alliance between Britain, France, the USA, Japan, China and others, including Russia until 1917.

Amphibious assault The practice of landing an infantry force ashore from the sea to launch an attack.

Anarcho-syndicalist An anarchic belief in which proponents desire the central authority of the state to be replaced by the operation of control by trade unions.

Annex To incorporate a territory into another country.

Anti-Comintern Pact Agreement initially between Japan and Germany to work together against Communist International (Comintern), an organization sponsored by the USSR to spread communism.

Appeasement A policy of giving concessions in order to avoid a more immediate confrontation.

Armistice An agreement to stop fighting.

Arms race A competition between nations for military superiority.

Army of Africa Spanish and Spanish Moroccan troops stationed in Spanish Morocco.

Assault Guards An armed police force, similar to the Civil Guard, established by the Republican government.

Atlantic Charter A declaration of goals of Allied nations in the Second World War.

Atoll An island formed from a coral reef.

Atomic bomb A large bomb that uses radioactive material to create an explosion large enough to destroy an entire city.

Auschwitz Germany's largest concentration camp, located in Poland, where over one million people, primarily Jews, were killed during the Second World War.

Axis The alliance in the Second World War that eventually consisted of Germany, Italy, Japan, Slovakia, Hungary, Bulgaria and Romania, as well as several states created in conquered areas.

Balkan Wars Two wars fought between 1912 and 1913 for possession of the European territories of the Ottoman Empire involving Bulgaria, Montenegro, Serbia, Greece and the Ottoman Empire.

Balkans A territorial area of south-eastern Europe from eastern Serbia through central Bulgaria to the Black Sea.

Barrage balloons Large balloons tethered with metal wires that were meant to prevent enemy aircraft from flying at lower altitudes, which would allow more accurate attacks.

Barrios Spanish word for a crowded, low-income city district.

Barter economy The exchange of goods or services without the use of money.

Battleship Heavily armed and armoured large warship.

Bay of Pigs A US-supported attack on Cuba by Cuban exiles in 1961 in which the exiles were heavily defeated.

Blockade To prevent enemy ships from reaching or leaving their ports usually to prevent the movement of supplies of food, raw materials or war goods.

Bolshevik Party The Russian Communist Party. It seized power in a revolution in October 1917.

Bolshevik Revolution The successful communist revolution in Russia in October 1917 led by the Bolshevik Party.

Bourgeois classes A term used to refer to a social class characterized by their ownership of property. It is largely synonymous with the middle classes.

Caciques Influential local 'bosses', usually wealthy landlords or industrialists.

Casa de Campo A large urban park to the west of Madrid.

Cash-and-carry Programme of the US government starting in September 1939 which allowed the sale of US-produced war goods to warring nations as long as they paid for items in cash and transported all goods on their own ships.

Central Powers First World War alliance of Germany, Austria-Hungary, Bulgaria and the Ottoman Empire.

Chancellor German equivalent to prime minister.

Charles Darwin A British natural scientist (1809–82) who formulated the theory of evolution.

Chinese Communist Party The communist party of China, established in 1921.

Civil marriage Marriage in which the ceremony is not performed by a religious official.

Civil rights movement Political movement in the USA that worked for equal rights for all citizens.

Coalition Government formed of a combination of political parties.

Codes A way of communicating information to prevent an enemy from understanding it.

Cold War The political hostilities in the era 1945–91 between capitalist and communist countries, in particular between the USA and the USSR. The conflict was primarily diplomatic, but serious military confrontation did break out on numerous occasions.

Collective farms Farms in which land was not individually owned but was managed by the collective.

Collective security The concept that a war against one member of the League of Nations is a war against all member states.

Collectives Factories, businesses or farms that are run collectively by workers for their own interests.

Communism A system in which all property of a nation is controlled by the state which represents all citizens; holds that nationalism is a creation by economically privileged classes to divide workers.

Communist partisans Communist guerrilla fighters who fought occupying armies as well as various nationalist groups in many countries during the war.

Conditional surrender Surrender in which terms have been agreed between the sides beforehand.

Condor Legion Units of Germany's air force that fought with the Nationalists.

Confederacion Espanola de Derechas Autonomas Spanish Confederation of Autonomous Rightist Parties.

Confederacion Nacional del Trabajo National Labour Confederation, an anarcho-syndicalist trade union.

Conscription Compulsory enrolment of civilians into an army.

Conservative A political position generally favouring the maintenance of a structured social hierarchy and minimal government intervention in social and economic life.

Conservatives Political groups dominated by major landowners that desired a closer relationship between the government and the Catholic Church.

Constitutional monarchy Governmental system in which a hereditary monarch is head of state, but whose powers are limited by a constitution.

Consultative Council Group that gives advice to a government.

Contras Various counter-revolutionary groups who fought against the Sandinistas in the 1980s. Contra is an abbreviation of the Spanish word for counter-revolution: *contrarrevolución*.

Convoy system The practice of ships sailing in large groups protected by naval destroyers rather than sailing individually.

Co-operative farms Farms in which individual plots of land continued to be individually owned but were managed and worked collectively by their owners.

Cortes Elected parliament.

Corvée Forced labour tax.

COSIP Nicaraguan group of businessmen opposed to Somozan domination of the economic system in the mid-1970s.

Coup An illegal takeover of power, often through the use of force.

Cruisers Fast, heavily armed warships that have less armour and fewer weapons than battleships.

Death camps Prisons established to kill prisoners.

Decolonization Process of granting independence to colonies of primarily European states.

Depth charge An explosive device fired from a battleship which is designed to detonate at a certain depth.

Destroyers Fast, lightly armoured ships built specifically to locate and destroy submarines.

Diplomatic sanctions The punishment of a country by the severing of normal relations.

Direct rule Ruling a country from a position of authority.

Domestic service Domestic servants provide household services for others, usually serving as cooks or maids.

Dominion A country which has its own autonomy (independent government) but which recognizes the sovereignty of a monarch from overseas.

Dual Alliance The alliance between Germany and Austria-Hungary established in 1878.

Embargo Ban on trade.

Enfranchise To give the right to vote in political elections.

Entente Cordiale The agreement signed between Britain and France in 1904 settling their imperial rivalries.

Expansionist A policy aimed at the enlargement of territorial/economic control.

Falange Fascist political party established in February 1933 by José Antonio Primo de Rivera, the son of Miguel Primo de Rivera.

Federacíon Anarquista Ibérica Iberian Anarchist Federation.

Fidel Castro Guerrilla fighter who overthrew a dictatorship in Cuba in 1959 and gradually introduced a communist form of government, allying with the USSR during the Cold War.

Firestorm A fire of such magnitude and intensity that it creates its own wind system, usually as a result of rising heat causing cool air to be pulled towards the fire, which provides more oxygen to make the fire more intense.

Five Year Plans Economic programmes of the USSR which initially focused on mass industrialization.

Foot binding The traditional practice of binding the feet of women from when they were children in order to keep feet dainty in size. It caused substantial physical discomfort.

Foreign concessions/enclaves Territorial areas within China which were essentially governed by foreign powers and where only foreign laws applied.

Fourteen Points speech Speech by US President Wilson in 1918 which presented 14 separate issues that he believed needed to be enacted to establish world peace.

Free French French troops who escaped the collapse of France in June 1940 and continued to fight with the Allies.

Free trade Ability to freely trade, usually with low or no taxes on goods crossing national borders.

French Indochina A French colony consisting of today's Laos, Cambodia and Vietnam.

Galicia A region of eastern Europe, now in south-east Poland.

General strike Large strike conducted by many labour unions.

Grand Alliance First World War alliance of Britain, France, Russia, Italy, Japan, the USA and many other countries.

Great Depression Economic depression which began in 1929 and adversely affected the world economy throughout much of the 1930s.

Greater Asia Co-prosperity Sphere Japanese-created and led organization of puppet-governments established in Japanese-occupied Asian nations that encouraged Asians to oppose European and US rule and to support Japan during the Second World War.

Green Gang An influential criminal organization operating in Shanghai in the early twentieth century.

Gross domestic product The market value of all goods and services produced in a country in a given time period.

Gross national product All economic activity of a nation, which includes production, exports and imports.

Guerrilla resistance movements Groups of fighters who oppose an occupying force using guerrilla tactics such as sabotage and assassination.

Guomindang The Chinese Nationalist Party. It can also be transliterated to Kuomintang (KMT).

Human rights violations Torture, illegal imprisonment, rape, executions and similar crimes.

Hurricane barrage A short, intensive artillery bombardment.

Hyperinflation When the value of a currency falls rapidly and leads to extremely high monetary inflation.

IJN Imperial Japanese Navy.

Imperialist Relating to imperialism, which is the extension of a nation's authority by territorial acquisition and political and economic domination over other nations.

Incendiary bombs Bombs designed to start fires.

Indirect rule Ruling a country unofficially through others.

Industrial revolution The rapid development of industry brought about by the introduction of machinery from the late eighteenth century.

Infiltration tactics The use of small, mobile detachments of infantry to infiltrate enemy lines by targeting previously identified weak points and thereby isolating strong points on the line for easier attack by more heavily armed troops.

Inter-American Development Bank Central and South American organization that works to alleviate poverty and promote economic development.

International Brigades Military units composed of volunteers from a range of countries.

International Court of Justice Court that deals with disputes between nations, located at The Hague, The Netherlands.

July Days The period during July 1914 in which diplomatic efforts failed to avert the outbreak of war.

Junta Military-led government.

Kaiser The German emperor.

Kamikazes Japanese pilots who flew aircraft into Allied ships, killing themselves in the process.

Korean War A military conflict between communist northern Korea and non-communist southern Korea which in the context of the Cold War attracted significant international involvement. It was fought between 1950 and 1953.

Labour camps Prisons where prisoners worked in factories.

Labour unions Organizations for workers that negotiate with business owners to improve working conditions.

League of Nations International organization established after the First World War to resolve conflicts between nations in order to prevent war.

Lend–Lease US programme begun in March 1941 that lent over $50 billion ($650 billion in today's terms) worth of war supplies to Allied nations.

Lenin Russian Marxist who led a revolution in Russia in 1917, establishing a communist state which became the USSR.

The Levant An area of the eastern Mediterranean, including what is now Lebanon, Syria and Israel.

Liberals Political groups mainly concerned with free trade and economic development.

Liberation theology Central American Catholic clergy movement, inspiring parishioners to work for change in this life, rather than waiting for their reward in heaven.

Lliga Regionalista Regionalist League, a separatist Catalan political party.

Maginot Line A complex system of fortresses and other defences established by France on the French–German border.

Manchuria A region in the far north-east of China bordering the then Soviet-controlled territory of Siberia, Mongolia and Korea. Manchuria contained China's largest deposits of coal, iron and gold, huge timber forests and 70 per cent of its heavy industry.

Mandate Territories of the German and Ottoman Empires that were administered primarily by Britain, France and Japan under supervision of the League of Nations.

Mao Zedong Leader of the CCP and ruler of China between 1949 and his death in 1976.

Marines Soldiers trained to invade territories from warships.

Matériel Equipment used in warfare.

Marx Wrote the Communist Manifesto and other writings which formed the basis of communism.

Marxism Marxism is also often referred to as communism. It is an economic and sociopolitical theory which identifies progress in history as coming about through class conflict and revolution, with the ultimate goal being the establishment of a society without government, private property or hierarchy. It is named after the originator of the theory, Karl Marx (1818–83).

Merchant shipping Non-military shipping, carrying supplies.

Mesopotamia A region of south-west Asia, part of what is now Iraq.

Militarism The principle or policy of maintaining a strong military and the glorification of military strength.

Militia A military force using civilians as opposed to professional soldiers.

Mine An explosive device which detonates on contact.

Mobile defence A military strategy that uses the guerrilla tactics of sabotage and ambush to weaken the enemy by disrupting supply lines and inflicting casualties It does not prioritize the enlargement of territorial control.

Nanjing Decade The period of Nationalist rule between 1927/8 and 1937. During this period the Nationalist Party's headquarters were in the city of Nanjing.

National Directorate Governing group of the Sandinistas which included members from all factions.

National unity government Government which includes a broad range of political parties working together.

Nationalism A devotion to the interests and culture of one's nation, often leading to the belief that certain nationalities are superior to others.

Native Americans Indigenous inhabitants of the Americas.

Nazi Party The German National Socialist Party led by Adolf Hitler, which held power in Germany from January 1933 until April 1945.

Neutrality Acts A series of US laws that prevented the USA from joining conflicts and from providing weapons for countries at war.

New Life Movement A cultural movement introduced by the Nationalists in the 1930s to encourage moral values and obedience to the state.

Nicaraguan Congress Parliament dominated by supporters of the Somoza family and co-operative minor opposition parties until 1979.

No-man's land The unclaimed land between the two opposing trench systems.

Northern Expedition A military expedition undertaken by the Nationalists and the Communists to reunify China by defeating the warlords between 1926 and 1927.

Organization of American States Organization of governments of North and South America that works to resolve crises that affect the region.

Ottoman Empire The former Turkish empire that incorporated territory in Europe, Africa and the Middle East, lasting from the thirteenth century to 1918.

Outflanking Gaining advantage by manoeuvring troops around an enemy's position.

Pan-Slavism A movement advocating the political and cultural union of Slavic nations and peoples.

Paramilitary A group of civilians organized and operating like an army.

Paratroops Soldiers who jump from planes, usually to establish positions behind enemy armies.

Partido Nacionalista Vasco Basque Nationalist Party, a Basque separatist political party.

Plebiscite A vote by all of a nation's voters on a particular issue.

Pontoon bridge Temporary bridge built on floating supports.

Popular Army Republican regular army organized in September 1937.

Potsdam Conference Meeting of Allied leaders in Germany in July 1945 where it was decided to divide Germany into four occupation zones, to prosecute war criminals and expel Germans from lands outside Germany, among other issues.

Proletariat The working classes in an industrialized society.

Provisional Government The government of Russia between March and October 1917.

Puppet-state Government that operates at the will of and for the benefit of another government.

Radiation sickness A series of illnesses that result from exposure to radiation released in a nuclear explosion, including cancer.

Radical Party Spanish political party founded by Alejandro Lerroux. Its political ideology represented the centre ground, favouring moderate social reform.

Railheads The point of a railway at which military supplies are unloaded.

Reagan Doctrine Policy of US President Ronald Reagan to remove governments friendly to the USSR, which included the arming and funding of rebel groups.

Rearmament Rebuilding of a fully equipped military force.

Reconnaissance The gathering of military information.

Red Cross International organization that provides emergency medical services.

Religious order In the Catholic Church one of many groups of priests, monks or nuns who follow a specific set of regulations, usually having distinctive clothing and goals.

Reparations Payments made by a defeated nation to a victorious one to compensate for war expenses and damage.

Reservations Territories within the USA operated with varying levels of autonomy by and for Native Americans.

Reserve forces Former, trained soldiers who can be quickly recalled from civilian life to expand a military.

Reunification Campaigns China's military campaigns to annex Tibet and Xinjiang to China.

Russo-Turkish War Conflict between the Ottoman and Russian Empires fought for territorial control in the Balkan region between 1877 and 1878.

Schlieffen Plan The German military plan by which they hoped to win the First World War by avoiding a substantial war on two fronts.

Second Sino-Japanese War Military conflict, primarily between Japan and China, 1937–45. It became one of the Asian theatres of the Second World War of 1939–45.

Self-determination The right of nations and nationalities to be independent and form their own governments.

Separatist Favouring a degree of political independence or autonomy for a particular region.

Siegfried Line System of anti-tank defences established by Germany on its borders with The Netherlands, Belgium and France.

Slavic An ethnic and linguistic grouping of eastern European peoples whose languages include Russian, Serbo-Croatian, Polish and Czech.

Small arms Firearms that can be carried by hand, such as rifles, pistols and small machine guns.

Socialism Political and economic system in which a nation's resources and means of production are controlled by the government to prevent extremes in wealth and poverty.

South Sea Mandate Large numbers of sparsely settled islands in the Pacific Ocean, formerly part of the German Empire.

Soviet 'Council' in Russian. The term was used to refer to communist organizations or assemblies.

Soviet satellites Nations allied to and dominated by the USSR.

Soviet Union Communist Russia and states under its control, also known as the USSR.

Spanish Morocco The significant proportion of Morocco that was controlled by Spain as a colony from 1906.

Standing army A permanent, professional army maintained in times of peace and war.

Stormtroopers German specialist infantry used in the First World War.

Strategic bombing The bombing of targets such as factories, transportation networks and even civilians, in an attempt to gain strategic advantage.

Stresa Front Agreement between Britain, France and Italy to work together diplomatically to isolate Germany from world affairs.

Suez Canal Canal located in Egypt connecting the Mediterranean and Red Seas, and therefore the Atlantic and Indian Oceans.

Superpowers Nations that have the ability to exert their influence on a global scale.

Taiwanese Strait The channel of sea separating mainland China and Taiwan.

Tehran Conference Conference held in Tehran, Iran, from 28 November 1943 where the Allies agreed to start a front against Germany in western Europe.

Theatre In warfare, a major area of fighting.

Trade union An organization of workers which pursues improvements in pay and working conditions for its members.

Triple Alliance The alliance between Germany, Austria-Hungary and Italy established in 1882.

Triple Entente The alliance between France, Britain and Russia established in 1907.

U-boats German submarines.

Ultra-nationalism Extreme form of nationalism that advocates national or racial superiority of a particular group.

Unconditional surrender An act of surrender in which you place yourself completely under the control of your opponent.

Union General de Trabajadores General Union of Labourers, the main union of the Socialist Party.

United Front An alliance between the Nationalist Party and the CCP between 1924 and 1927 which was revived between 1936 and 1945.

United Nations International organization whose member states work to resolve crises.

Universal male suffrage When all adult males are entitled to vote in elections.

US secretary of state The head of the government department of foreign affairs.

Vichy France The remnant of France that was a German puppet-state between 1940 and late 1942, ruled from the city of Vichy.

Victory Programme US government initiative to increase the size of its armed forces in mid-1941 although it was not at war with any country.

War of attrition A strategy in which the main goal is to achieve victory by wearing down the enemy's strength and will to fight, through the infliction of mass casualties and the limitation of their essential resources.

Warlords Wealthy, powerful individuals whose control of private armies enabled them to establish themselves as virtual dictators in the regions of China following the collapse of imperial rule.

Warsaw Ghetto Section of Warsaw, Poland, where Jews were required to live.

Washington Naval Conference A conference in 1922 that led to several treaties, limiting the size of the navies of Britain, Japan and the USA, as well as settling other problems.

Weltpolitik Literally world policy. Kaiser Wilhelm II's foreign policy objectives to make Germany a world power particularly through the pursuit of expansive colonial and naval policies.

White-collar employment Non-manual employment, typically office work.

World Health Organization International body that works to prevent disease and promotes health.

Yalta Conference Meeting of Allied leaders in the USSR in February 1945 where many agreements were made about what the governments and borders of Europe would be after the war's end.

Yuan A unit of currency in China.

Zeppelin A large cylindrical airship that uses gas to stay aloft.

Further reading

First World War

World War I by H.P. Willmott *et al.* Dorling Kindersley, London, 2003.
A general history focusing on the military aspects of the First World War. Contains superb visual material to accompany a detailed narrative of the fighting in different theatres.

The Experience of World War I by J.M. Winter, Andromeda, Oxford, 1995.
An interesting thematic presentation of the First World War organized from the perspective of the politicians, the generals, the soldiers and the civilians. Illustrated with excellent visual material.

The Origins of the First World War: Controversies and Consensus by Annika Mombauer. Pearson, Harlow, 2002.
A thorough and analytical discussion of the historiography of the First World War.

The War that Ended Peace: The Road to 1914, by Margaret MacMillan. Random House, New York, 2013.
A fascinating, detailed book that thoroughly reviews the major causes of the First World War. The book has been praised by many journals, newspapers and magazines as one of the best written on the subject.

Thirteen Days: The Road to the First World War by Clive Ponting. Pimlico, London, 2003.
An extremely thorough account of the diplomatic attempts at peace which took place during July 1914. It rejects both the argument that German aggression was primarily to blame and that war was likely by 1914, emphasizing instead the importance of the short-term causes of the war.

Minds at War: The Poetry and Experience of the First World War by David Roberts. Saxon, London, 1996.
A superb collection of poetry, prose and factual data relating to the First World War.

Peacemakers: Six Months that Changed the World by Margaret MacMillan. John Murray, London, 2001.
A detailed and thoughtful analysis of the peace treaties and their impact.

Spanish Civil War

Franco and the Spanish Civil War by Filipe Ribeiro de Meneses. Routledge, London, 2001.
A clear and concise general introduction to the Spanish Civil War.

The Spanish Civil War: Origins, Course and Outcomes by Francisco J. Romero Salvadó. Palgrave Macmillan, Basingstoke, 2005.
An excellent overview providing detailed, comprehensive coverage of the Spanish Civil War.

Revolution and War in Spain 1931–1939 edited by Paul Preston. Methuen, London, 1984.
An interesting, wide-ranging and thought-provoking collection of essays on various aspects of the civil war from some of the leading authorities on the subject.

The Spanish Civil War: A Modern Tragedy by George R. Esenwein. Routledge, London, 2005.
Provides excellent primary source material on a variety of aspects of the war, accompanied by clear, concise explanations.

The Spanish Civil War 1936–1939 by Frances Lannon. Osprey, Oxford, 2002.
Focuses on the military issues of the war, with clear narrative and useful maps.

Homage to Catalonia by George Orwell. Penguin, London, 2000.
An engaging and lively contemporary account of the British journalist George Orwell's experiences of fighting in the Spanish Civil War. Particularly good for its analysis of the militias and the internal conflicts of the Republicans.

Second World War in Europe and north Africa

The Origins of the Second World War by A.J.P. Taylor. Penguin Books, London, 2001.
A most famous book by one of the world's most famous historians that continues to inspire and provoke controversy.

The Origins of the Second World War Reconsidered: A.J.P. Taylor and the Historians, second edition, edited by Gordon Martel. Routledge, London, 1999.
An analysis of Taylor's *The Origins of the Second World War* 40 years after its publication.

The Origins of the Second World War in Europe, third edition, by P.M.H. Bell. Pearson, London, 2007.

A highly useful and readable work that exhibits excellent scholarship on the interwar period.

The Road to War, second edition, by Richard Overy and Andrew Wheatcroft. Penguin Books, London, 2000.
A work that expands on A.J.P. Taylor's earlier views.

A World in Flames: A Short History of the Second World War in Europe and Asia, 1939–45 by Martin Kitchen. Longman, London, 1990.
Very detailed description of all aspects of the Second World War with illustrations and maps.

The Strategic Bombing of Germany, 1940–45 by Alan J. Levine. Praeger, Westport, Connecticut, 1992.
Thorough work on all aspects of the Allied air campaign against Germany during the Second World War.

World War II: A Student Companion by William L. O'Neill. Oxford University Press, 1999.
An encyclopaedia of information regarding most aspects of the Second World War.

Russia's War: 1941–45 by Richard Overy. Penguin Books, London, 1997.
A comprehensive review of the Second World War in Europe's Eastern Front.

World War II by H.P. Willmott *et al*. Dorling Kindersley, London, 2004.
Overview of entire Second World War in Europe, north Africa, Asia and the Pacific with illustrations, timelines and maps.

France and the Second World War: Occupation, Collaboration, and Resistance by Peter Davies. Routledge, London, 2001.
A seminal work regarding the occupation of France by Germany during the Second World War in Europe.

The Other Price of Hitler's War: Germany Military and Civilian Losses Resulting from World War II by Martin K. Sorge. Greenwood Press, Westport, Connecticut, 1986.
A highly informative discussion of the effects of the Second World War on Germany.

Second World War in Asia and the Pacific

World War II by H.P. Willmott *et al*. Dorling Kindersley, London, 2004.
Overview of entire Second World War in Europe, north Africa, Asia and the Pacific with illustrations, timelines and maps.

World War II: A Student Companion by William L. O'Neill. Oxford University Press, 1999.
An encyclopaedia of information regarding most aspects of the Second World War.

A World in Flames: A Short History of the Second World War in Europe and Asia, 1939–45 by Martin Kitchen. Longman, London, 1990.
Very detailed description of all aspects of the Second World War with illustrations and maps.

A Modern History of Japan: From Tokugawa Times to the Present by Andrew Gordon. Oxford University Press, 2003.
A survey of Japanese history which places Japanese imperialism in context.

The Pacific War: Japan Versus the Allies by Alan J. Levine. Praeger, Westport, Connecticut, 1995.
An overview of the Second World War between Japan and the Allies, including a detailed chapter about Japan's land war in China and Burma.

Stars and Stripes Across the Pacific: The United States, Japan, and Asia/Pacific Region 1895–1945 by William F. Nimmo. Praeger, Westport, Connecticut, 2001.
Discusses growing economic and colonial rivalries between Japan and the USA in the late nineteenth century to the end of the Second World War.

Embracing Defeat: Japan in the Aftermath of World War II by John Dower. Penguin Books, London, 1999.
Excellent work detailing the conditions of Japan in the last months of the Second World War through changing political and economic events after the conflict ended.

Modern China: The Fall and Rise of a Great Power, 1850 to the Present by Jonathan Fenby. HarperCollins, New York, 2008.
Highly praised work that thoroughly covers Japan's wars with China in the twentieth century.

Battle at Sea: 3000 Years of Naval Warfare by R.G. Grant. Dorling Kindersley, London, 2010.
Includes information on modern naval warfare with examples from the Second World War in Asia and the Pacific.

Chinese Civil War

The Chinese Civil War, 1945–49 by Michael Lynch. Osprey, Oxford, 2010.
Focuses on the military aspects of the war, with a clear concise narrative and useful maps.

Modern China: The Fall and Rise of a Great Power, 1850 to the Present by Jonathan Fenby. HarperCollins, New York, 2008.
Highly praised work that thoroughly covers Japan's wars with China in the twentieth century.

The Third Chinese Revolutionary Civil War, 1945–49: An Analysis of Communist Strategy and Leadership by Christopher R. Lew. Routledge, London, 2011.
Provides a detailed analysis of the military aspects of the war, emphasizing the importance of communist strategy and tactics in determining their victory.

The Chinese Century: A Photographic History by Jonathan Spence and Annping Chin. HarperCollins, London, 1996.
A general history of twentieth-century China, including a significant section on the war and superbly illustrated.

Mao by Michael Lynch. Routledge, London, 2004.
A clear, concise biography of Mao, including information on the civil war.

Mao: The Unknown Story by Jung Chang and Jon Halliday. Vintage, London, 2005.
A highly readable, detailed and controversial biography of Mao which challenges many of the previous accepted interpretations of twentieth-century Chinese history.

Wild Swans: Three Daughters of China by Jung Chang. Flamingo, London, 1991.
An engaging memoir based on the experiences of three generations of women within a Chinese family, set against the backdrop of the main events in modern China.

Nicaraguan Revolution

US Intervention and Regime Change in Nicaragua by Mauricio Solaún. University of Nebraska Press, Lincoln, Nebraska, 2005.
Detailed review and analysis of US political and economic involvement in Nicaragua during the twentieth century.

Nicaragua: Revolution in the Family by Shirley Christian. Vintage Books, New York, 1986.
Engaging work based on interviews with many of those involved in the Nicaraguan Revolution.

Death of Somoza by Claribel Alegría and Darwin Flakoll. Curbstone Press, Willimantic, Connecticut, 1996.
Reviews historical events of Somoza's last days in power until his death by assassination.

Visual sources

The First World War DVD series by Channel 4 in the UK, based on *The First World War* by Hew Strachan, 2004.
An excellent, easy to understand yet academically sound review of the First World War, including coverage of post-war revolutions and other events often neglected.

The World at War DVD series narrated by Laurence Olivier, 2001.
An older series that includes interviews with German officials, civilians, soldiers and others while covering the events of the Second World War in incredible detail.

CNN's Cold War DVD series, 2012.
An acclaimed series now available on DVD which thoroughly discusses and analyses the beginnings of the Cold War as the result of the Second World War in Europe.

World War II: The War in the Pacific DVD series by the History Channel, 2010.
A thorough review of the Second World War in the Pacific.

Nicaragua No Pasaran DVD by Frontline Films, 2008.
One of the few documentaries on the Nicaraguan Revolution.

Websites

Fordham University's Internet Modern History Sourcebook: www.fordham.edu/halsall/mod/modsbook.asp
One of the largest databases of primary documents available for any era of history.

Firstworldwar.com: www.firstworldwar.com
Tremendous site with timelines, primary documents, discussion on impact of war on women, lots of statistics, examples of propaganda from most active participants in the war and much more. Includes all treaties from the Paris Peace Conference of 1919–20.

BBC History: www.bbc.co.uk/history
British perspectives of twentieth-century events including both world wars.

The History Place: www.historyplace.com/index.html
US perspectives of twentieth-century events including both world wars, includes timelines and historical photographs.

The Spanish War History: www.spanishwars.net
Site regarding Spain's wars over several hundred years, including the Spanish Civil War.

Internal assessment

The internal assessment is a historical investigation on a historical topic that is required of all IB History students. This book has many key and leading questions which may be adapted for use as a research question for your internal assessment. In addition to those, you may wish to consider questions such as the following.

First World War 1914–18

1 To what extent was the British naval blockade of Germany responsible for Germany's defeat in the First World War?
2 How successful was British food rationing compared to food rationing in Germany during the First World War?
3 In what ways and for what reasons were propaganda posters of Austria-Hungary different from those of Italy during the First World War?
4 Why was the Treaty of Versailles completed before any other treaties during the Paris Peace Conference after the First World War?
5 How did the First World War affect the economies of the neutral countries of Switzerland and Sweden?

Second World War in Europe and north Africa 1939–45

1 To what extent did Germany integrate the economic resources of conquered areas into its economy during the Second World War?
2 Why did the Allies not bomb the industrially important city of Prague during the Second World War?
3 How did US and British military strategy in western Europe in 1944–5 differ from military strategy used by the USSR in eastern Europe during the same period?
4 Why were the Partisans in Yugoslavia more successful than rival groups in the same country during the Second World War?
5 What was the importance of Gibraltar for Britain during the Second World War?

Second World War in Asia and the Pacific 1941–5

1 How were civilian populations on Japanese-occupied islands in the Pacific Ocean affected by the Second World War?
2 Was the Battle of the Coral Sea or Midway the more important battle for the USA?
3 To what extent was Japan's defeat during the Second World War the result of its occupation of China?
4 How did Japan's puppet-states in China contribute to Japan's wartime economy during the Second World War?
5 Which anti-Japanese resistance movement in Japanese-occupied territories used guerrilla warfare most effectively?

Spanish Civil War 1936–9

1 How did Republican propaganda compare to Nationalist propaganda during the Spanish Civil War?
2 To what extent was the outcome of the Spanish Civil War the result of Republican political weakness?
3 How did the experience of Basque civilians differ from that of Catalan civilians during the Spanish Civil War?
4 Why did Germany militarily support the Nationalist cause?
5 How significant was Soviet assistance to the Republican government?

Chinese Civil War 1927–37 and 1945–9

1 To what extent was the Chinese Communist Party supported by peasants during the Chinese Civil War?
2 How did the Chinese Civil War affect minority populations in China?
3 What was the role of the USSR in the Chinese Civil War?
4 Why were the Nationalists unable to combat guerrilla warfare of the Chinese Communist Party effectively during the Chinese Civil War?"
5 To what extent was Mao personally responsible for the victory of the Chinese Communist Party during the Chinese Civil War?

Nicaraguan Revolution 1976–9

1 How did the Nicaraguan Revolution affect Honduras?
2 To what extent was the authority of the Roman Catholic Church affected by the rise of the Sandinista government in Nicaragua in 1979?
3 Was the Nicaraguan Revolution the result of US diplomacy or Sandinista military success?
4 How was the Nicaraguan economy affected by revolution between 1976 and 1979?
5 Why were the Sandinistas more successful than other political groups during the Nicaraguan Revolution?

Index